Takane & Hana

2

STORY AND ART BY

Yuki Shiwasu

Takane
&Hana

2

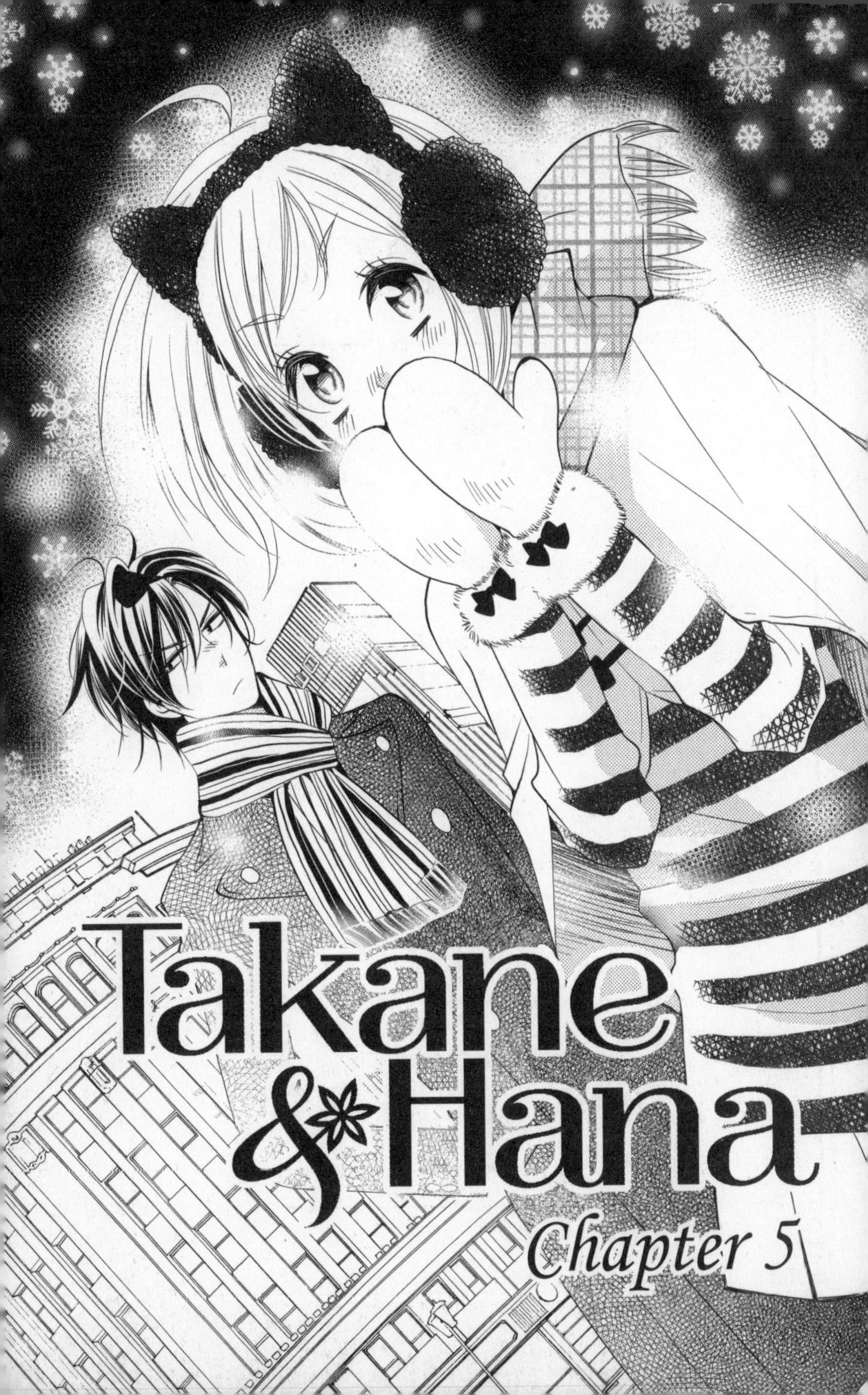
Takane & Hana
Chapter 5

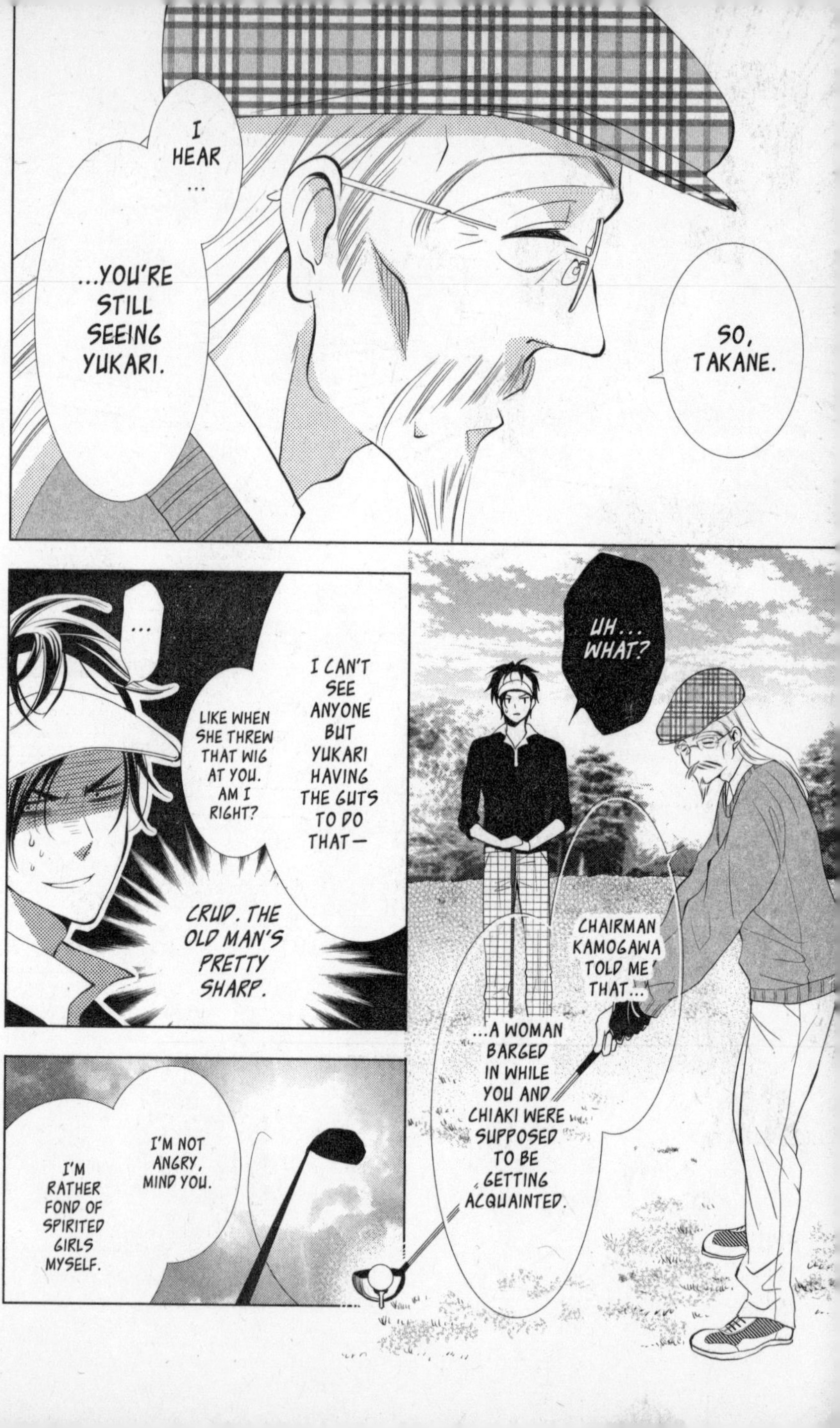
SO, TAKANE.
I HEAR ...
...YOU'RE STILL SEEING YUKARI.
UH... WHAT?
CHAIRMAN KAMOGAWA TOLD ME THAT...
...A WOMAN BARGED IN WHILE YOU AND CHIAKI WERE SUPPOSED TO BE GETTING ACQUAINTED.
I CAN'T SEE ANYONE BUT YUKARI HAVING THE GUTS TO DO THAT—
...
LIKE WHEN SHE THREW THAT WIG AT YOU. AM I RIGHT?
CRUD. THE OLD MAN'S PRETTY SHARP.
I'M NOT ANGRY, MIND YOU.
I'M RATHER FOND OF SPIRITED GIRLS MYSELF.

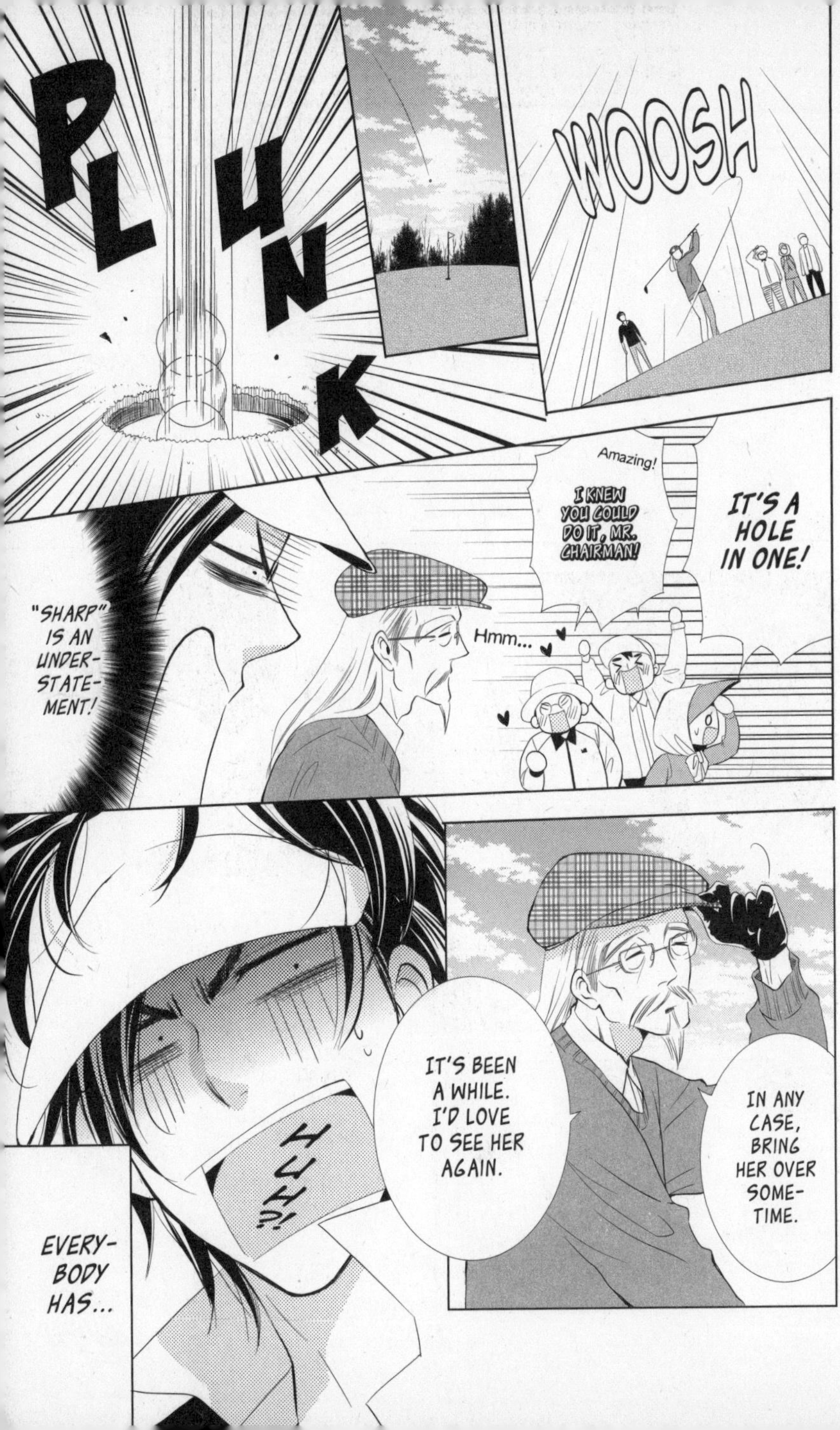
WOOSH
PLUNK
IT'S A HOLE IN ONE!
Amazing!
I KNEW YOU COULD DO IT, MR. CHAIRMAN!
Hmm...
"SHARP" IS AN UNDER-STATE-MENT!
IN ANY CASE, BRING HER OVER SOME-TIME.
IT'S BEEN A WHILE. I'D LOVE TO SEE HER AGAIN.
HUH?!
EVERY-BODY HAS...

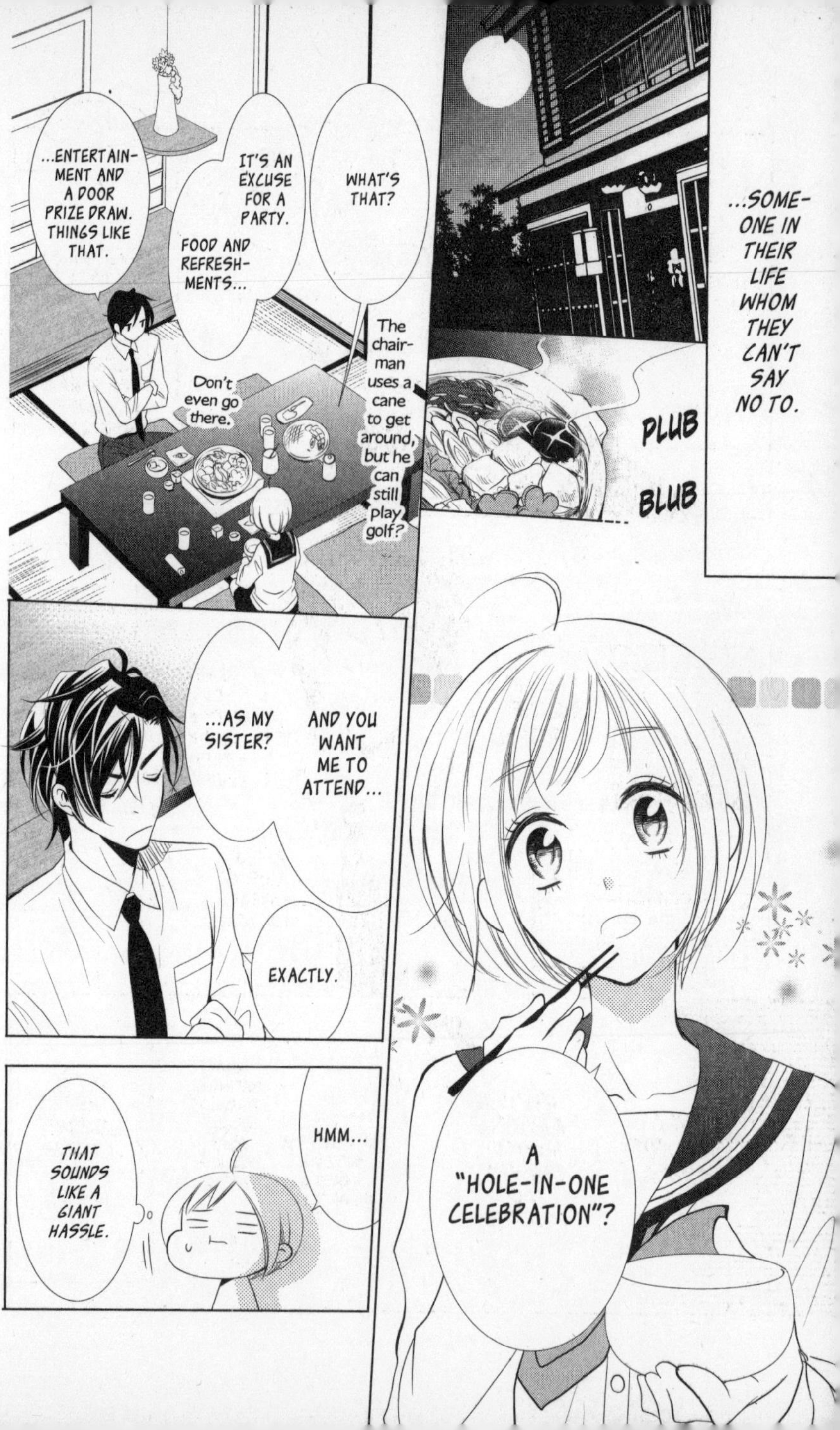
...SOMEONE IN THEIR LIFE WHOM THEY CAN'T SAY NO TO.
PLUB
BLUB
A "HOLE-IN-ONE CELEBRATION"?
WHAT'S THAT?
The chairman uses a cane to get around, but he can still play golf?
IT'S AN EXCUSE FOR A PARTY.
FOOD AND REFRESHMENTS...
...ENTERTAINMENT AND A DOOR PRIZE DRAW. THINGS LIKE THAT.
Don't even go there.
AND YOU WANT ME TO ATTEND...
...AS MY SISTER?
EXACTLY.
HMM...
THAT SOUNDS LIKE A GIANT HASSLE.

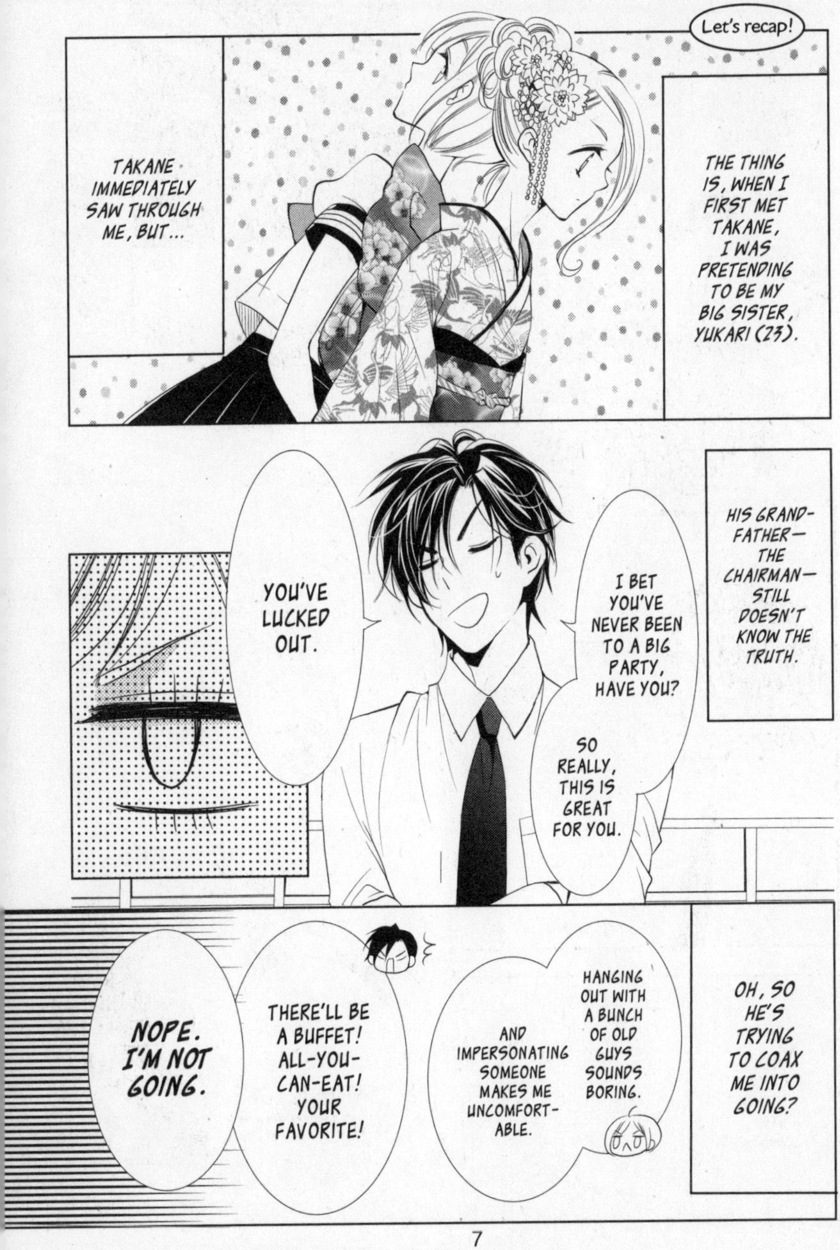
Let's recap!
THE THING IS, WHEN I FIRST MET TAKANE, I WAS PRETENDING TO BE MY BIG SISTER, YUKARI (23).
TAKANE IMMEDIATELY SAW THROUGH ME, BUT...
HIS GRANDFATHER—THE CHAIRMAN—STILL DOESN'T KNOW THE TRUTH.
I BET YOU'VE NEVER BEEN TO A BIG PARTY, HAVE YOU?
SO REALLY, THIS IS GREAT FOR YOU.
YOU'VE LUCKED OUT.
OH, SO HE'S TRYING TO COAX ME INTO GOING?
HANGING OUT WITH A BUNCH OF OLD GUYS SOUNDS BORING.
AND IMPERSONATING SOMEONE MAKES ME UNCOMFORTABLE.
THERE'LL BE A BUFFET! ALL-YOU-CAN-EAT! YOUR FAVORITE!
NOPE. I'M NOT GOING.

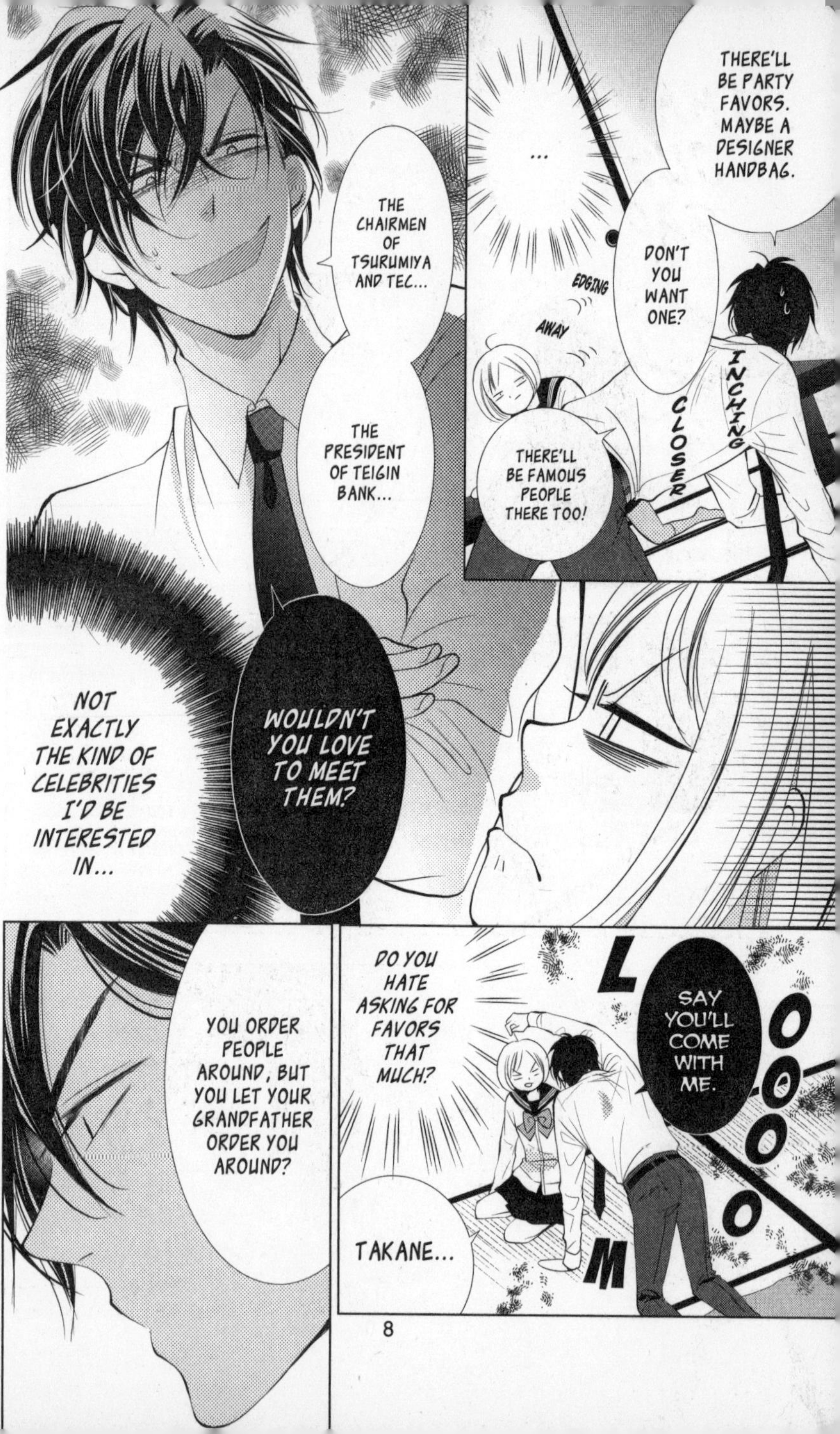
...
THERE'LL BE PARTY FAVORS. MAYBE A DESIGNER HANDBAG.
DON'T YOU WANT ONE?
EDGING AWAY
INCHING CLOSER
THERE'LL BE FAMOUS PEOPLE THERE TOO!
THE CHAIRMEN OF TSURUMIYA AND TEC...
THE PRESIDENT OF TEIGIN BANK...
WOULDN'T YOU LOVE TO MEET THEM?
NOT EXACTLY THE KIND OF CELEBRITIES I'D BE INTERESTED IN...
SAY YOU'LL COME WITH ME.
LOOOOOM
DO YOU HATE ASKING FOR FAVORS THAT MUCH?
TAKANE...
YOU ORDER PEOPLE AROUND, BUT YOU LET YOUR GRANDFATHER ORDER YOU AROUND?

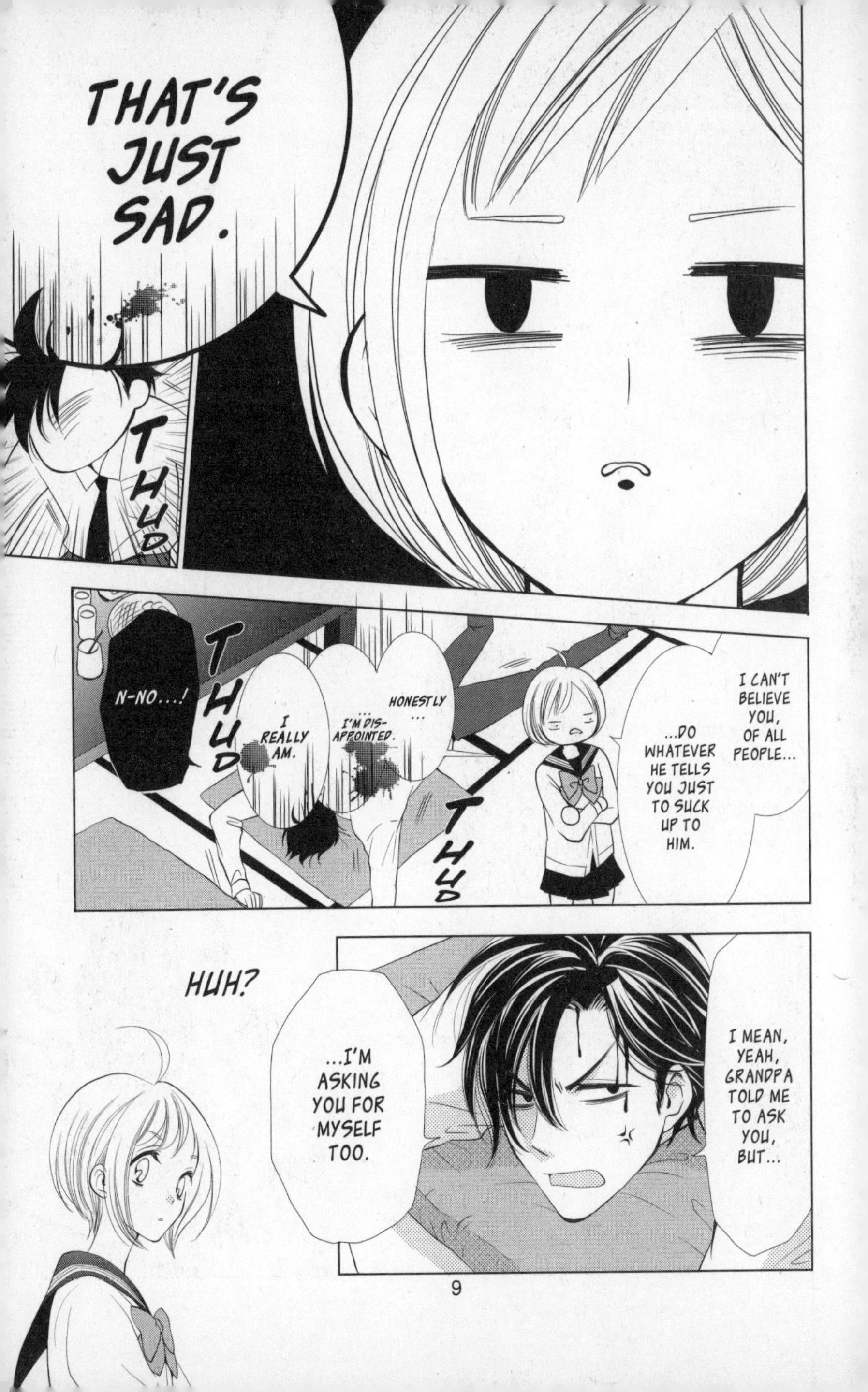
THAT'S JUST SAD.
THUD
I CAN'T BELIEVE YOU, OF ALL PEOPLE...
...DO WHATEVER HE TELLS YOU JUST TO SUCK UP TO HIM.
THUD
HONESTLY... ...I'M DIS-APPOINTED.
I REALLY AM.
THUD
N-NO...!
I MEAN, YEAH, GRANDPA TOLD ME TO ASK YOU, BUT...
...I'M ASKING YOU FOR MYSELF TOO.
HUH?

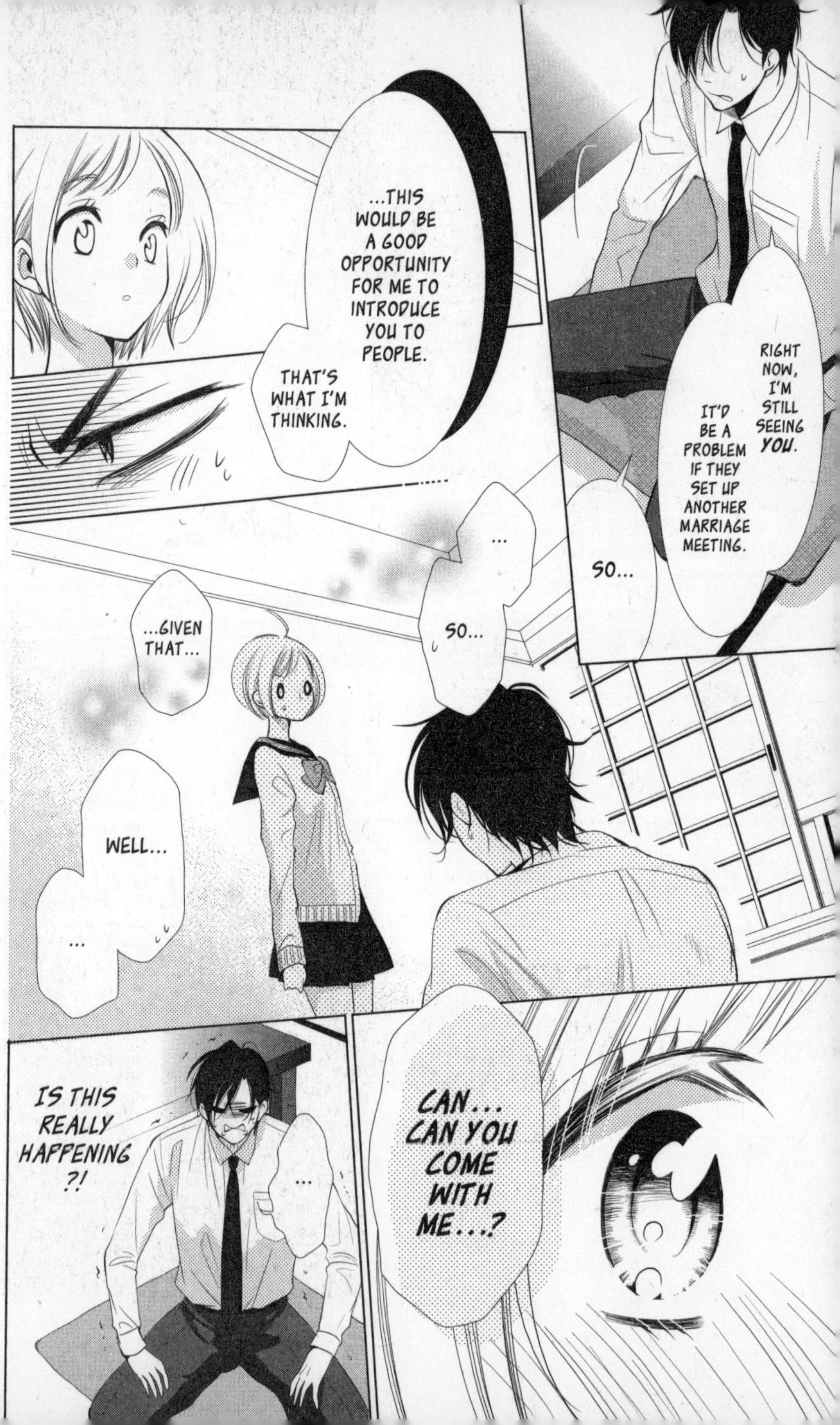
RIGHT NOW, I'M STILL SEEING YOU.
IT'D BE A PROBLEM IF THEY SET UP ANOTHER MARRIAGE MEETING.
SO...
...THIS WOULD BE A GOOD OPPORTUNITY FOR ME TO INTRODUCE YOU TO PEOPLE.
THAT'S WHAT I'M THINKING.
...
SO...
...GIVEN THAT...
WELL...
...
CAN... CAN YOU COME WITH ME...?
...
IS THIS REALLY HAPPENING ?!

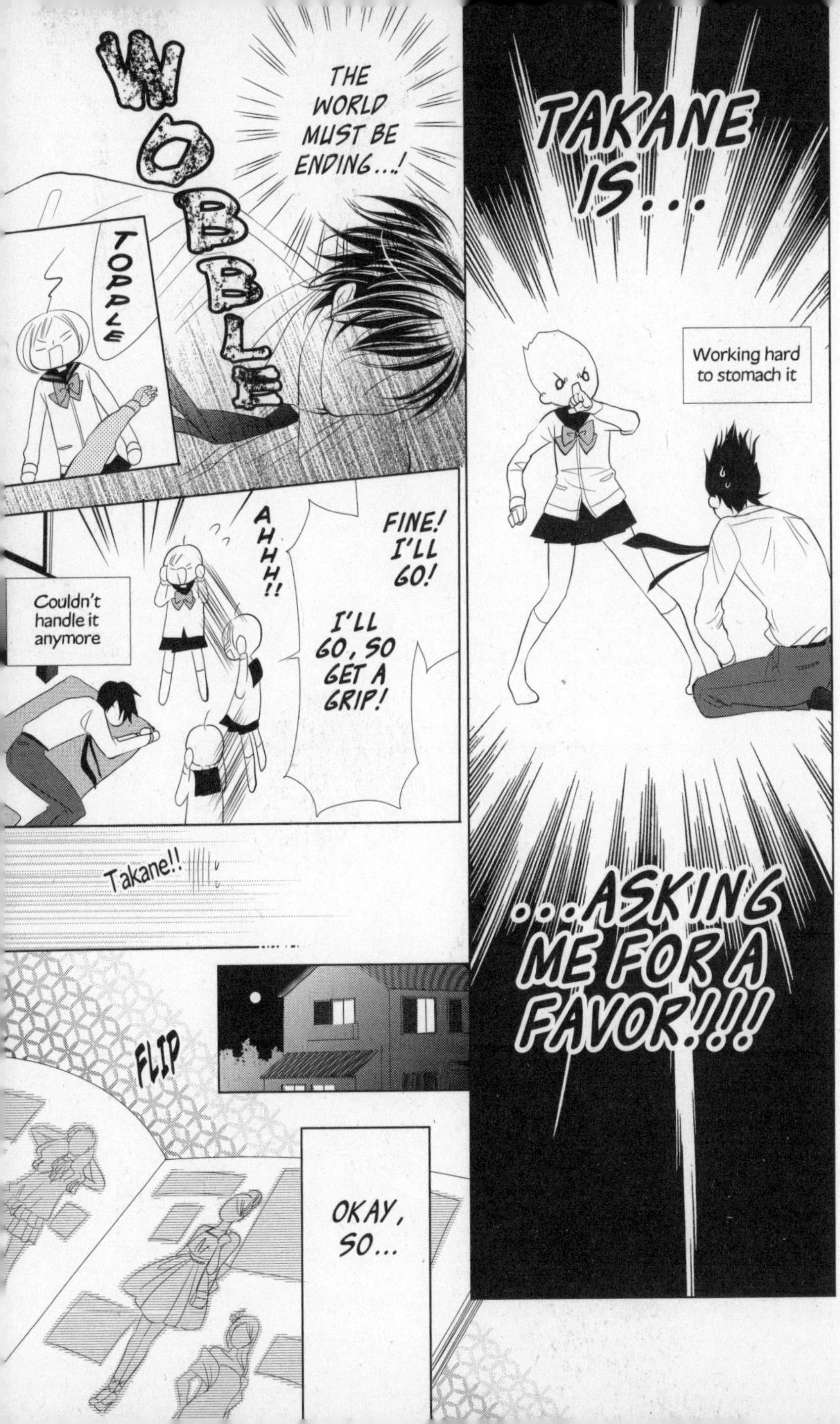
TAKANE IS...
Working hard to stomach it
...ASKING ME FOR A FAVOR!!!
THE WORLD MUST BE ENDING...!
WOBBLE
TOPPLE
FINE! I'LL GO!
I'LL GO, SO GET A GRIP!
AHHH!!
Couldn't handle it anymore
Takane!!
FLIP
OKAY, SO...

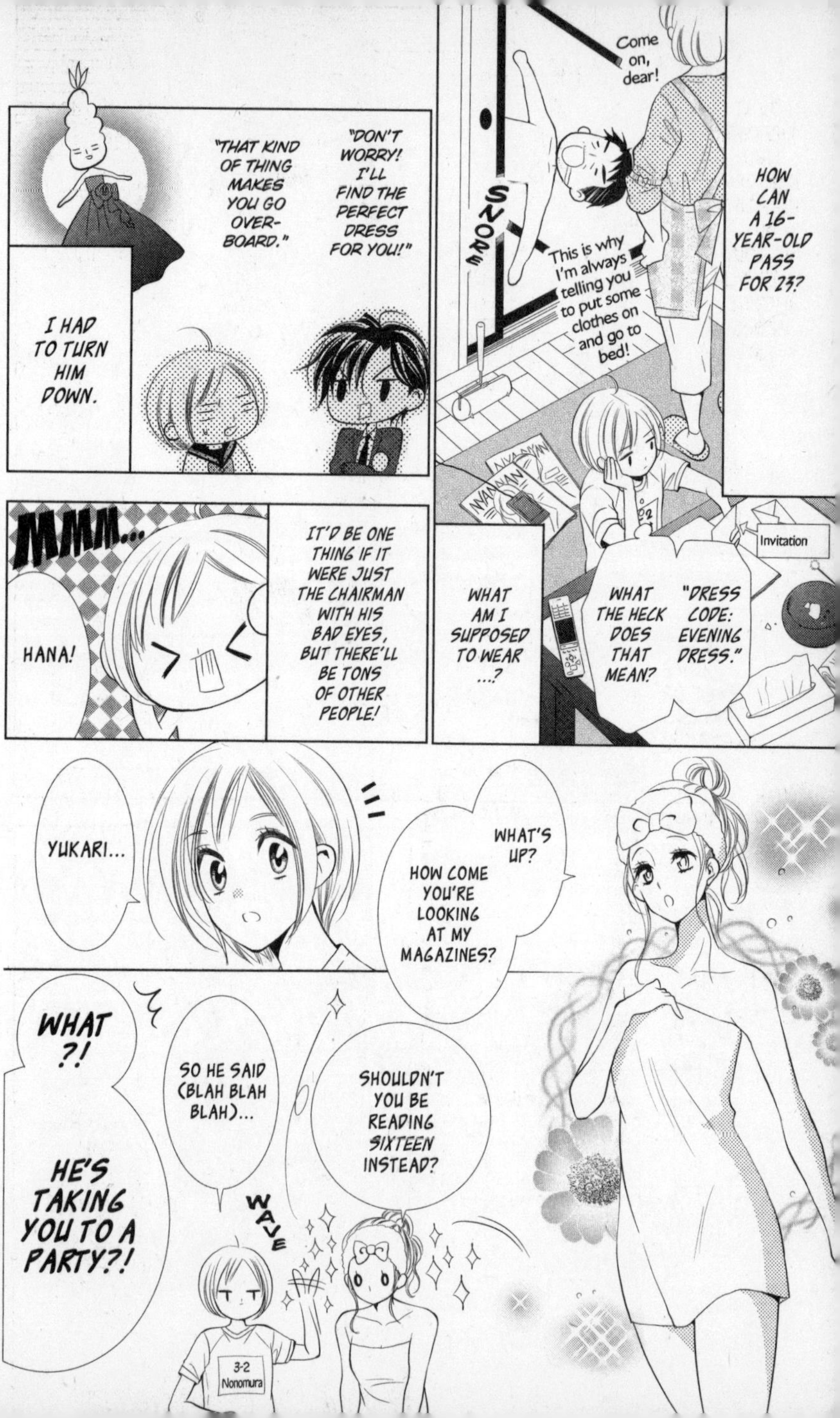
HOW CAN A 16-YEAR-OLD PASS FOR 23?
Come on, dear!
This is why I'm always telling you to put some clothes on and go to bed!
SNORE
"DON'T WORRY! I'LL FIND THE PERFECT DRESS FOR YOU!"
"THAT KIND OF THING MAKES YOU GO OVER-BOARD."
I HAD TO TURN HIM DOWN.
Invitation
"DRESS CODE: EVENING DRESS."
WHAT THE HECK DOES THAT MEAN?
WHAT AM I SUPPOSED TO WEAR ...?
IT'D BE ONE THING IF IT WERE JUST THE CHAIRMAN WITH HIS BAD EYES, BUT THERE'LL BE TONS OF OTHER PEOPLE!
MMM...
HANA!
WHAT'S UP?
HOW COME YOU'RE LOOKING AT MY MAGAZINES?
YUKARI...
SHOULDN'T YOU BE READING SIXTEEN INSTEAD?
SO HE SAID (BLAH BLAH BLAH)...
WHAT?!
HE'S TAKING YOU TO A PARTY?!
WAVE
3-2
Nonomura

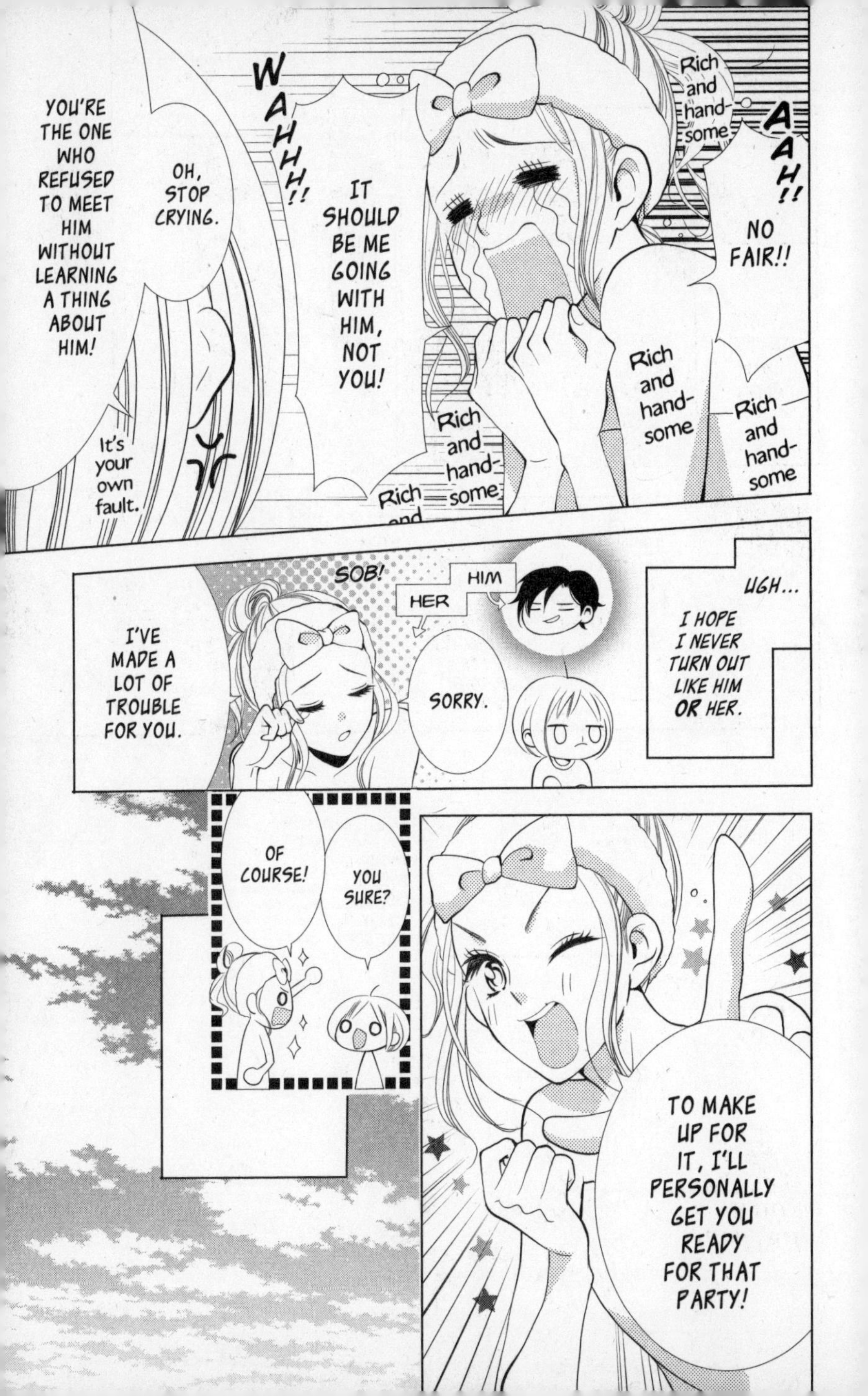
Rich and hand-some
AAAH!!
NO FAIR!!
Rich and hand-some
Rich and hand-some
Rich and hand-some
Rich
WAHHH!!
IT SHOULD BE ME GOING WITH HIM, NOT YOU!
OH, STOP CRYING.
YOU'RE THE ONE WHO REFUSED TO MEET HIM WITHOUT LEARNING A THING ABOUT HIM!
It's your own fault.
UGH...
I HOPE I NEVER TURN OUT LIKE HIM OR HER.
HIM
HER
SOB!
SORRY.
I'VE MADE A LOT OF TROUBLE FOR YOU.
TO MAKE UP FOR IT, I'LL PERSONALLY GET YOU READY FOR THAT PARTY!
YOU SURE?
OF COURSE!

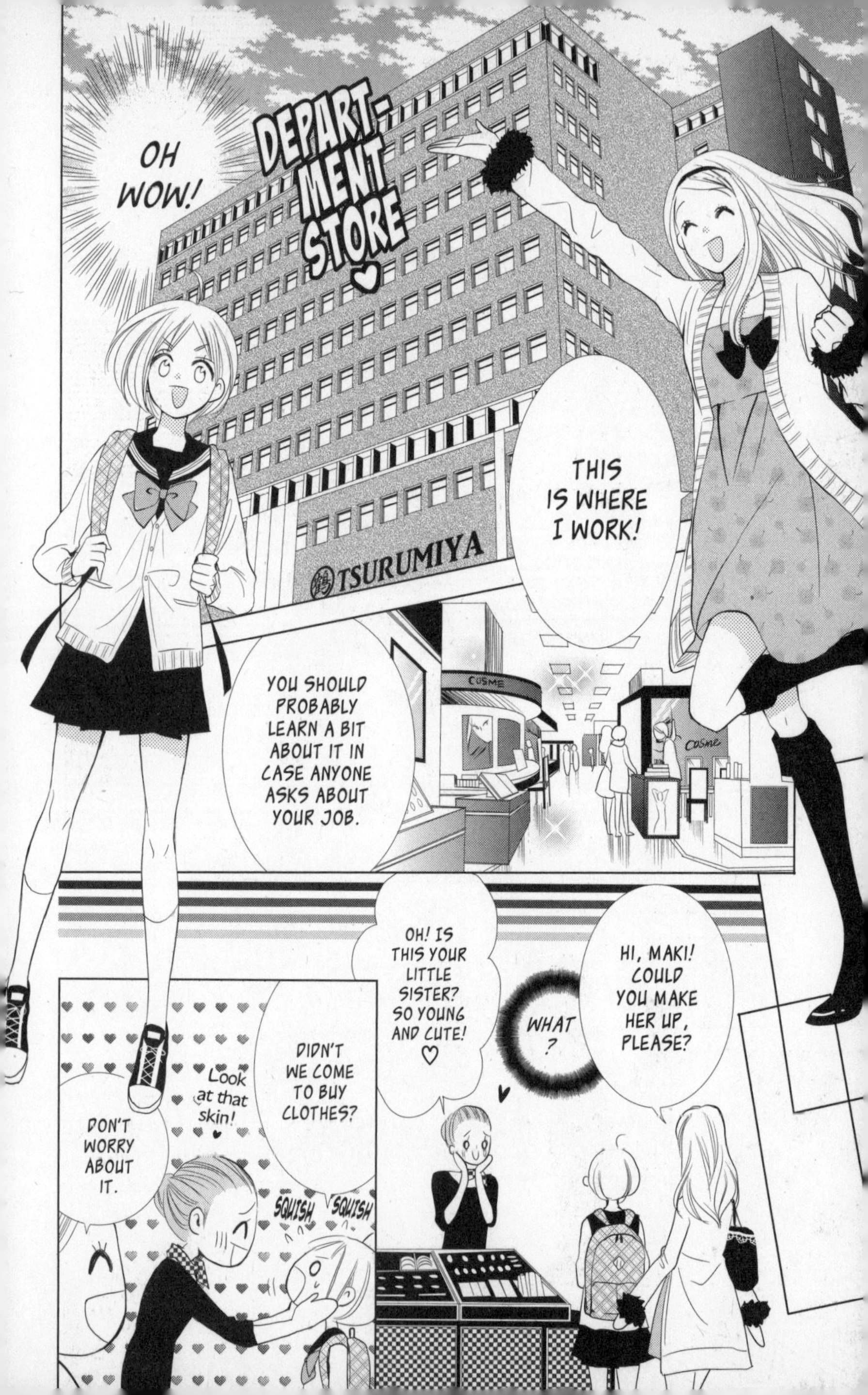
THIS IS WHERE I WORK!
DEPART-MENT STORE ♥
TSURUMIYA
COSME
COSME
YOU SHOULD PROBABLY LEARN A BIT ABOUT IT IN CASE ANYONE ASKS ABOUT YOUR JOB.
OH WOW!
HI, MAKI! COULD YOU MAKE HER UP, PLEASE?
WHAT?
OH! IS THIS YOUR LITTLE SISTER? SO YOUNG AND CUTE! ♥
DIDN'T WE COME TO BUY CLOTHES?
Look at that skin! ♥
SQUISH SQUISH
DON'T WORRY ABOUT IT.

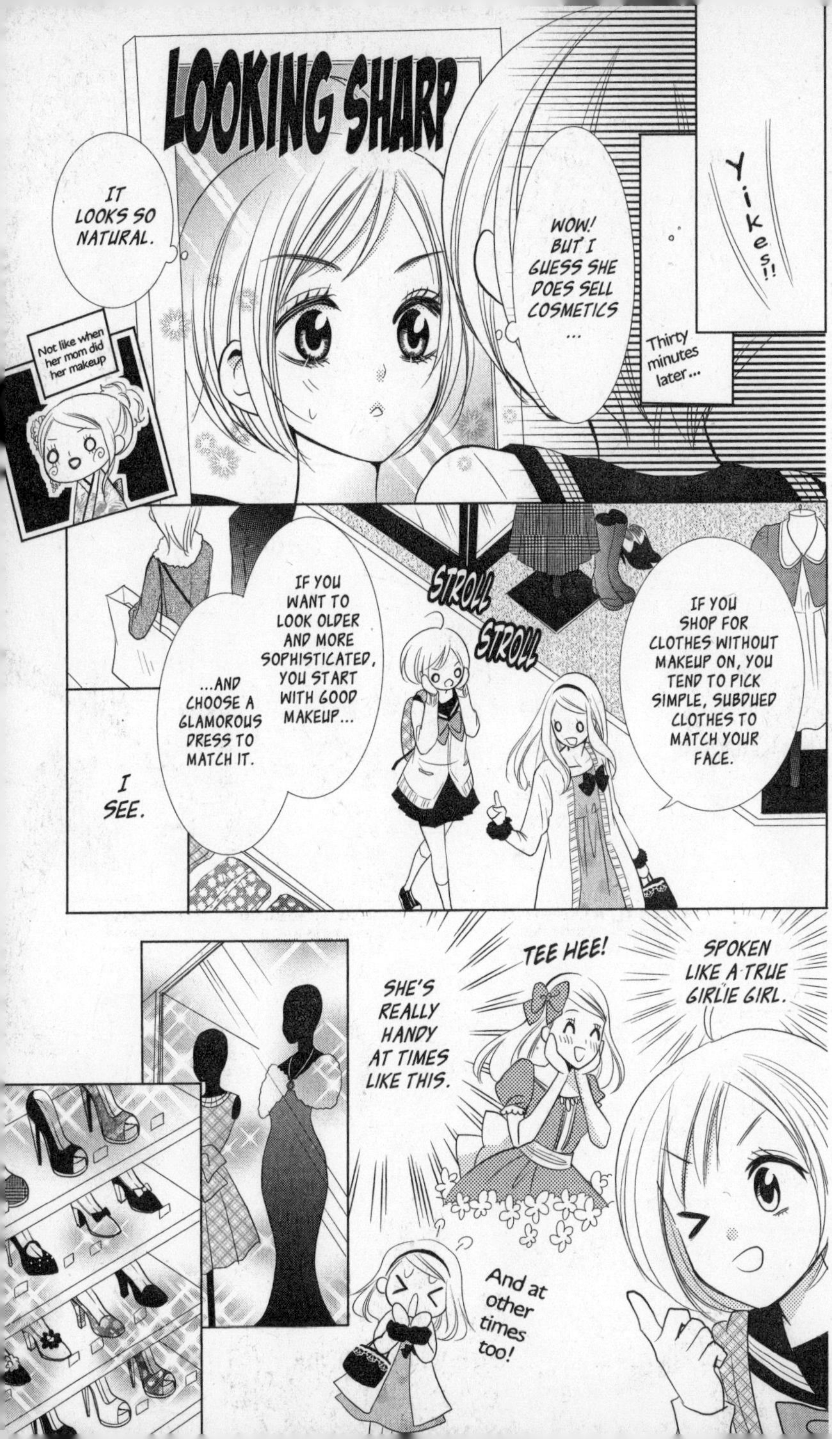
LOOKING SHARP
Yikes!!
Thirty minutes later...
WOW! BUT I GUESS SHE DOES SELL COSMETICS...
IT LOOKS SO NATURAL.
Not like when her mom did her makeup
IF YOU SHOP FOR CLOTHES WITHOUT MAKEUP ON, YOU TEND TO PICK SIMPLE, SUBDUED CLOTHES TO MATCH YOUR FACE.
STROLL
STROLL
IF YOU WANT TO LOOK OLDER AND MORE SOPHISTICATED, YOU START WITH GOOD MAKEUP...
...AND CHOOSE A GLAMOROUS DRESS TO MATCH IT.
I SEE.
SPOKEN LIKE A TRUE GIRLIE GIRL.
TEE HEE!
SHE'S REALLY HANDY AT TIMES LIKE THIS.
And at other times too!

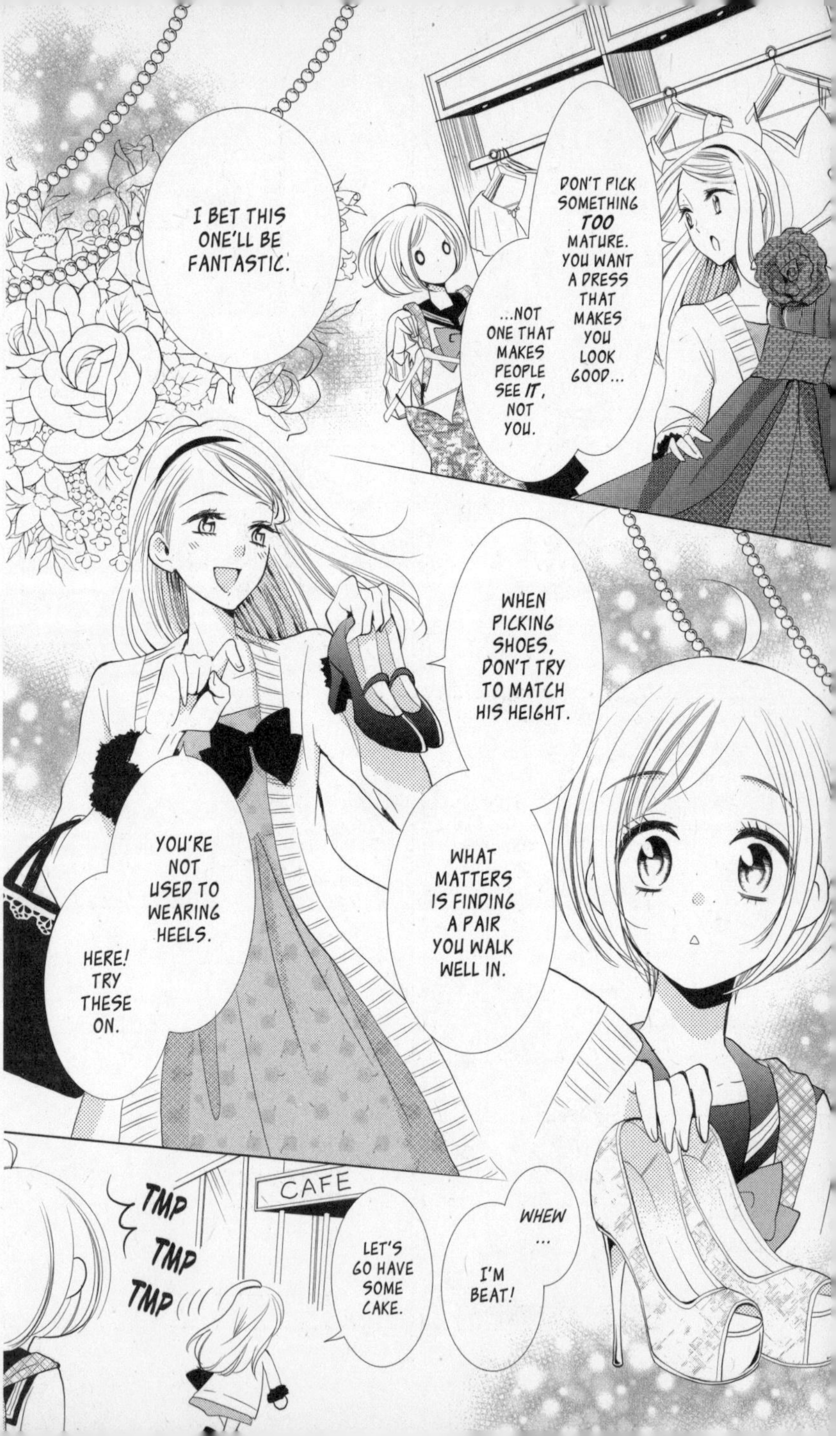
DON'T PICK SOMETHING **TOO** MATURE. YOU WANT A DRESS THAT MAKES YOU LOOK GOOD...
...NOT ONE THAT MAKES PEOPLE SEE *IT*, NOT YOU.
I BET THIS ONE'LL BE FANTASTIC.
WHEN PICKING SHOES, DON'T TRY TO MATCH HIS HEIGHT.
WHAT MATTERS IS FINDING A PAIR YOU WALK WELL IN.
YOU'RE NOT USED TO WEARING HEELS.
HERE! TRY THESE ON.
WHEW...
I'M BEAT!
CAFE
LET'S GO HAVE SOME CAKE.
TMP TMP TMP

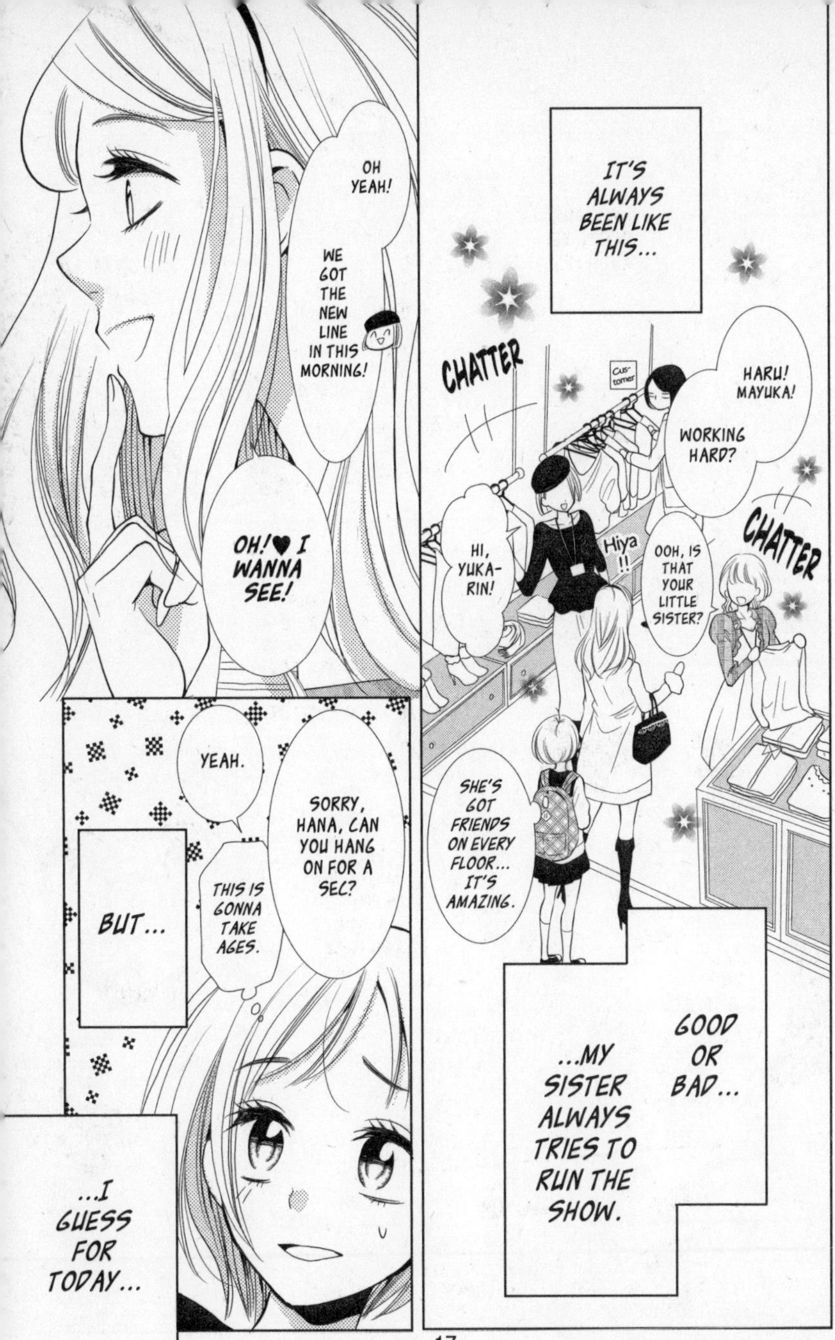
IT'S ALWAYS BEEN LIKE THIS...
CHATTER
HARU! MAYUKA!
WORKING HARD?
Cus-tomer
CHATTER
HI, YUKA-RIN!
Hiya!!
OOH, IS THAT YOUR LITTLE SISTER?
SHE'S GOT FRIENDS ON EVERY FLOOR... IT'S AMAZING.
GOOD OR BAD...
...MY SISTER ALWAYS TRIES TO RUN THE SHOW.
OH YEAH!
WE GOT THE NEW LINE IN THIS MORNING!
OH!♥ I WANNA SEE!
SORRY, HANA, CAN YOU HANG ON FOR A SEC?
YEAH.
THIS IS GONNA TAKE AGES.
BUT...
...I GUESS FOR TODAY...

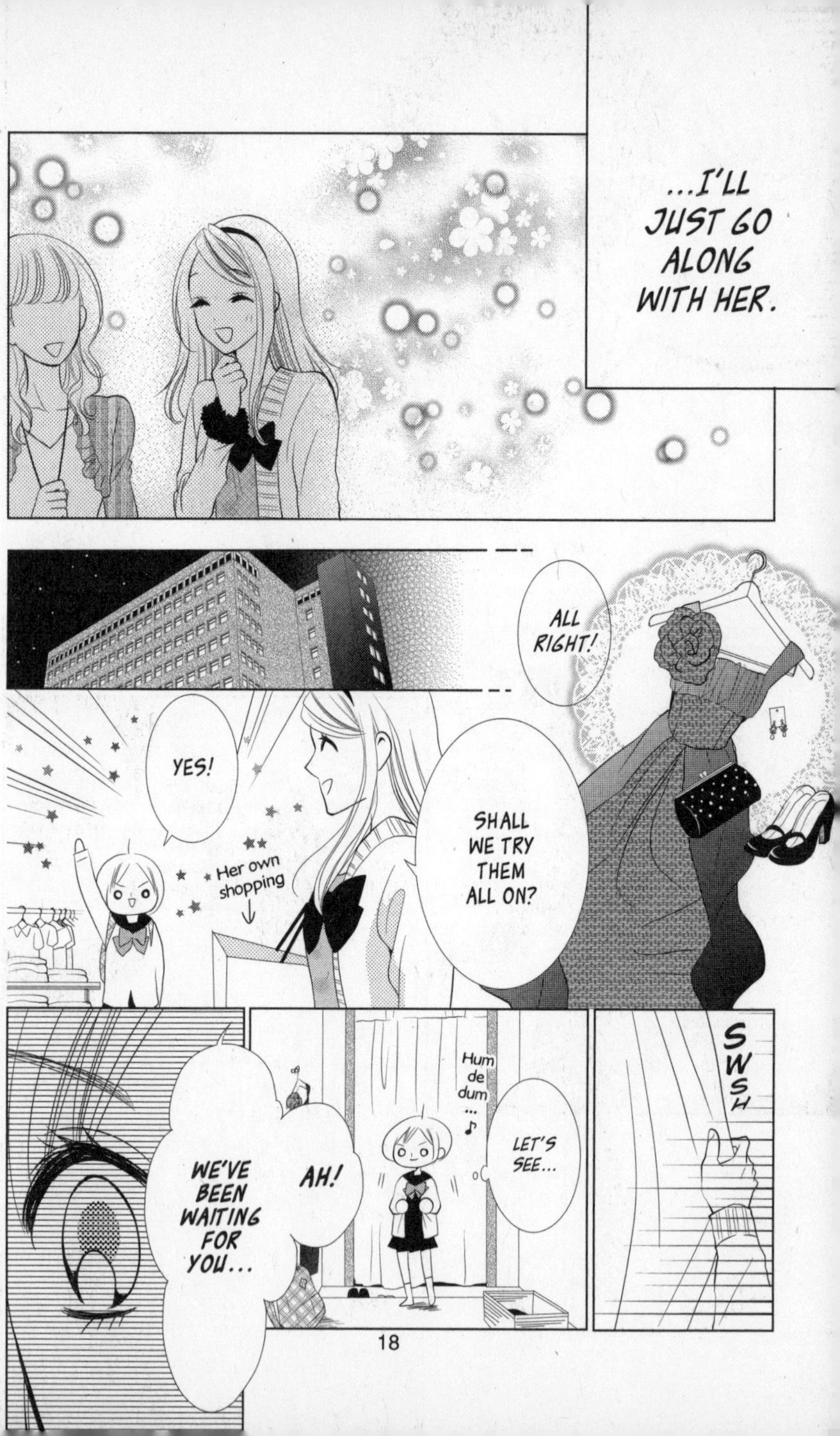
...I'LL JUST GO ALONG WITH HER.
ALL RIGHT!
SHALL WE TRY THEM ALL ON?
YES!
Her own shopping
SWSH
LET'S SEE...
Hum de dum...♪
AH!
WE'VE BEEN WAITING FOR YOU...

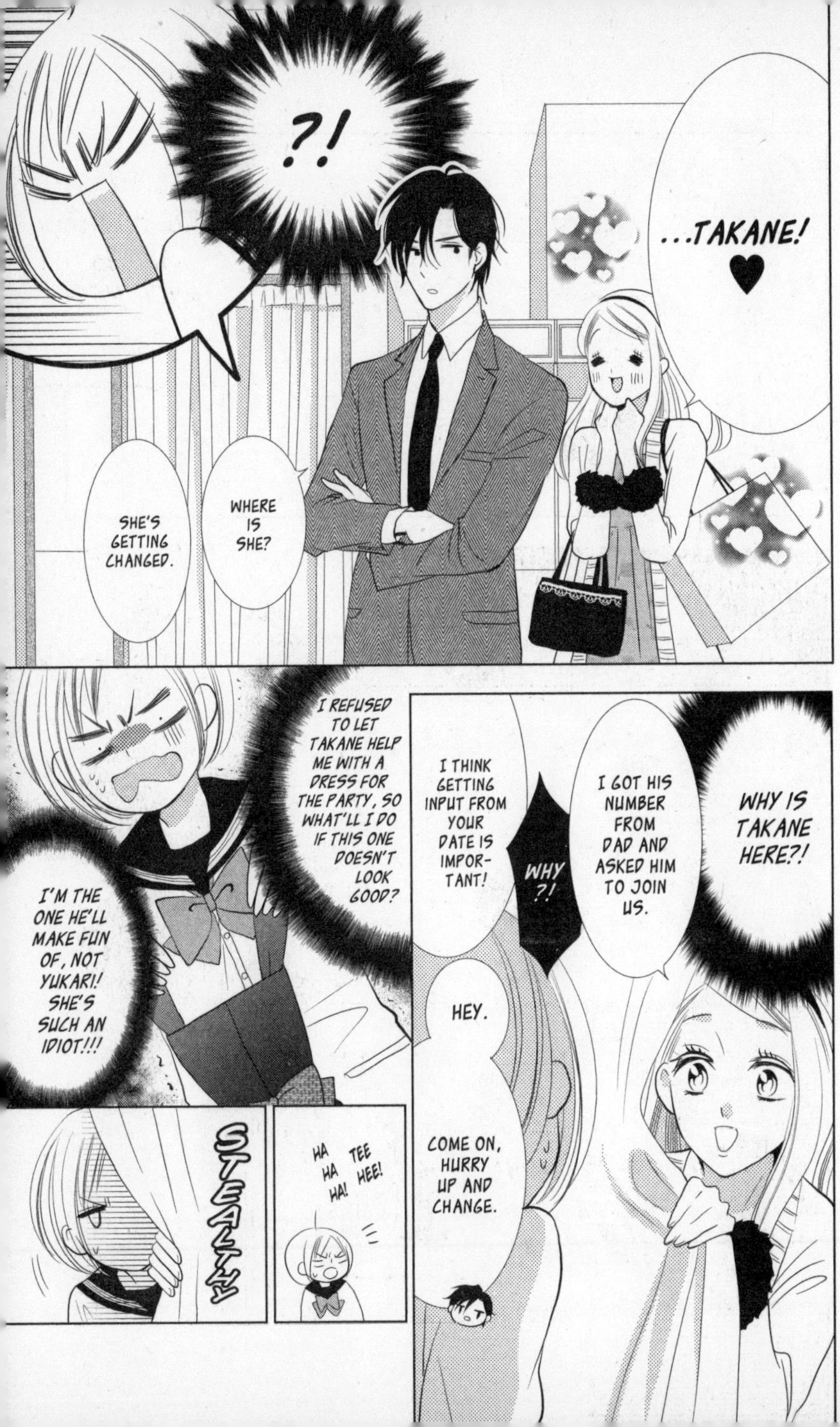
...TAKANE! ♥
?!
WHERE IS SHE?
SHE'S GETTING CHANGED.
WHY IS TAKANE HERE?!
I GOT HIS NUMBER FROM DAD AND ASKED HIM TO JOIN US.
WHY?!
I THINK GETTING INPUT FROM YOUR DATE IS IMPORTANT!
HEY.
COME ON, HURRY UP AND CHANGE.
I REFUSED TO LET TAKANE HELP ME WITH A DRESS FOR THE PARTY, SO WHAT'LL I DO IF THIS ONE DOESN'T LOOK GOOD?
I'M THE ONE HE'LL MAKE FUN OF, NOT YUKARI! SHE'S SUCH AN IDIOT!!!
HA HA HA! TEE HEE!
STEALTHY

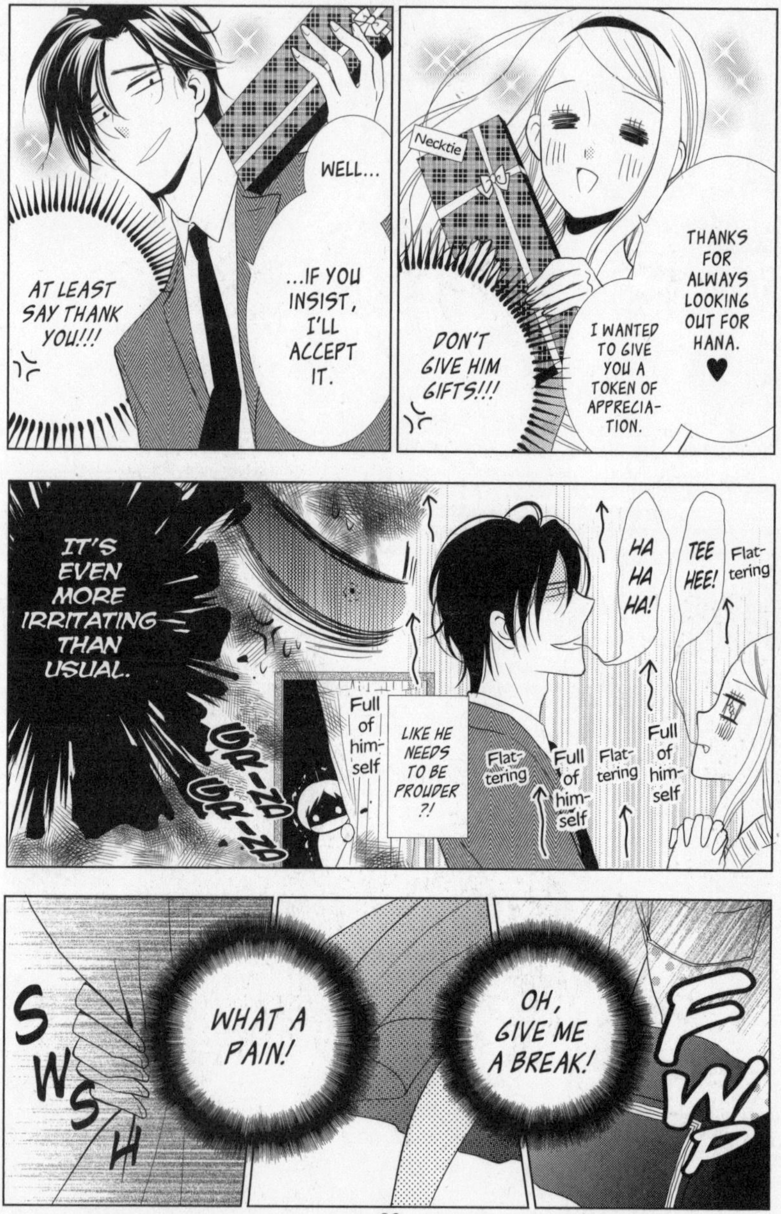
THANKS FOR ALWAYS LOOKING OUT FOR HANA. ♥
I WANTED TO GIVE YOU A TOKEN OF APPRECIATION.
Necktie
DON'T GIVE HIM GIFTS!!!
WELL...
...IF YOU INSIST, I'LL ACCEPT IT.
AT LEAST SAY THANK YOU!!!
Flattering
TEE HEE!
HA HA HA!
Full of himself
Flattering
Full of himself
Flattering
LIKE HE NEEDS TO BE PROUDER?!
Full of himself
GRIND GRIND
IT'S EVEN MORE IRRITATING THAN USUAL.
FWP
OH, GIVE ME A BREAK!
WHAT A PAIN!
SWSH

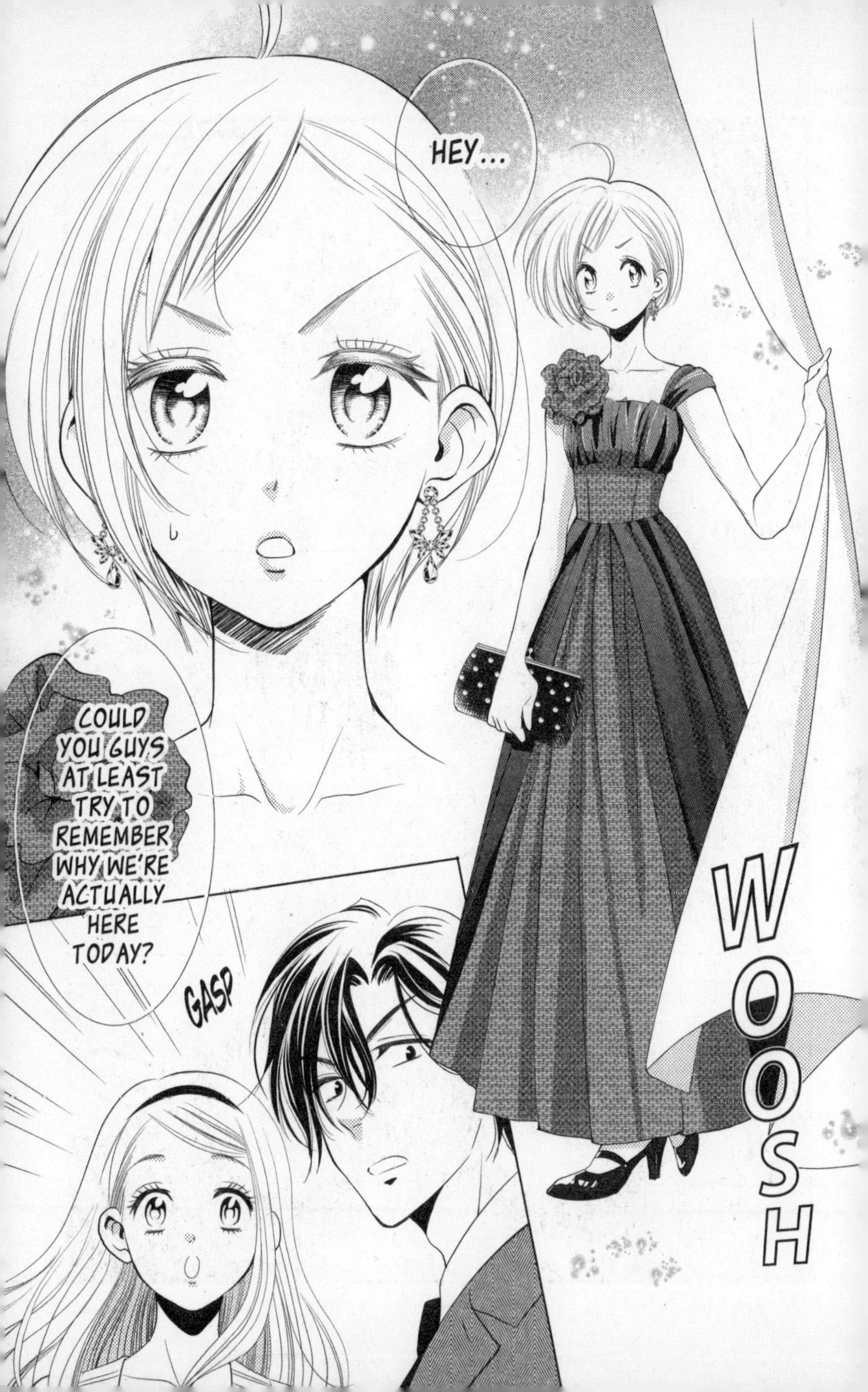
HEY...
WOOSH
COULD YOU GUYS AT LEAST TRY TO REMEMBER WHY WE'RE ACTUALLY HERE TODAY?
GASP

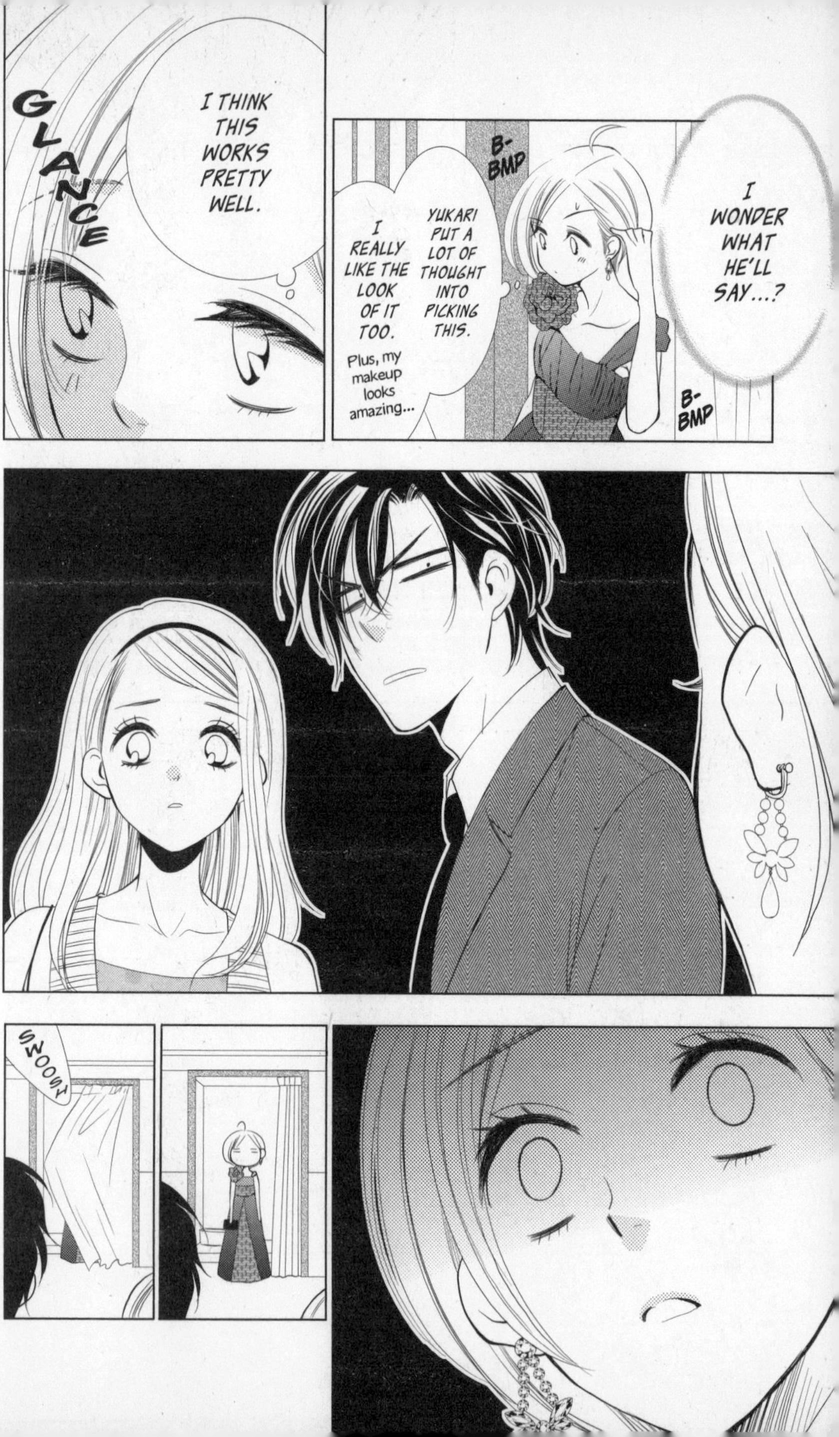
I WONDER WHAT HE'LL SAY...?
B-BMP
YUKARI PUT A LOT OF THOUGHT INTO PICKING THIS.
I REALLY LIKE THE LOOK OF IT TOO.
Plus, my makeup looks amazing...
B-BMP
I THINK THIS WORKS PRETTY WELL.
GLANCE
SWOOSH

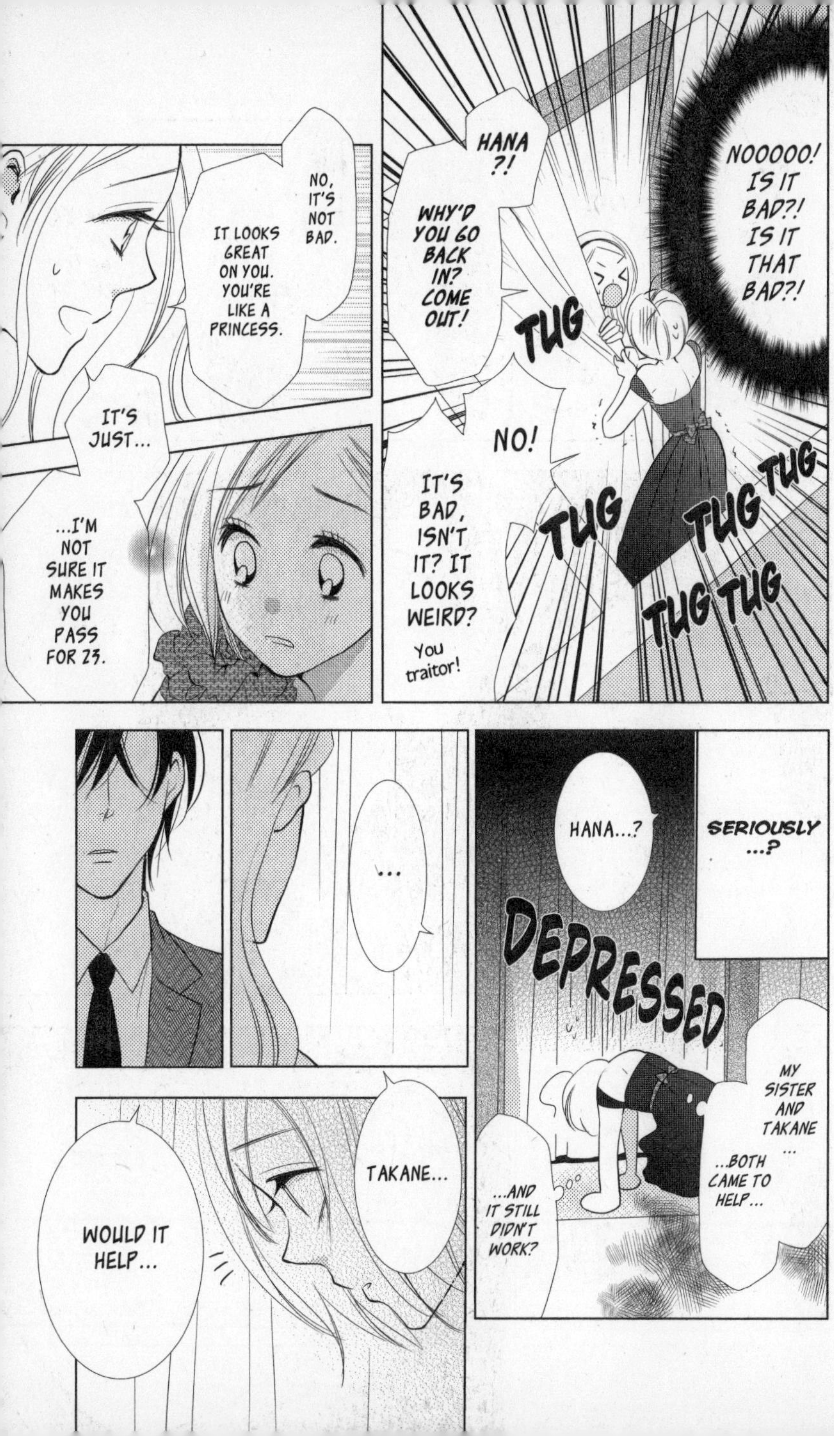
NOOOOO! IS IT BAD?! IS IT THAT BAD?!
HANA ?!
WHY'D YOU GO BACK IN? COME OUT!
TUG
NO!
TUG TUG
IT'S BAD, ISN'T IT? IT LOOKS WEIRD?
TUG
TUG TUG
You traitor!
NO, IT'S NOT BAD.
IT LOOKS GREAT ON YOU. YOU'RE LIKE A PRINCESS.
IT'S JUST...
...I'M NOT SURE IT MAKES YOU PASS FOR 23.
SERIOUSLY ...?
HANA...?
DEPRESSED
MY SISTER AND TAKANE ...
...BOTH CAME TO HELP...
...AND IT STILL DIDN'T WORK?
...
TAKANE...
WOULD IT HELP...

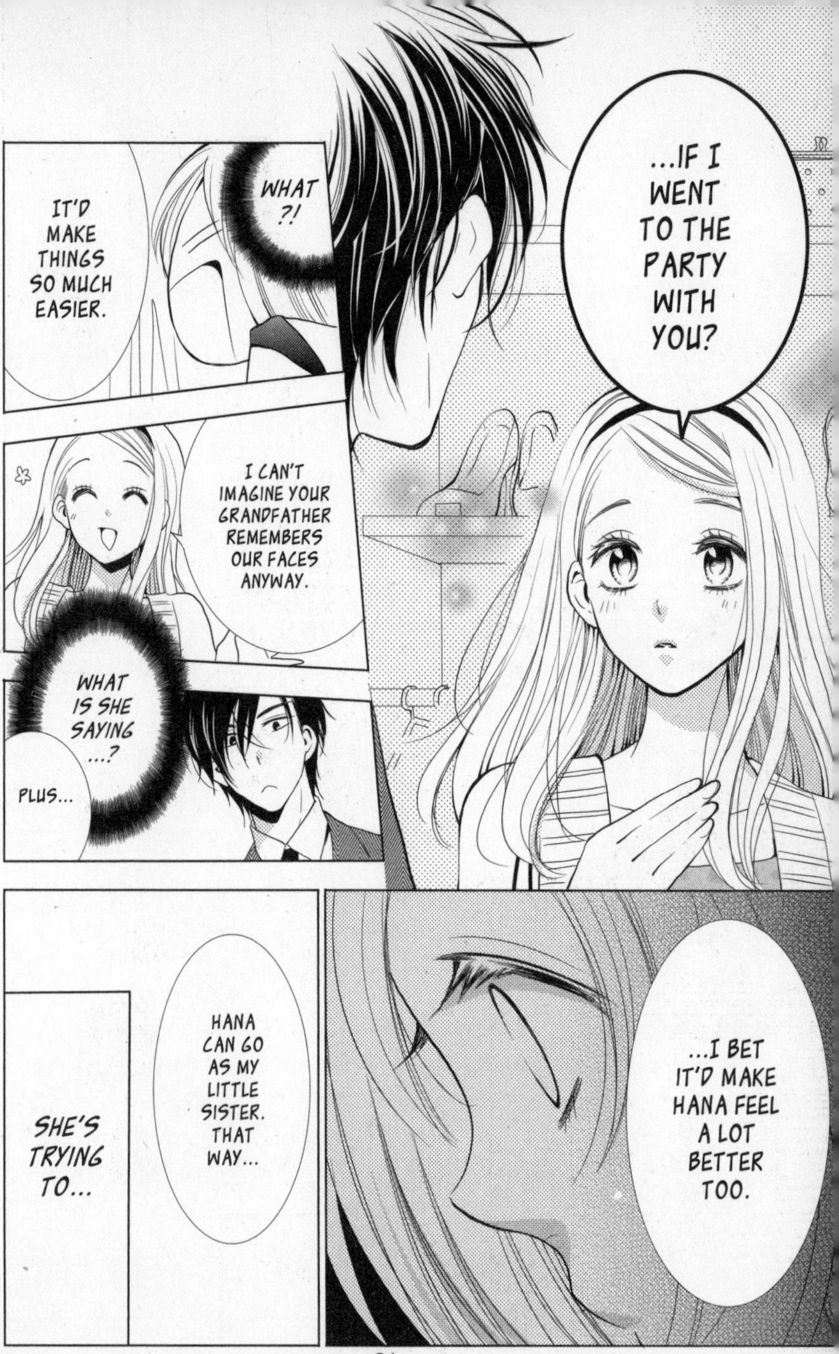
...IF I WENT TO THE PARTY WITH YOU?
WHAT?!
IT'D MAKE THINGS SO MUCH EASIER.
I CAN'T IMAGINE YOUR GRANDFATHER REMEMBERS OUR FACES ANYWAY.
WHAT IS SHE SAYING...?
PLUS...
...I BET IT'D MAKE HANA FEEL A LOT BETTER TOO.
HANA CAN GO AS MY LITTLE SISTER. THAT WAY...
SHE'S TRYING TO...

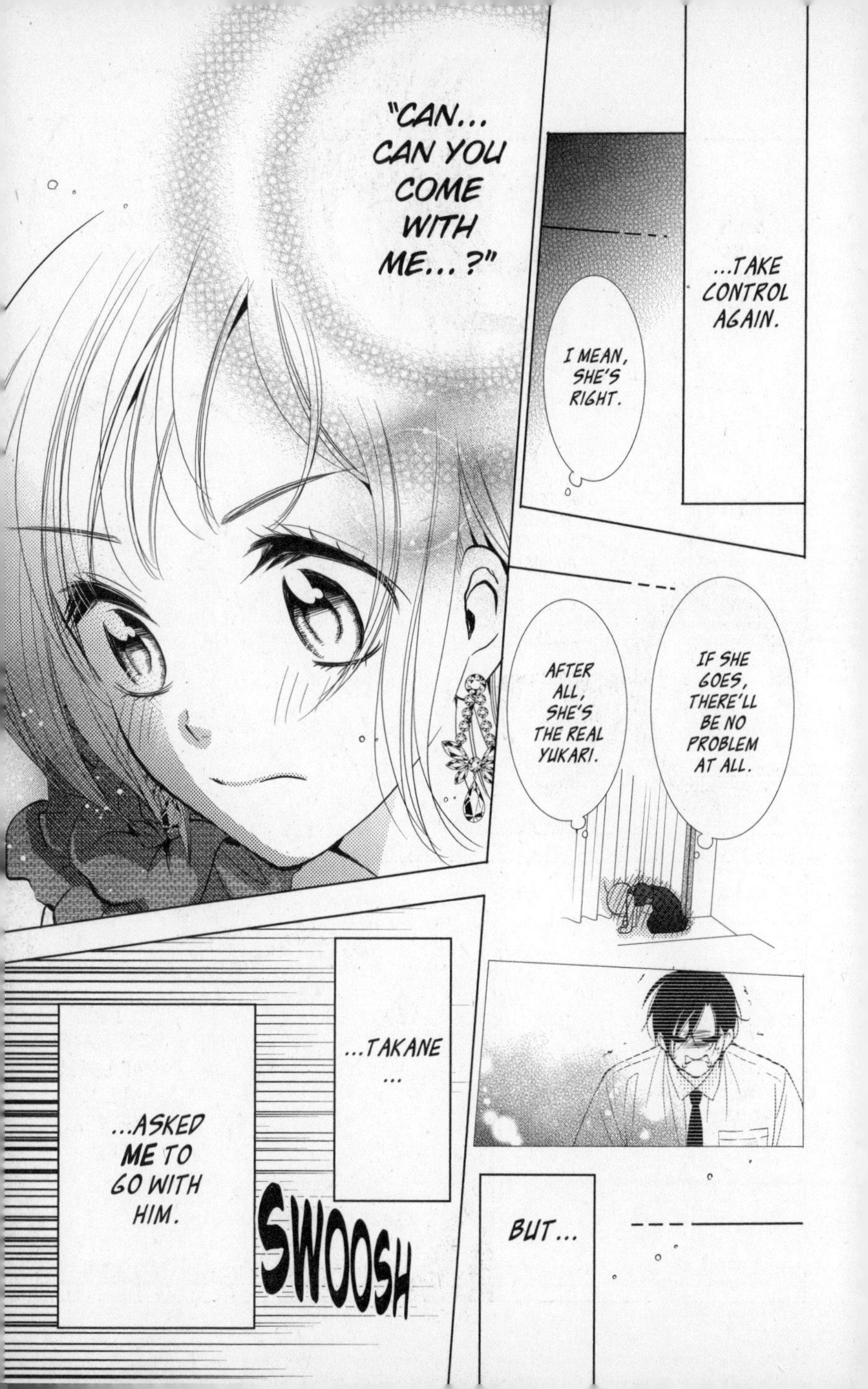
...TAKE CONTROL AGAIN.
I MEAN, SHE'S RIGHT.
IF SHE GOES, THERE'LL BE NO PROBLEM AT ALL.
AFTER ALL, SHE'S THE REAL YUKARI.
"CAN... CAN YOU COME WITH ME...?"
...TAKANE ...
...ASKED ME TO GO WITH HIM.
SWOOSH
BUT...

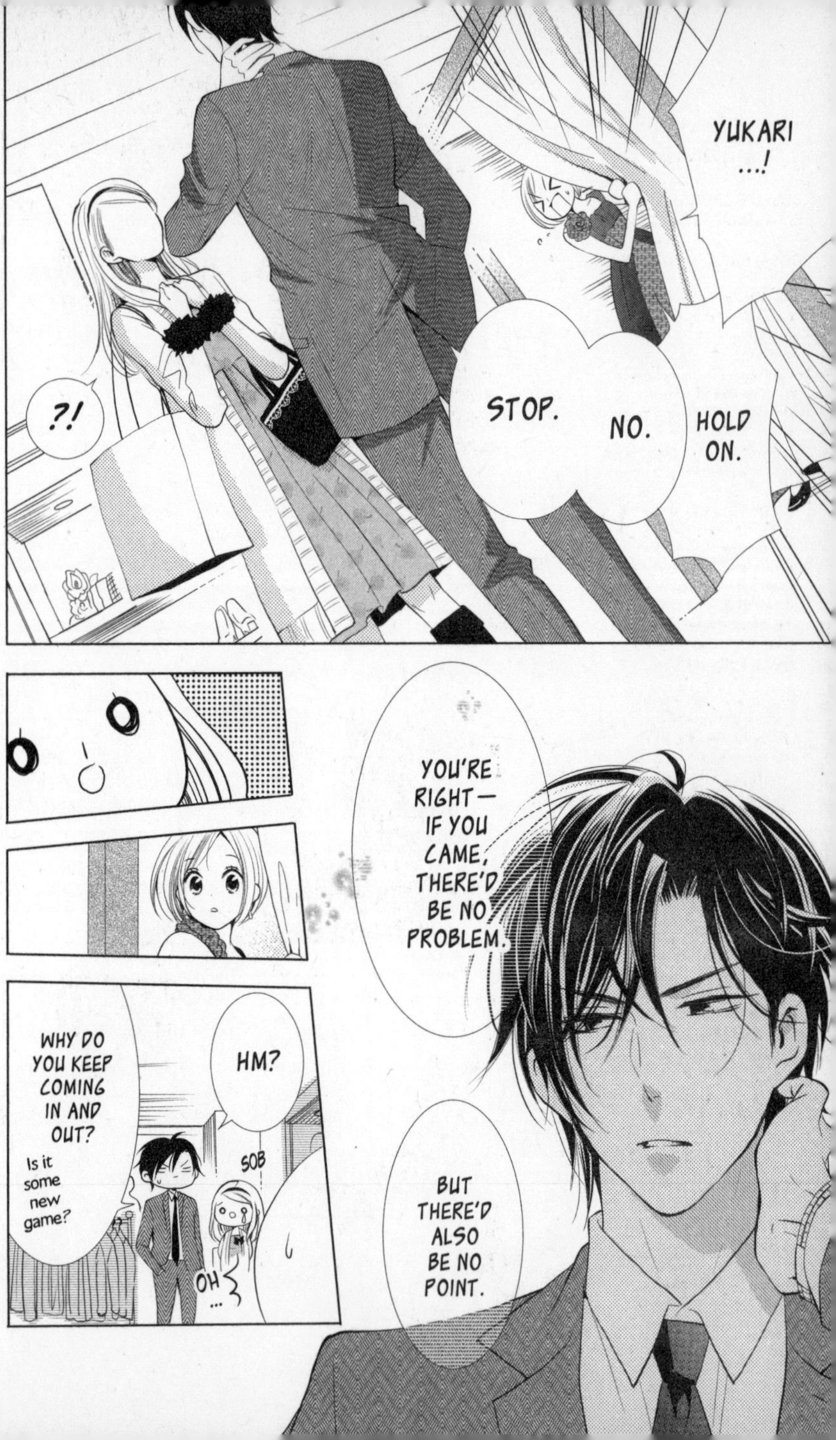
YUKARI ...!
STOP.
NO.
HOLD ON.
?!
YOU'RE RIGHT— IF YOU CAME, THERE'D BE NO PROBLEM.
BUT THERE'D ALSO BE NO POINT.
HM?
WHY DO YOU KEEP COMING IN AND OUT?
Is it some new game?
SOB
OH ...

● Hello! ●

Thanks to all of you, I've reached volume 2.

It's my first serialization!

I'm so happy to be able to keep writing about Hana and Takane.

The longer I write a character, the more I become attached to them and am able to discover new sides to them. It's also fun to get to explore deeper story lines.

The stories in volume 1 were created as one-shots, so I imagined my audience as people reading it for the first time. But with volume 2, I'm gradually coming to think of it more as a series. I've had to really change the way I approach it. It's hard.

I'm beginning to understand just how different the challenges posed by one-shots are compared to the challenges of doing a series.

● About the Cover ●

In volume 1, they were buried under money in the Yukichi desert.* I wanted them to be buried in something else for this volume, so I came up with a sea of roses.

I'm not good at thinking of cover designs. They often get rejected for looking too old-fashioned, but I got instant approval on this one.

The Yukichi desert, a sea of roses... What will be next? Trying to keep the "buried" theme going will be a challenge.

*Yukichi Fukuzawa is on the 10,000 yen bill.

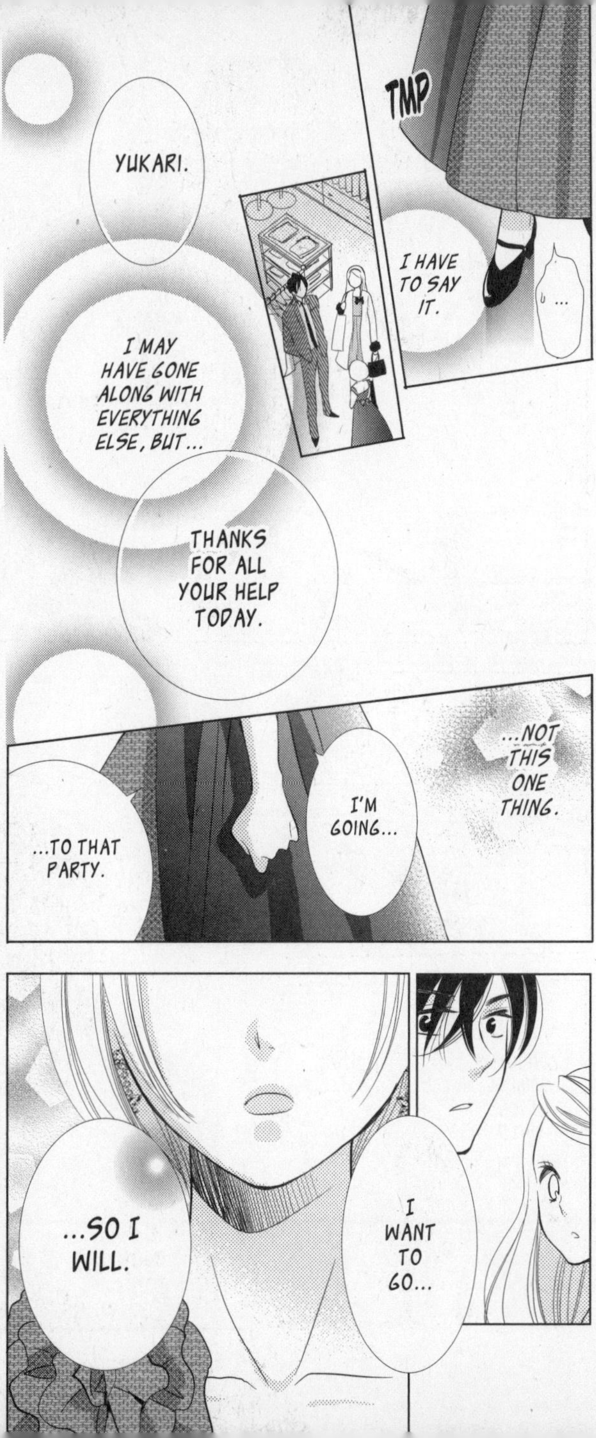
TMP
I HAVE TO SAY IT.
...
YUKARI.
I MAY HAVE GONE ALONG WITH EVERYTHING ELSE, BUT...
THANKS FOR ALL YOUR HELP TODAY.
...NOT THIS ONE THING.
I'M GOING...
...TO THAT PARTY.
I WANT TO GO...
...SO I WILL.

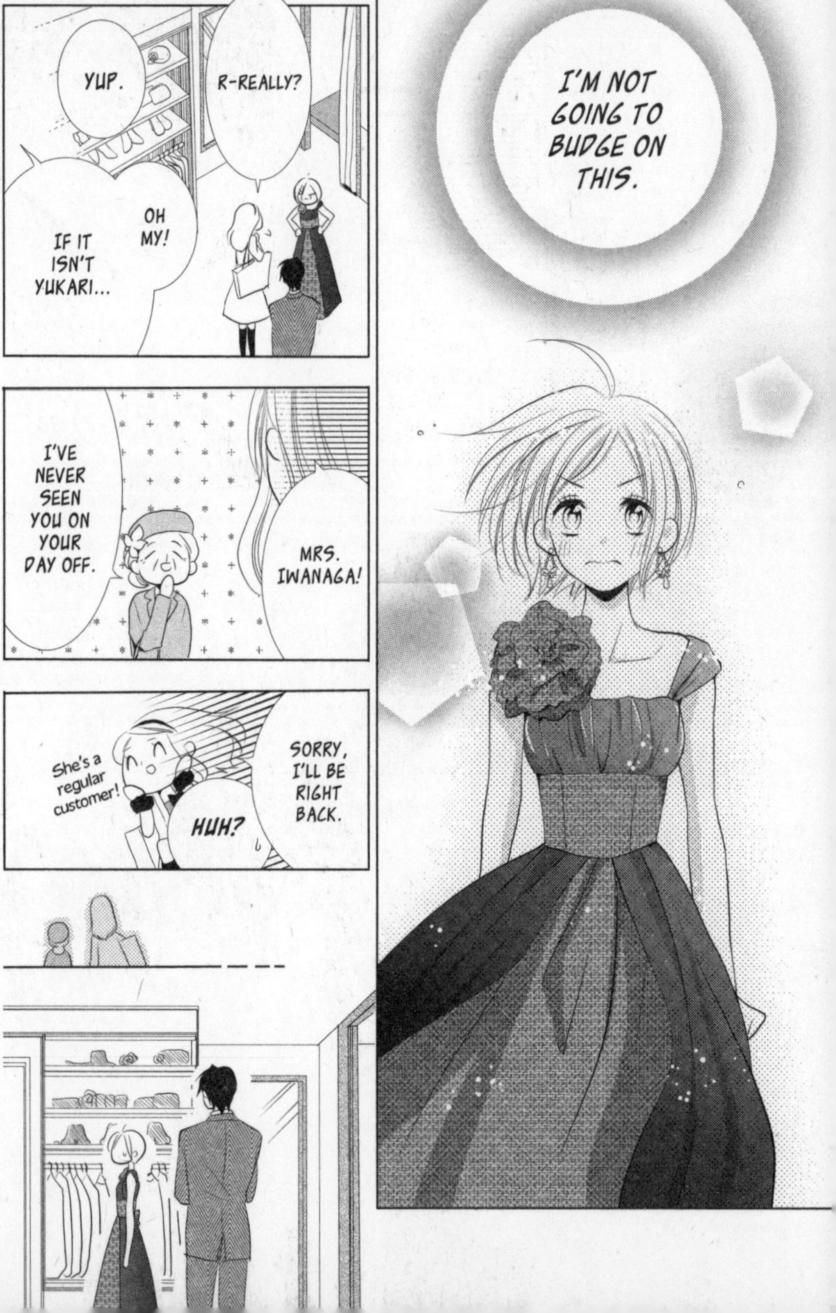
I'M NOT GOING TO BUDGE ON THIS.
R-REALLY?
YUP.
OH MY!
IF IT ISN'T YUKARI...
MRS. IWANAGA!
I'VE NEVER SEEN YOU ON YOUR DAY OFF.
SORRY, I'LL BE RIGHT BACK.
HUH?
She's a regular customer!

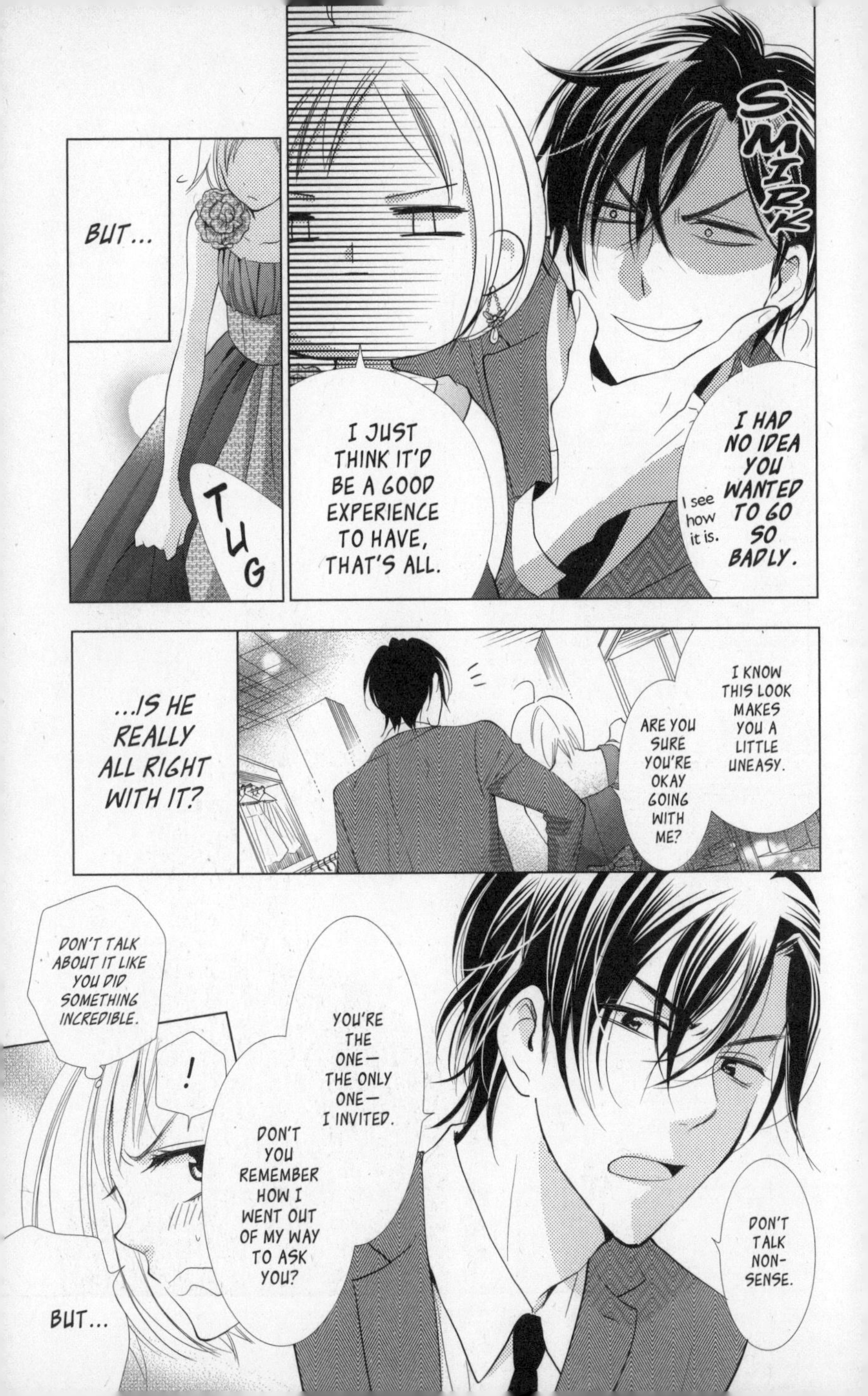
SMIRK
I HAD NO IDEA YOU WANTED TO GO SO BADLY.
I see how it is.
I JUST THINK IT'D BE A GOOD EXPERIENCE TO HAVE, THAT'S ALL.
TUG
BUT...
I KNOW THIS LOOK MAKES YOU A LITTLE UNEASY.
ARE YOU SURE YOU'RE OKAY GOING WITH ME?
...IS HE REALLY ALL RIGHT WITH IT?
DON'T TALK NON-SENSE.
YOU'RE THE ONE— THE ONLY ONE— I INVITED.
DON'T YOU REMEMBER HOW I WENT OUT OF MY WAY TO ASK YOU?
!
DON'T TALK ABOUT IT LIKE YOU DID SOMETHING INCREDIBLE.
BUT...

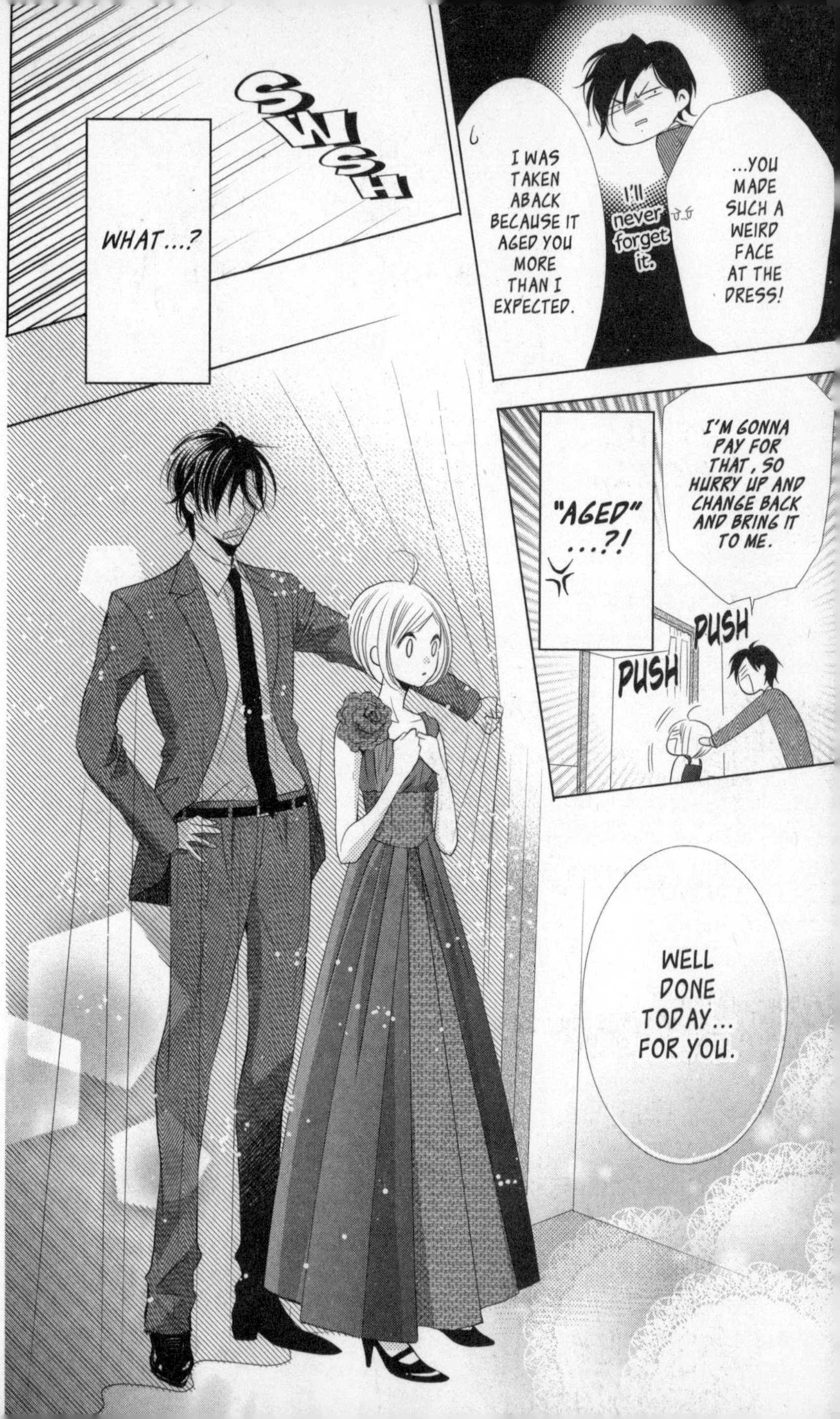
...YOU MADE SUCH A WEIRD FACE AT THE DRESS!
I'll never forget it.
I WAS TAKEN ABACK BECAUSE IT AGED YOU MORE THAN I EXPECTED.
SWSH
WHAT...?
I'M GONNA PAY FOR THAT, SO HURRY UP AND CHANGE BACK AND BRING IT TO ME.
"AGED" ...?!
PUSH
PUSH
WELL DONE TODAY... FOR YOU.

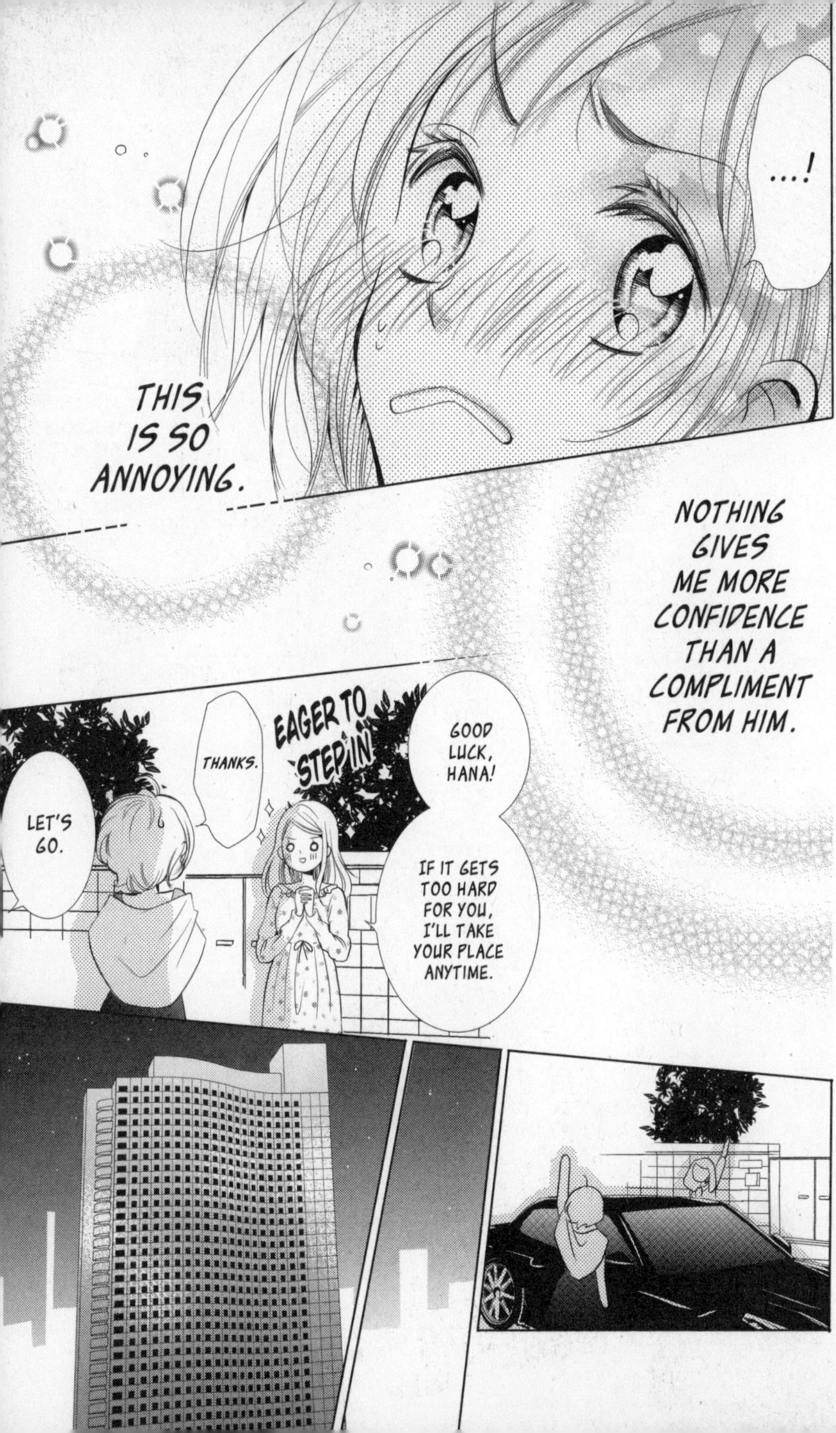
...!
THIS IS SO ANNOYING.
NOTHING GIVES ME MORE CONFIDENCE THAN A COMPLIMENT FROM HIM.
GOOD LUCK, HANA!
IF IT GETS TOO HARD FOR YOU, I'LL TAKE YOUR PLACE ANYTIME.
EAGER TO STEP IN
THANKS.
LET'S GO.

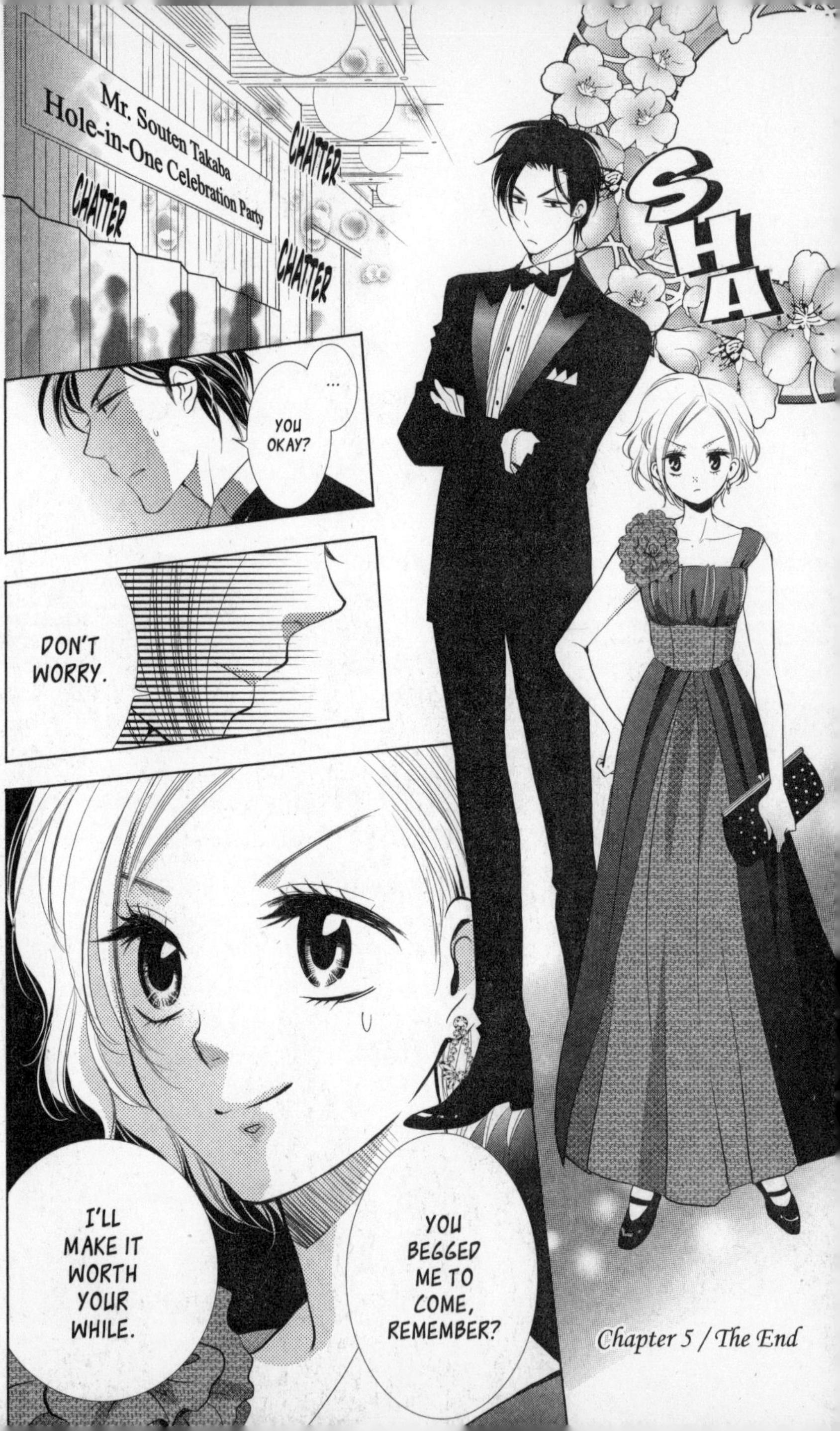
SHA
Chapter 5 / The End
Mr. Souten Takaba Hole-in-One Celebration Party
CHATTER
CHATTER
CHATTER
...
YOU OKAY?
DON'T WORRY.
YOU BEGGED ME TO COME, REMEMBER?
I'LL MAKE IT WORTH YOUR WHILE.

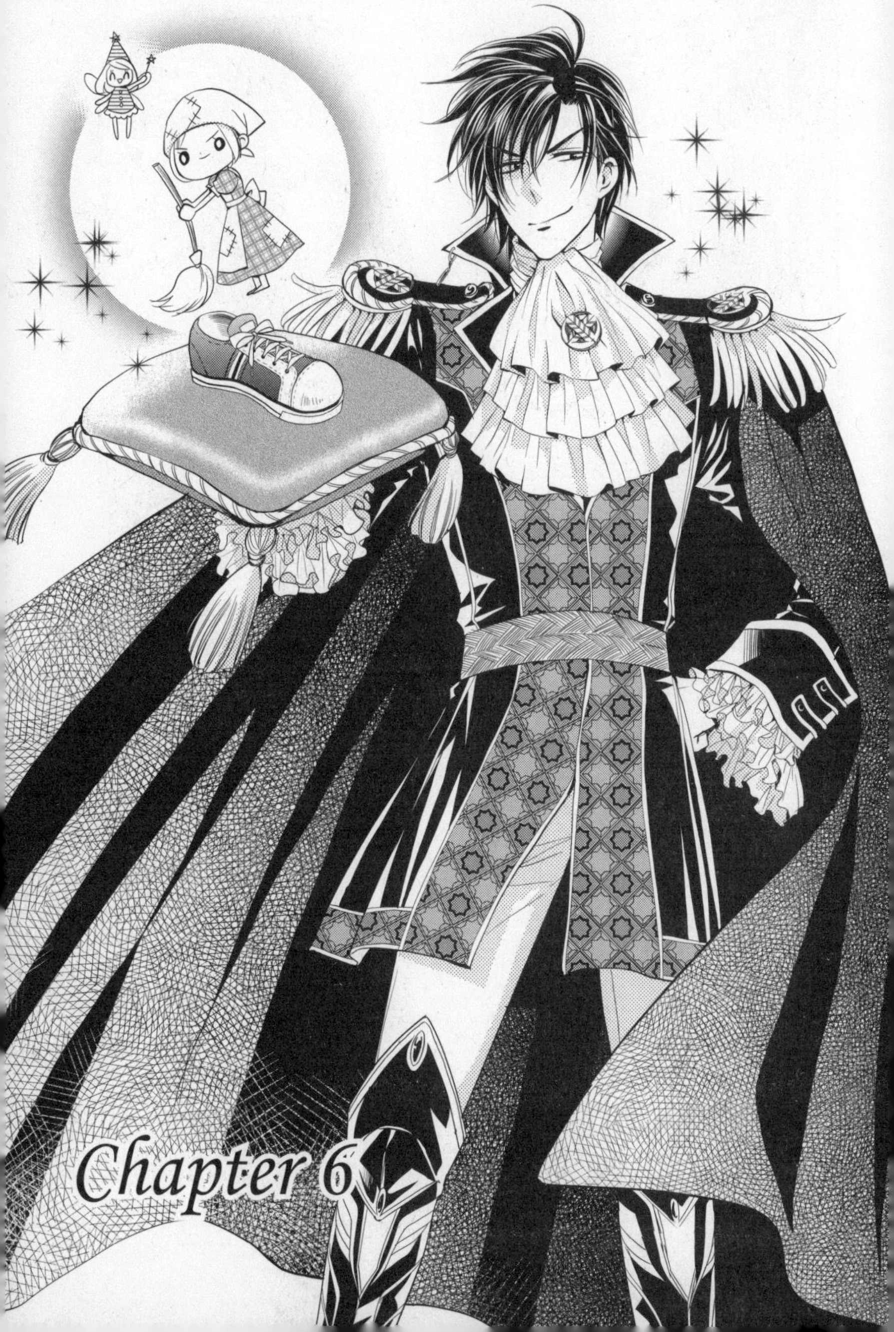
Chapter 6

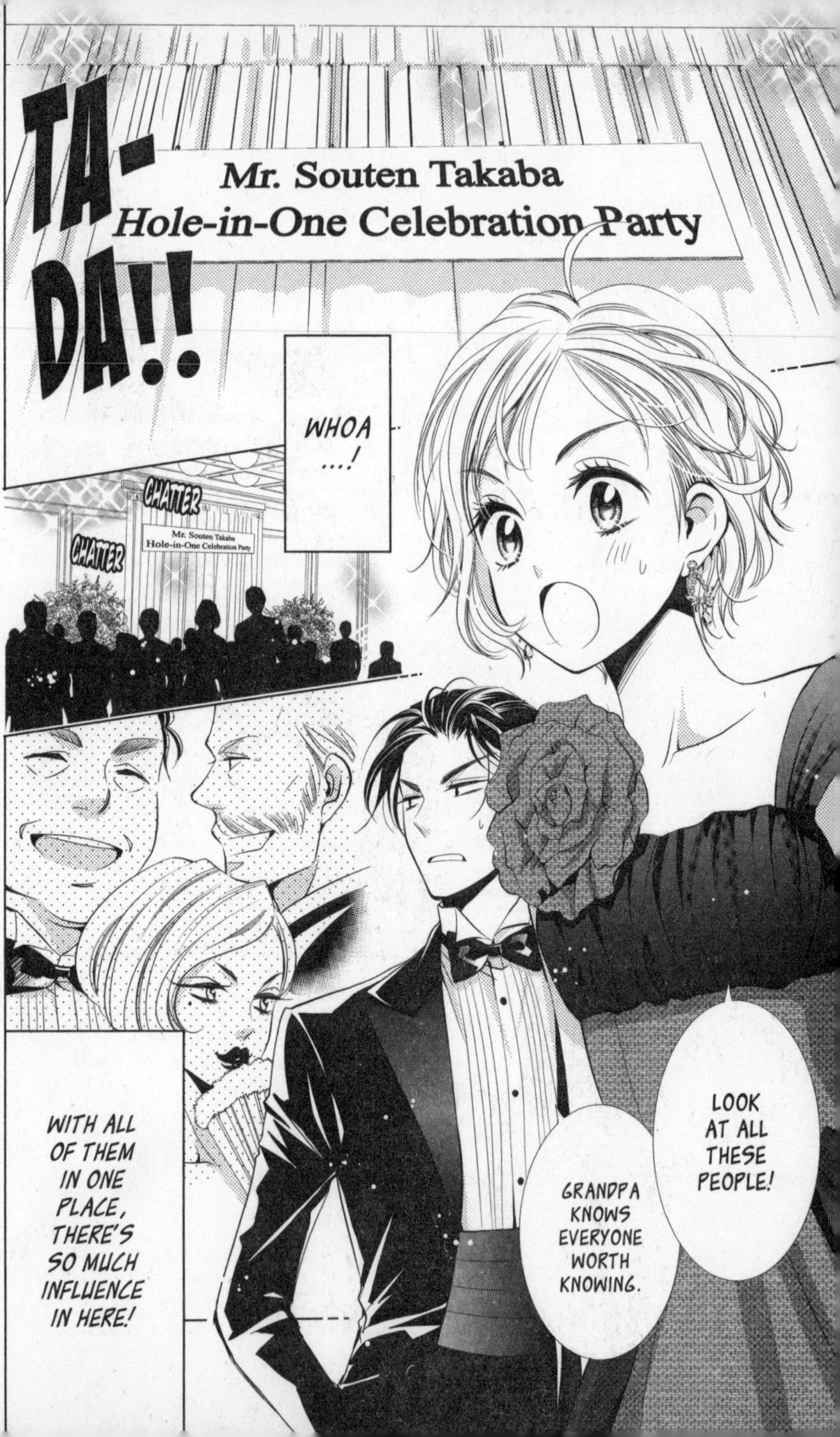
Mr. Souten Takaba
Hole-in-One Celebration Party
TA-DA!!
WHOA ...!
CHATTER
Mr. Souten Takaba
Hole-in-One Celebration Party
CHATTER
LOOK AT ALL THESE PEOPLE!
GRANDPA KNOWS EVERYONE WORTH KNOWING.
WITH ALL OF THEM IN ONE PLACE, THERE'S SO MUCH INFLUENCE IN HERE!

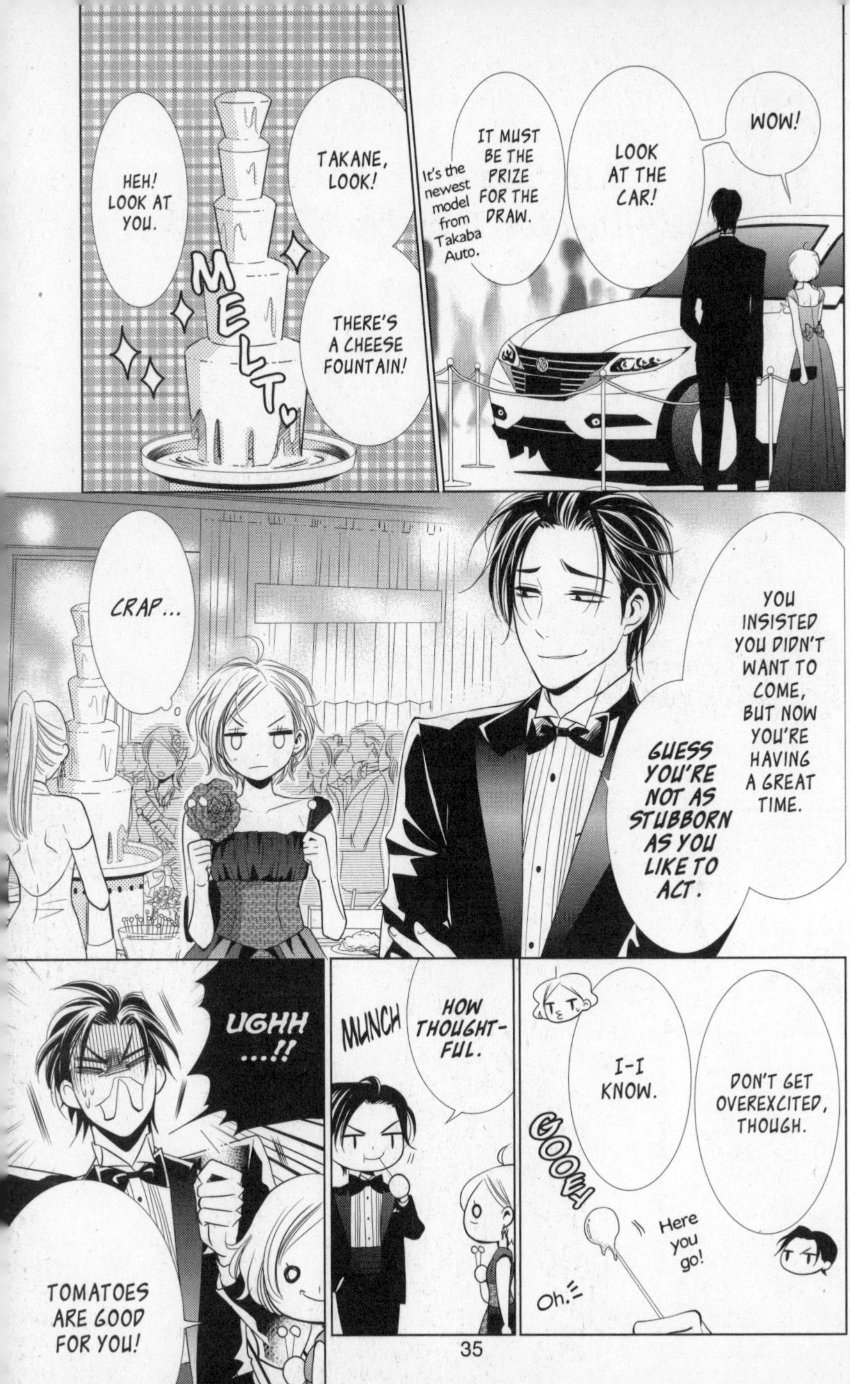
WOW!
LOOK AT THE CAR!
IT MUST BE THE PRIZE FOR THE DRAW.
It's the newest model from Takaba Auto.
TAKANE, LOOK!
THERE'S A CHEESE FOUNTAIN!
MELT
HEH! LOOK AT YOU.
YOU INSISTED YOU DIDN'T WANT TO COME, BUT NOW YOU'RE HAVING A GREAT TIME.
GUESS YOU'RE NOT AS STUBBORN AS YOU LIKE TO ACT.
CRAP...
DON'T GET OVEREXCITED, THOUGH.
I-I KNOW.
Here you go!
Oh.
HOW THOUGHT-FUL.
MUNCH
UGHH ...!!
TOMATOES ARE GOOD FOR YOU!

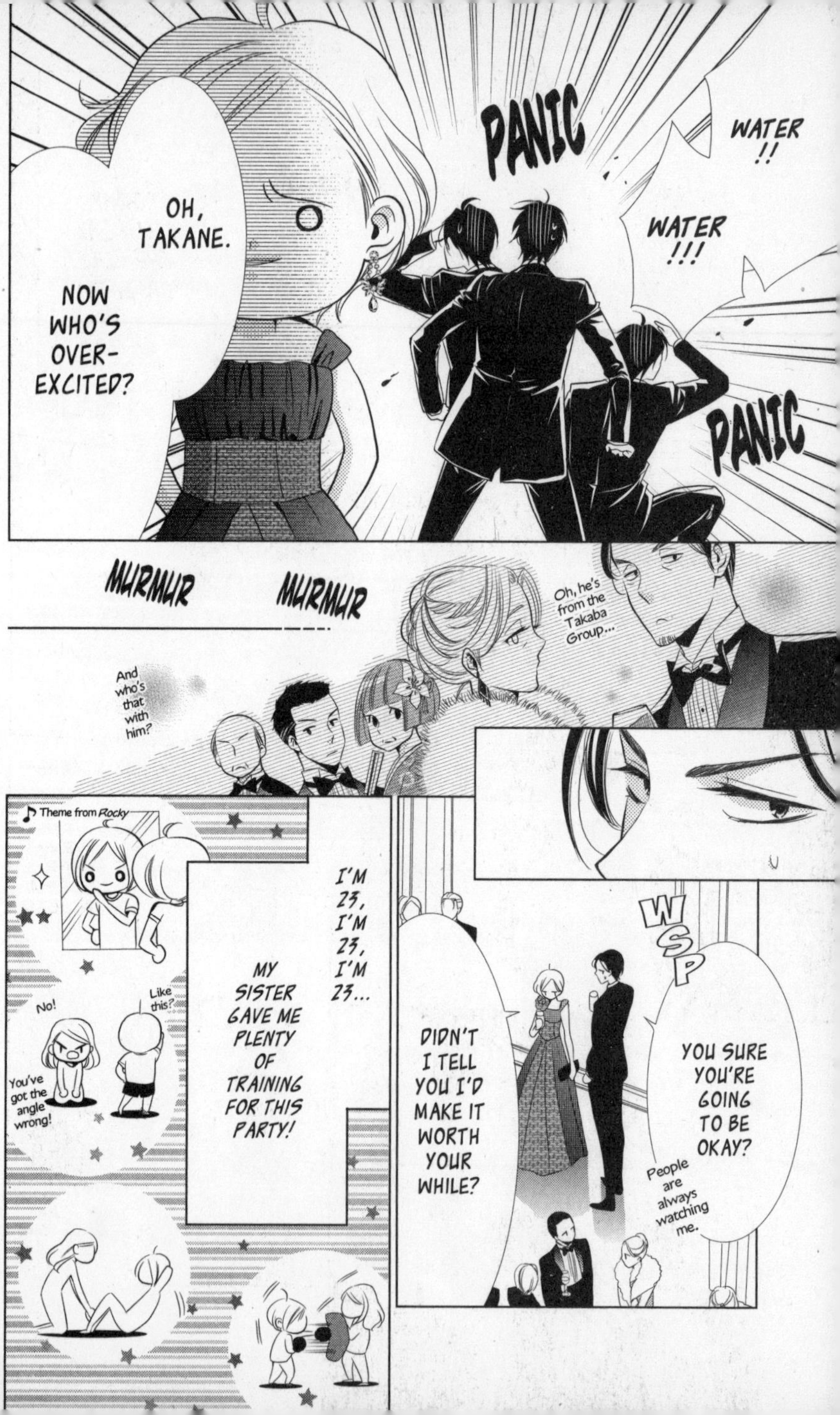
WATER !!
WATER !!!
PANIC
PANIC
OH, TAKANE.
NOW WHO'S OVER-EXCITED?
Oh, he's from the Takaba Group...
MURMUR
MURMUR
And who's that with him?
WSP
YOU SURE YOU'RE GOING TO BE OKAY?
People are always watching me.
DIDN'T I TELL YOU I'D MAKE IT WORTH YOUR WHILE?
I'M 23, I'M 23, I'M 23...
MY SISTER GAVE ME PLENTY OF TRAINING FOR THIS PARTY!
♪ Theme from Rocky
Like this?
No!
You've got the angle wrong!

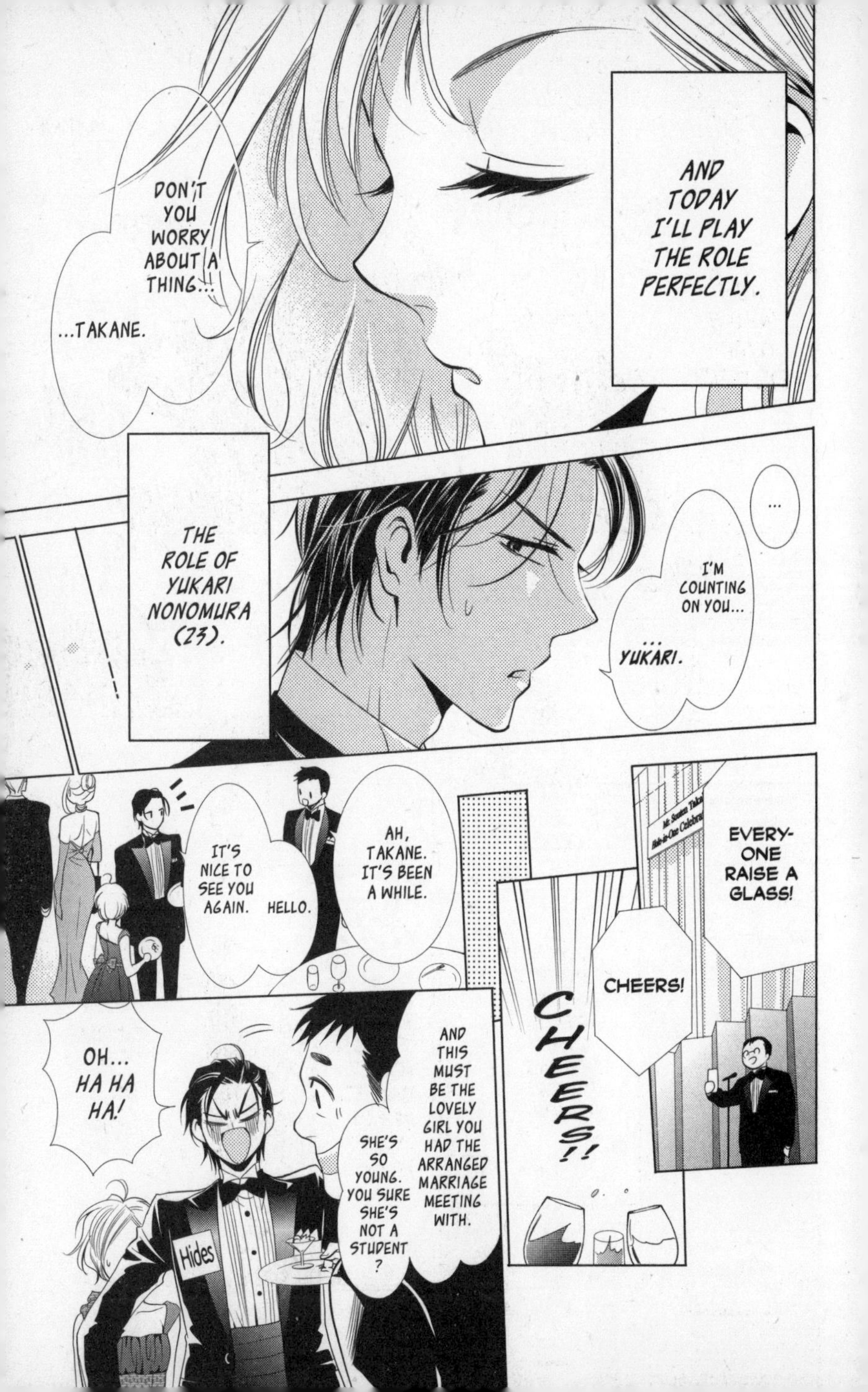
AND TODAY I'LL PLAY THE ROLE PERFECTLY.
DON'T YOU WORRY ABOUT A THING...
...TAKANE.
...
I'M COUNTING ON YOU...
...YUKARI.
THE ROLE OF YUKARI NONOMURA (23).
EVERY-ONE RAISE A GLASS!
CHEERS!
CHEERS!!
AH, TAKANE. IT'S BEEN A WHILE.
HELLO.
IT'S NICE TO SEE YOU AGAIN.
AND THIS MUST BE THE LOVELY GIRL YOU HAD THE ARRANGED MARRIAGE MEETING WITH.
SHE'S SO YOUNG. YOU SURE SHE'S NOT A STUDENT?
OH... HA HA HA!
Hides

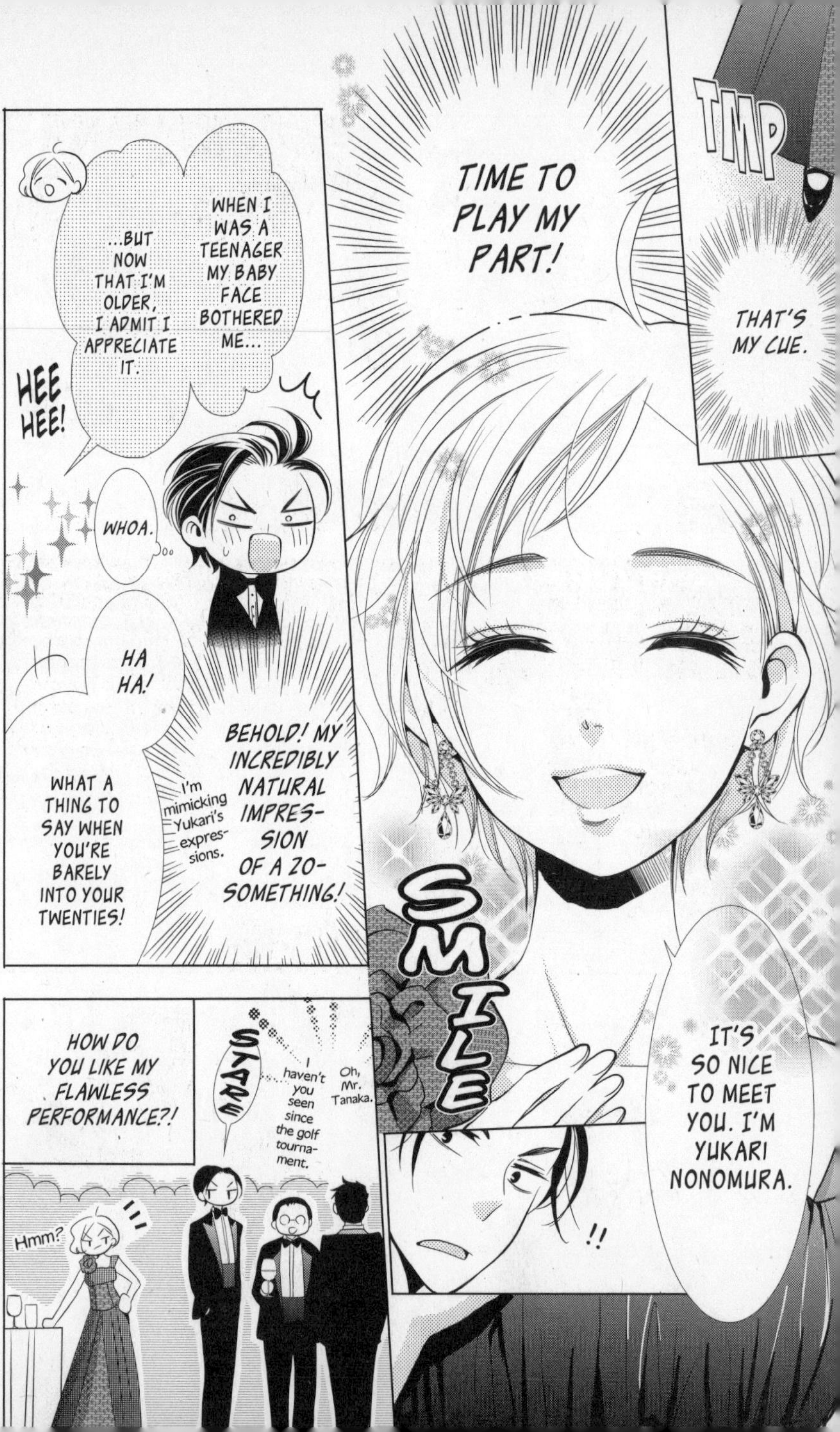
TMP
THAT'S MY CUE.
TIME TO PLAY MY PART!
SMILE
IT'S SO NICE TO MEET YOU. I'M YUKARI NONOMURA.
!!
WHEN I WAS A TEENAGER MY BABY FACE BOTHERED ME...
...BUT NOW THAT I'M OLDER, I ADMIT I APPRECIATE IT.
HEE HEE!
WHOA.
HA HA!
BEHOLD! MY INCREDIBLY NATURAL IMPRES-SION OF A 20-SOMETHING!
I'm mimicking Yukari's expres-sions.
WHAT A THING TO SAY WHEN YOU'RE BARELY INTO YOUR TWENTIES!
Oh, Mr. Tanaka.
I haven't you seen since the golf tourna-ment.
STARE
HOW DO YOU LIKE MY FLAWLESS PERFORMANCE?!
Hmm?

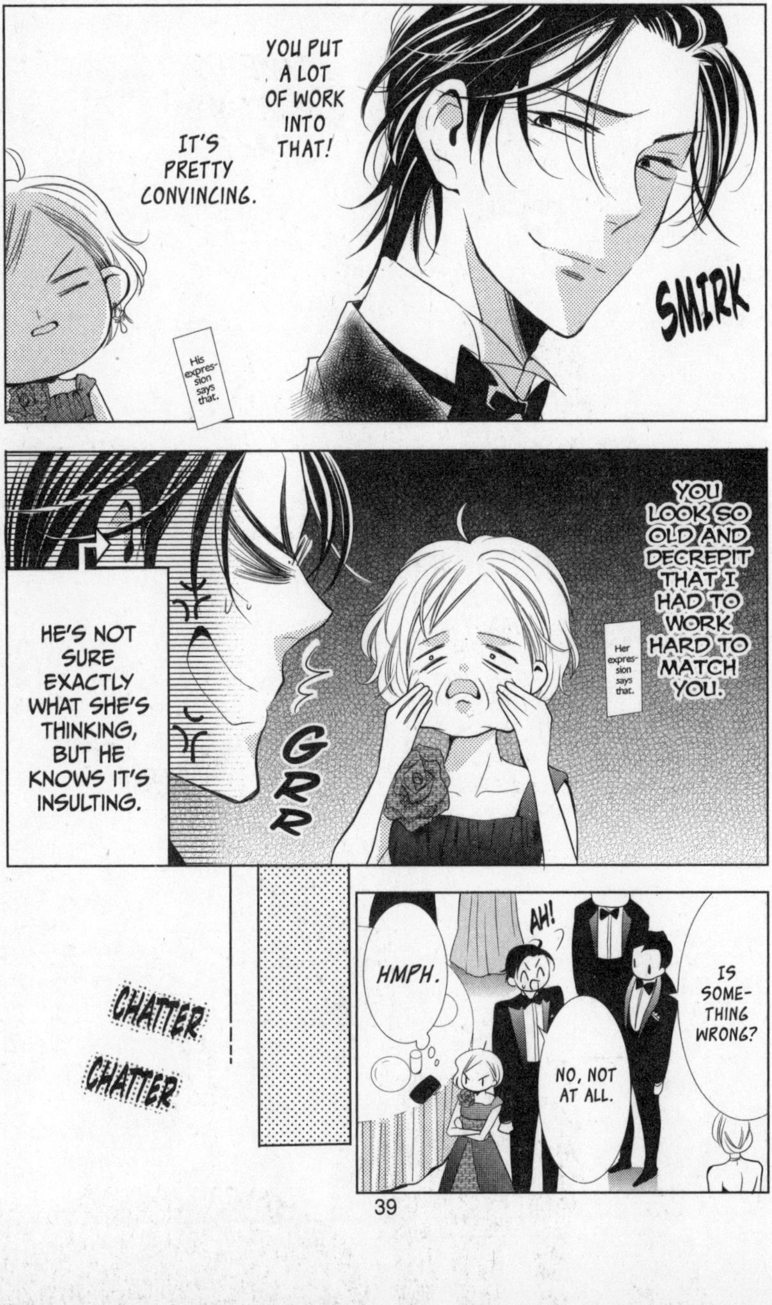
YOU PUT A LOT OF WORK INTO THAT!
IT'S PRETTY CONVINCING.
SMIRK
His expression says that.
YOU LOOK SO OLD AND DECREPIT THAT I HAD TO WORK HARD TO MATCH YOU.
Her expression says that.
GRR
HE'S NOT SURE EXACTLY WHAT SHE'S THINKING, BUT HE KNOWS IT'S INSULTING.
IS SOME-THING WRONG?
AH!
NO, NOT AT ALL.
HMPH.
CHATTER
CHATTER

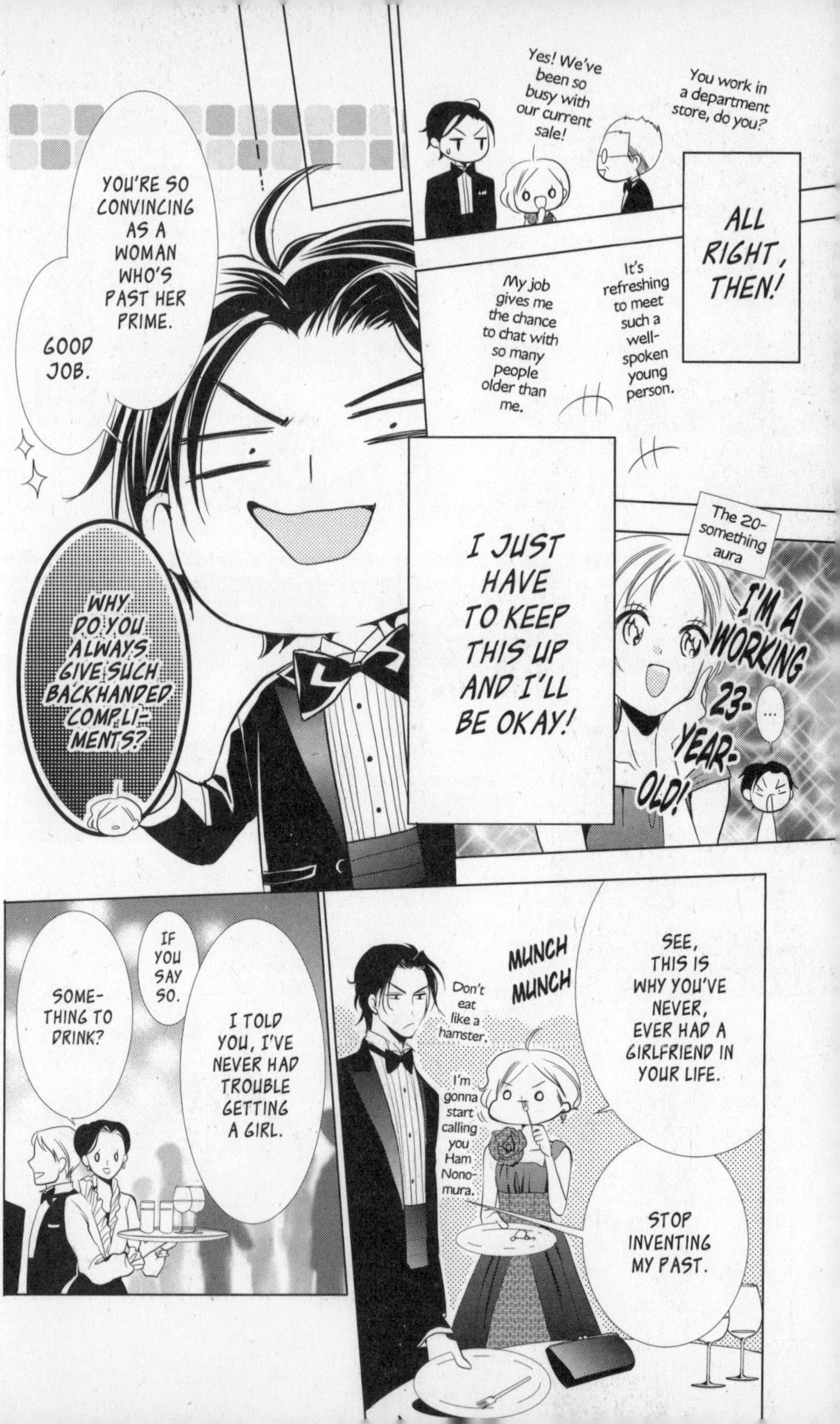
You work in a department store, do you?
Yes! We've been so busy with our current sale!
ALL RIGHT, THEN!
It's refreshing to meet such a well-spoken young person.
My job gives me the chance to chat with so many people older than me.
I JUST HAVE TO KEEP THIS UP AND I'LL BE OKAY!
The 20-something aura
I'M A WORKING 23-YEAR-OLD!
...
YOU'RE SO CONVINCING AS A WOMAN WHO'S PAST HER PRIME.
GOOD JOB.
WHY DO YOU ALWAYS GIVE SUCH BACKHANDED COMPLI-MENTS?
SEE, THIS IS WHY YOU'VE NEVER, EVER HAD A GIRLFRIEND IN YOUR LIFE.
MUNCH MUNCH
Don't eat like a hamster.
I'm gonna start calling you Ham Nonomura.
STOP INVENTING MY PAST.
I TOLD YOU, I'VE NEVER HAD TROUBLE GETTING A GIRL.
IF YOU SAY SO.
SOME-THING TO DRINK?

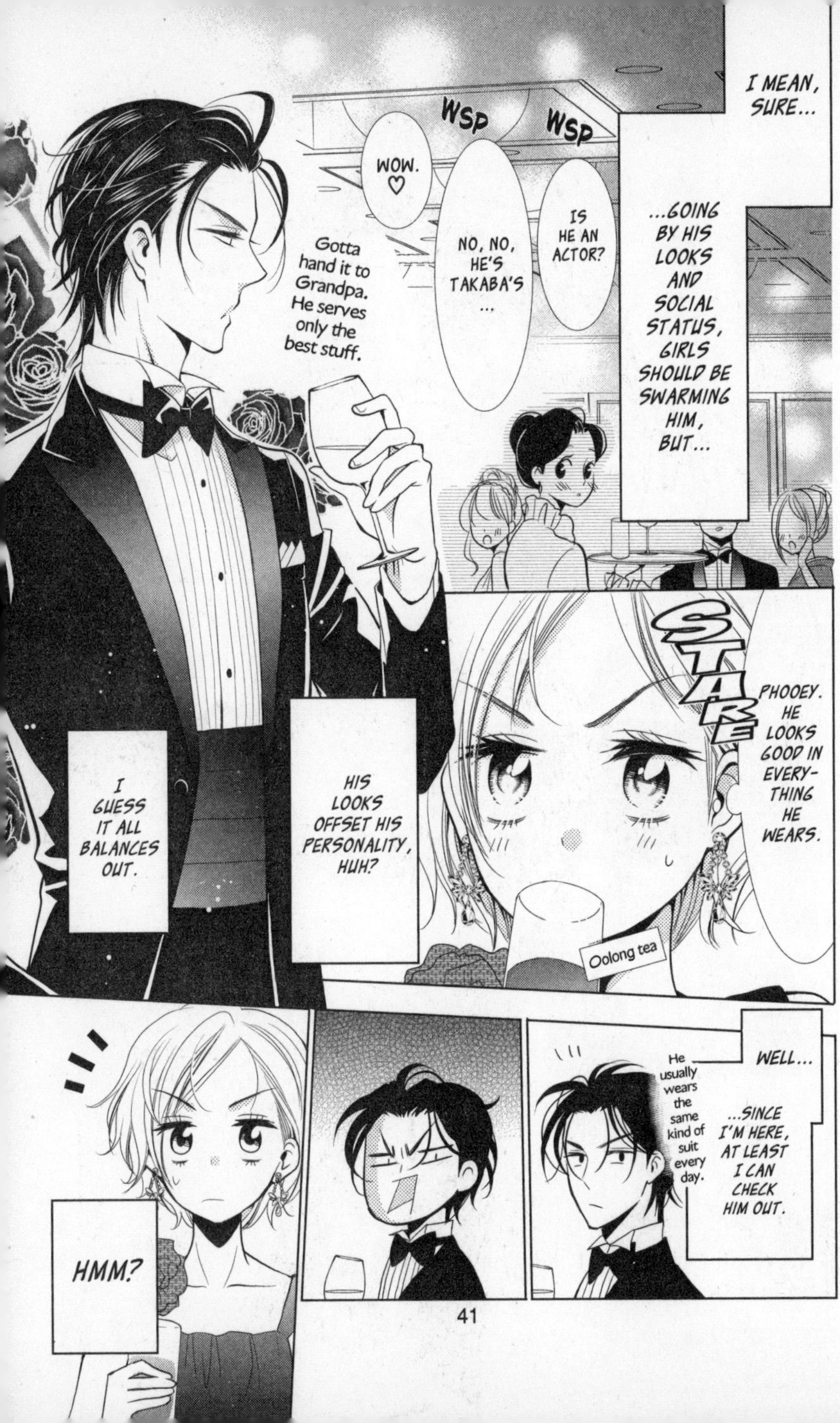

I MEAN, SURE...
...GOING BY HIS LOOKS AND SOCIAL STATUS, GIRLS SHOULD BE SWARMING HIM, BUT...
WSP
WSP
IS HE AN ACTOR?
NO, NO, HE'S TAKABA'S ...
WOW. ♡
STARE
PHOOEY. HE LOOKS GOOD IN EVERYTHING HE WEARS.
Oolong tea
Gotta hand it to Grandpa. He serves only the best stuff.
HIS LOOKS OFFSET HIS PERSONALITY, HUH?
I GUESS IT ALL BALANCES OUT.
WELL...
...SINCE I'M HERE, AT LEAST I CAN CHECK HIM OUT.
He usually wears the same kind of suit every day.
HMM?

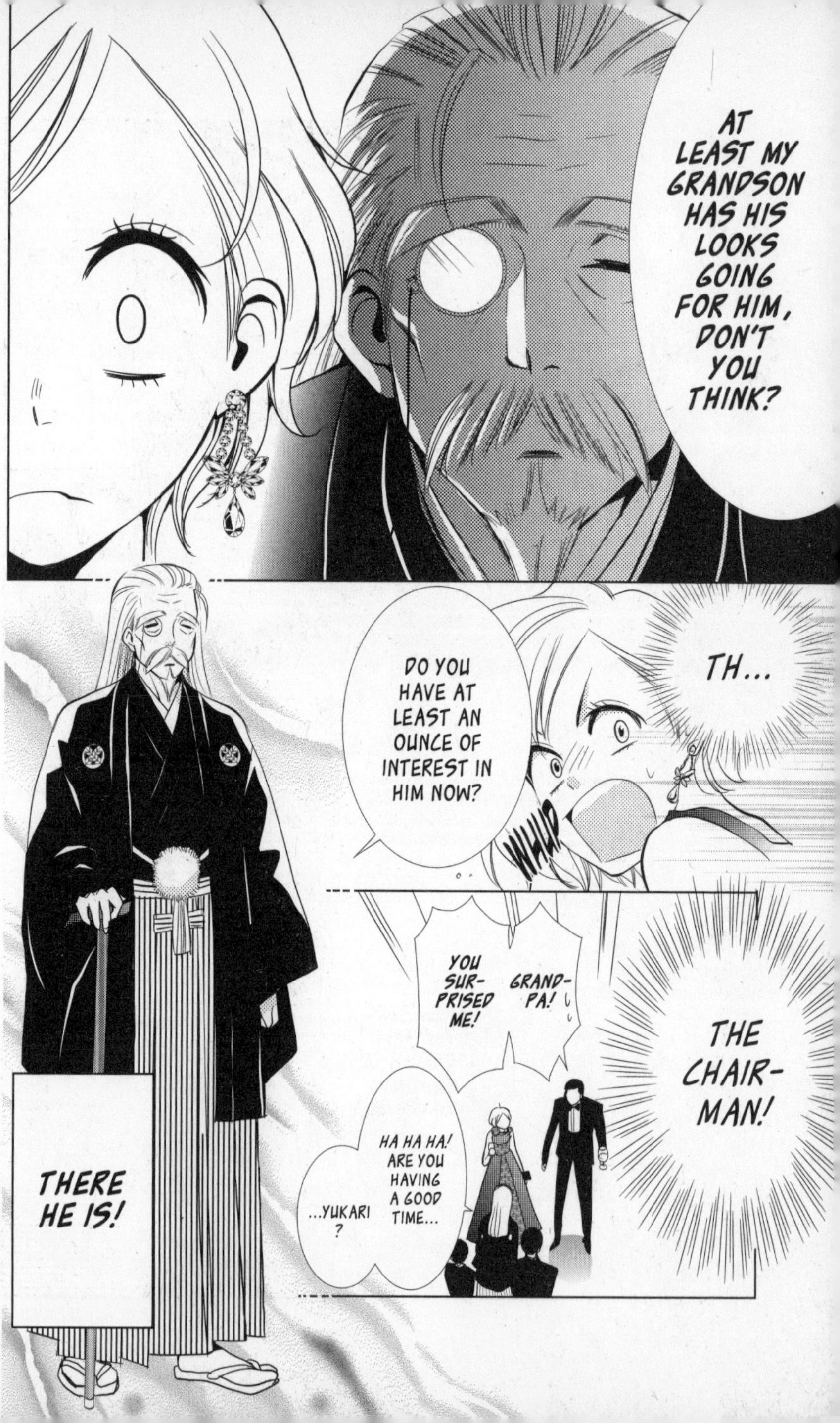
AT LEAST MY GRANDSON HAS HIS LOOKS GOING FOR HIM, DON'T YOU THINK?
TH...
DO YOU HAVE AT LEAST AN OUNCE OF INTEREST IN HIM NOW?
WHUP
THE CHAIR-MAN!
GRAND-PA!
YOU SUR-PRISED ME!
HA HA HA! ARE YOU HAVING A GOOD TIME...
...YUKARI?
THERE HE IS!

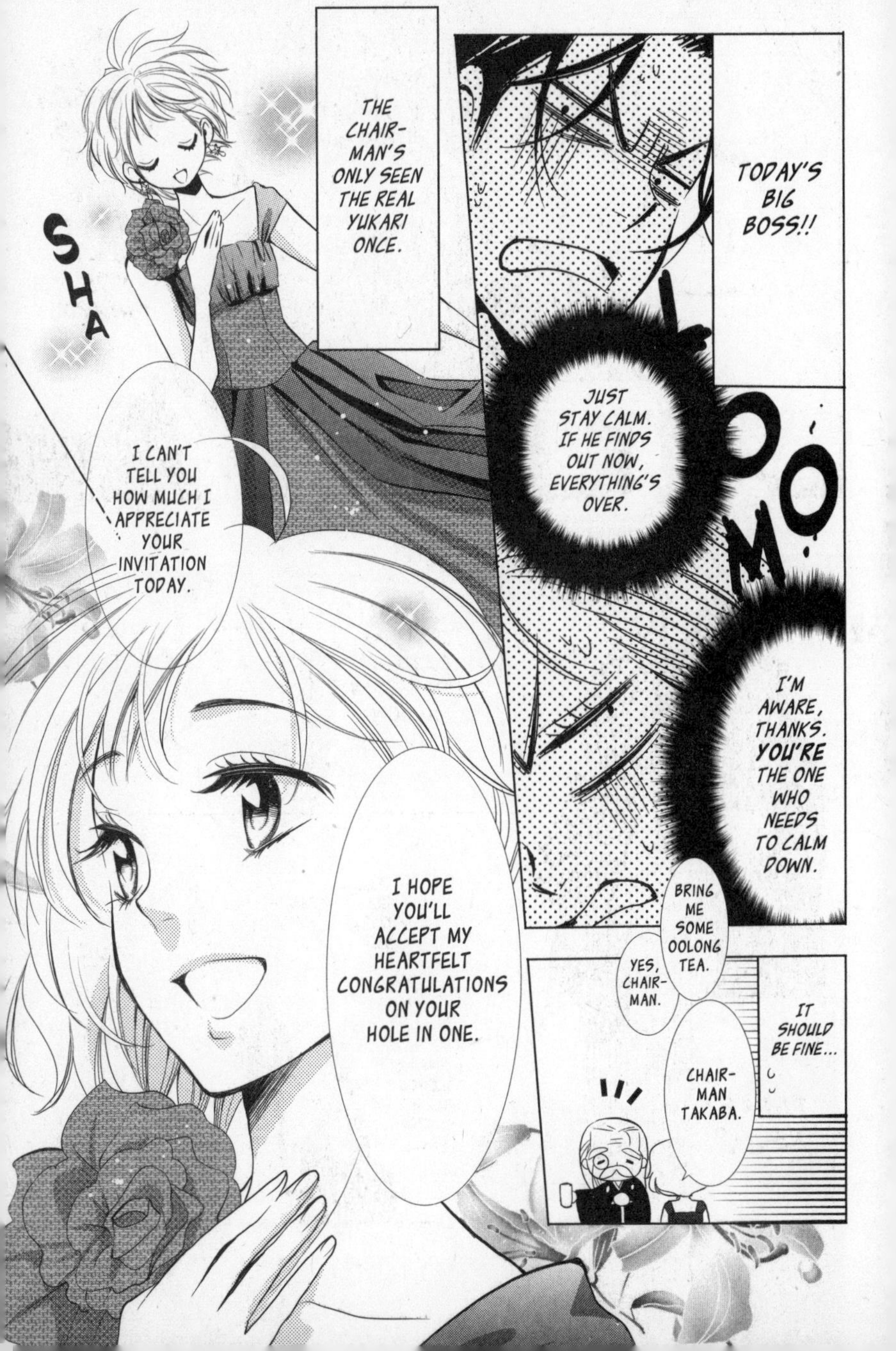
TODAY'S BIG BOSS!!
THE CHAIRMAN'S ONLY SEEN THE REAL YUKARI ONCE.
DOOM
JUST STAY CALM. IF HE FINDS OUT NOW, EVERYTHING'S OVER.
I'M AWARE, THANKS. **YOU'RE** THE ONE WHO NEEDS TO CALM DOWN.
BRING ME SOME OOLONG TEA.
YES, CHAIRMAN.
IT SHOULD BE FINE...
CHAIRMAN TAKABA.
SHA
I CAN'T TELL YOU HOW MUCH I APPRECIATE YOUR INVITATION TODAY.
I HOPE YOU'LL ACCEPT MY HEARTFELT CONGRATULATIONS ON YOUR HOLE IN ONE.

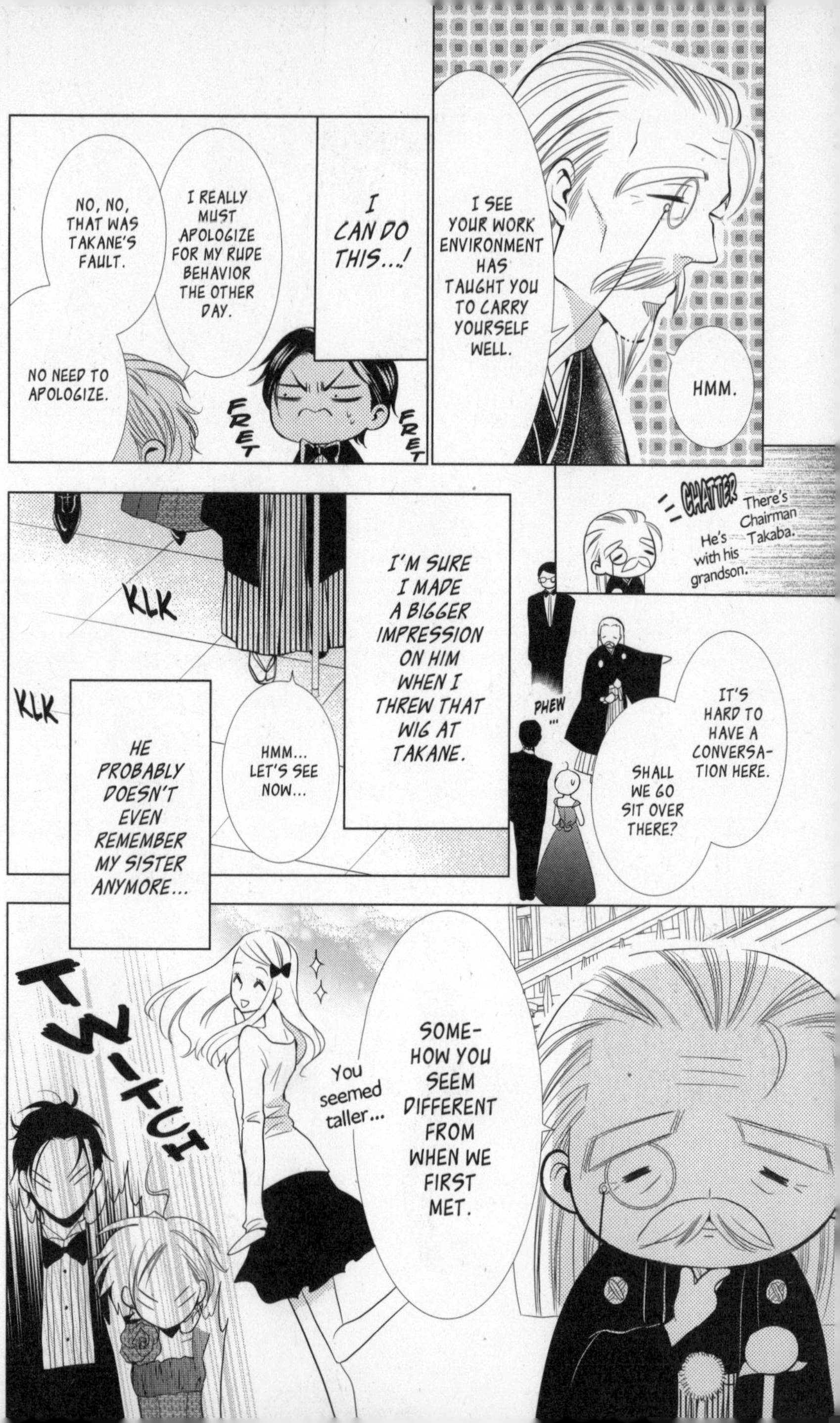
I SEE YOUR WORK ENVIRONMENT HAS TAUGHT YOU TO CARRY YOURSELF WELL.
HMM.
I CAN DO THIS...!
I REALLY MUST APOLOGIZE FOR MY RUDE BEHAVIOR THE OTHER DAY.
NO, NO, THAT WAS TAKANE'S FAULT.
NO NEED TO APOLOGIZE.
FRET
FRET
CHATTER
There's Chairman Takaba.
He's with his grandson.
IT'S HARD TO HAVE A CONVERSA-TION HERE.
SHALL WE GO SIT OVER THERE?
PHEW...
I'M SURE I MADE A BIGGER IMPRESSION ON HIM WHEN I THREW THAT WIG AT TAKANE.
KLK
HMM... LET'S SEE NOW...
KLK
HE PROBABLY DOESN'T EVEN REMEMBER MY SISTER ANYMORE...
SOME-HOW YOU SEEM DIFFERENT FROM WHEN WE FIRST MET.
You seemed taller...
TWITCH

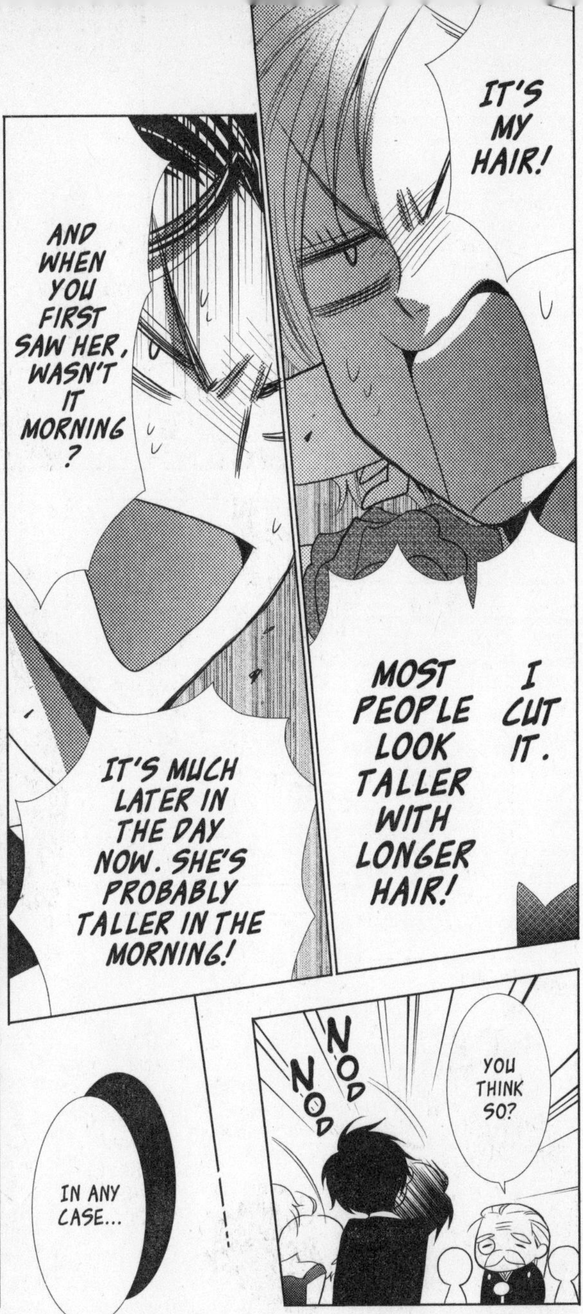
IT'S MY HAIR!
I CUT IT.
MOST PEOPLE LOOK TALLER WITH LONGER HAIR!
AND WHEN YOU FIRST SAW HER, WASN'T IT MORNING?
IT'S MUCH LATER IN THE DAY NOW. SHE'S PROBABLY TALLER IN THE MORNING!
YOU THINK SO?
NOD NOD
IN ANY CASE...

●Yukari Nonomura●

She acts on her gut feelings. Her carefree attitude attracts some people...and probably repels others. (LOL) But her intentions are always good. She loves clothing that's both sophisticated and feminine.

Without Yukari for an older sister, Hana would probably be a totally different person, and she never would have met Takane. In that respect, Yukari's a very important character. I chose her name because it means "connection."

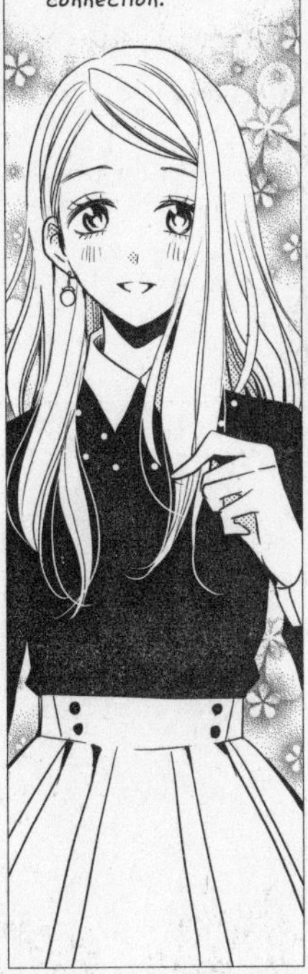

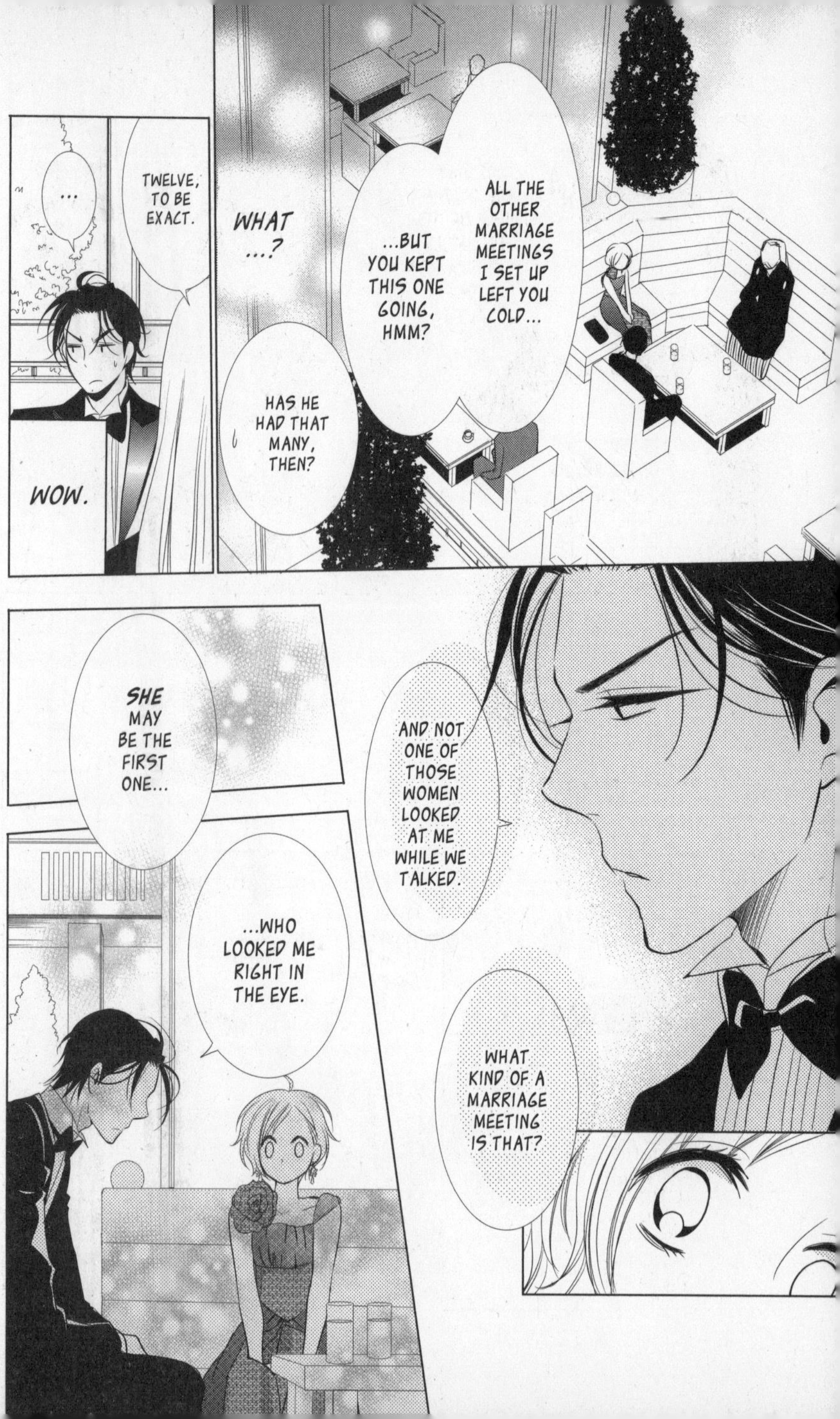
ALL THE OTHER MARRIAGE MEETINGS I SET UP LEFT YOU COLD...
...BUT YOU KEPT THIS ONE GOING, HMM?
WHAT ...?
HAS HE HAD THAT MANY, THEN?
TWELVE, TO BE EXACT.
...
WOW.
AND NOT ONE OF THOSE WOMEN LOOKED AT ME WHILE WE TALKED.
WHAT KIND OF A MARRIAGE MEETING IS THAT?
SHE MAY BE THE FIRST ONE...
...WHO LOOKED ME RIGHT IN THE EYE.

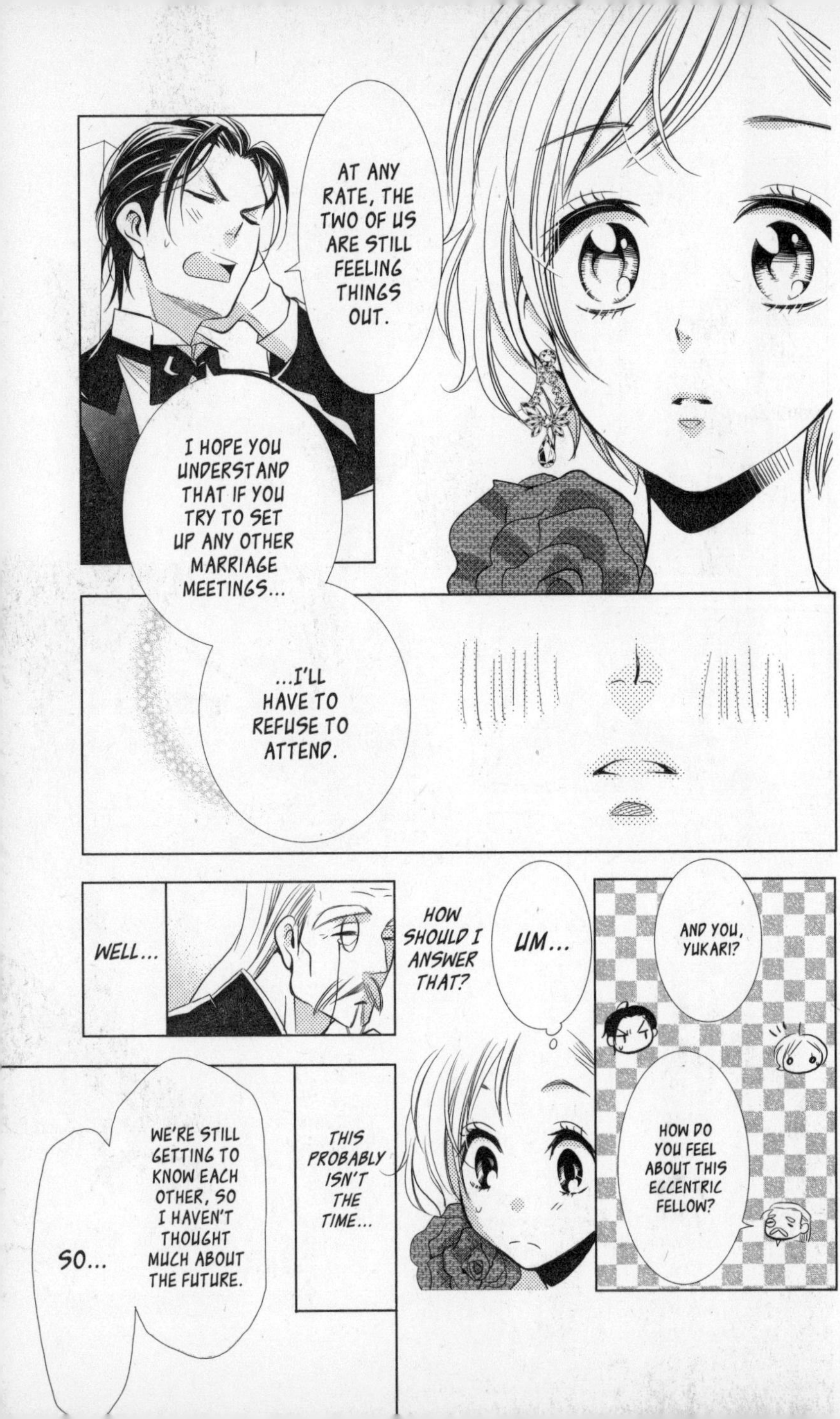
AT ANY RATE, THE TWO OF US ARE STILL FEELING THINGS OUT.
I HOPE YOU UNDERSTAND THAT IF YOU TRY TO SET UP ANY OTHER MARRIAGE MEETINGS...
...I'LL HAVE TO REFUSE TO ATTEND.
AND YOU, YUKARI?
HOW DO YOU FEEL ABOUT THIS ECCENTRIC FELLOW?
UM...
HOW SHOULD I ANSWER THAT?
WELL...
THIS PROBABLY ISN'T THE TIME...
WE'RE STILL GETTING TO KNOW EACH OTHER, SO I HAVEN'T THOUGHT MUCH ABOUT THE FUTURE.
SO...

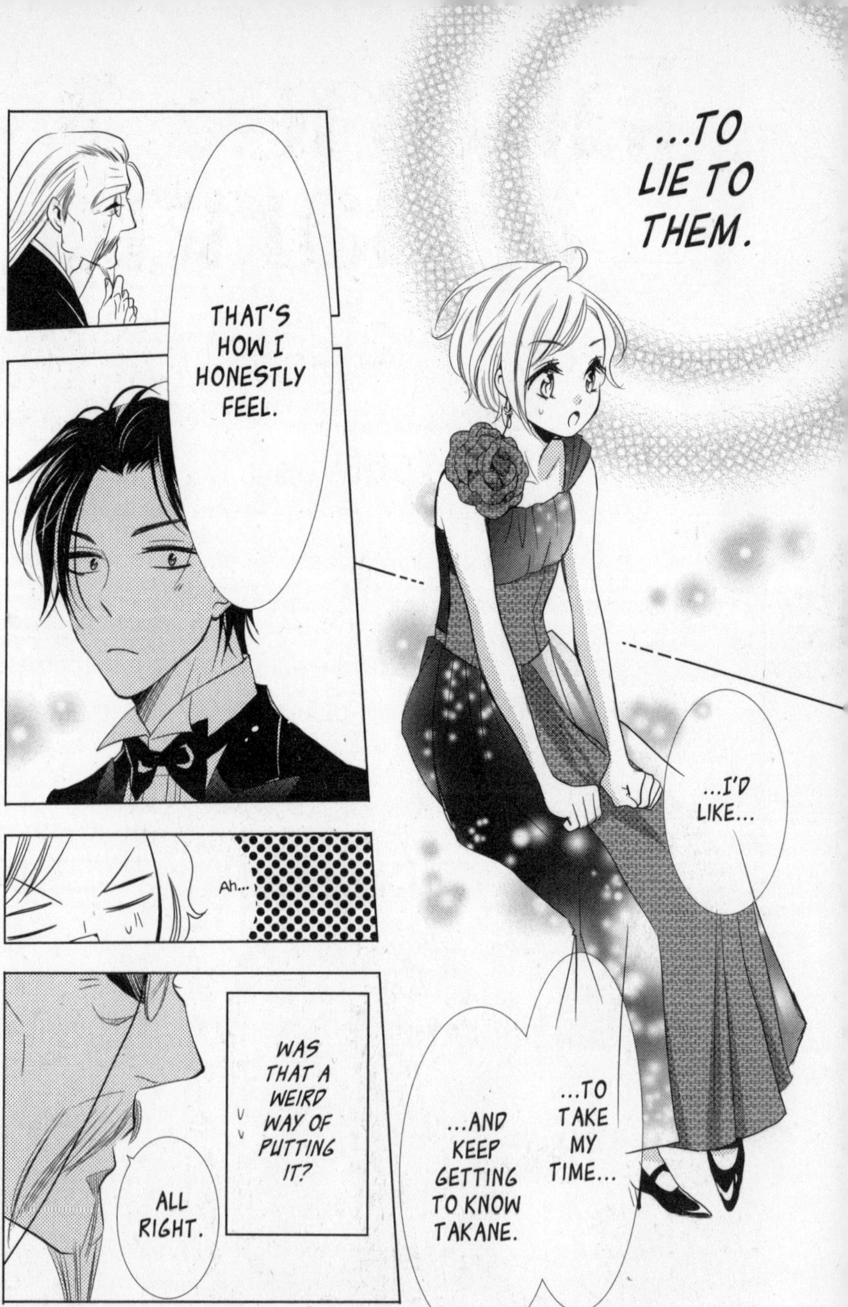
...TO LIE TO THEM.
...I'D LIKE...
...TO TAKE MY TIME...
...AND KEEP GETTING TO KNOW TAKANE.
THAT'S HOW I HONESTLY FEEL.
Ah...
WAS THAT A WEIRD WAY OF PUTTING IT?
ALL RIGHT.

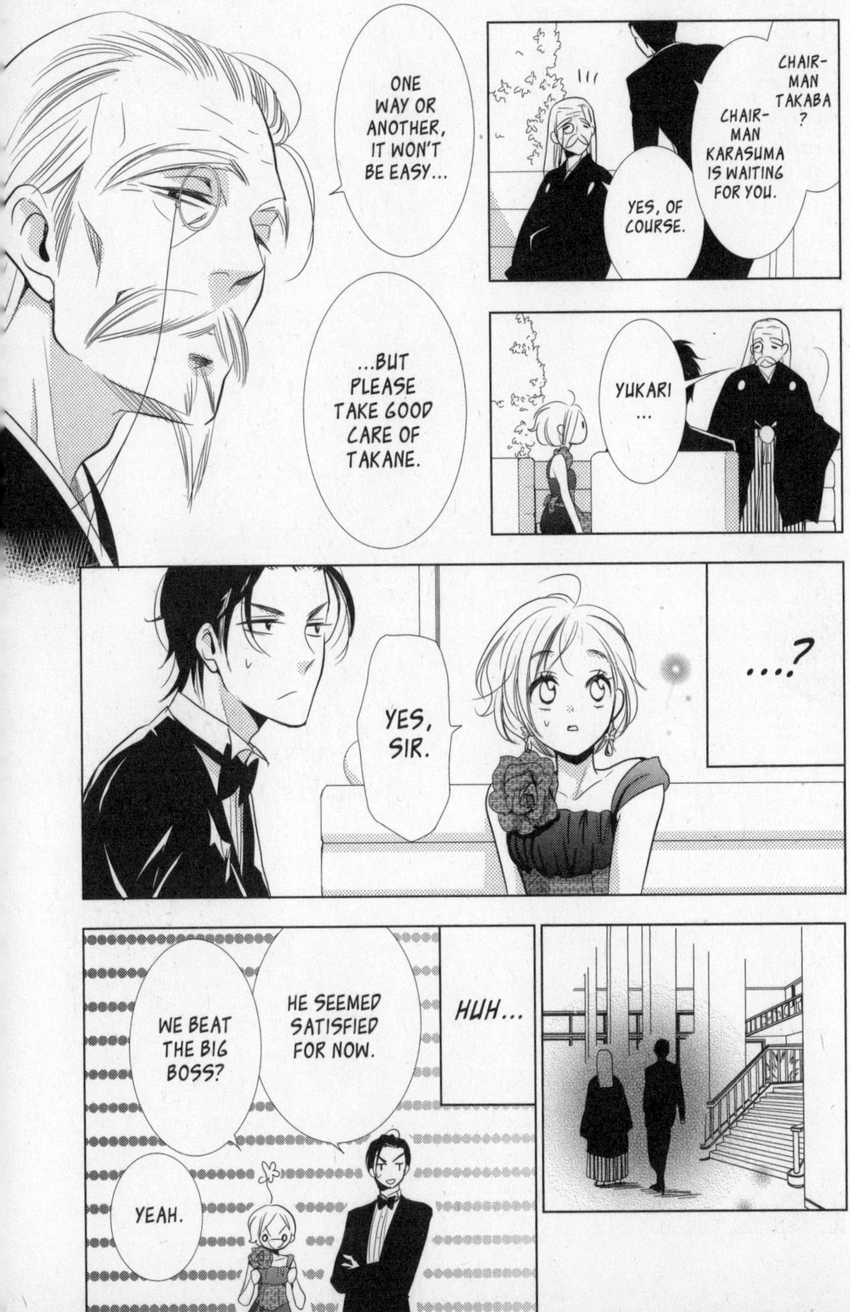
CHAIRMAN TAKABA?
CHAIRMAN KARASUMA IS WAITING FOR YOU.
YES, OF COURSE.
YUKARI ...
ONE WAY OR ANOTHER, IT WON'T BE EASY...
...BUT PLEASE TAKE GOOD CARE OF TAKANE.
...?
YES, SIR.
HUH...
HE SEEMED SATISFIED FOR NOW.
WE BEAT THE BIG BOSS?
YEAH.

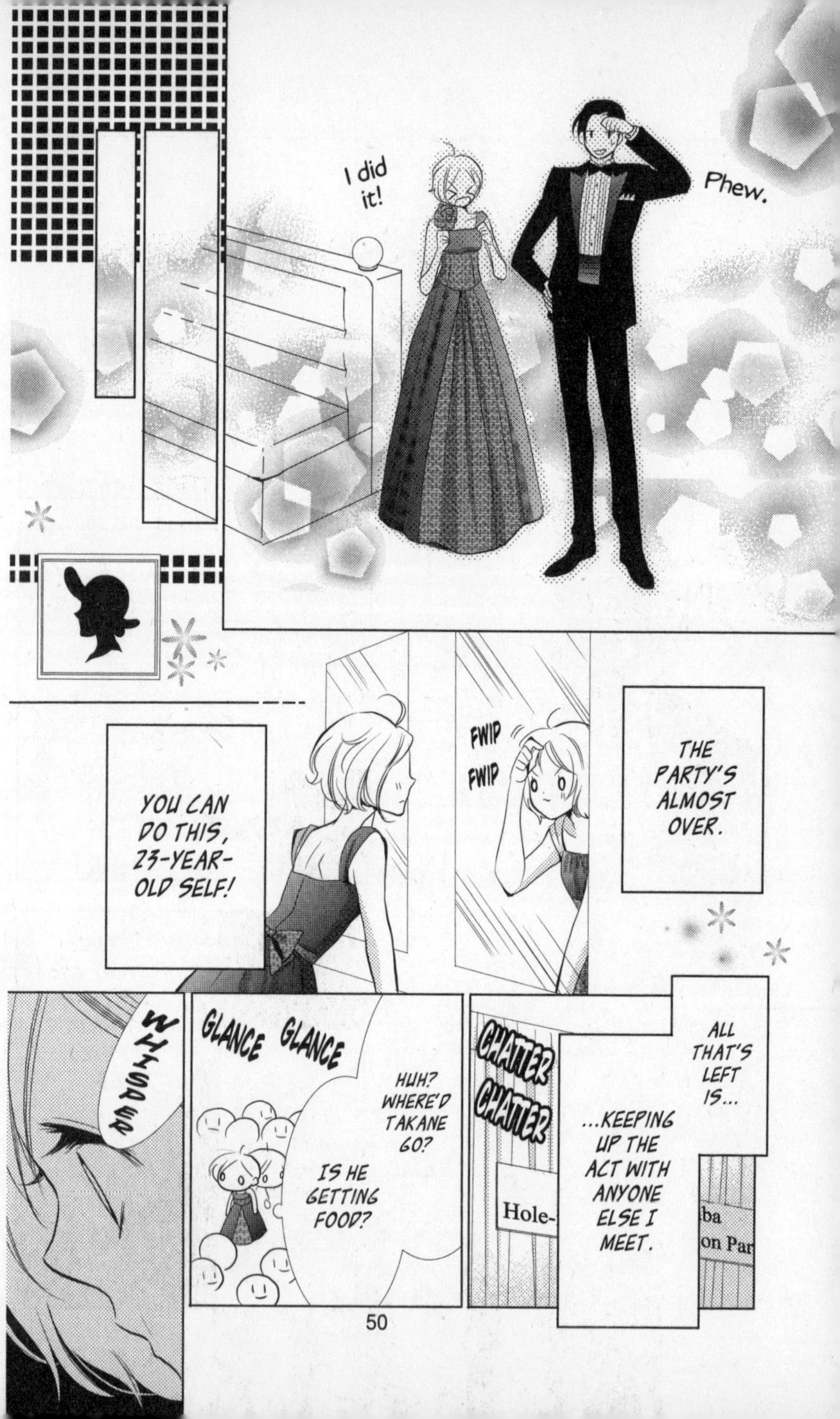
Phew.
I did it!
THE PARTY'S ALMOST OVER.
FWIP
FWIP
YOU CAN DO THIS, 23-YEAR-OLD SELF!
ALL THAT'S LEFT IS...
...KEEPING UP THE ACT WITH ANYONE ELSE I MEET.
CHATTER
CHATTER
GLANCE
GLANCE
HUH? WHERE'D TAKANE GO?
IS HE GETTING FOOD?
WHISPER

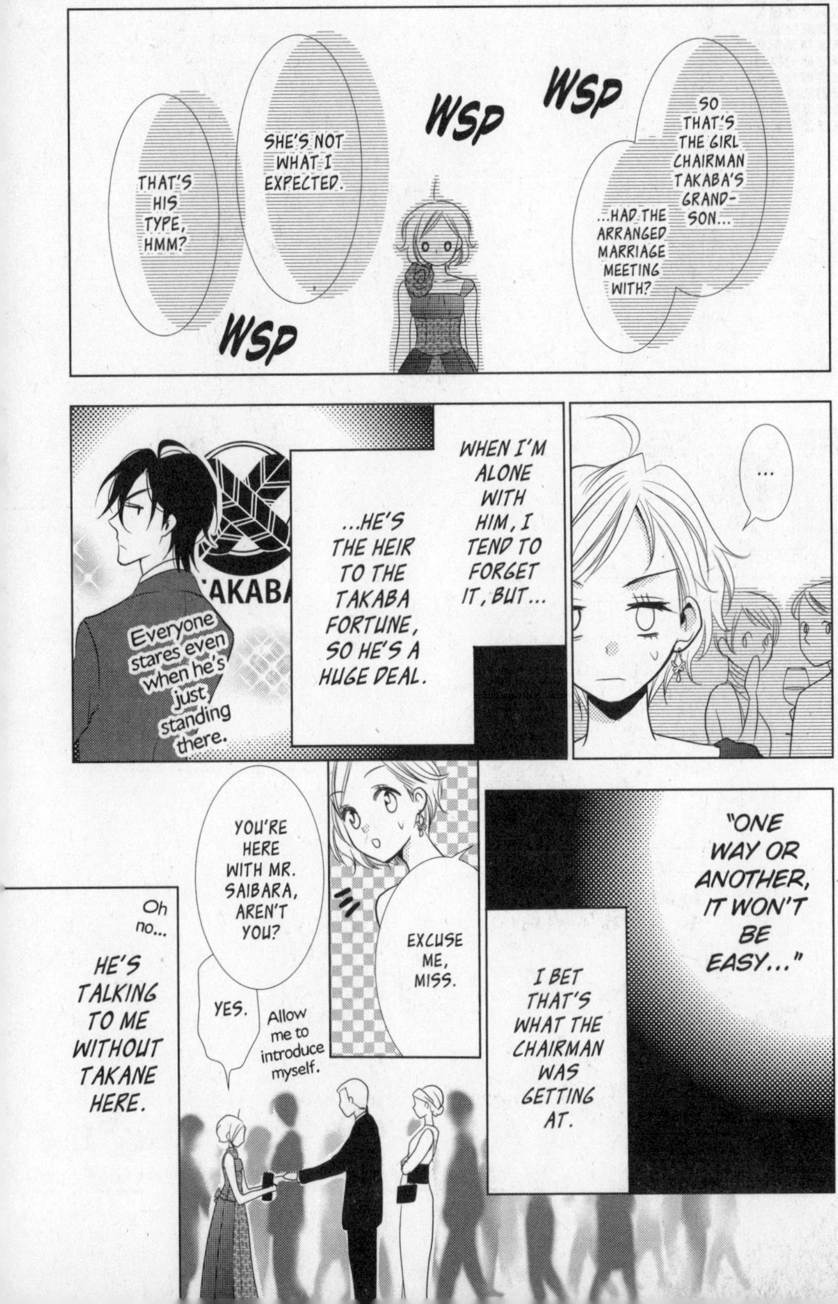
WSP
SO THAT'S THE GIRL CHAIRMAN TAKABA'S GRAND-SON...
...HAD THE ARRANGED MARRIAGE MEETING WITH?
WSP
SHE'S NOT WHAT I EXPECTED.
THAT'S HIS TYPE, HMM?
WSP
...
WHEN I'M ALONE WITH HIM, I TEND TO FORGET IT, BUT...
...HE'S THE HEIR TO THE TAKABA FORTUNE, SO HE'S A HUGE DEAL.
TAKABA
Everyone stares even when he's just standing there.
"ONE WAY OR ANOTHER, IT WON'T BE EASY..."
I BET THAT'S WHAT THE CHAIRMAN WAS GETTING AT.
EXCUSE ME, MISS.
YOU'RE HERE WITH MR. SAIBARA, AREN'T YOU?
YES.
Allow me to introduce myself.
Oh no...
HE'S TALKING TO ME WITHOUT TAKANE HERE.

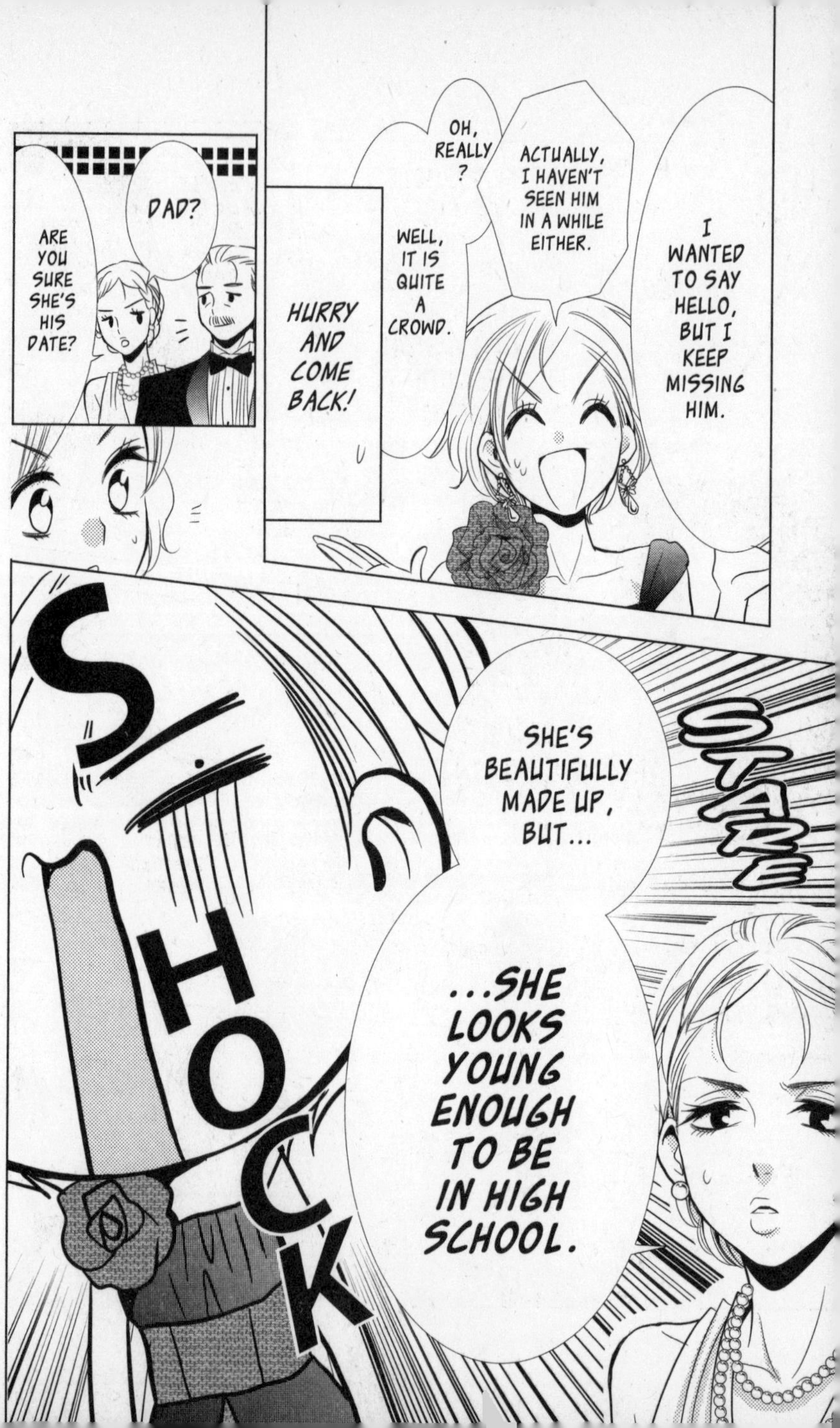
I WANTED TO SAY HELLO, BUT I KEEP MISSING HIM.
ACTUALLY, I HAVEN'T SEEN HIM IN A WHILE EITHER.
OH, REALLY?
WELL, IT IS QUITE A CROWD.
HURRY AND COME BACK!
DAD?
ARE YOU SURE SHE'S HIS DATE?
STARE
SHE'S BEAUTIFULLY MADE UP, BUT...
...SHE LOOKS YOUNG ENOUGH TO BE IN HIGH SCHOOL.
SHOCK

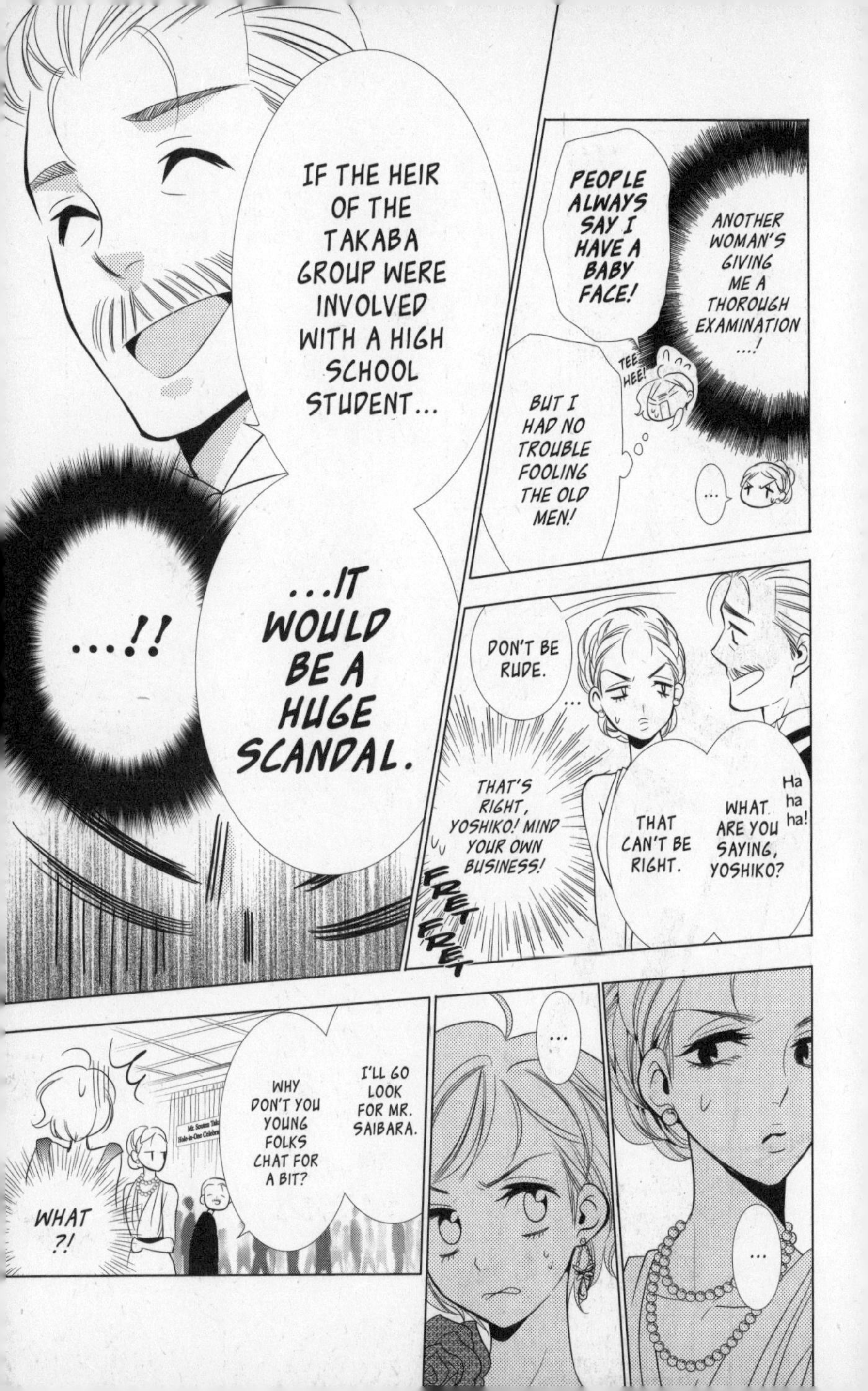
ANOTHER WOMAN'S GIVING ME A THOROUGH EXAMINATION ...!
PEOPLE ALWAYS SAY I HAVE A BABY FACE!
TEE HEE!
...
BUT I HAD NO TROUBLE FOOLING THE OLD MEN!
Ha ha ha!
WHAT ARE YOU SAYING, YOSHIKO?
THAT CAN'T BE RIGHT.
DON'T BE RUDE.
...
THAT'S RIGHT, YOSHIKO! MIND YOUR OWN BUSINESS!
FRET FRET
IF THE HEIR OF THE TAKABA GROUP WERE INVOLVED WITH A HIGH SCHOOL STUDENT...
...IT WOULD BE A HUGE SCANDAL.
...!!
...
...
I'LL GO LOOK FOR MR. SAIBARA.
WHY DON'T YOU YOUNG FOLKS CHAT FOR A BIT?
WHAT ?!

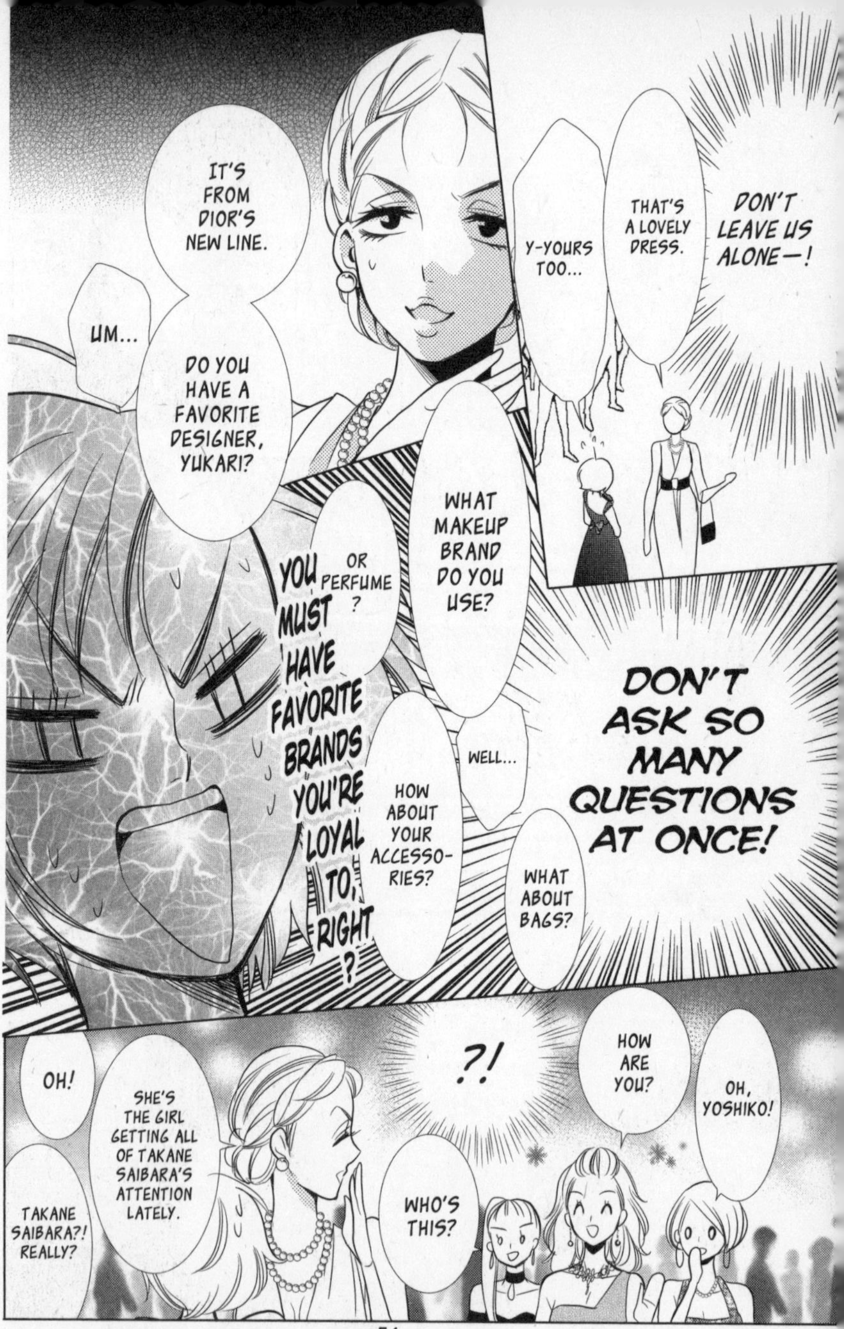
DON'T LEAVE US ALONE—!
THAT'S A LOVELY DRESS.
Y-YOURS TOO...
IT'S FROM DIOR'S NEW LINE.
DO YOU HAVE A FAVORITE DESIGNER, YUKARI?
UM...
DON'T ASK SO MANY QUESTIONS AT ONCE!
WHAT MAKEUP BRAND DO YOU USE?
OR PERFUME?
WELL...
WHAT ABOUT BAGS?
HOW ABOUT YOUR ACCESSORIES?
YOU MUST HAVE FAVORITE BRANDS YOU'RE LOYAL TO, RIGHT?
OH, YOSHIKO!
HOW ARE YOU?
?!
WHO'S THIS?
SHE'S THE GIRL GETTING ALL OF TAKANE SAIBARA'S ATTENTION LATELY.
OH!
TAKANE SAIBARA?! REALLY?

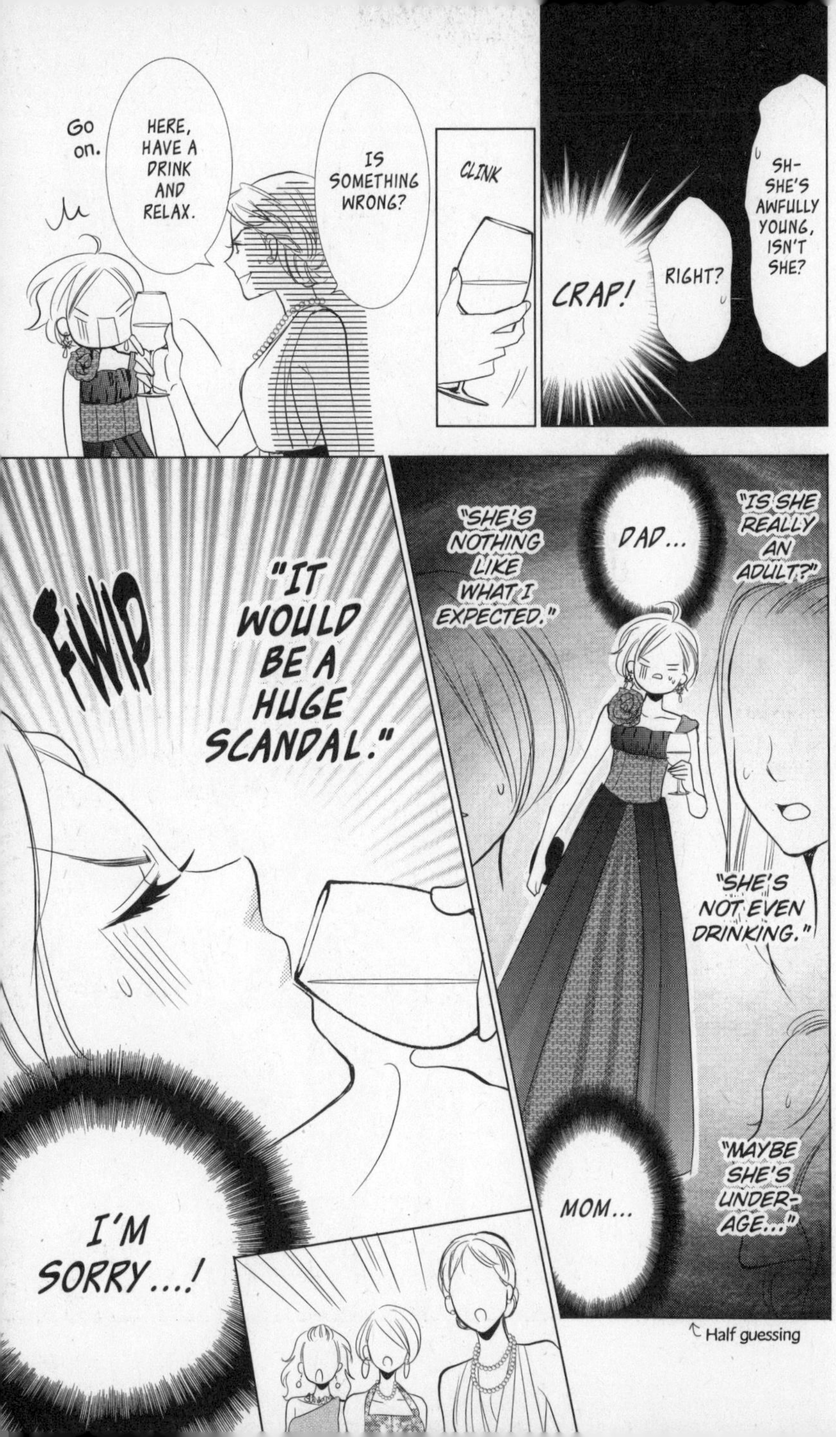
SH-SHE'S AWFULLY YOUNG, ISN'T SHE?
RIGHT?
CRAP!
CLINK
IS SOMETHING WRONG?
HERE, HAVE A DRINK AND RELAX.
Go on.
"IS SHE REALLY AN ADULT?"
DAD...
"SHE'S NOTHING LIKE WHAT I EXPECTED."
"SHE'S NOT EVEN DRINKING."
"MAYBE SHE'S UNDER-AGE..."
MOM...
↑ Half guessing
"IT WOULD BE A HUGE SCANDAL."
FWIP
I'M SORRY...!

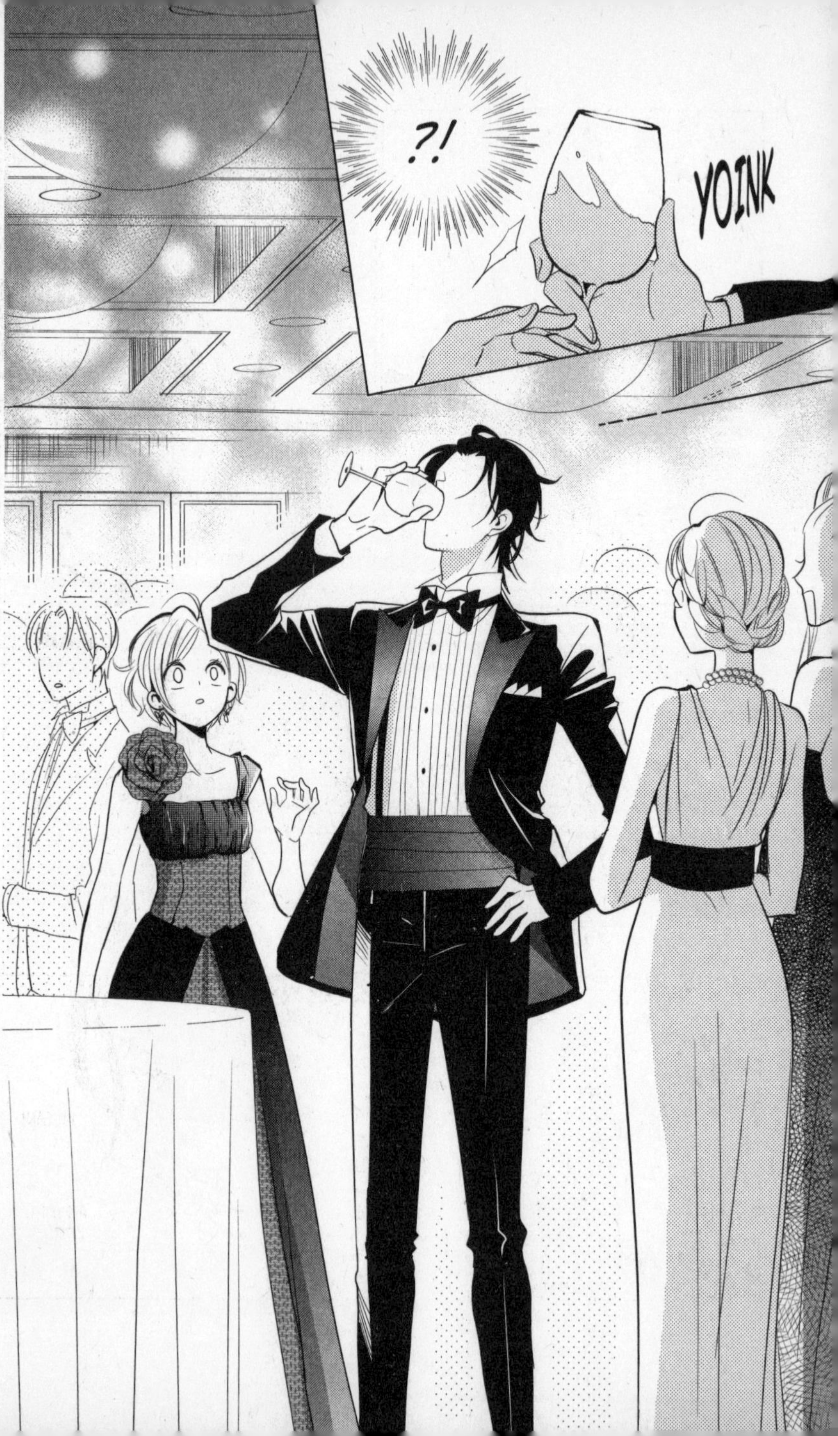
YOINK
?!

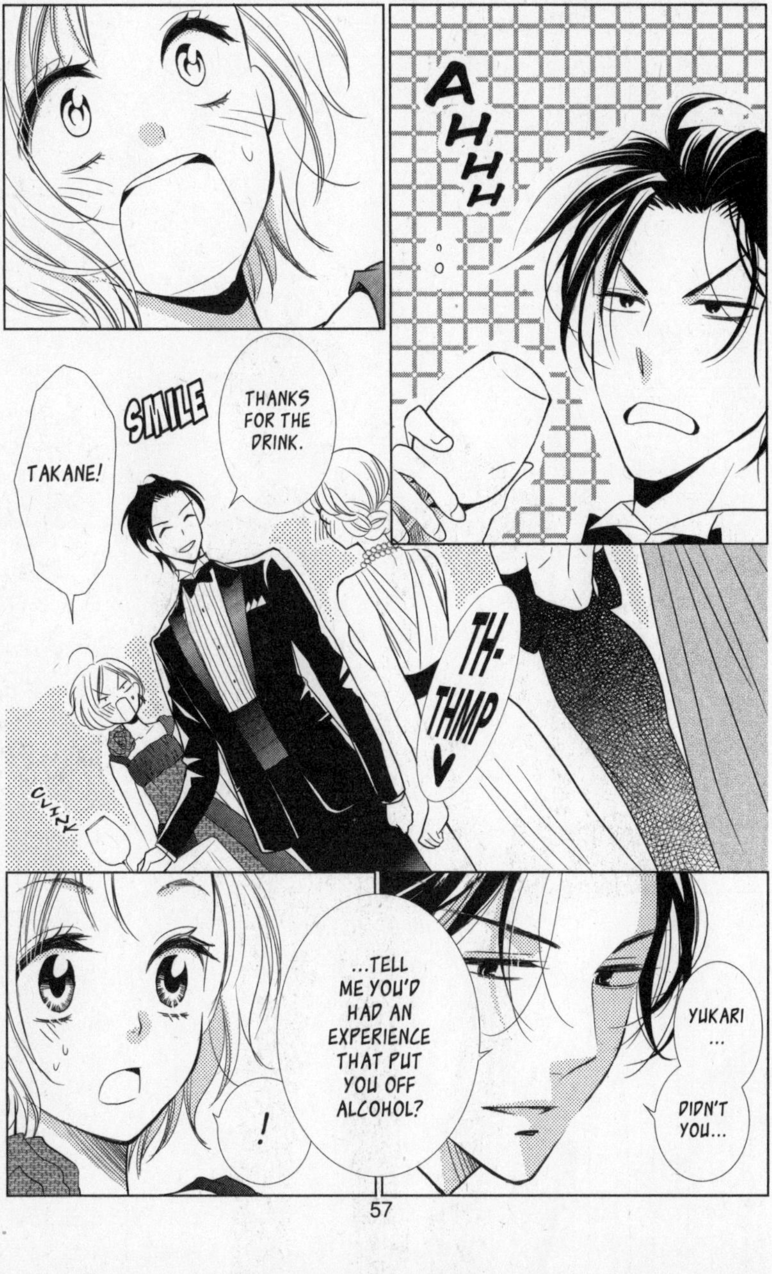
AHHH
...
TH-THMP
THANKS FOR THE DRINK.
SMILE
TAKANE!
CLINK
YUKARI ... DIDN'T YOU...
...TELL ME YOU'D HAD AN EXPERIENCE THAT PUT YOU OFF ALCOHOL?
!

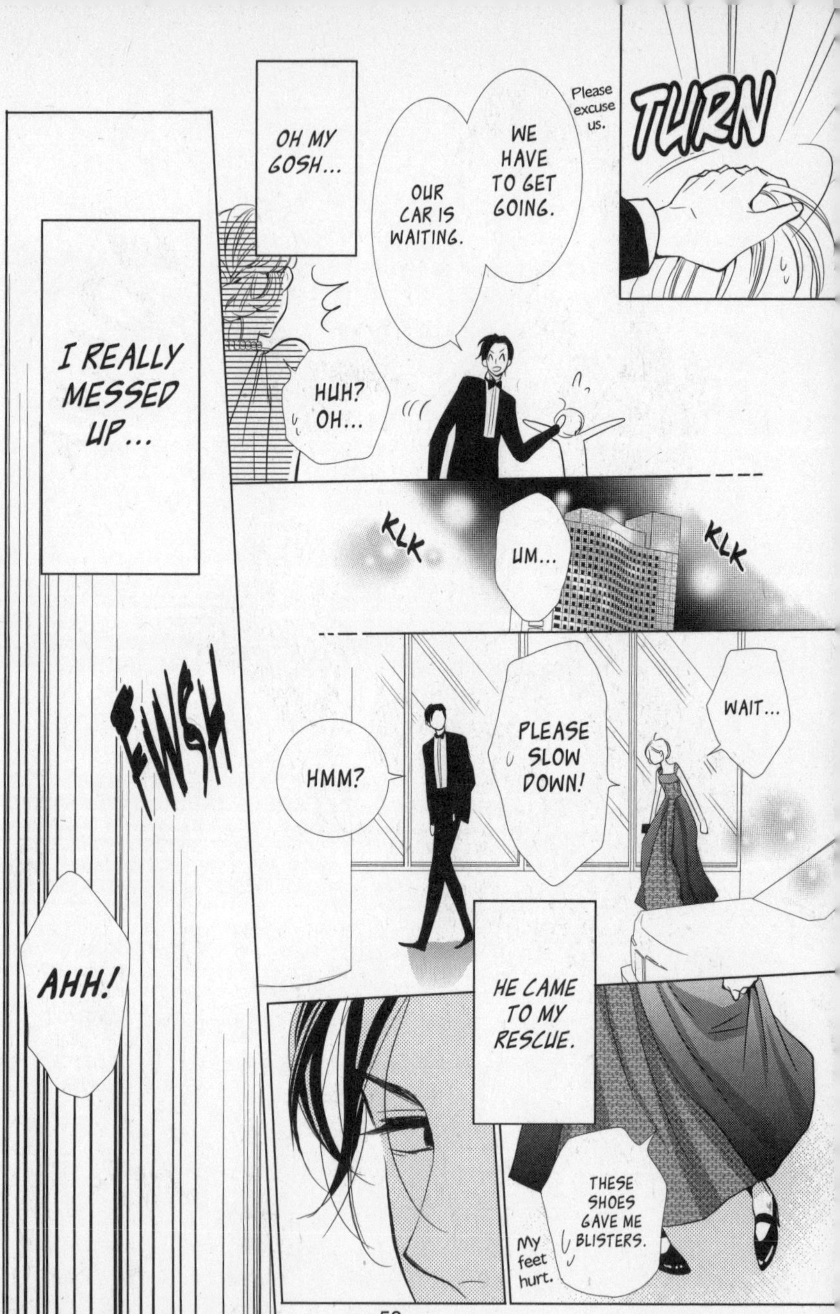
TURN
Please excuse us.
WE HAVE TO GET GOING.
OUR CAR IS WAITING.
OH MY GOSH...
HUH? OH...
KLK
UM...
KLK
WAIT...
PLEASE SLOW DOWN!
HMM?
THESE SHOES GAVE ME BLISTERS.
My feet hurt.
HE CAME TO MY RESCUE.
I REALLY MESSED UP...
FWSH
AHH!

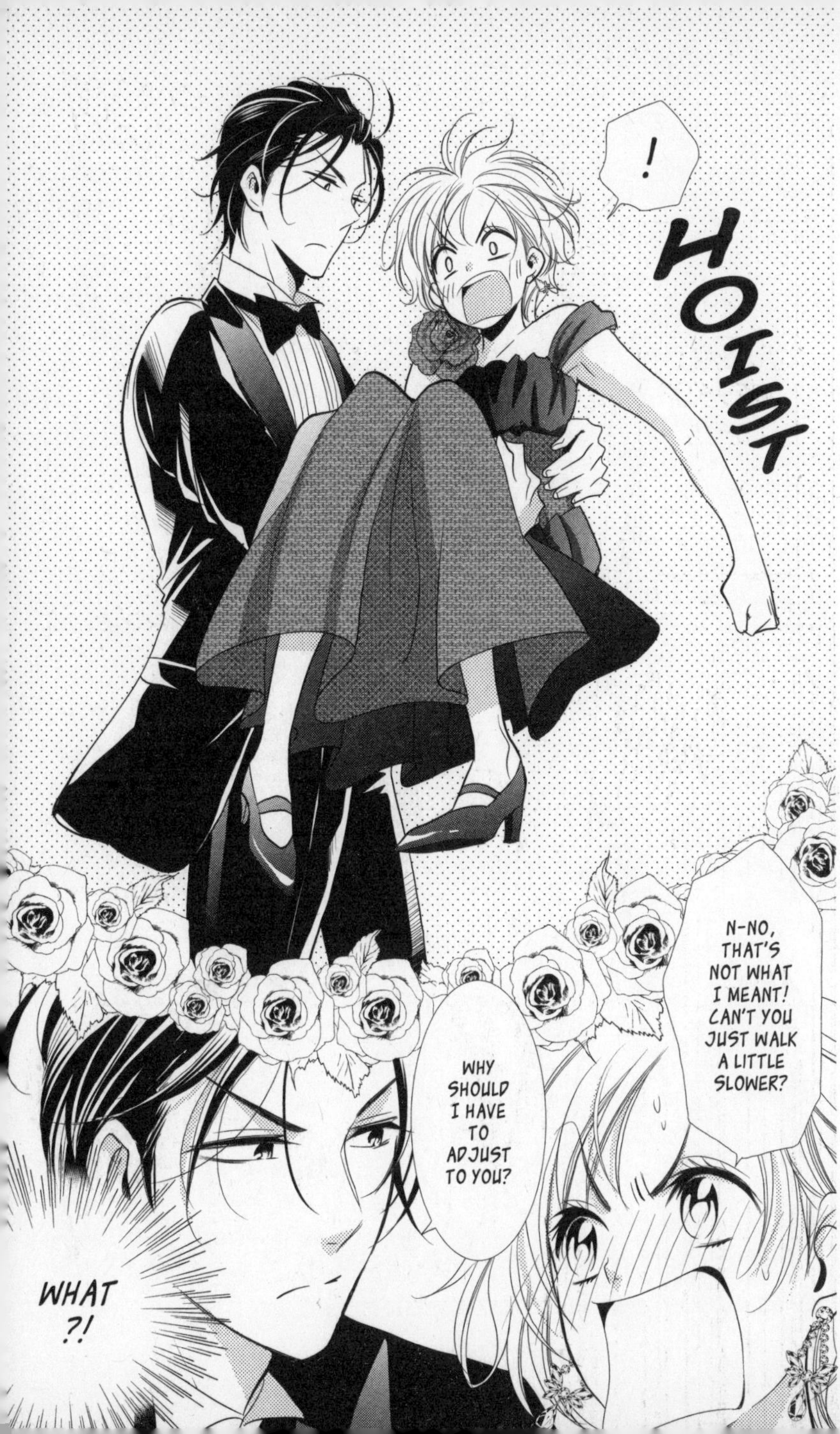
!
HOIST
N-NO, THAT'S NOT WHAT I MEANT! CAN'T YOU JUST WALK A LITTLE SLOWER?
WHY SHOULD I HAVE TO ADJUST TO YOU?
WHAT?!

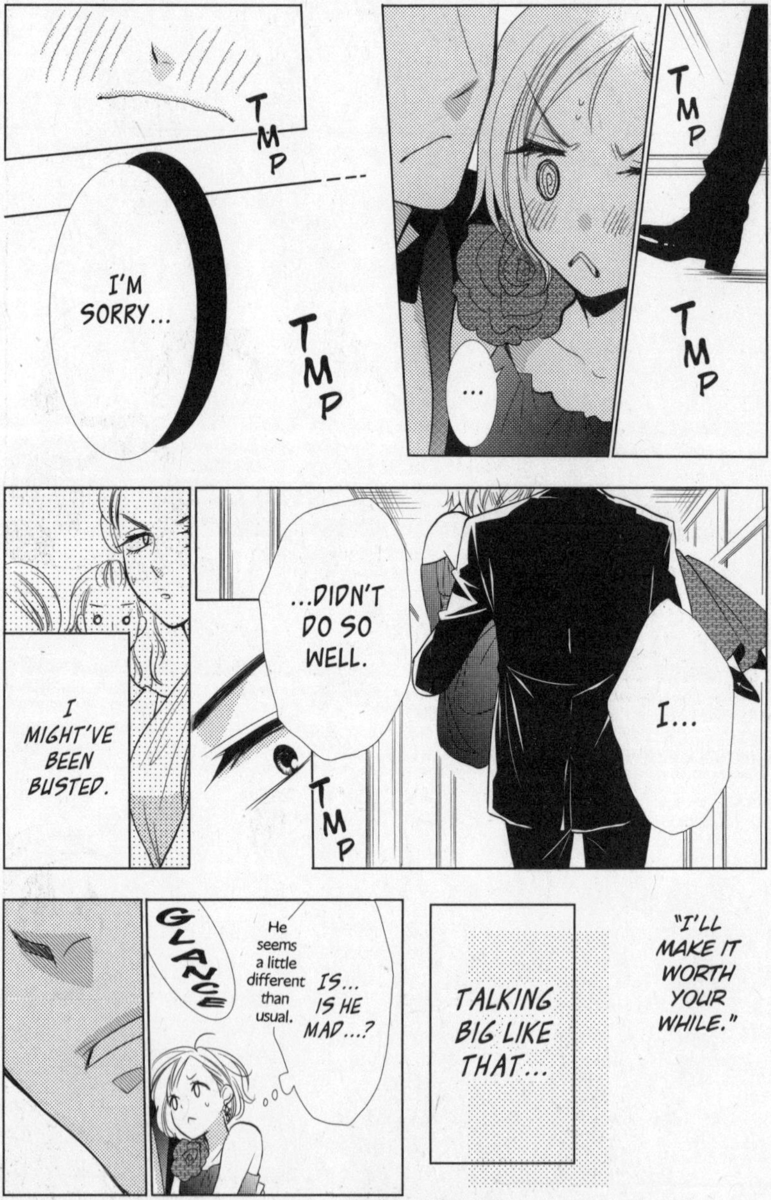
TMP
TMP
...
TMP
I'M SORRY...
TMP
I...
...DIDN'T DO SO WELL.
TMP
I MIGHT'VE BEEN BUSTED.
"I'LL MAKE IT WORTH YOUR WHILE."
TALKING BIG LIKE THAT...
IS... IS HE MAD...?
He seems a little different than usual.
GLANCE

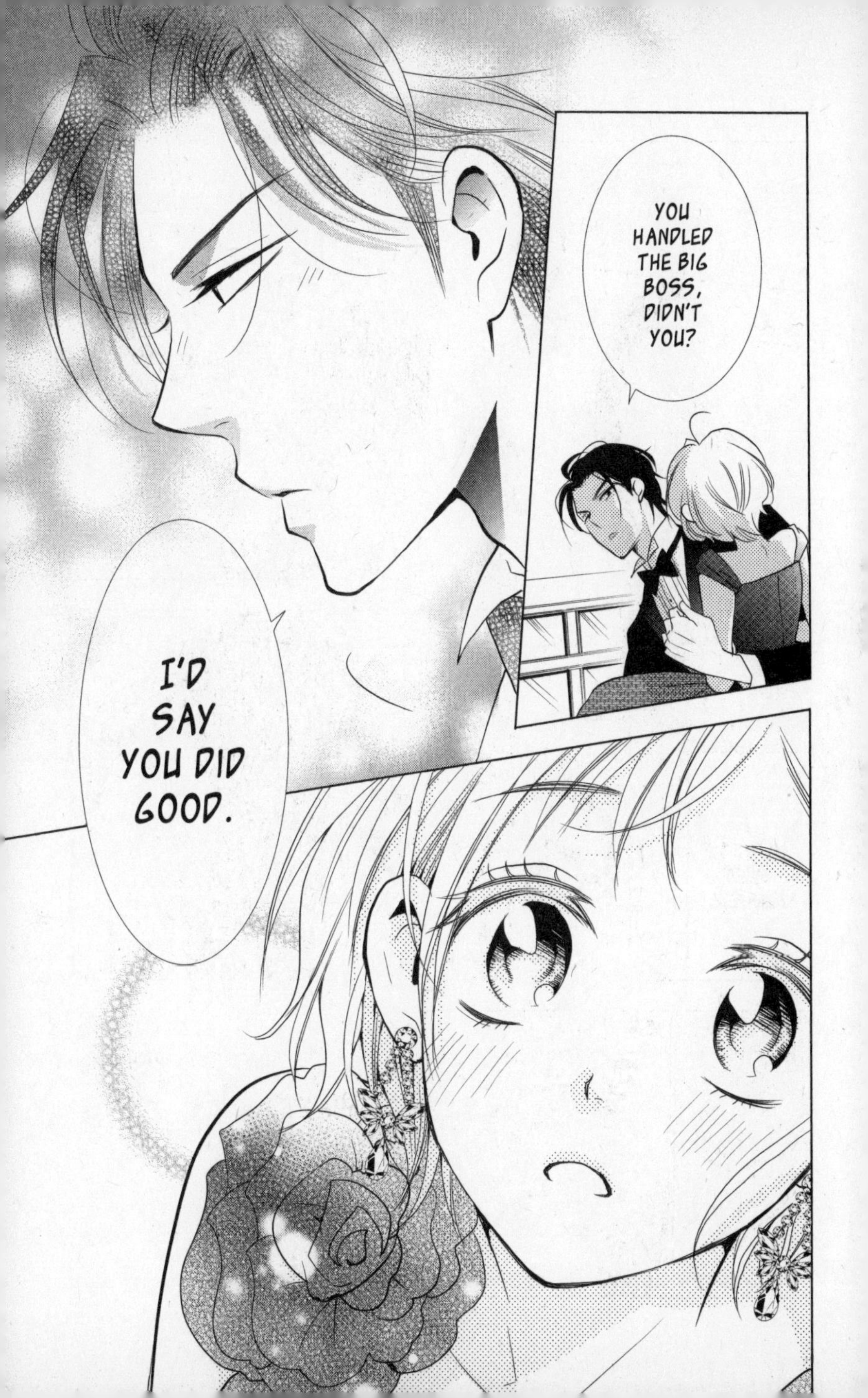
YOU HANDLED THE BIG BOSS, DIDN'T YOU?
I'D SAY YOU DID GOOD.

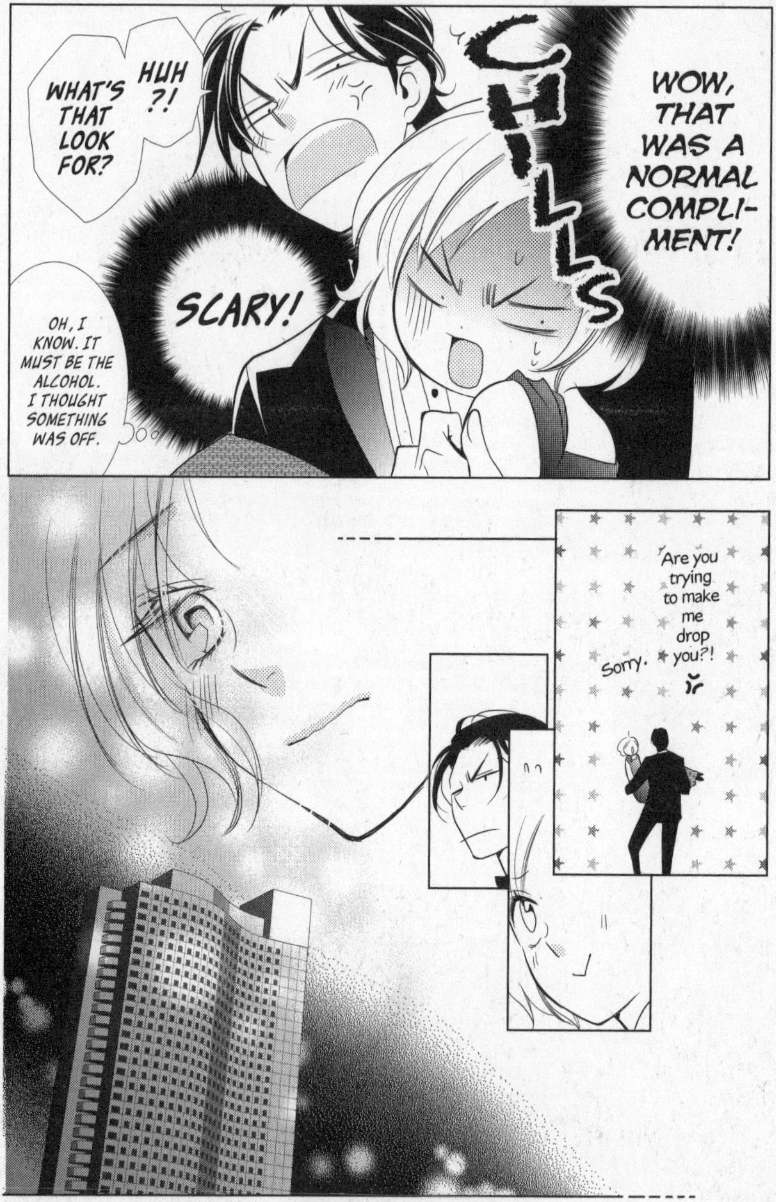
WOW, THAT WAS A NORMAL COMPLIMENT!
CHILLS
HUH?!
WHAT'S THAT LOOK FOR?
SCARY!
OH, I KNOW. IT MUST BE THE ALCOHOL. I THOUGHT SOMETHING WAS OFF.
Are you trying to make me drop you?!
Sorry.

Chapter 6 / The End

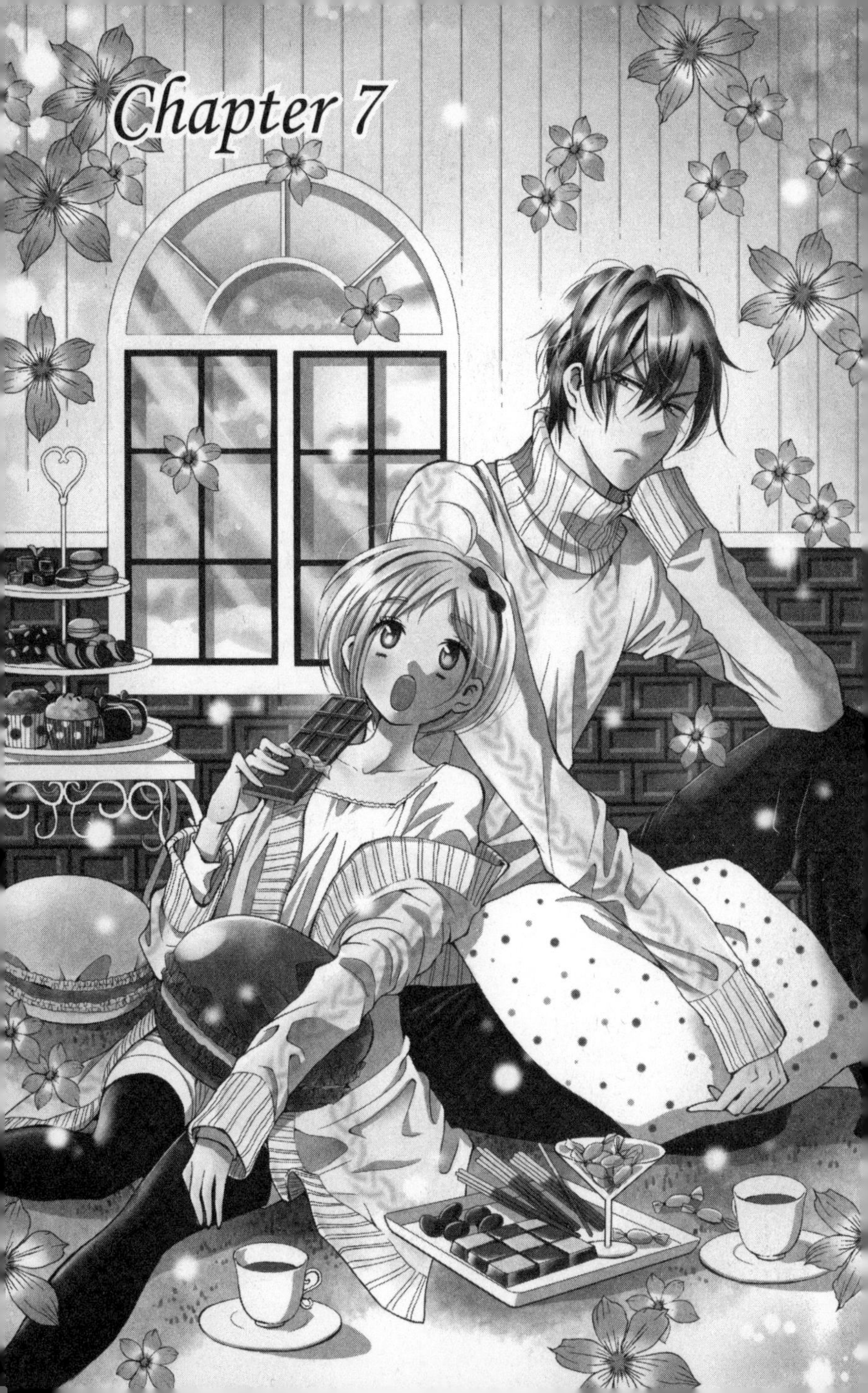
Chapter 7

At the Celebration Party

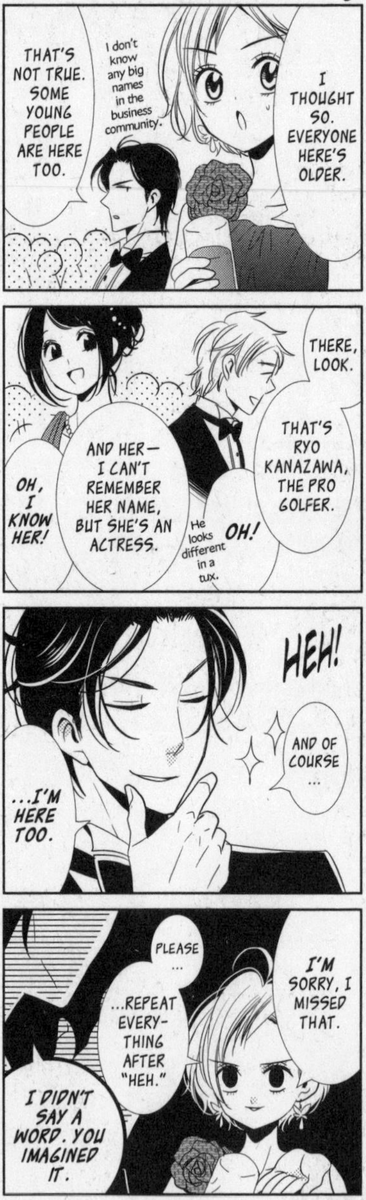
I THOUGHT SO. EVERYONE HERE'S OLDER.
I don't know any big names in the business community.
THAT'S NOT TRUE. SOME YOUNG PEOPLE ARE HERE TOO.
THERE, LOOK.
THAT'S RYO KANAZAWA, THE PRO GOLFER.
OH!
He looks different in a tux.
AND HER— I CAN'T REMEMBER HER NAME, BUT SHE'S AN ACTRESS.
OH, I KNOW HER!
HEH!
AND OF COURSE ...
...I'M HERE TOO.
I'M SORRY, I MISSED THAT.
PLEASE ...
...REPEAT EVERY-THING AFTER "HEH."
I DIDN'T SAY A WORD. YOU IMAGINED IT.

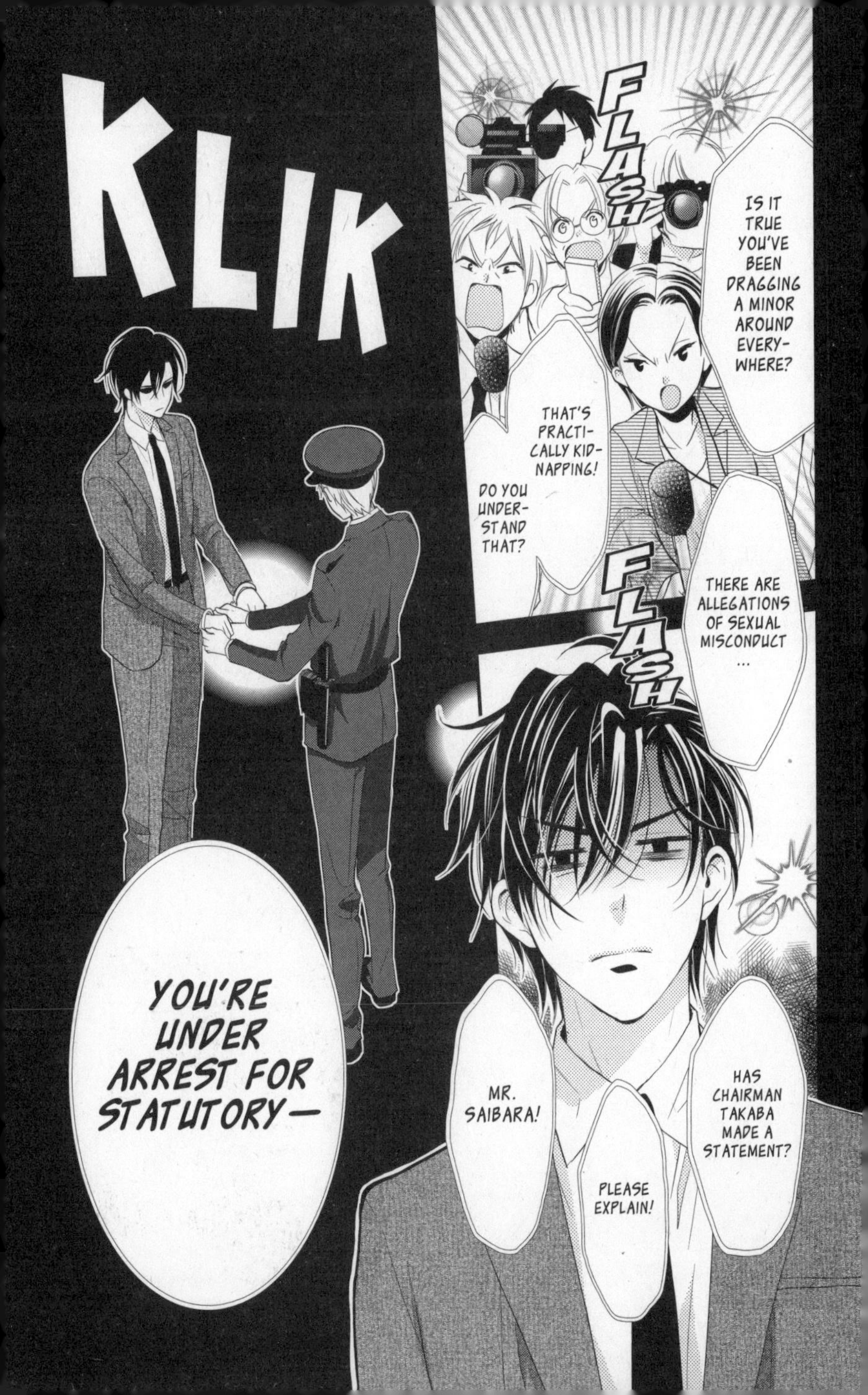
FLASH
IS IT TRUE YOU'VE BEEN DRAGGING A MINOR AROUND EVERY-WHERE?
THAT'S PRACTI-CALLY KID-NAPPING!
DO YOU UNDER-STAND THAT?
FLASH
THERE ARE ALLEGATIONS OF SEXUAL MISCONDUCT ...
HAS CHAIRMAN TAKABA MADE A STATEMENT?
PLEASE EXPLAIN!
MR. SAIBARA!
KLIK
YOU'RE UNDER ARREST FOR STATUTORY—

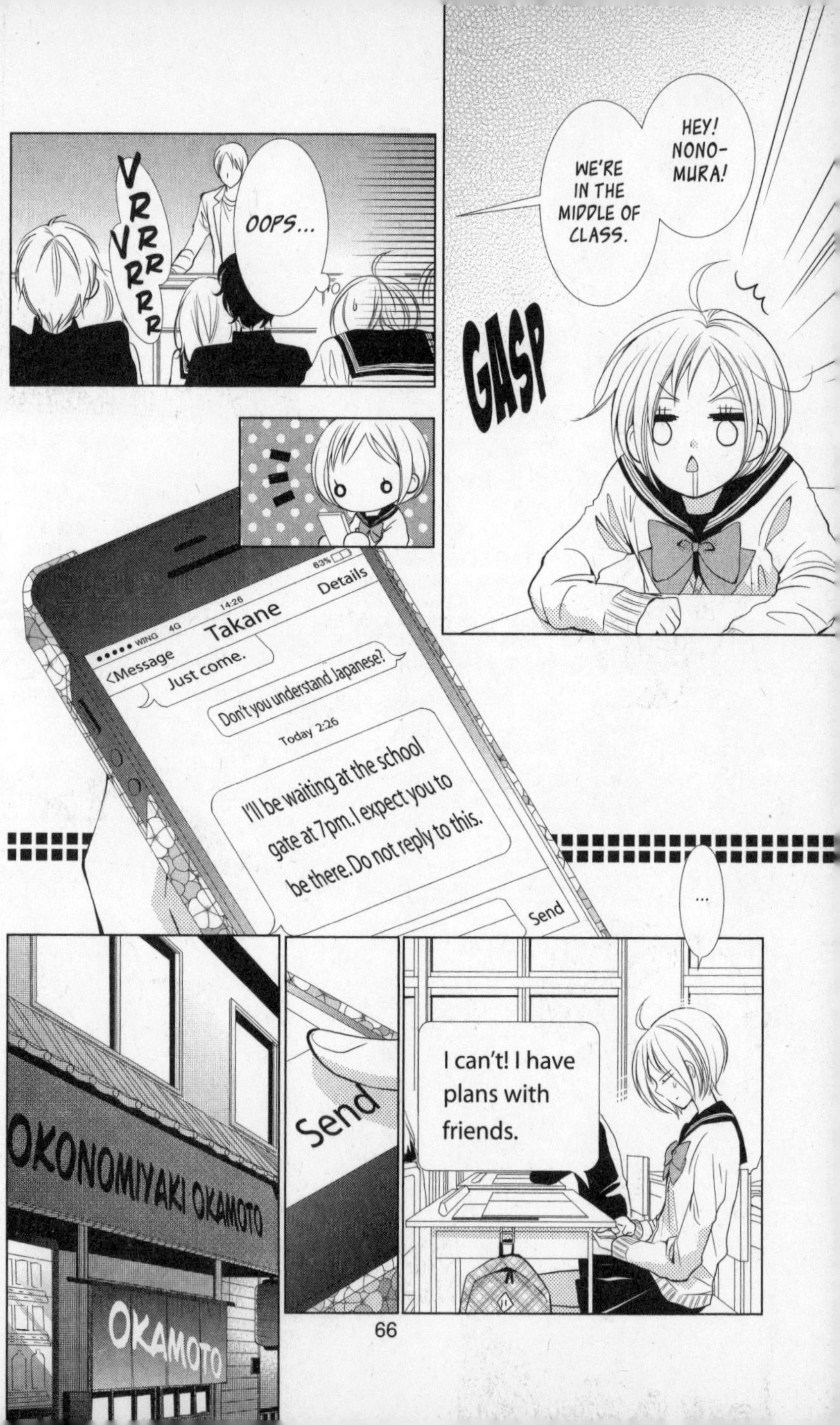
HEY! NONOMURA!
WE'RE IN THE MIDDLE OF CLASS.
GASP
OOPS...
VRRRVRRRR
WING 4G
14:26
83%
<Message
Takane
Details
Just come.
Don't you understand Japanese?
Today 2:26
I'll be waiting at the school gate at 7pm. I expect you to be there. Do not reply to this.
Send
...
I can't! I have plans with friends.
Send
OKONOMIYAKI OKAMOTO
OKAMOTO

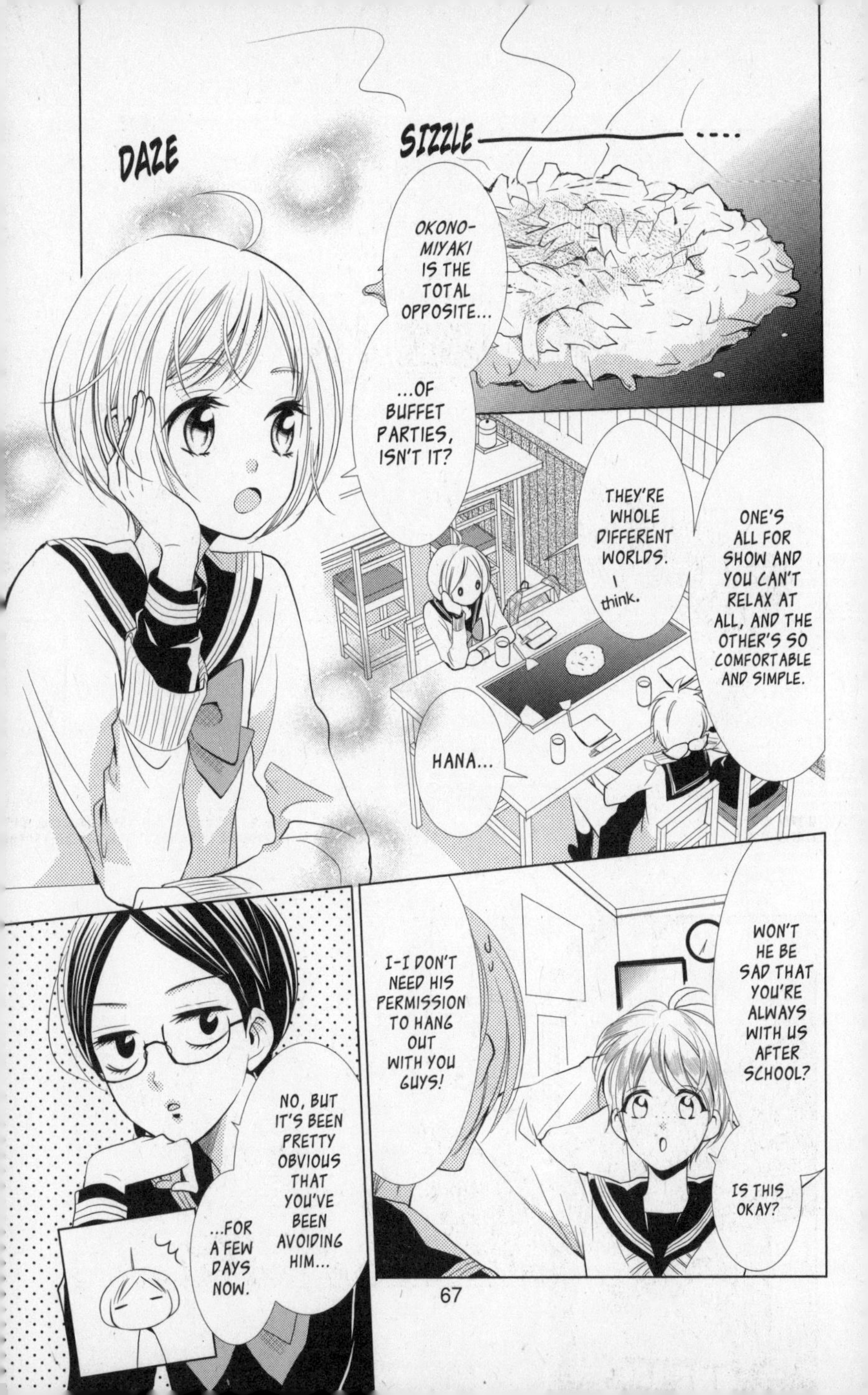
SIZZLE ....
OKONOMIYAKI IS THE TOTAL OPPOSITE...
...OF BUFFET PARTIES, ISN'T IT?
DAZE
ONE'S ALL FOR SHOW AND YOU CAN'T RELAX AT ALL, AND THE OTHER'S SO COMFORTABLE AND SIMPLE.
THEY'RE WHOLE DIFFERENT WORLDS. I think.
HANA...
WON'T HE BE SAD THAT YOU'RE ALWAYS WITH US AFTER SCHOOL?
IS THIS OKAY?
I-I DON'T NEED HIS PERMISSION TO HANG OUT WITH YOU GUYS!
NO, BUT IT'S BEEN PRETTY OBVIOUS THAT YOU'VE BEEN AVOIDING HIM...
...FOR A FEW DAYS NOW.

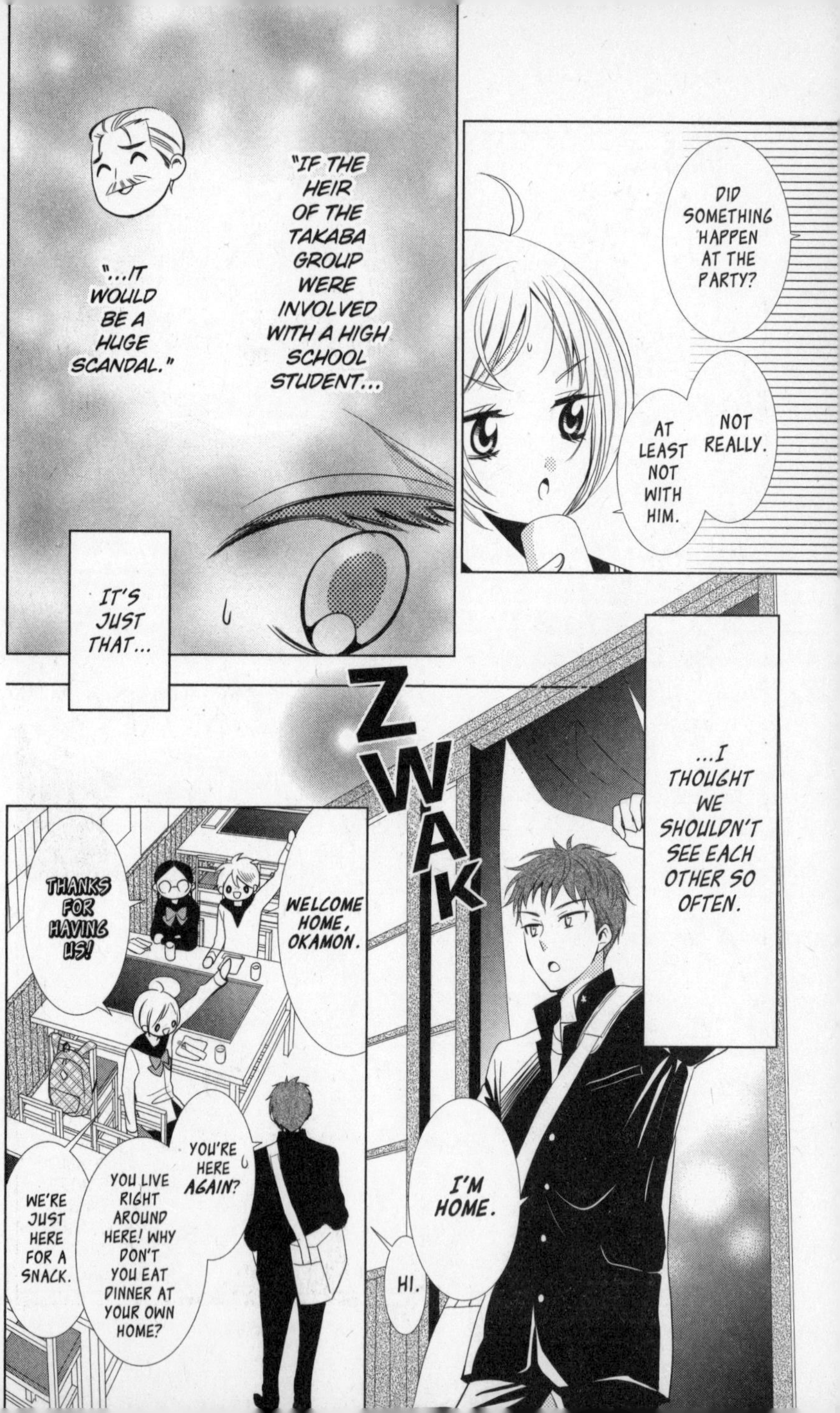
DID SOMETHING HAPPEN AT THE PARTY?
NOT REALLY.
AT LEAST NOT WITH HIM.
"IF THE HEIR OF THE TAKABA GROUP WERE INVOLVED WITH A HIGH SCHOOL STUDENT...
"...IT WOULD BE A HUGE SCANDAL."
IT'S JUST THAT...
...I THOUGHT WE SHOULDN'T SEE EACH OTHER SO OFTEN.
ZWAK
I'M HOME.
HI.
WELCOME HOME, OKAMON.
THANKS FOR HAVING US!
YOU'RE HERE AGAIN?
YOU LIVE RIGHT AROUND HERE! WHY DON'T YOU EAT DINNER AT YOUR OWN HOME?
WE'RE JUST HERE FOR A SNACK.

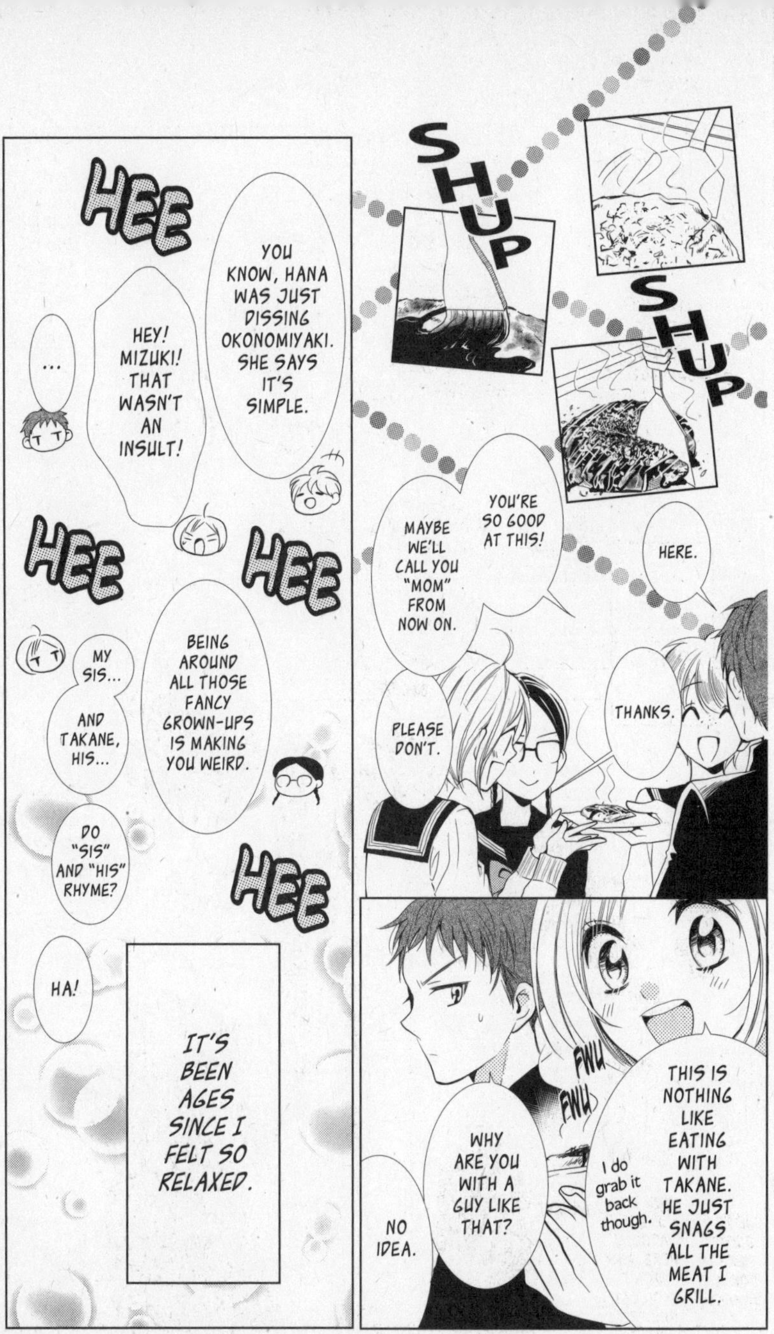
SHUP
SHUP
HERE.
THANKS.
YOU'RE SO GOOD AT THIS!
MAYBE WE'LL CALL YOU "MOM" FROM NOW ON.
PLEASE DON'T.
THIS IS NOTHING LIKE EATING WITH TAKANE. HE JUST SNAGS ALL THE MEAT I GRILL.
I do grab it back though.
FWU FWU
WHY ARE YOU WITH A GUY LIKE THAT?
NO IDEA.
HEE
YOU KNOW, HANA WAS JUST DISSING OKONOMIYAKI. SHE SAYS IT'S SIMPLE.
HEY! MIZUKI! THAT WASN'T AN INSULT!
...
HEE
HEE
BEING AROUND ALL THOSE FANCY GROWN-UPS IS MAKING YOU WEIRD.
MY SIS...
AND TAKANE, HIS...
DO "SIS" AND "HIS" RHYME?
HEE
HA!
IT'S BEEN AGES SINCE I FELT SO RELAXED.

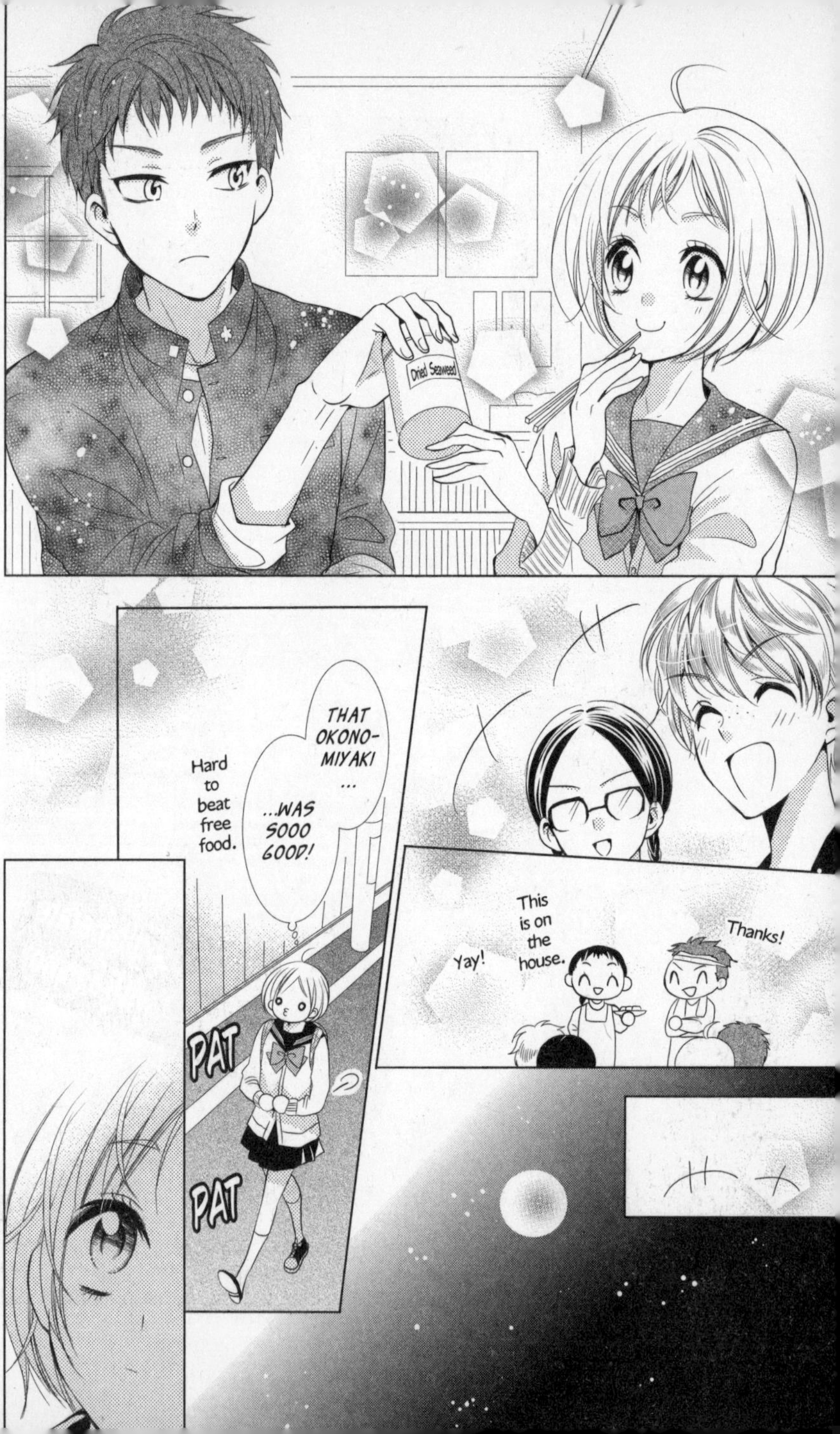
Dried Seaweed
Thanks!
This is on the house.
Yay!
THAT OKONOMIYAKI...
...WAS SOOO GOOD!
Hard to beat free food.
PAT
PAT

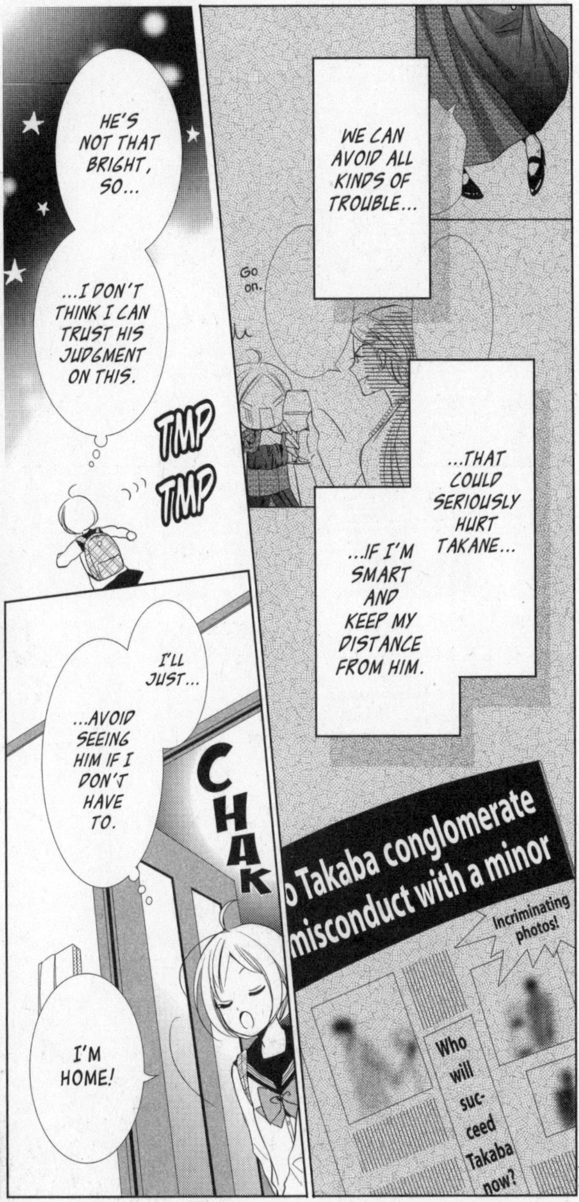
WE CAN AVOID ALL KINDS OF TROUBLE...
Go on.
...THAT COULD SERIOUSLY HURT TAKANE...
...IF I'M SMART AND KEEP MY DISTANCE FROM HIM.
o Takaba conglomerate misconduct with a minor
Incriminating photos!
Who will suc-ceed Takaba now?
HE'S NOT THAT BRIGHT, SO...
...I DON'T THINK I CAN TRUST HIS JUDGMENT ON THIS.
TMP TMP
I'LL JUST...
...AVOID SEEING HIM IF I DON'T HAVE TO.
CHAK
I'M HOME!

●Souten Takaba●

Character concept: a key player. Visually, I tried to create a look that gave that impression. Also, I wanted his name to sound super strong, so I named him Souten ("sky"), which is higher than Takane ("mountain").

He's the chairman of Takaba Holdings, which controls the Takaba Group. He's an excellent golfer. (Since he's always wearing traditional kimono, I had a hard time coming up with his golf wear.)

He has a cane, but he can still play golf. What exactly is that cane for, then? Self-defense, maybe...?

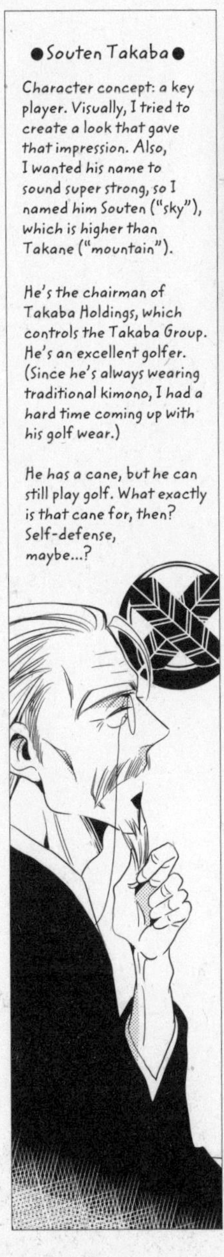

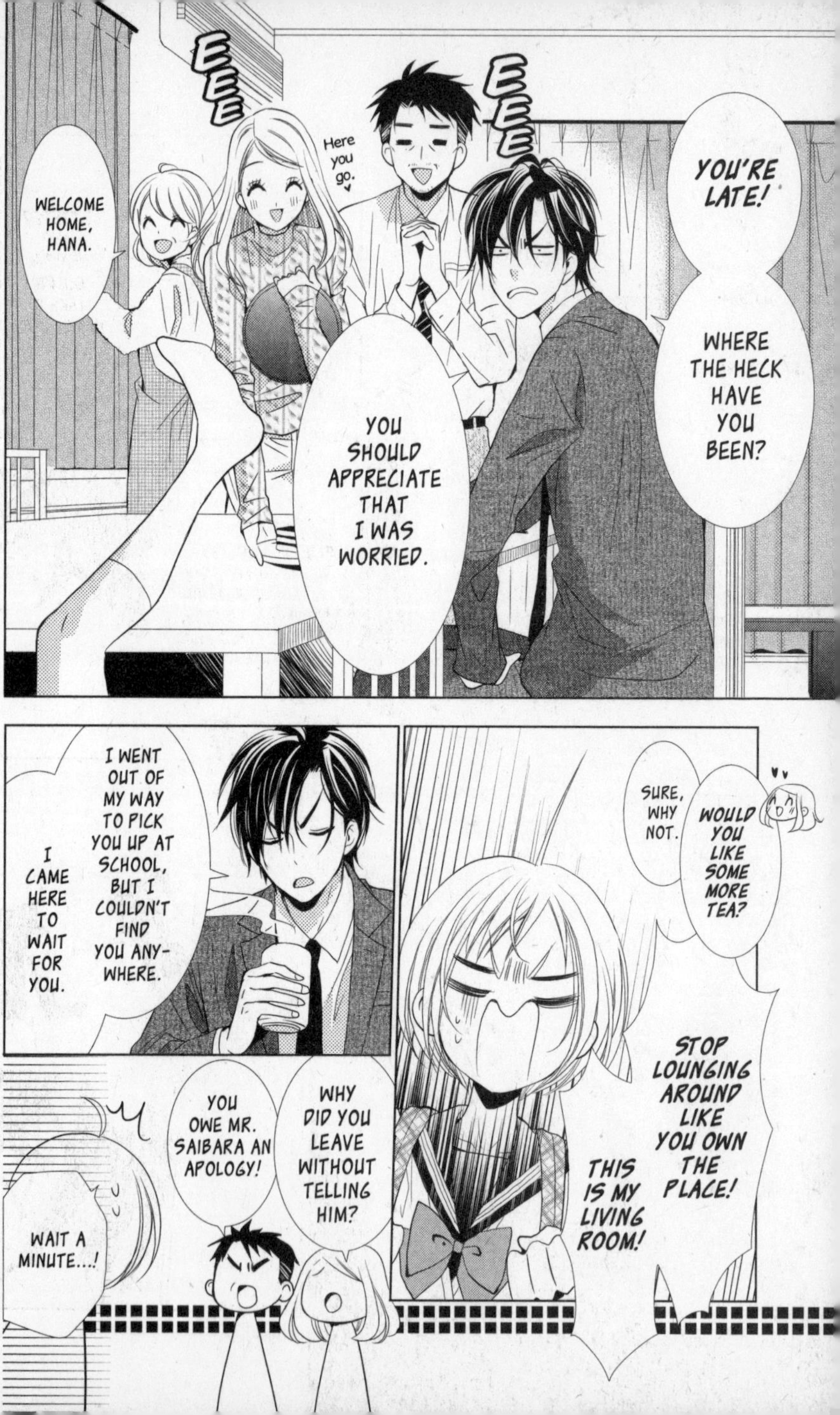
EEE
EEE
YOU'RE LATE!
WHERE THE HECK HAVE YOU BEEN?
YOU SHOULD APPRECIATE THAT I WAS WORRIED.
Here you go.
WELCOME HOME, HANA.
WOULD YOU LIKE SOME MORE TEA?
SURE, WHY NOT.
STOP LOUNGING AROUND LIKE YOU OWN THE PLACE!
THIS IS MY LIVING ROOM!
I WENT OUT OF MY WAY TO PICK YOU UP AT SCHOOL, BUT I COULDN'T FIND YOU ANYWHERE.
I CAME HERE TO WAIT FOR YOU.
WHY DID YOU LEAVE WITHOUT TELLING HIM?
YOU OWE MR. SAIBARA AN APOLOGY!
WAIT A MINUTE...!

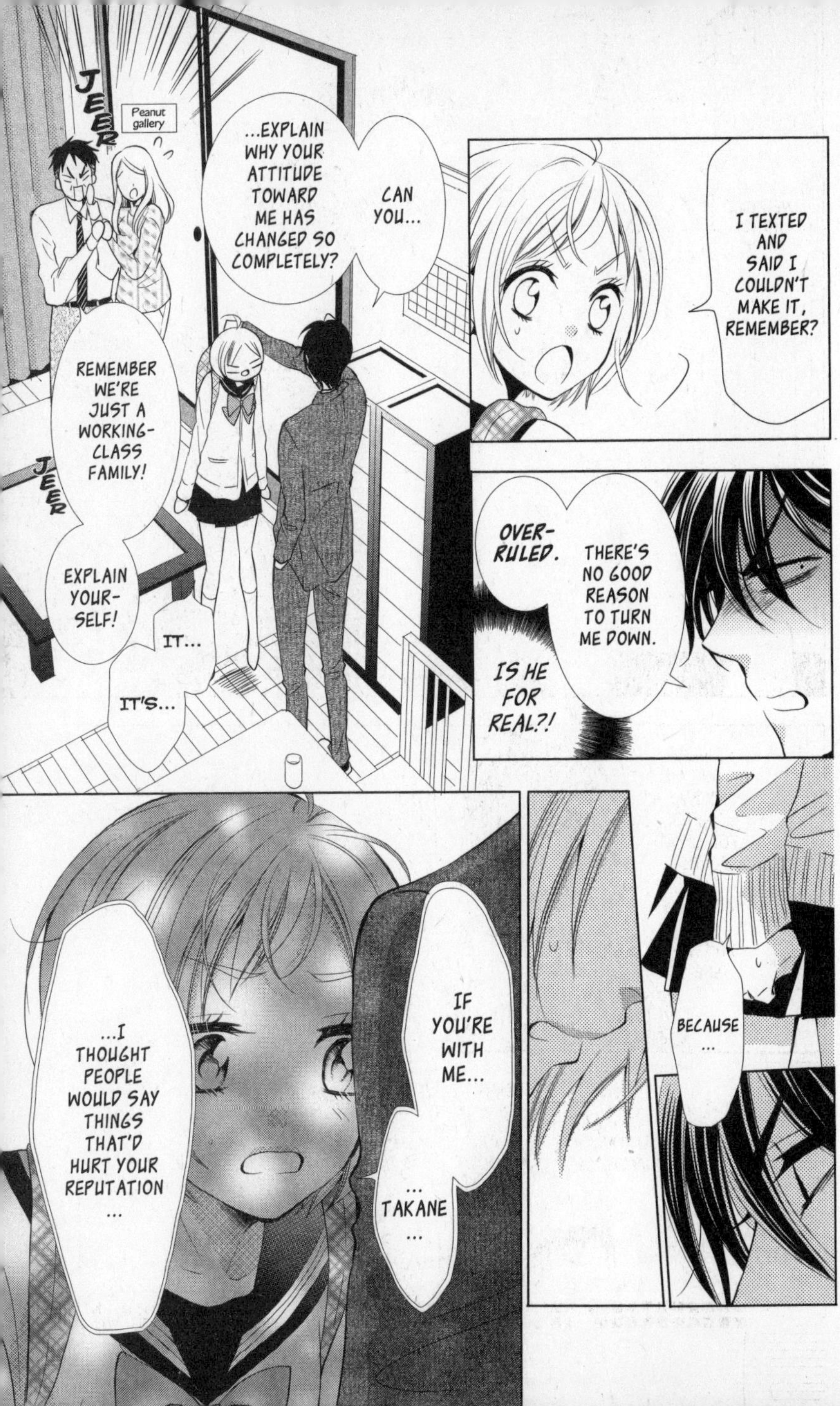
I TEXTED AND SAID I COULDN'T MAKE IT, REMEMBER?
OVER-RULED.
THERE'S NO GOOD REASON TO TURN ME DOWN.
IS HE FOR REAL?!
CAN YOU...
...EXPLAIN WHY YOUR ATTITUDE TOWARD ME HAS CHANGED SO COMPLETELY?
JEER
Peanut gallery
REMEMBER WE'RE JUST A WORKING-CLASS FAMILY!
JEER
EXPLAIN YOUR-SELF!
IT...
IT'S...
BECAUSE...
IF YOU'RE WITH ME...
...TAKANE...
...I THOUGHT PEOPLE WOULD SAY THINGS THAT'D HURT YOUR REPUTATION...

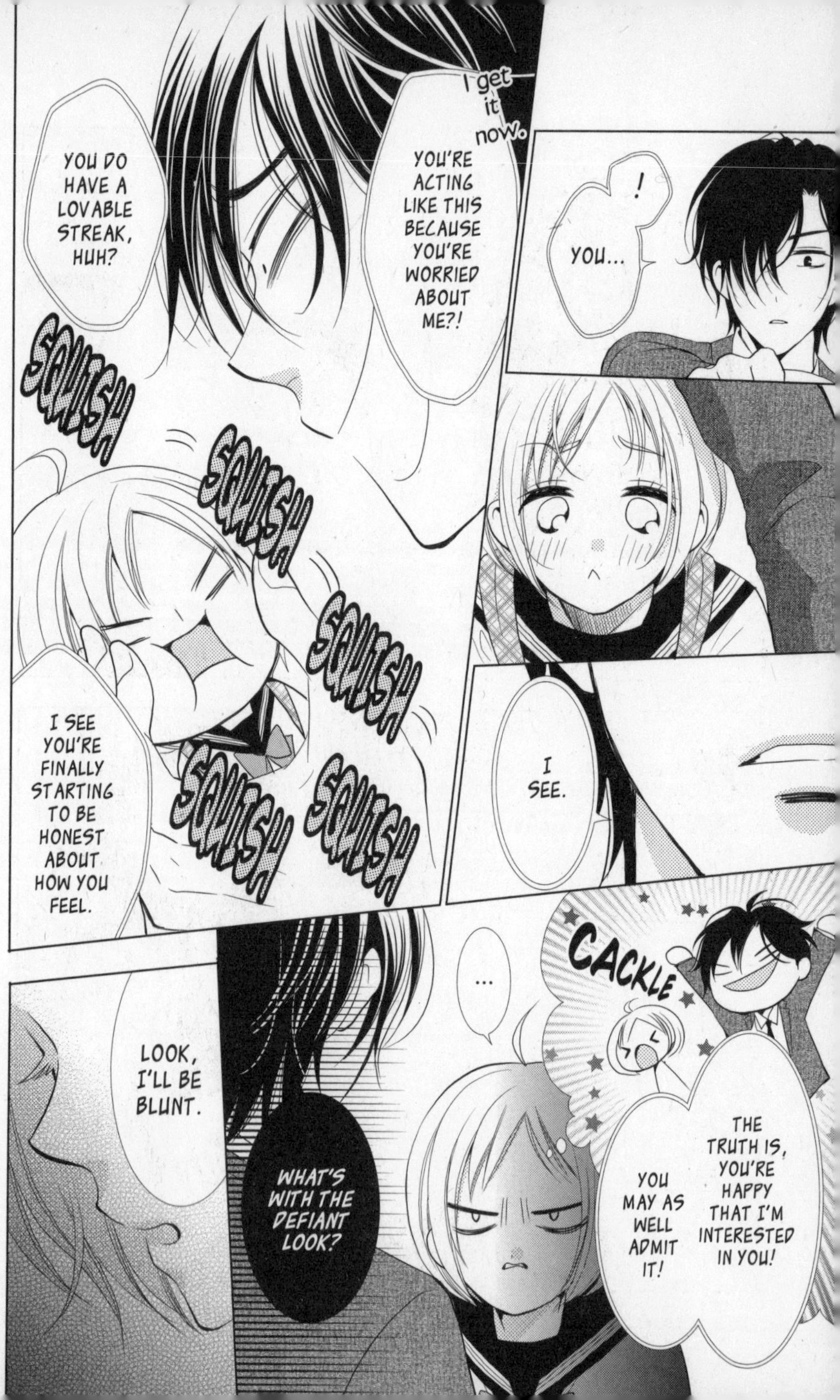
YOU...
!
I SEE.
I get it now.
YOU'RE ACTING LIKE THIS BECAUSE YOU'RE WORRIED ABOUT ME?!
YOU DO HAVE A LOVABLE STREAK, HUH?
SQUISH
SQUISH
SQUISH
SQUISH
SQUISH
I SEE YOU'RE FINALLY STARTING TO BE HONEST ABOUT HOW YOU FEEL.
...
CACKLE
THE TRUTH IS, YOU'RE HAPPY THAT I'M INTERESTED IN YOU!
YOU MAY AS WELL ADMIT IT!
WHAT'S WITH THE DEFIANT LOOK?
LOOK, I'LL BE BLUNT.

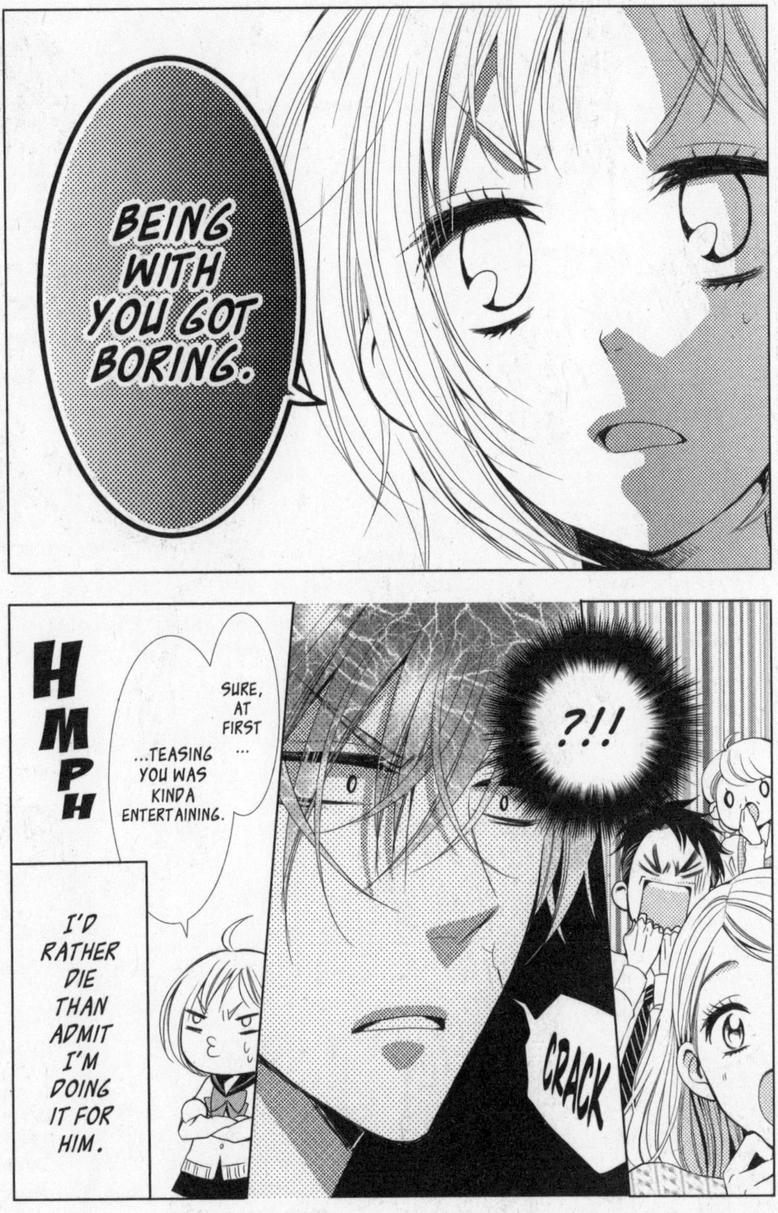
BEING WITH YOU GOT BORING.
?!!
CRACK
SURE, AT FIRST ... ...TEASING YOU WAS KINDA ENTERTAINING.
HMPH
I'D RATHER DIE THAN ADMIT I'M DOING IT FOR HIM.

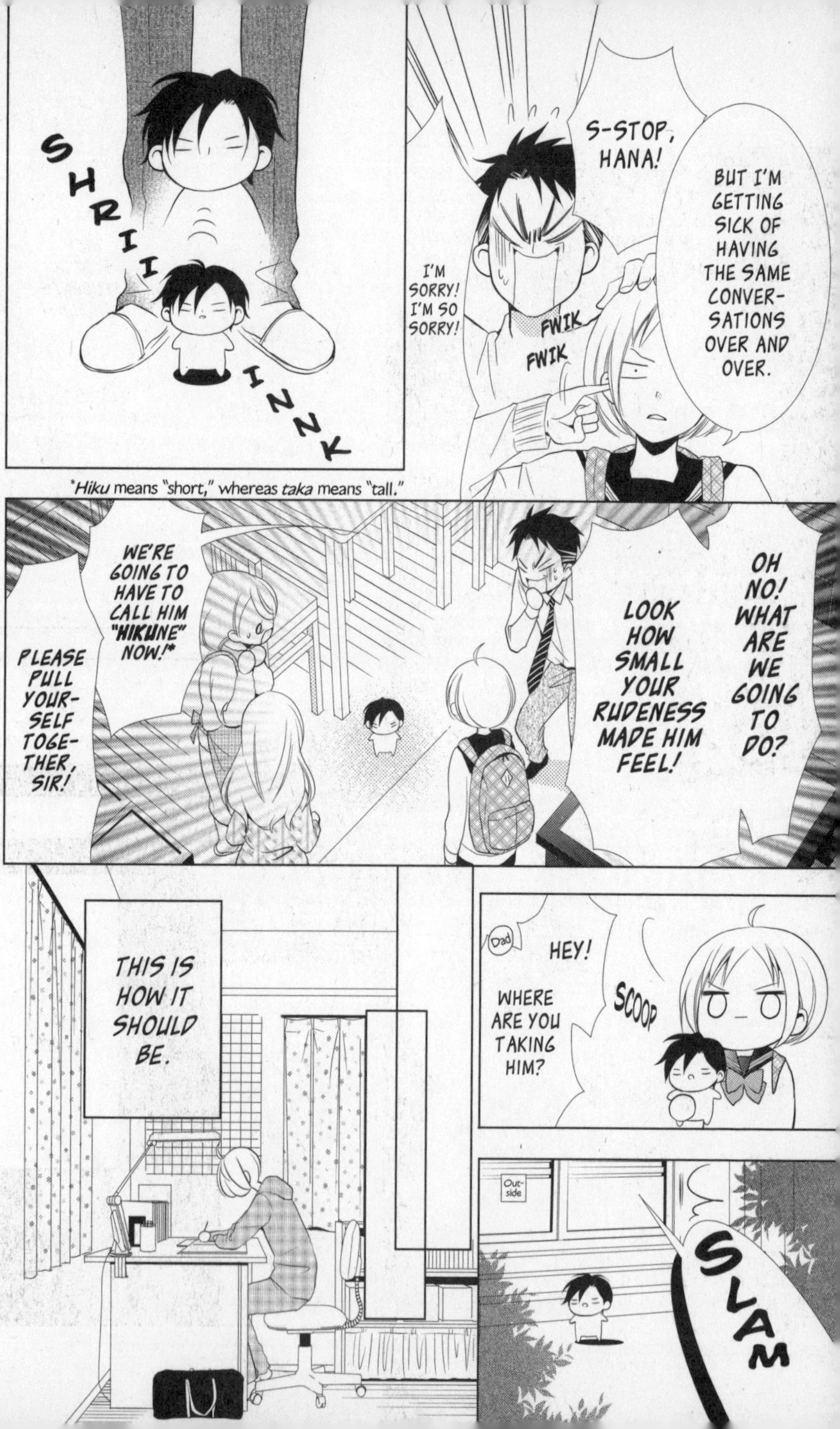
S-STOP, HANA!
BUT I'M GETTING SICK OF HAVING THE SAME CONVER-SATIONS OVER AND OVER.
I'M SORRY! I'M SO SORRY!
FWIK
FWIK
SHRIIINNK
OH NO! WHAT ARE WE GOING TO DO?
LOOK HOW SMALL YOUR RUDENESS MADE HIM FEEL!
WE'RE GOING TO HAVE TO CALL HIM "HIKUNE" NOW!*
PLEASE PULL YOUR-SELF TOGE-THER, SIR!
Dad
HEY!
WHERE ARE YOU TAKING HIM?
SCOOP
Out-side
SLAM
THIS IS HOW IT SHOULD BE.

*Hiku means "short," whereas taka means "tall."

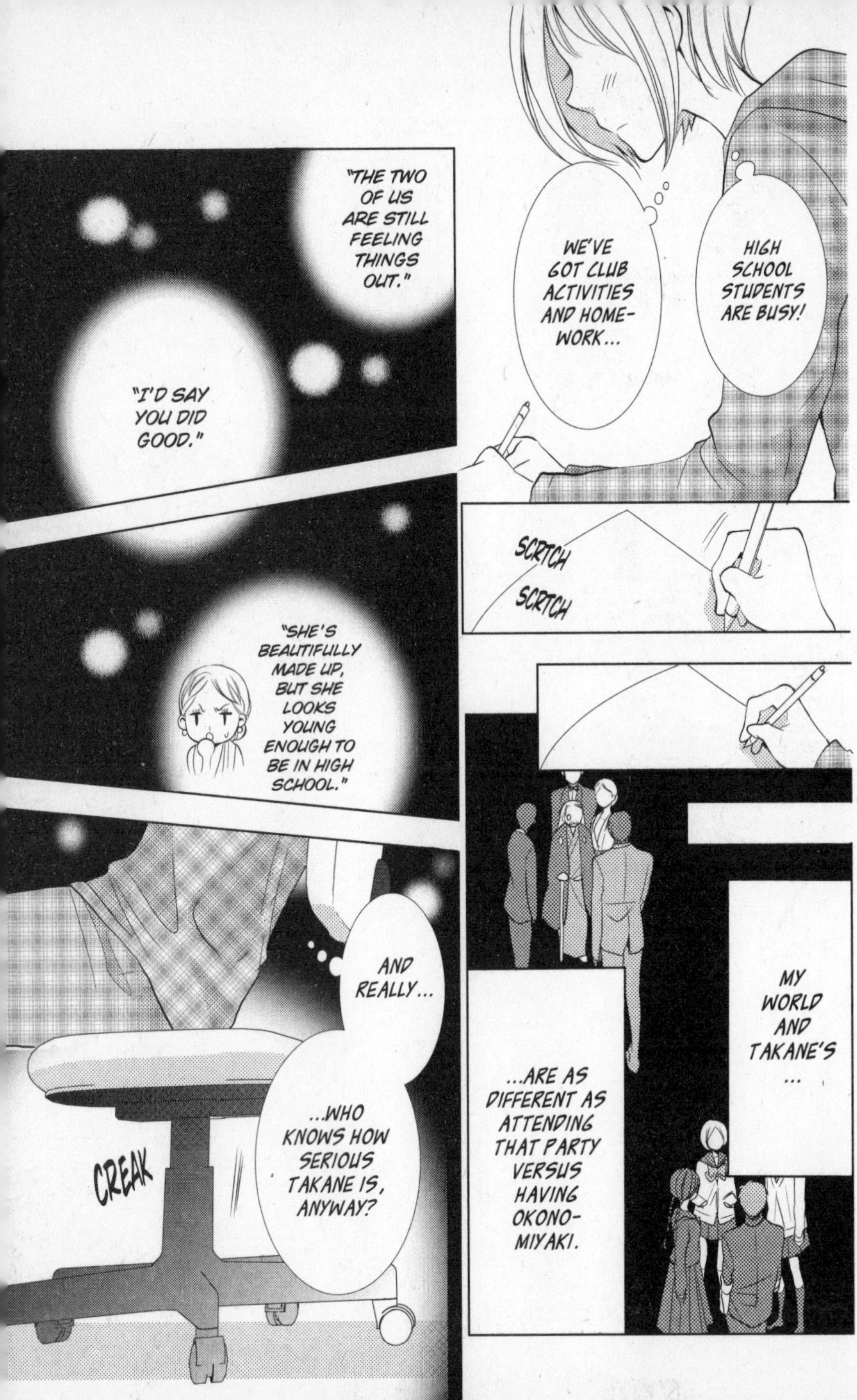
HIGH SCHOOL STUDENTS ARE BUSY!
WE'VE GOT CLUB ACTIVITIES AND HOME-WORK...
SCRTCH
SCRTCH
MY WORLD AND TAKANE'S...
...ARE AS DIFFERENT AS ATTENDING THAT PARTY VERSUS HAVING OKONO-MIYAKI.
"THE TWO OF US ARE STILL FEELING THINGS OUT."
"I'D SAY YOU DID GOOD."
"SHE'S BEAUTIFULLY MADE UP, BUT SHE LOOKS YOUNG ENOUGH TO BE IN HIGH SCHOOL."
AND REALLY...
...WHO KNOWS HOW SERIOUS TAKANE IS, ANYWAY?
CREAK

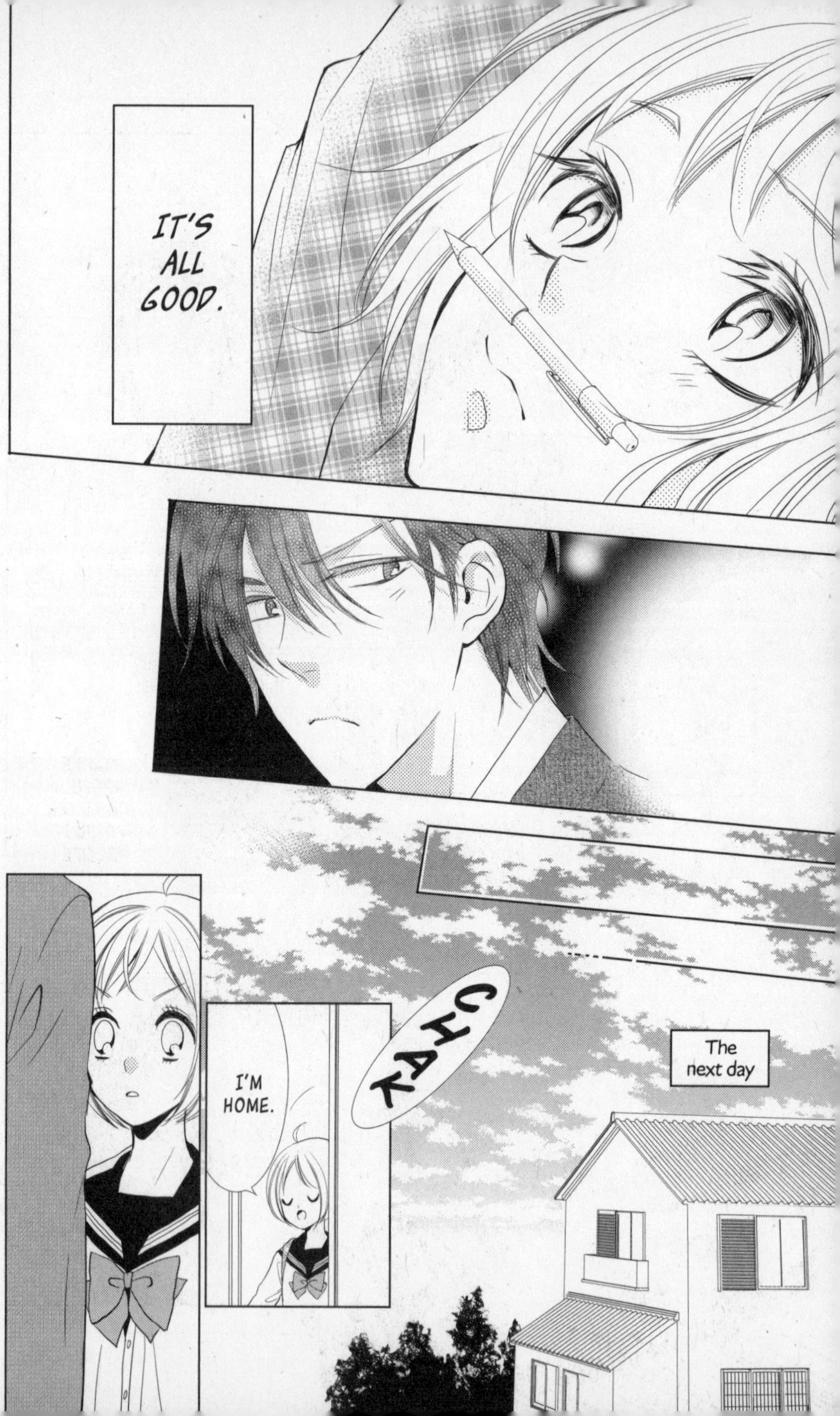
IT'S ALL GOOD.
The next day
CHAK
I'M HOME.

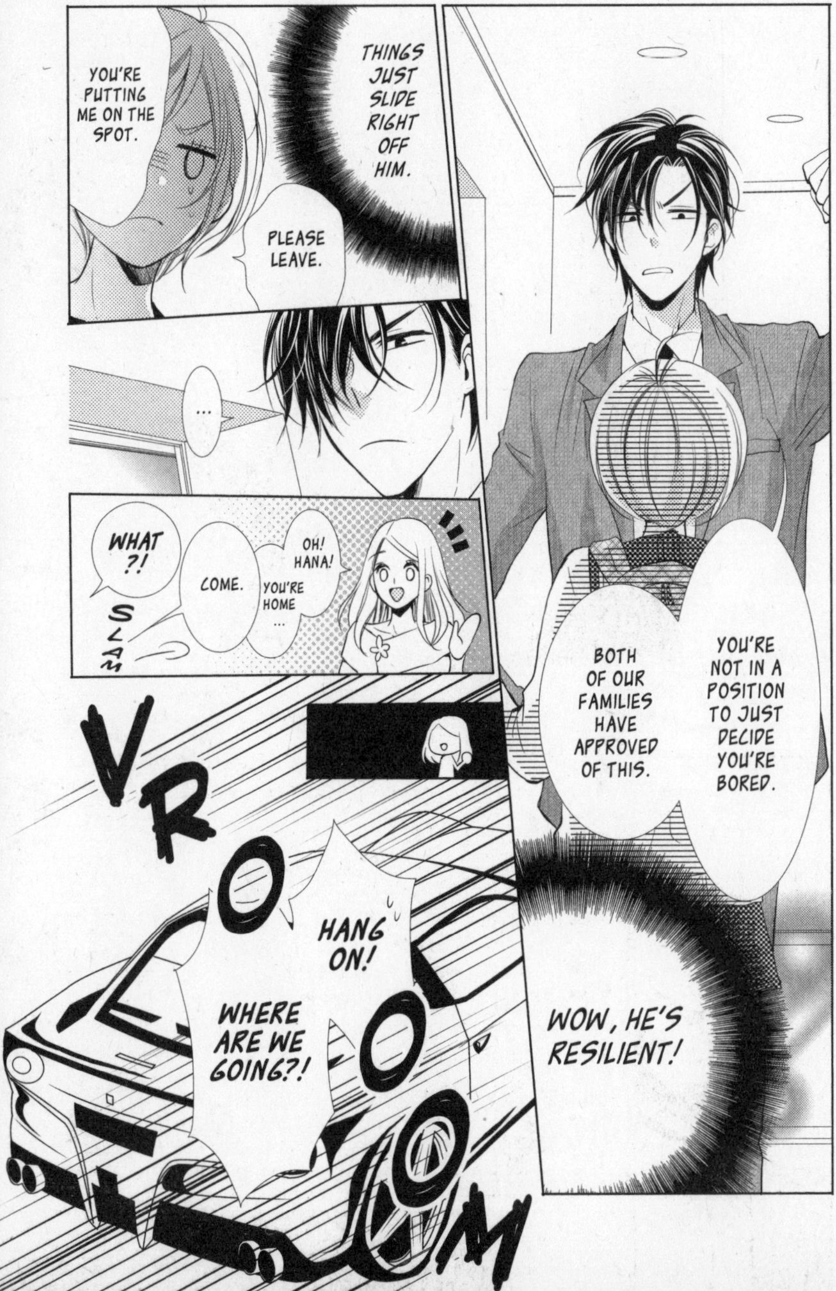
YOU'RE NOT IN A POSITION TO JUST DECIDE YOU'RE BORED.
BOTH OF OUR FAMILIES HAVE APPROVED OF THIS.
WOW, HE'S RESILIENT!
THINGS JUST SLIDE RIGHT OFF HIM.
YOU'RE PUTTING ME ON THE SPOT.
PLEASE LEAVE.
...
OH! HANA!
YOU'RE HOME ...
COME.
WHAT ?!
SLAM
VROOM
HANG ON!
WHERE ARE WE GOING?!

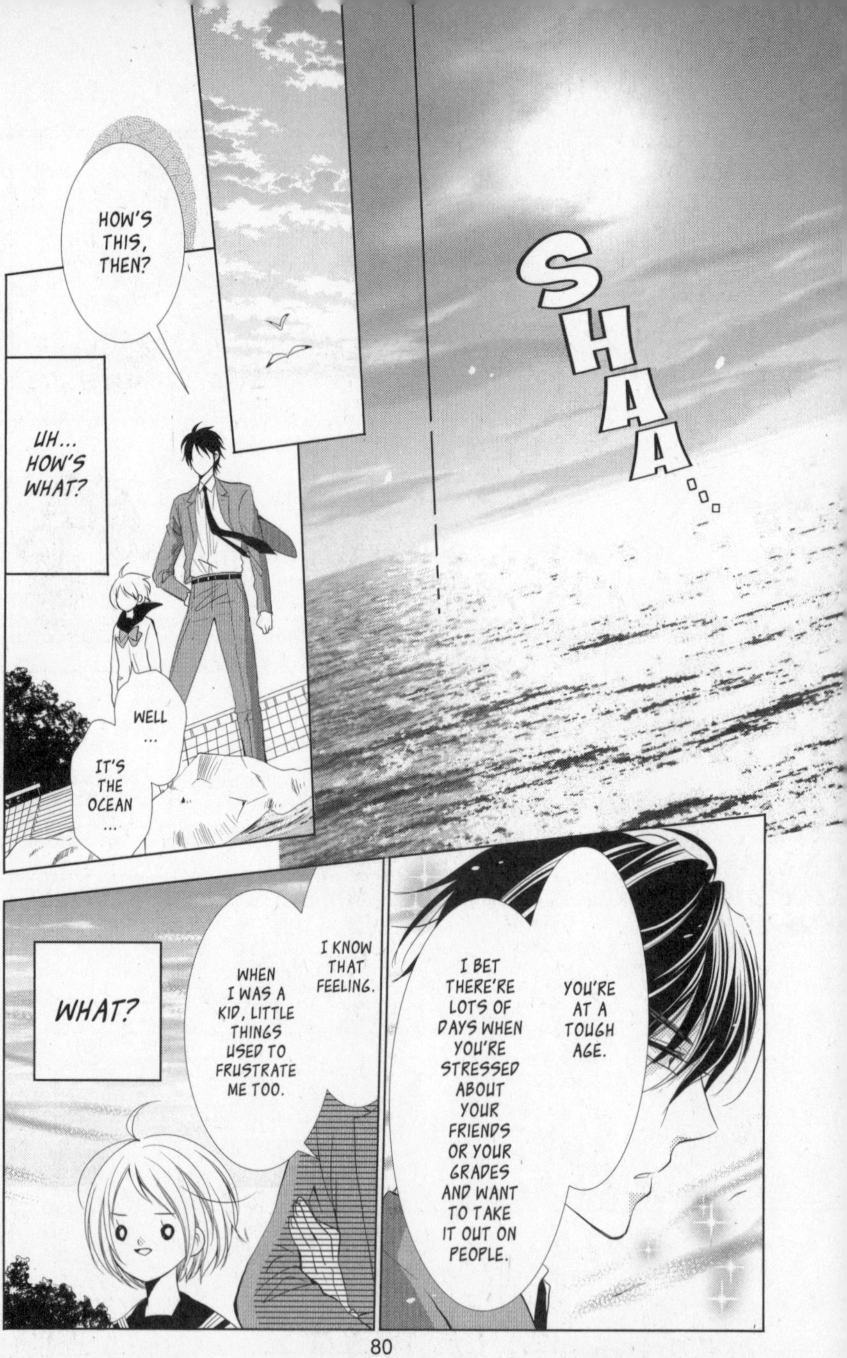
SHAA...
HOW'S THIS, THEN?
UH... HOW'S WHAT?
WELL... IT'S THE OCEAN...
YOU'RE AT A TOUGH AGE.
I BET THERE'RE LOTS OF DAYS WHEN YOU'RE STRESSED ABOUT YOUR FRIENDS OR YOUR GRADES AND WANT TO TAKE IT OUT ON PEOPLE.
I KNOW THAT FEELING.
WHEN I WAS A KID, LITTLE THINGS USED TO FRUSTRATE ME TOO.
WHAT?

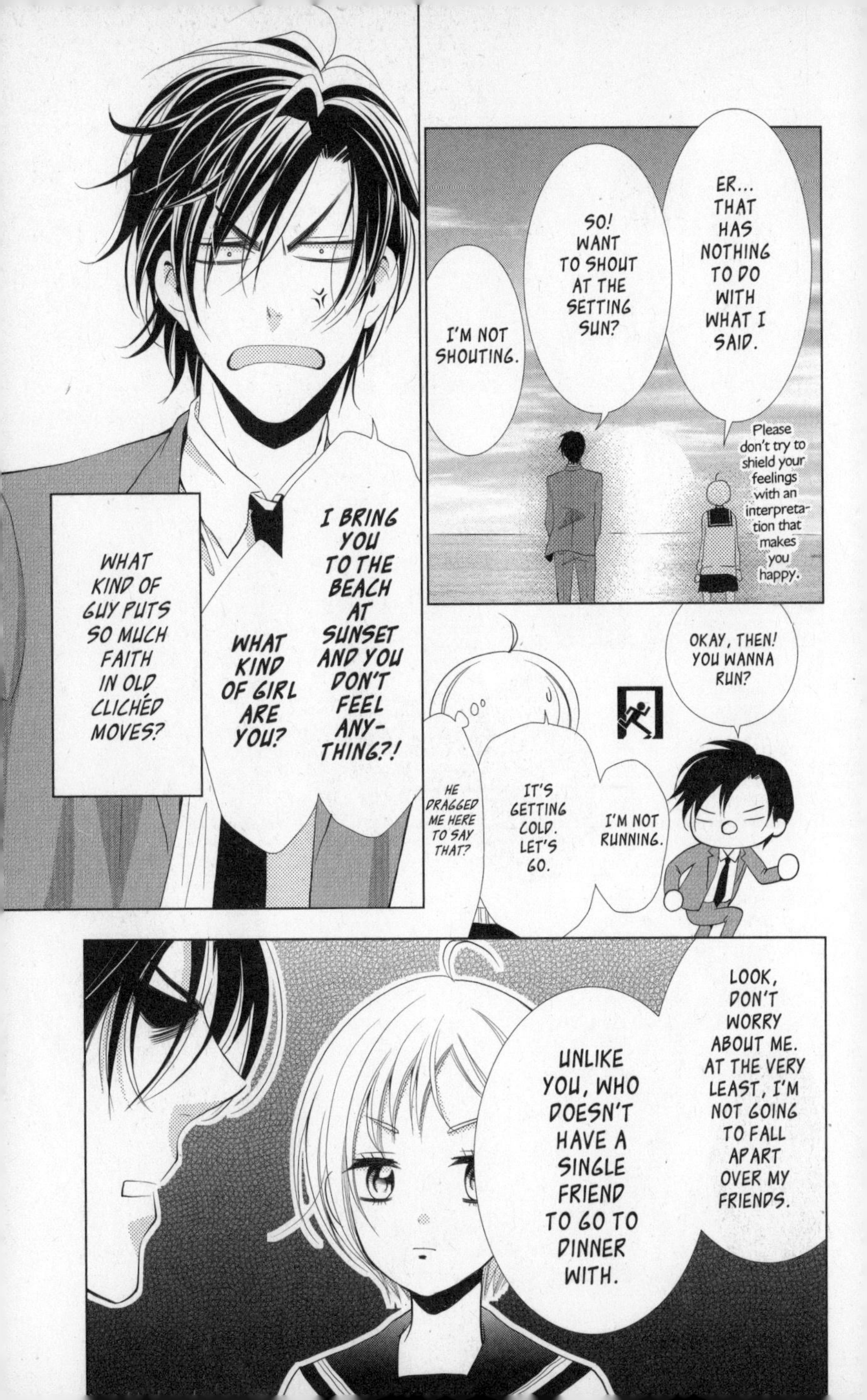
ER... THAT HAS NOTHING TO DO WITH WHAT I SAID.
SO! WANT TO SHOUT AT THE SETTING SUN?
I'M NOT SHOUTING.
Please don't try to shield your feelings with an interpretation that makes you happy.
OKAY, THEN! YOU WANNA RUN?
I'M NOT RUNNING.
IT'S GETTING COLD. LET'S GO.
HE DRAGGED ME HERE TO SAY THAT?
I BRING YOU TO THE BEACH AT SUNSET AND YOU DON'T FEEL ANYTHING?!
WHAT KIND OF GIRL ARE YOU?
WHAT KIND OF GUY PUTS SO MUCH FAITH IN OLD CLICHÉD MOVES?
LOOK, DON'T WORRY ABOUT ME. AT THE VERY LEAST, I'M NOT GOING TO FALL APART OVER MY FRIENDS.
UNLIKE YOU, WHO DOESN'T HAVE A SINGLE FRIEND TO GO TO DINNER WITH.

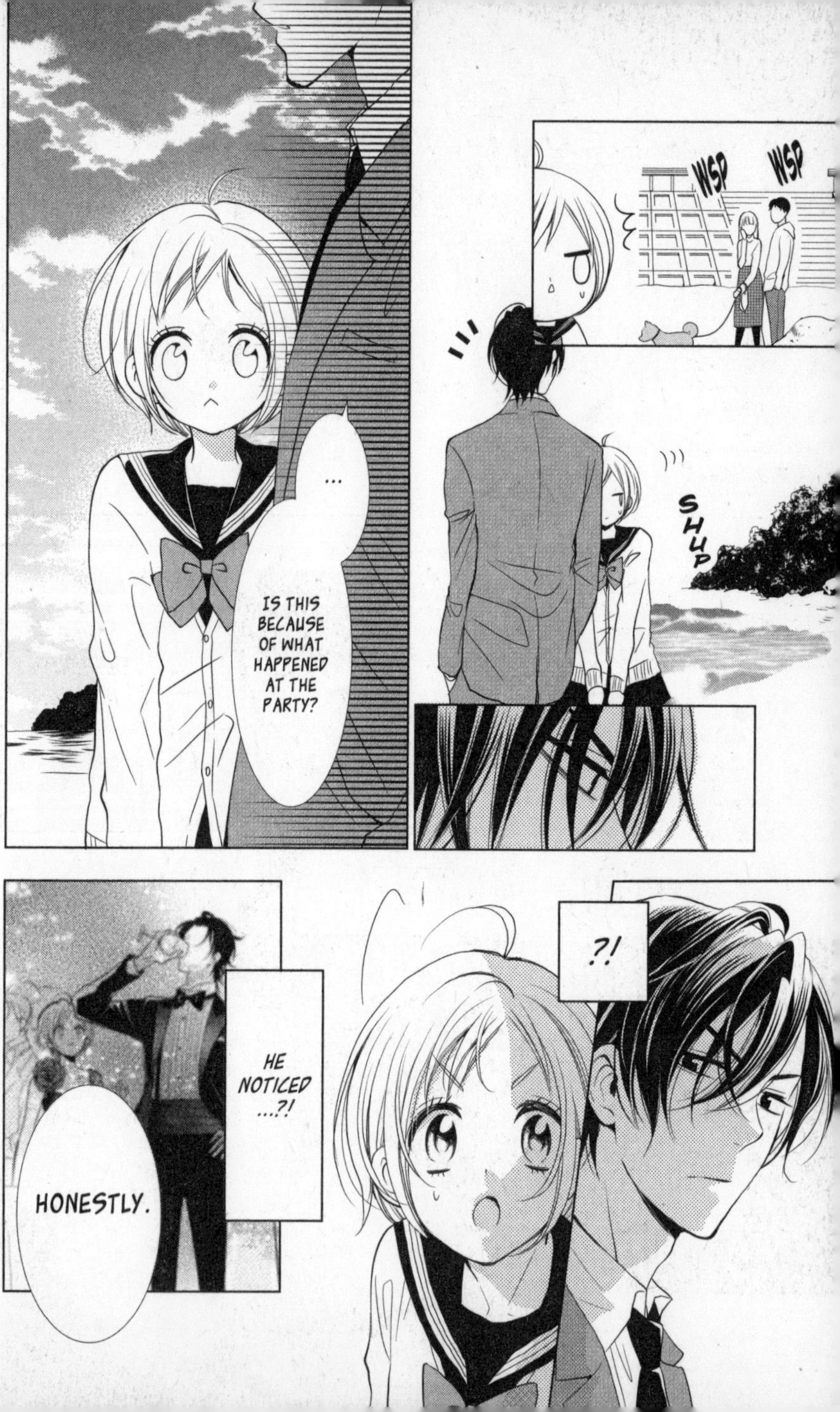
WSP
WSP
SHUP
...
IS THIS BECAUSE OF WHAT HAPPENED AT THE PARTY?
?!
HE NOTICED ...?!
HONESTLY.

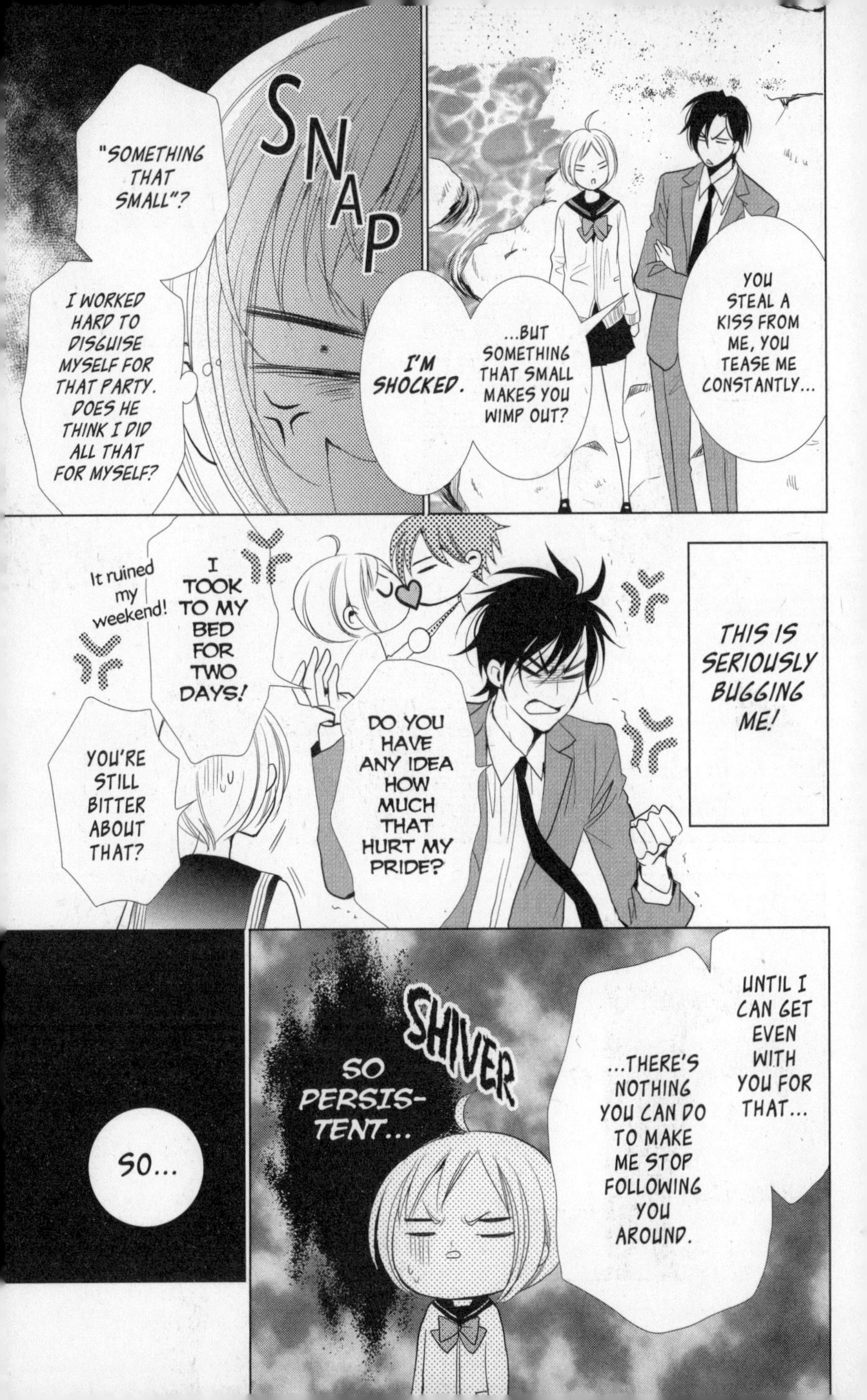

YOU STEAL A KISS FROM ME, YOU TEASE ME CONSTANTLY...
...BUT SOMETHING THAT SMALL MAKES YOU WIMP OUT?
I'M SHOCKED.
SNAP
"SOMETHING THAT SMALL"?
I WORKED HARD TO DISGUISE MYSELF FOR THAT PARTY. DOES HE THINK I DID ALL THAT FOR MYSELF?
THIS IS SERIOUSLY BUGGING ME!
DO YOU HAVE ANY IDEA HOW MUCH THAT HURT MY PRIDE?
I TOOK TO MY BED FOR TWO DAYS!
It ruined my weekend!
YOU'RE STILL BITTER ABOUT THAT?
UNTIL I CAN GET EVEN WITH YOU FOR THAT...
...THERE'S NOTHING YOU CAN DO TO MAKE ME STOP FOLLOWING YOU AROUND.
SHIVER
SO PERSIS-TENT...
SO...

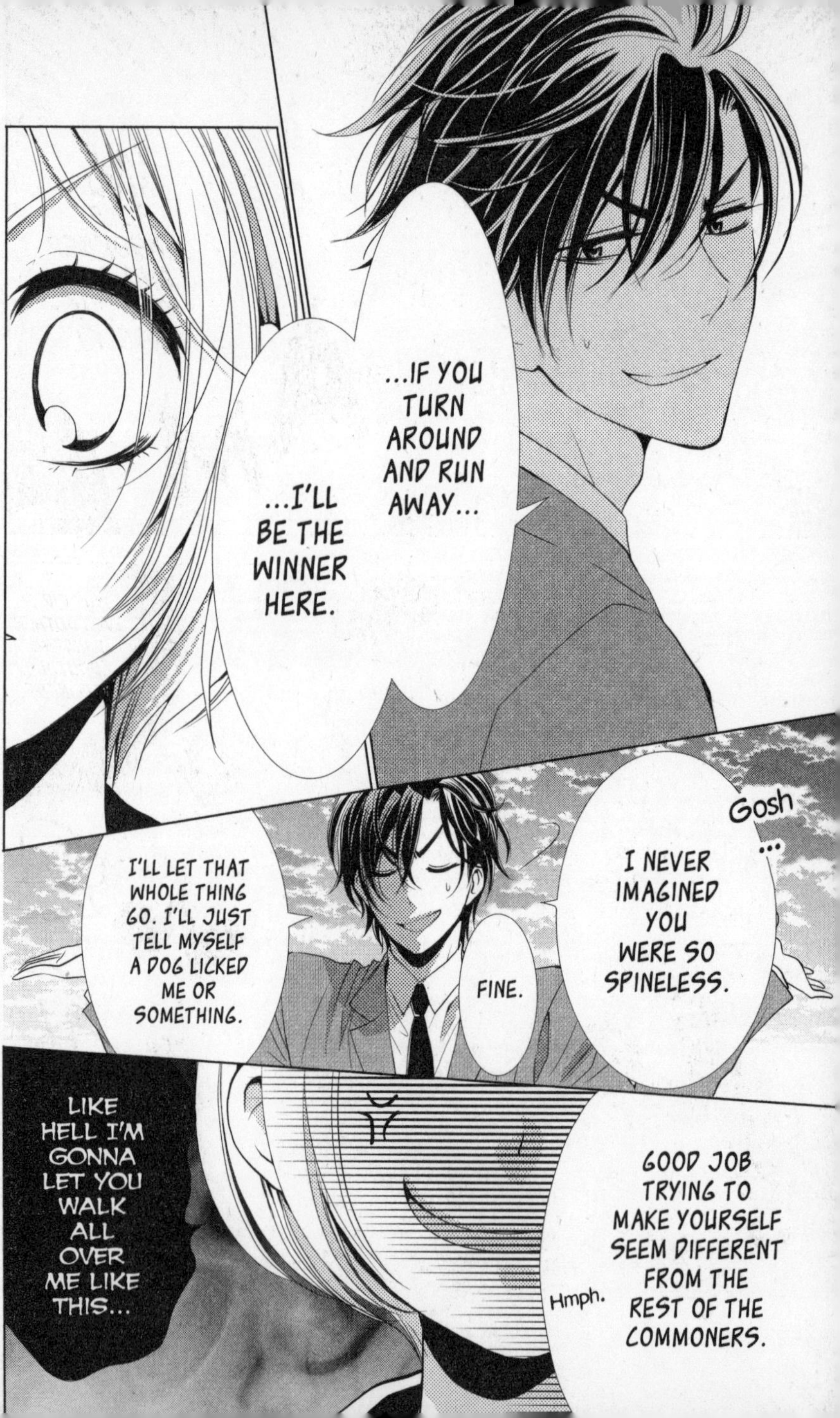
...IF YOU TURN AROUND AND RUN AWAY...
...I'LL BE THE WINNER HERE.
Gosh...
I NEVER IMAGINED YOU WERE SO SPINELESS.
FINE.
I'LL LET THAT WHOLE THING GO. I'LL JUST TELL MYSELF A DOG LICKED ME OR SOMETHING.
GOOD JOB TRYING TO MAKE YOURSELF SEEM DIFFERENT FROM THE REST OF THE COMMONERS.
Hmph.
LIKE HELL I'M GONNA LET YOU WALK ALL OVER ME LIKE THIS...

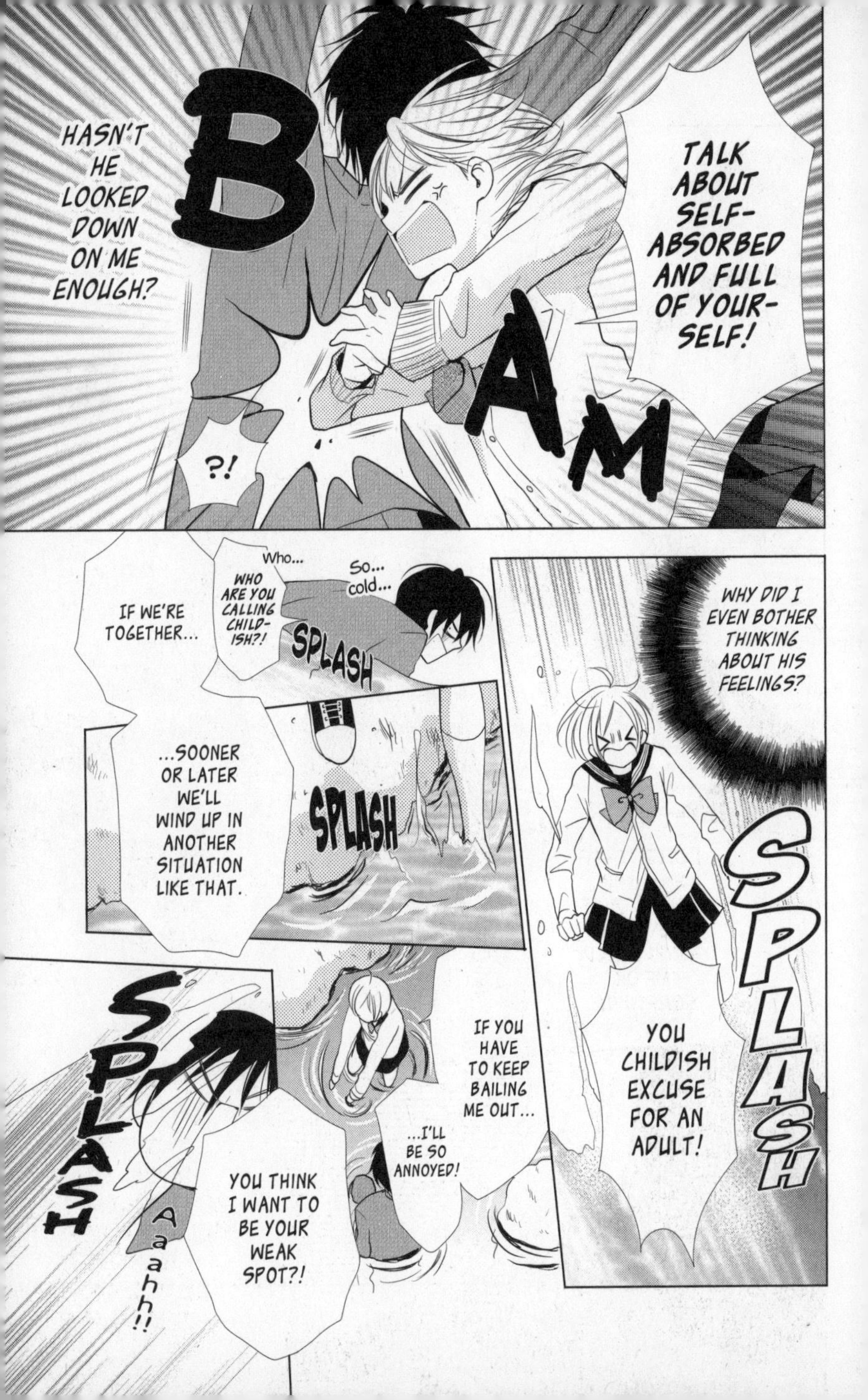
TALK ABOUT SELF-ABSORBED AND FULL OF YOURSELF!
HASN'T HE LOOKED DOWN ON ME ENOUGH?
BAM
?!
WHY DID I EVEN BOTHER THINKING ABOUT HIS FEELINGS?
SPLASH
YOU CHILDISH EXCUSE FOR AN ADULT!
So... cold...
Who...
WHO ARE YOU CALLING CHILDISH?!
SPLASH
IF WE'RE TOGETHER...
SPLASH
...SOONER OR LATER WE'LL WIND UP IN ANOTHER SITUATION LIKE THAT.
IF YOU HAVE TO KEEP BAILING ME OUT...
...I'LL BE SO ANNOYED!
YOU THINK I WANT TO BE YOUR WEAK SPOT?!
SPLASH
Aaahh!!

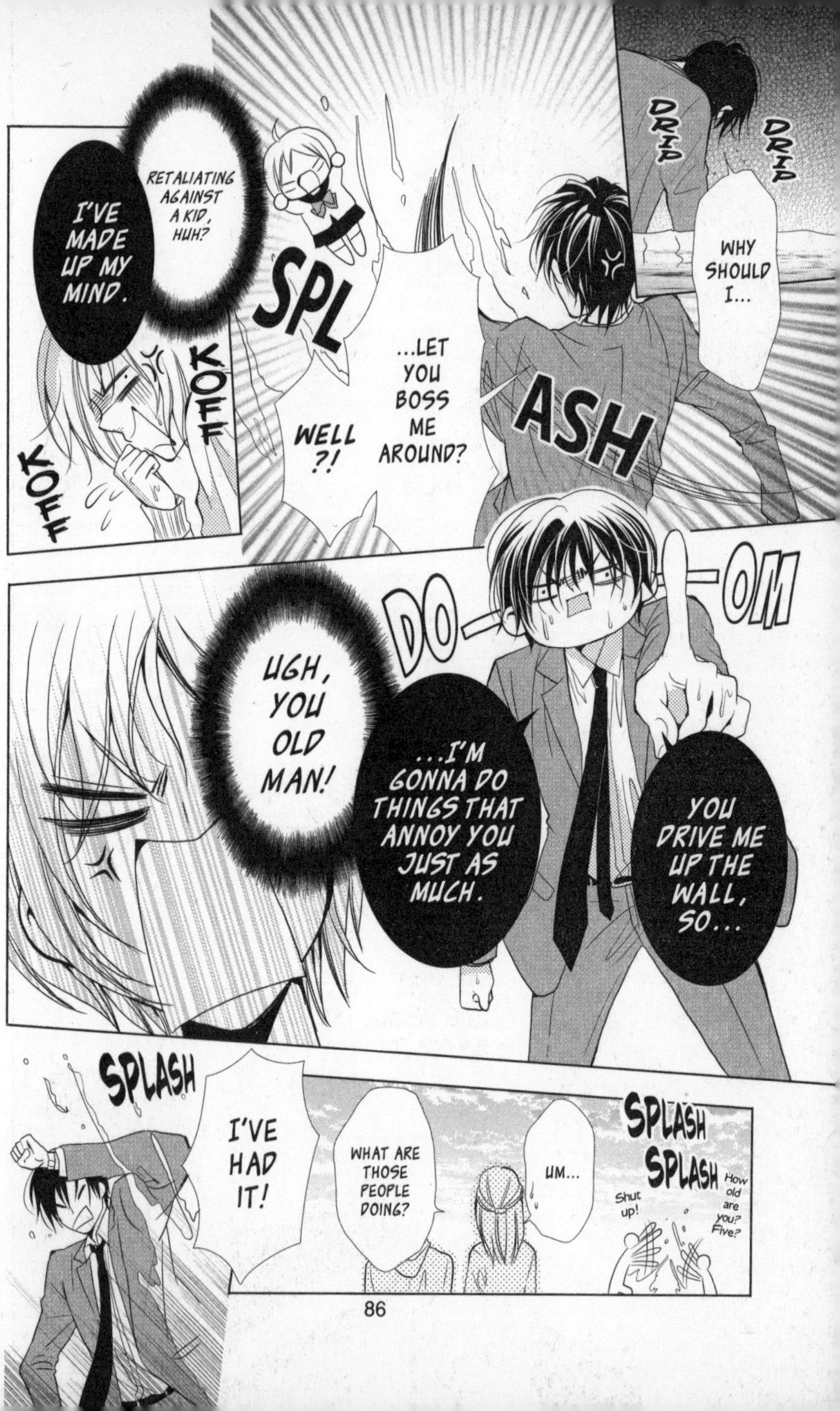
DRIP
DRIP
WHY SHOULD I...
...LET YOU BOSS ME AROUND?
ASH
SPL
WELL?!
RETALIATING AGAINST A KID, HUH?
I'VE MADE UP MY MIND.
KOFF
KOFF
DO-OM
YOU DRIVE ME UP THE WALL, SO...
...I'M GONNA DO THINGS THAT ANNOY YOU JUST AS MUCH.
UGH, YOU OLD MAN!
SPLASH SPLASH
How old are you? Five?
Shut up!
UM...
WHAT ARE THOSE PEOPLE DOING?
SPLASH
I'VE HAD IT!

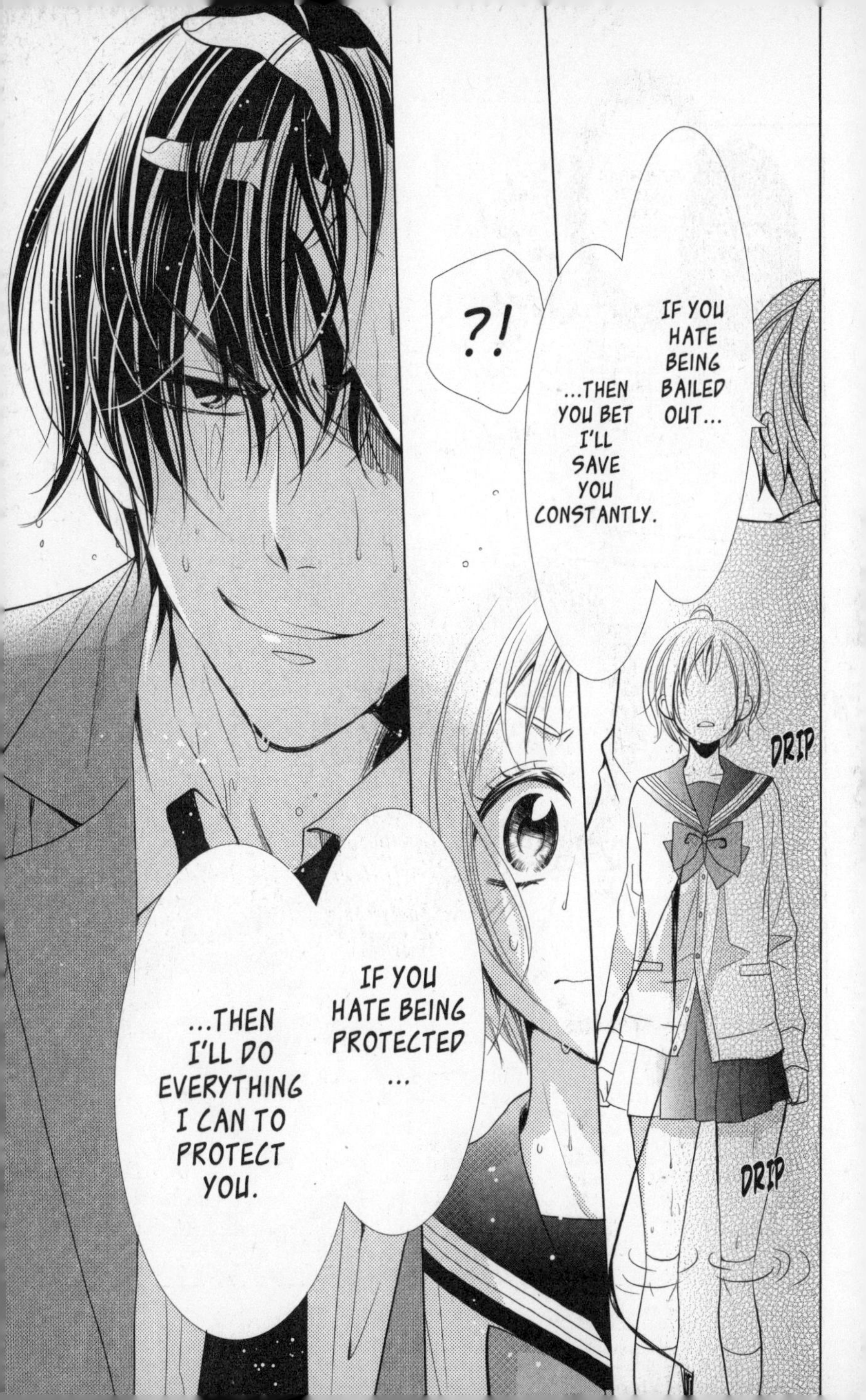
IF YOU HATE BEING BAILED OUT... ...THEN YOU BET I'LL SAVE YOU CONSTANTLY.
DRIP
DRIP
?!
IF YOU HATE BEING PROTECTED ... ...THEN I'LL DO EVERYTHING I CAN TO PROTECT YOU.

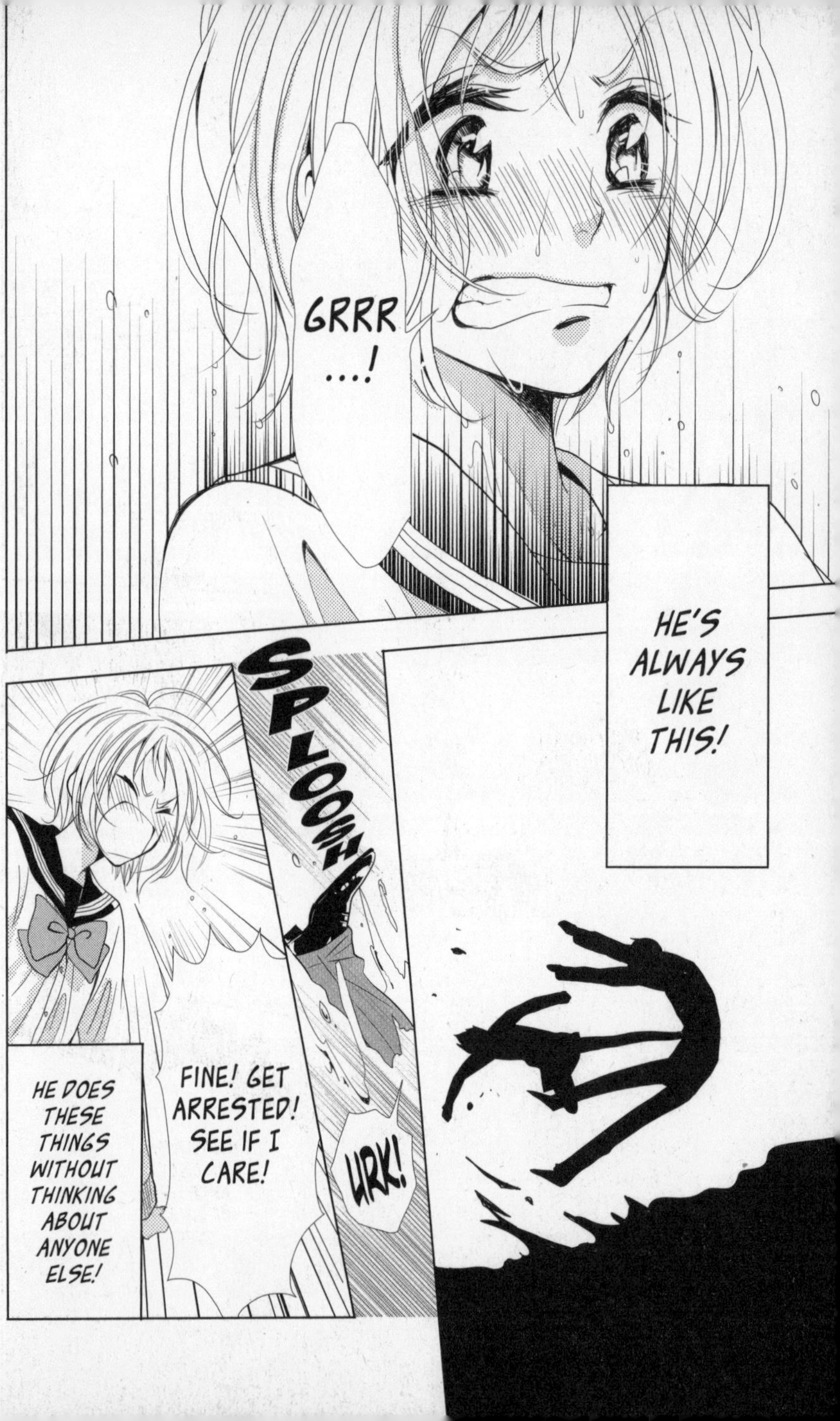
GRRR ...!
HE'S ALWAYS LIKE THIS!
SPLOOSH
URK!
FINE! GET ARRESTED! SEE IF I CARE!
HE DOES THESE THINGS WITHOUT THINKING ABOUT ANYONE ELSE!

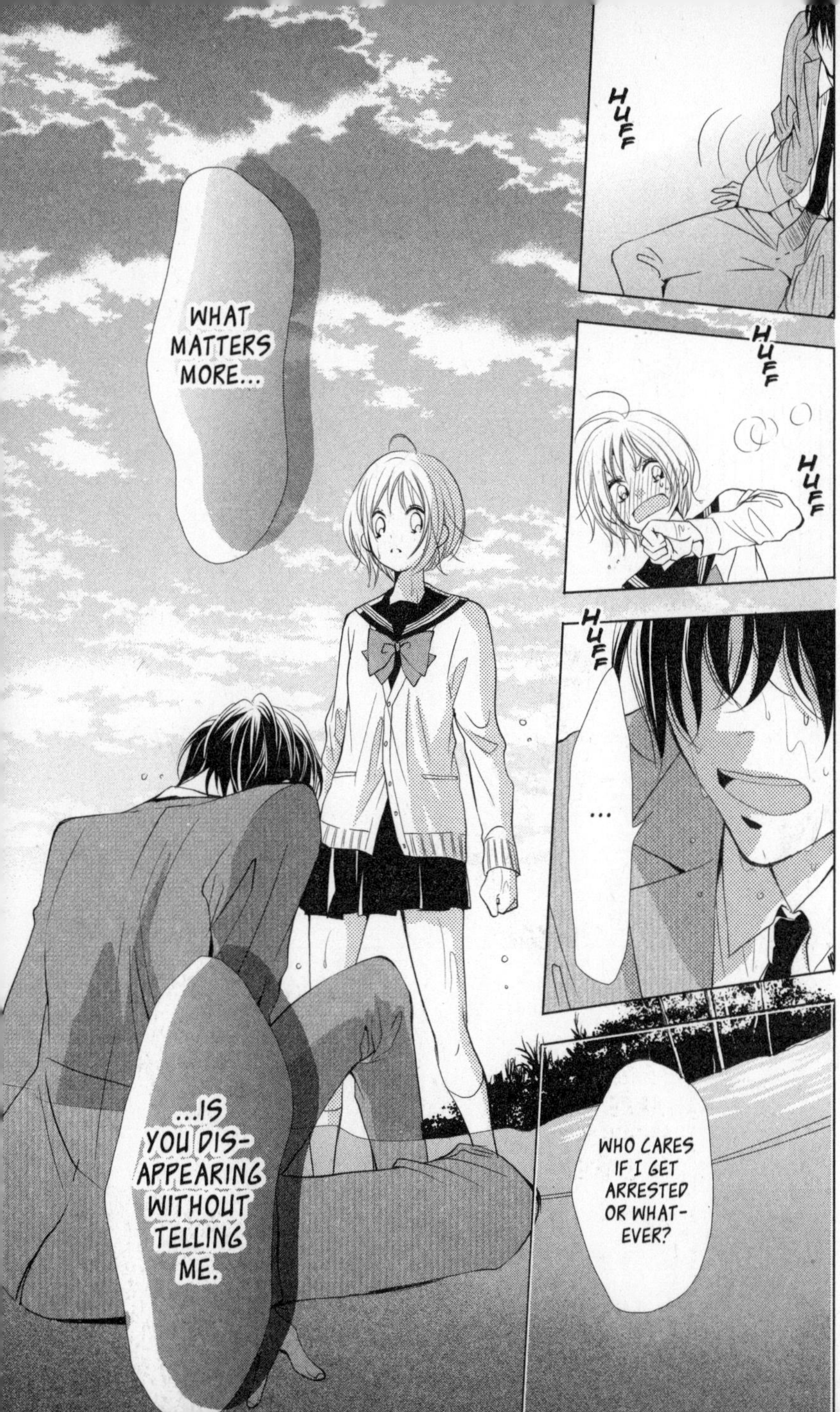
HUFF
HUFF
HUFF
HUFF
...
WHO CARES IF I GET ARRESTED OR WHAT-EVER?
WHAT MATTERS MORE...
...IS YOU DIS-APPEARING WITHOUT TELLING ME.

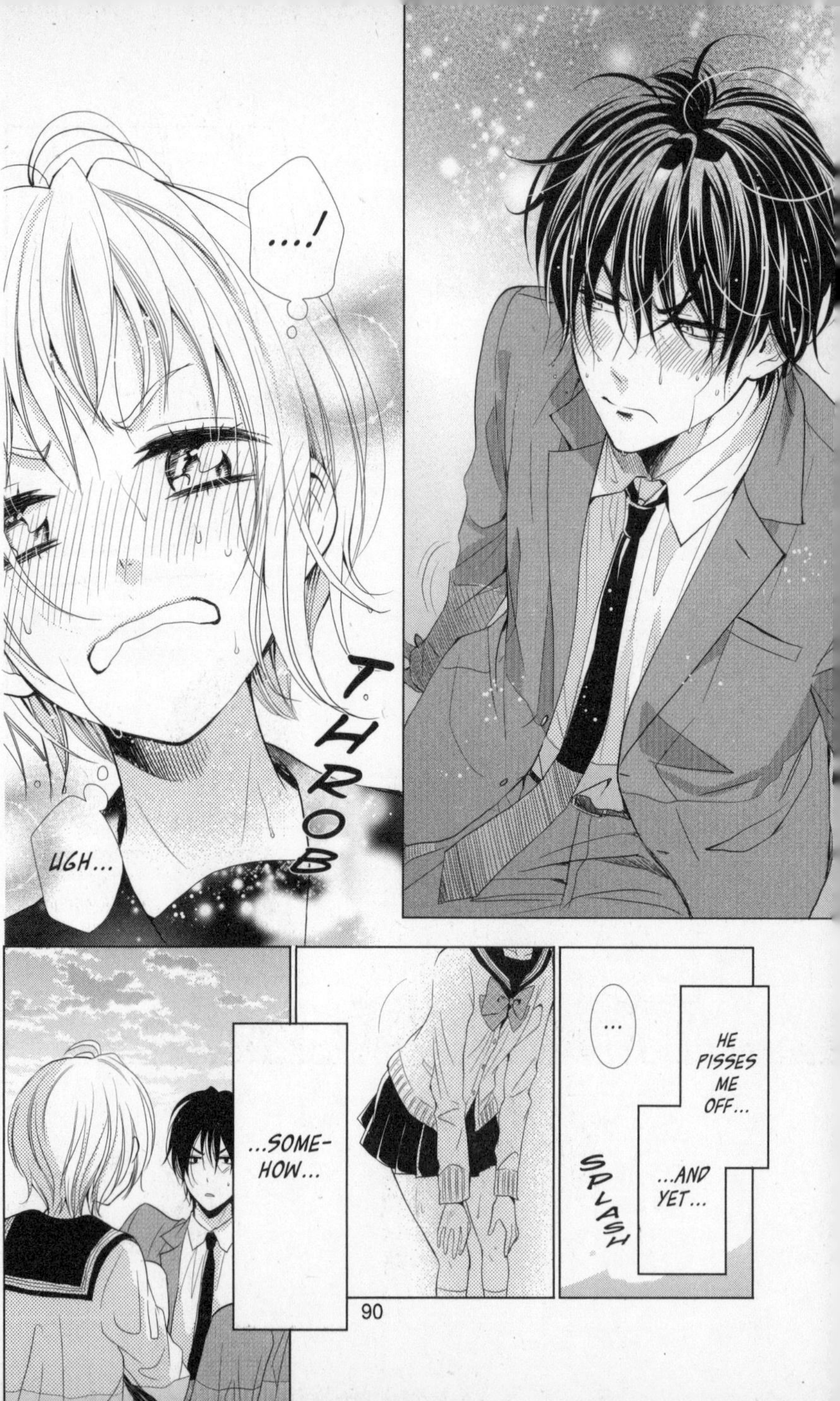
...!
THROB
UGH...
...
HE PISSES ME OFF...
SPLASH
...AND YET...
...SOME-HOW...

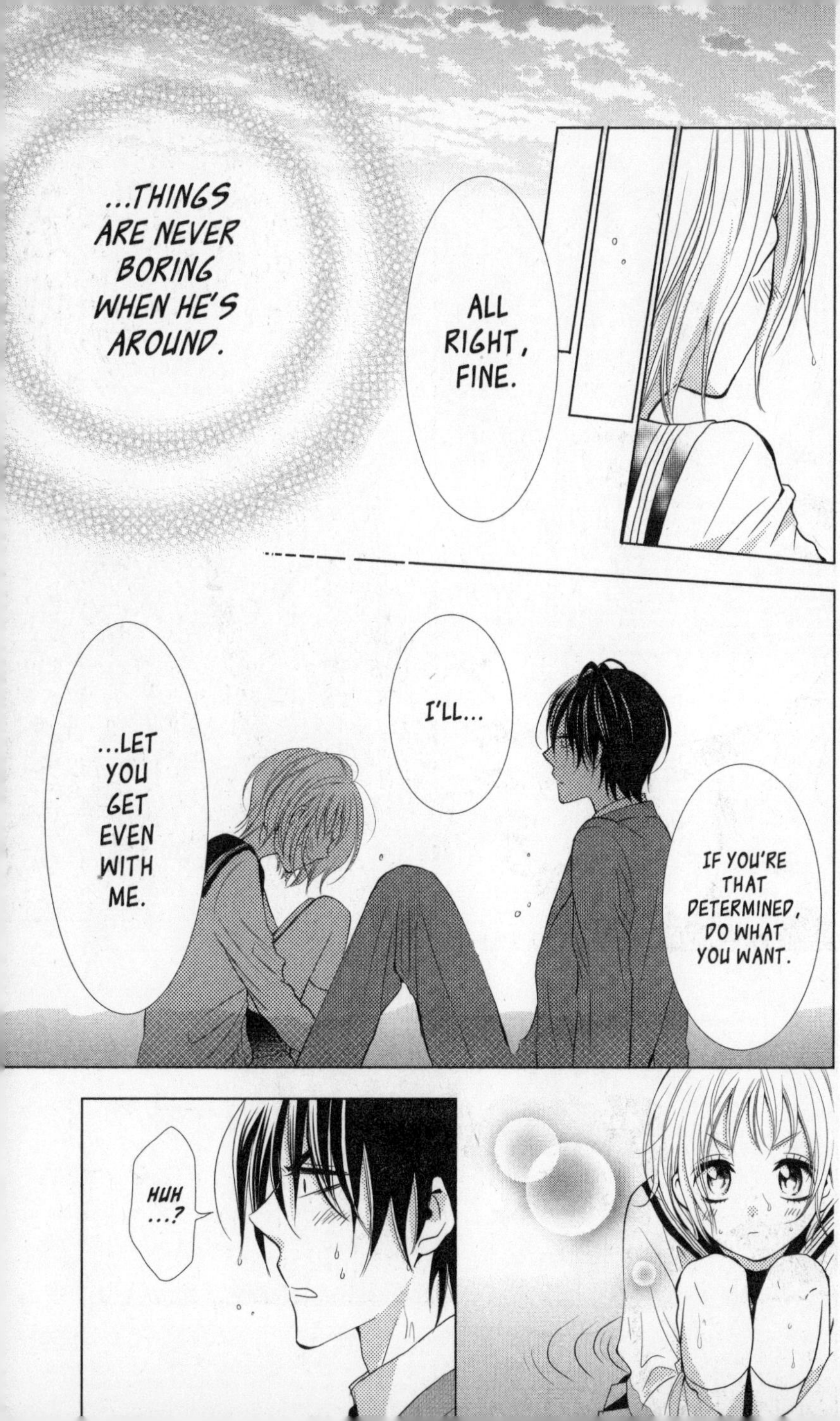
ALL RIGHT, FINE.
...THINGS ARE NEVER BORING WHEN HE'S AROUND.
IF YOU'RE THAT DETERMINED, DO WHAT YOU WANT.
I'LL...
...LET YOU GET EVEN WITH ME.
HUH ...?

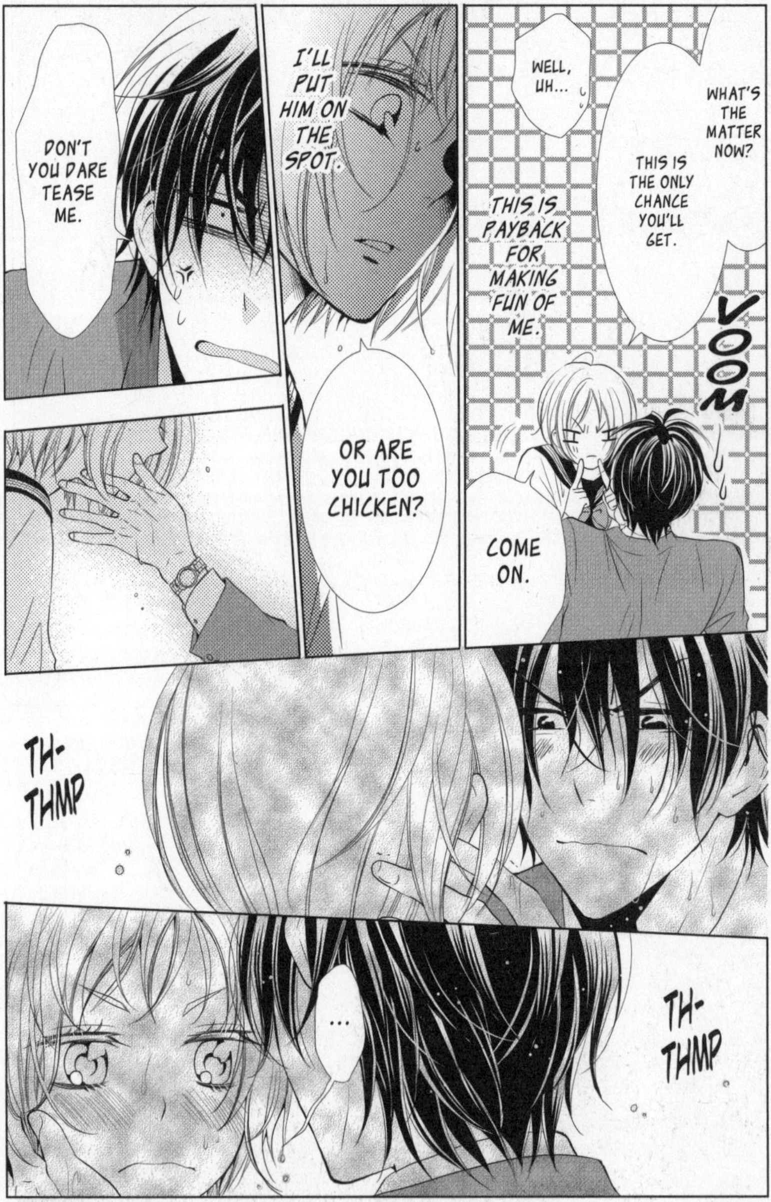
WHAT'S THE MATTER NOW?
THIS IS THE ONLY CHANCE YOU'LL GET.
WELL, UH...
VOOM
THIS IS PAYBACK FOR MAKING FUN OF ME.
COME ON.
I'LL PUT HIM ON THE SPOT.
OR ARE YOU TOO CHICKEN?
DON'T YOU DARE TEASE ME.
TH-THMP
TH-THMP
...

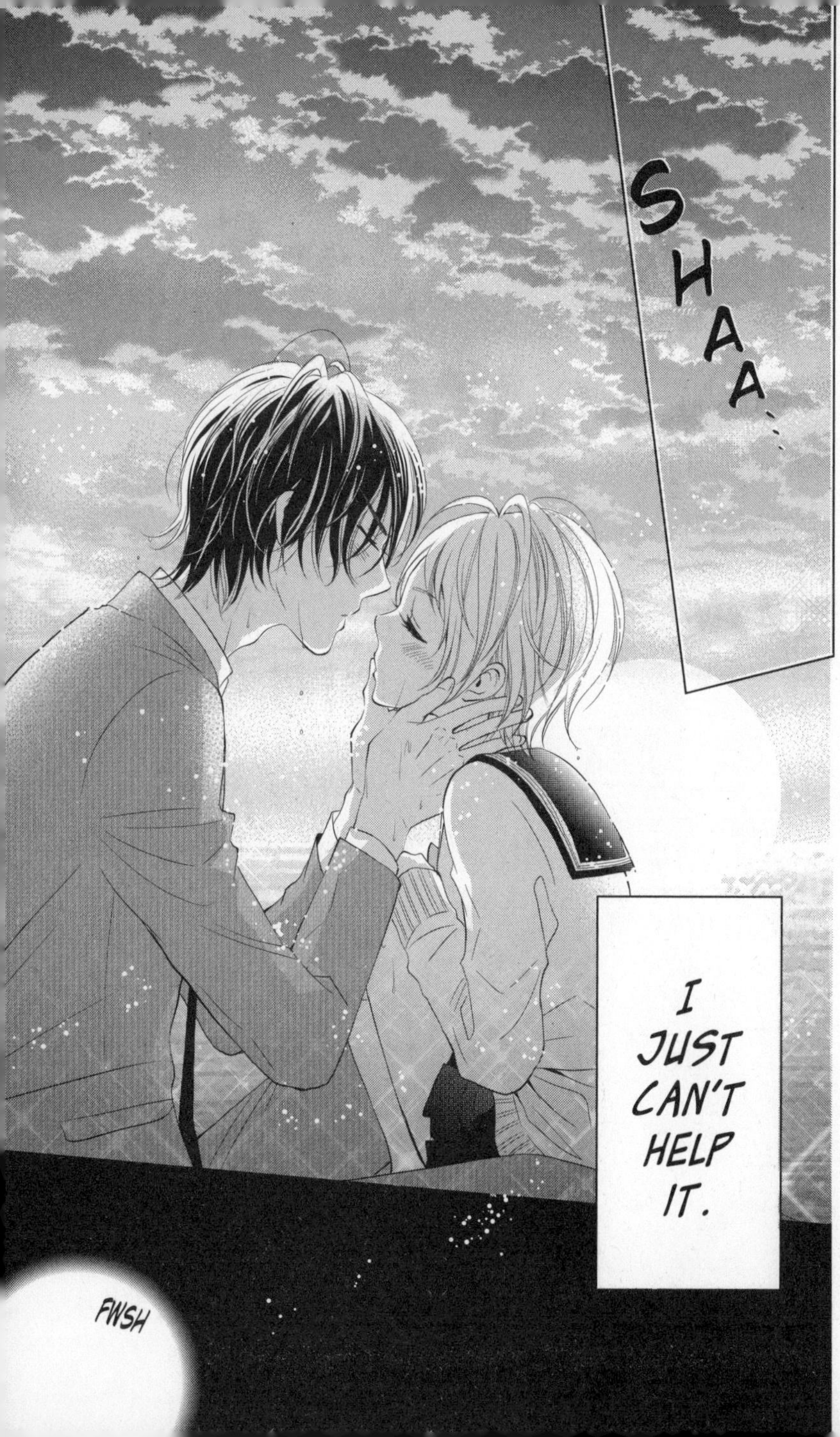
SHAA...
I JUST CAN'T HELP IT.
FWSH

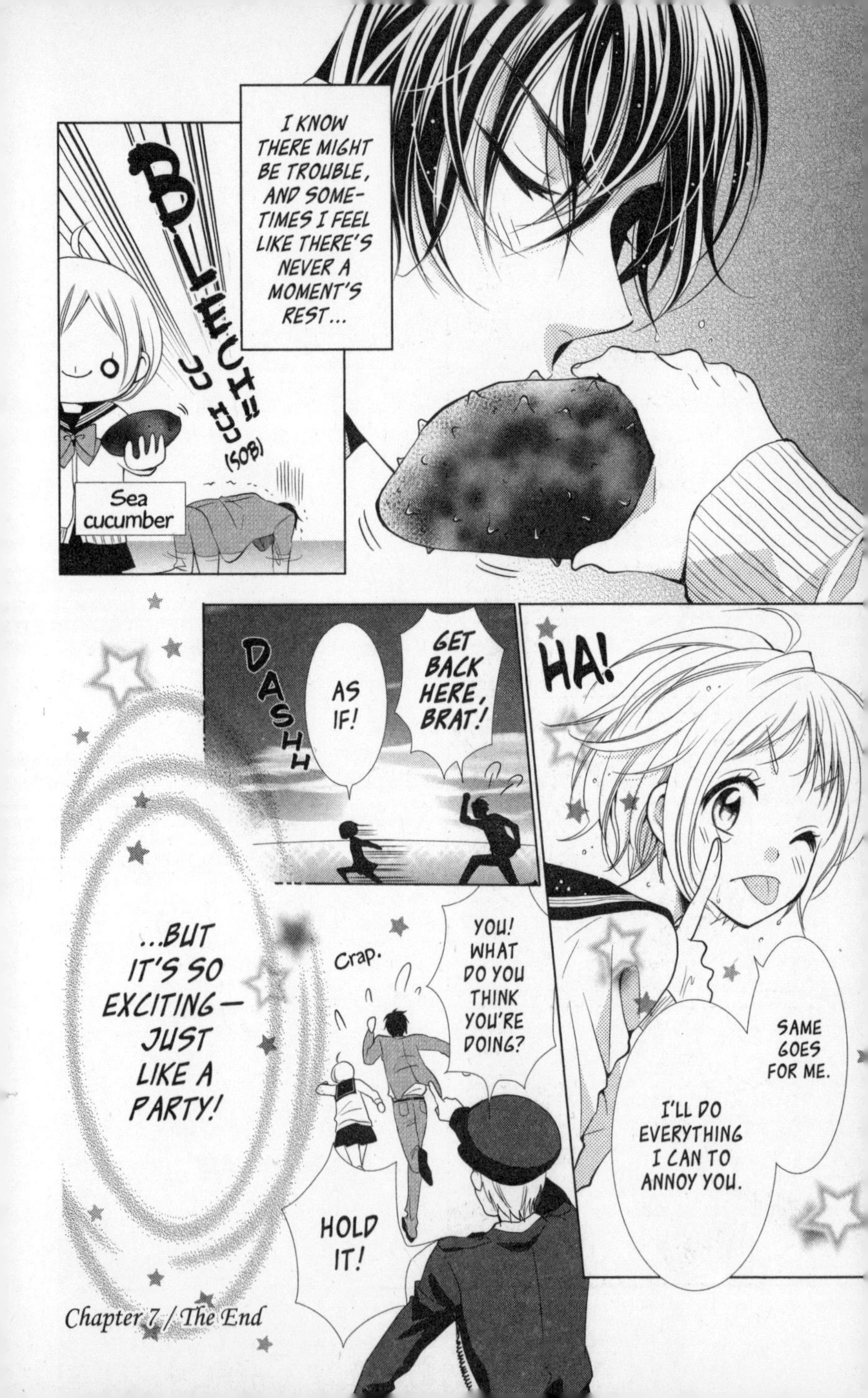
I KNOW THERE MIGHT BE TROUBLE, AND SOME-TIMES I FEEL LIKE THERE'S NEVER A MOMENT'S REST...
BLECH!!
UU HUU
(SOB)
Sea cucumber
HA!
SAME GOES FOR ME.
I'LL DO EVERYTHING I CAN TO ANNOY YOU.
GET BACK HERE, BRAT!
AS IF!
DASHH
YOU! WHAT DO YOU THINK YOU'RE DOING?
Crap.
HOLD IT!
...BUT IT'S SO EXCITING—JUST LIKE A PARTY!
Chapter 7 / The End

Hikune 1

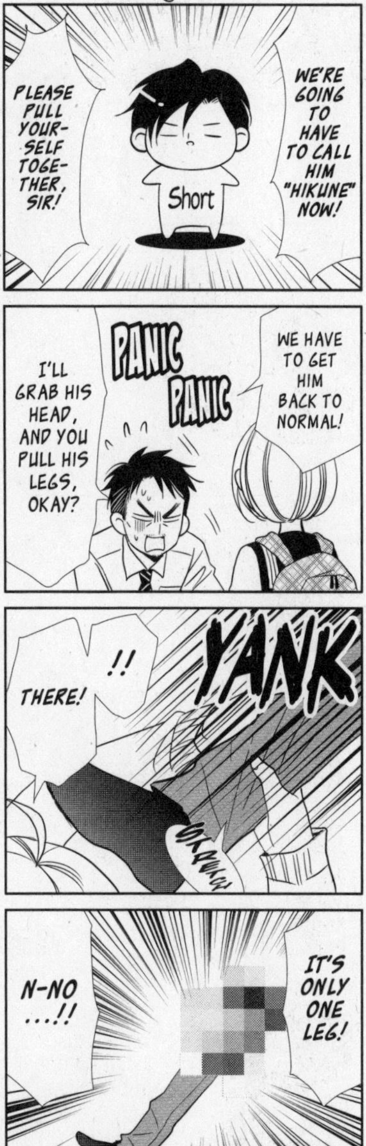
WE'RE GOING TO HAVE TO CALL HIM "HIKUNE" NOW!
Short
PLEASE PULL YOURSELF TOGETHER, SIR!
WE HAVE TO GET HIM BACK TO NORMAL!
PANIC PANIC
I'LL GRAB HIS HEAD, AND YOU PULL HIS LEGS, OKAY?
YANK
!!
THERE!
IT'S ONLY ONE LEG!
N-NO ...!!

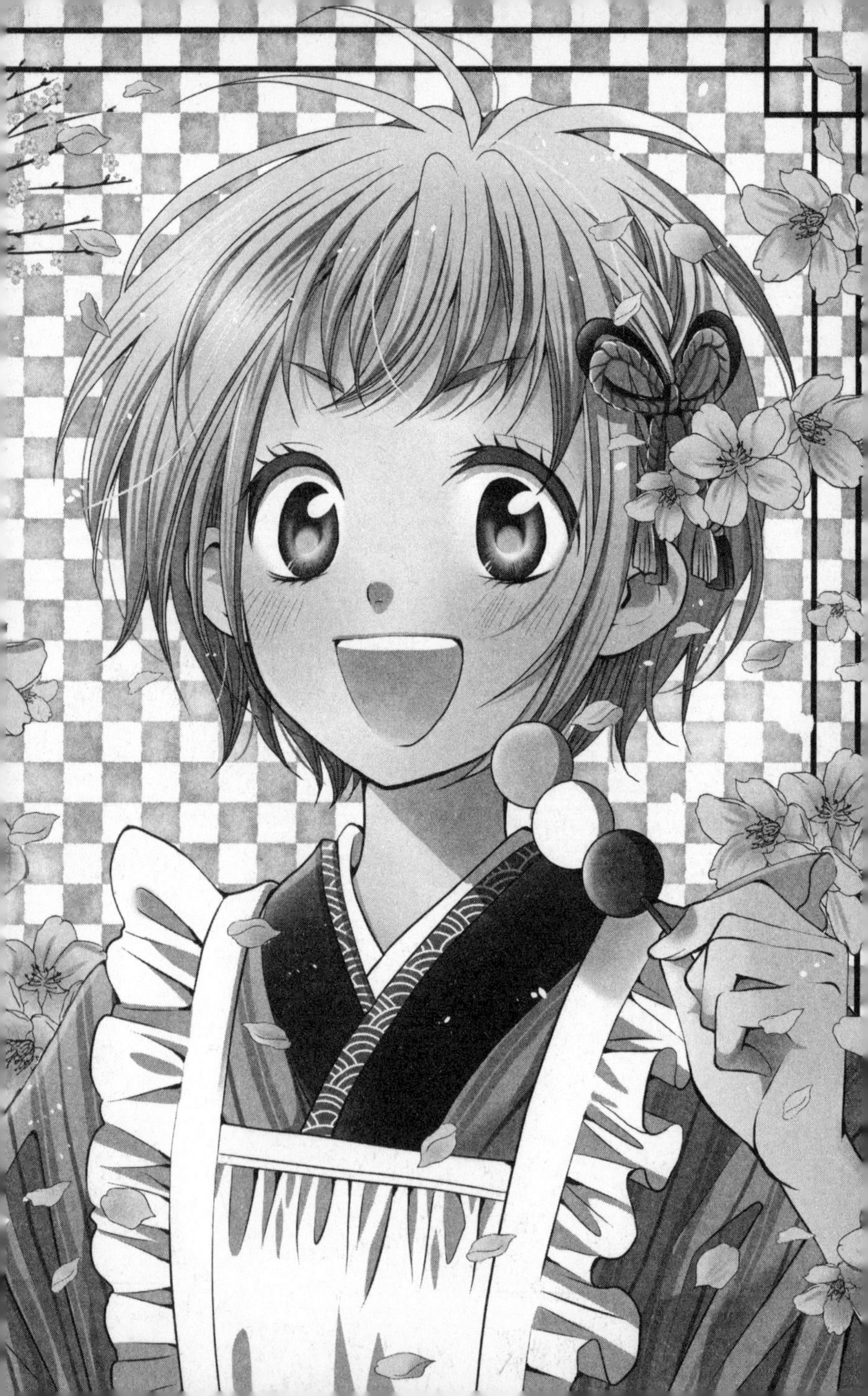

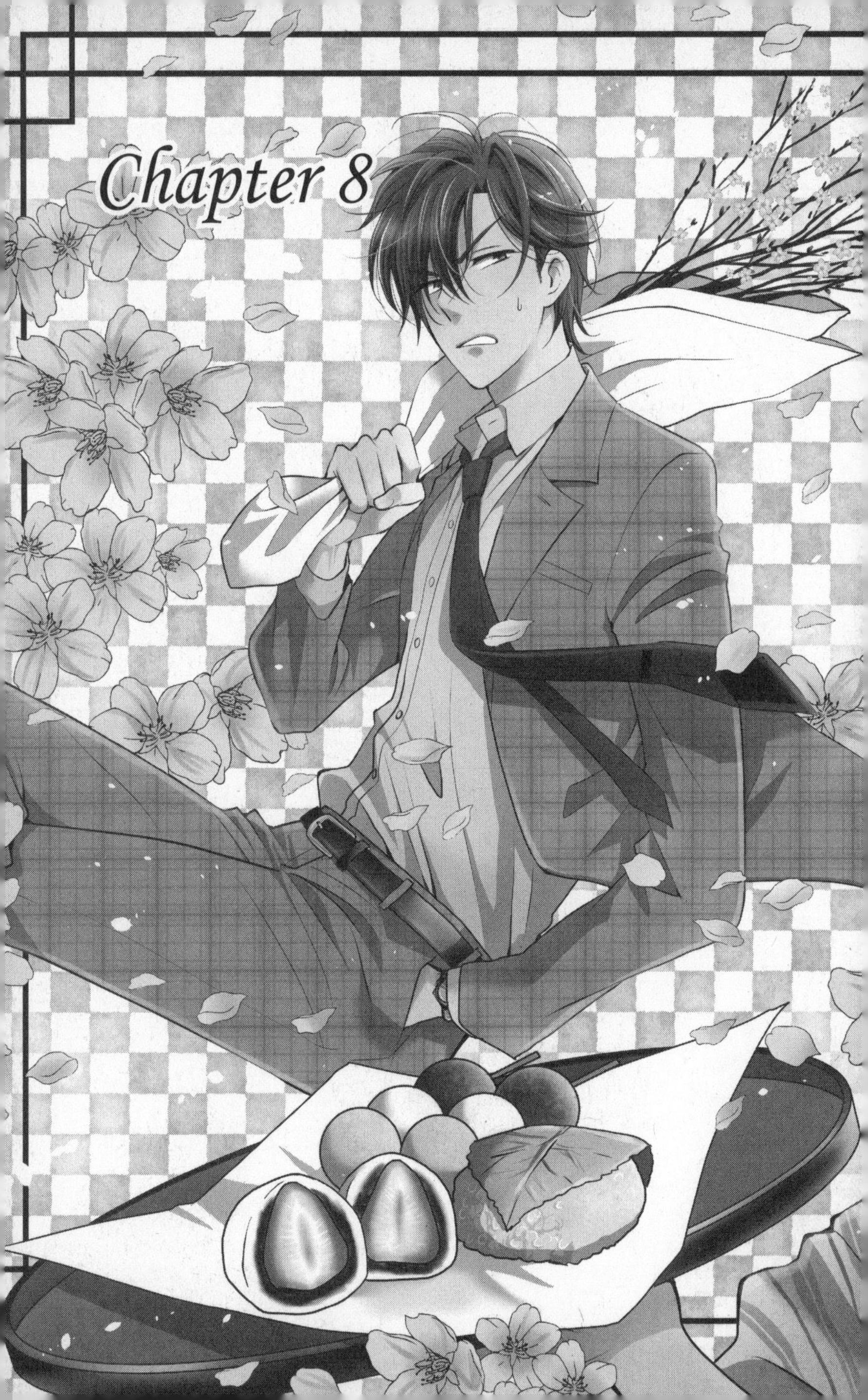
Chapter 8

Hikune 2

A STOLEN KISS...
BY A SEA CUCUMBER.
A STOLEN KISS...
BY A SEA CUCUMBER.
BY A SEA CUCUMBER.
HEY, DO YOU SMELL SOME-THING BRINY?
I THINK IT'S THAT GUY'S BREATH.
*AUDITORY HALLUCINA-TIONS
*AUDITORY HALLUCINA-TIONS
DO YOU SMELL SEA CUCUM-BERS?
LET'S CALL THAT GUY "SEA CUCUMBER LIPS"!
TAKANE TURNED INTO HIKUNE AGAIN.
STROLL
STROLL
HE STAYED LIKE THAT FOR A FEW DAYS.

To be continued in "Hikune 3"

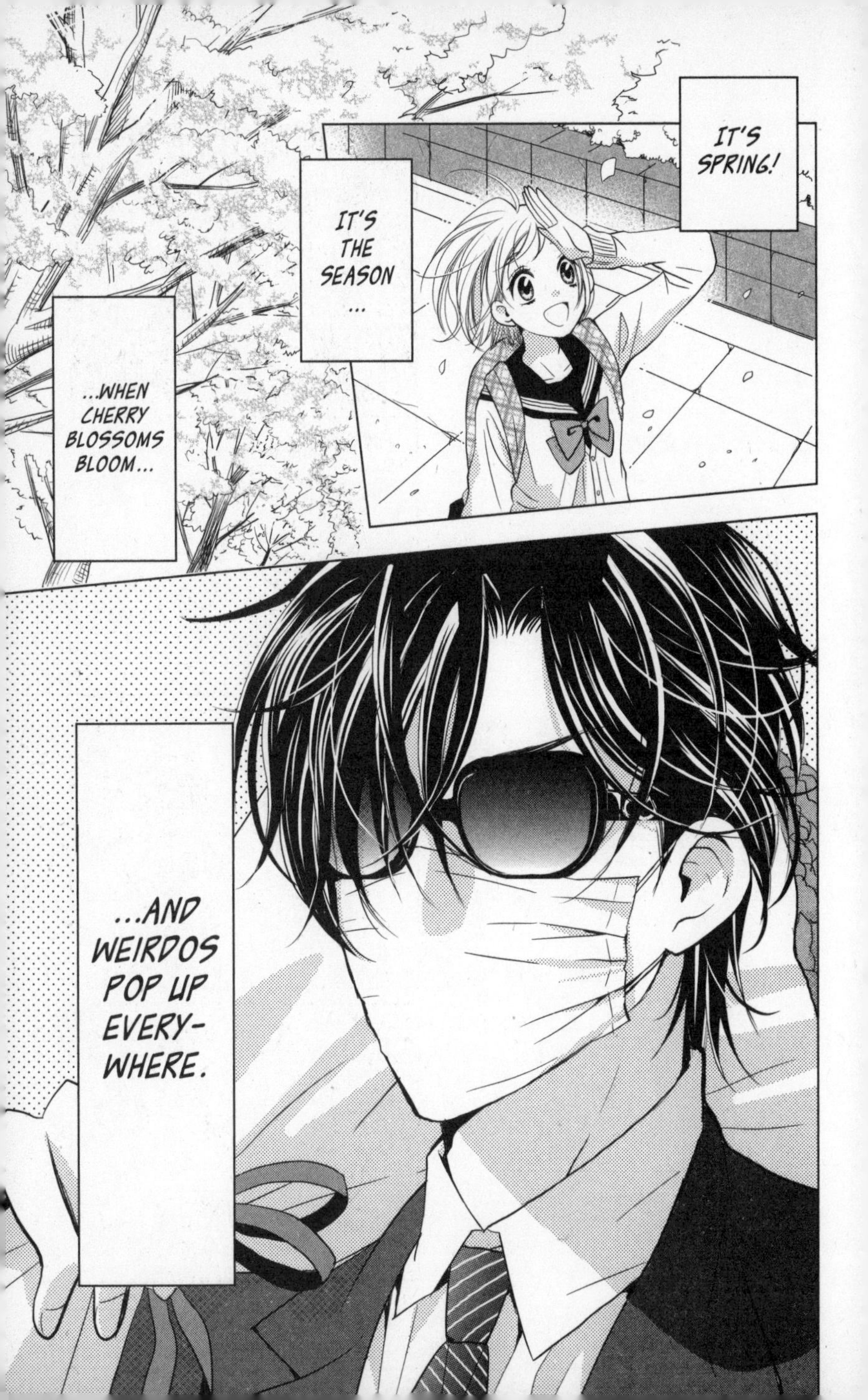
IT'S SPRING!
IT'S THE SEASON...
...WHEN CHERRY BLOSSOMS BLOOM...
...AND WEIRDOS POP UP EVERY-WHERE.

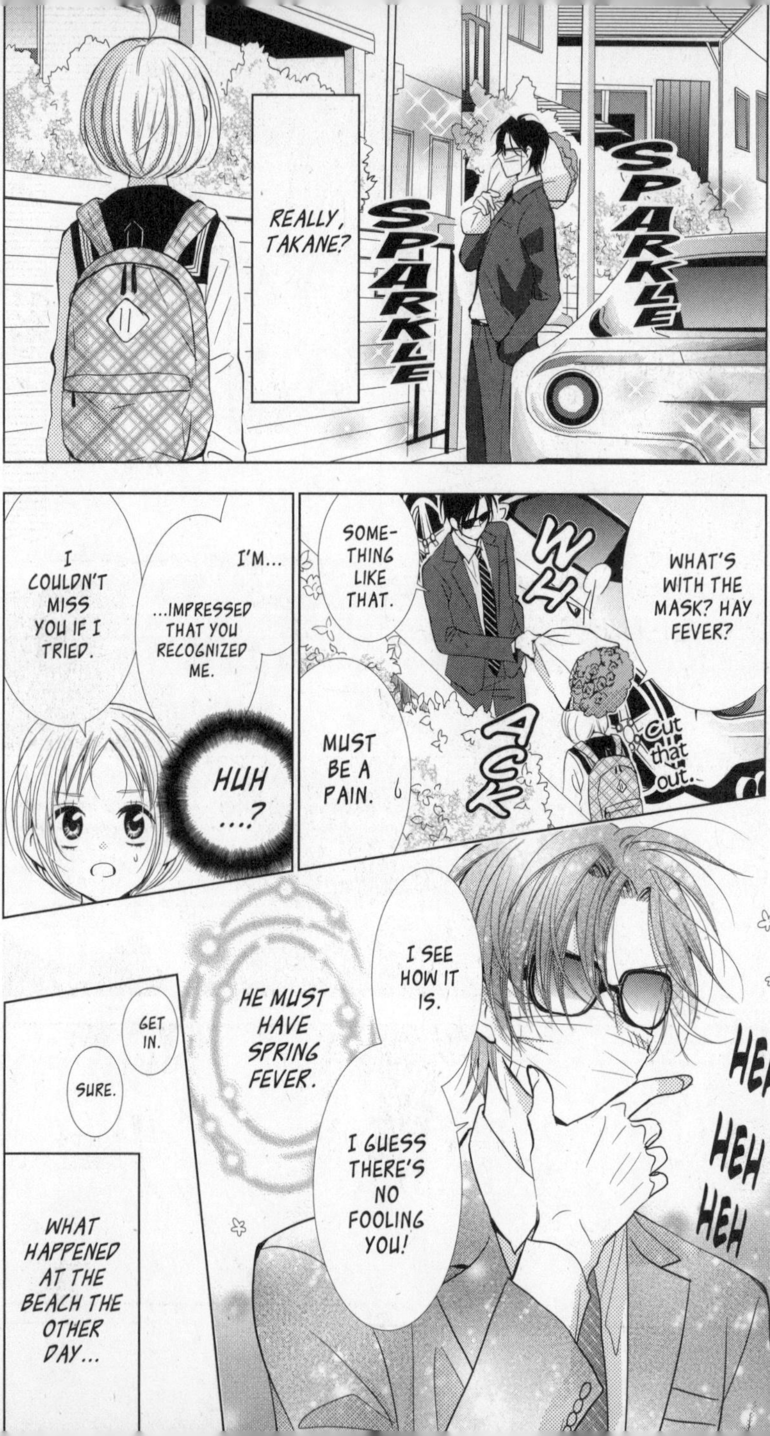
REALLY, TAKANE?
SPARKLE
SPARKLE
WHAT'S WITH THE MASK? HAY FEVER?
WH
ACK
Cut that out.
SOME-THING LIKE THAT.
MUST BE A PAIN.
I'M...
...IMPRESSED THAT YOU RECOGNIZED ME.
I COULDN'T MISS YOU IF I TRIED.
HUH ...?
HEH HEH HEH
I SEE HOW IT IS.
I GUESS THERE'S NO FOOLING YOU!
HE MUST HAVE SPRING FEVER.
GET IN.
SURE.
WHAT HAPPENED AT THE BEACH THE OTHER DAY...

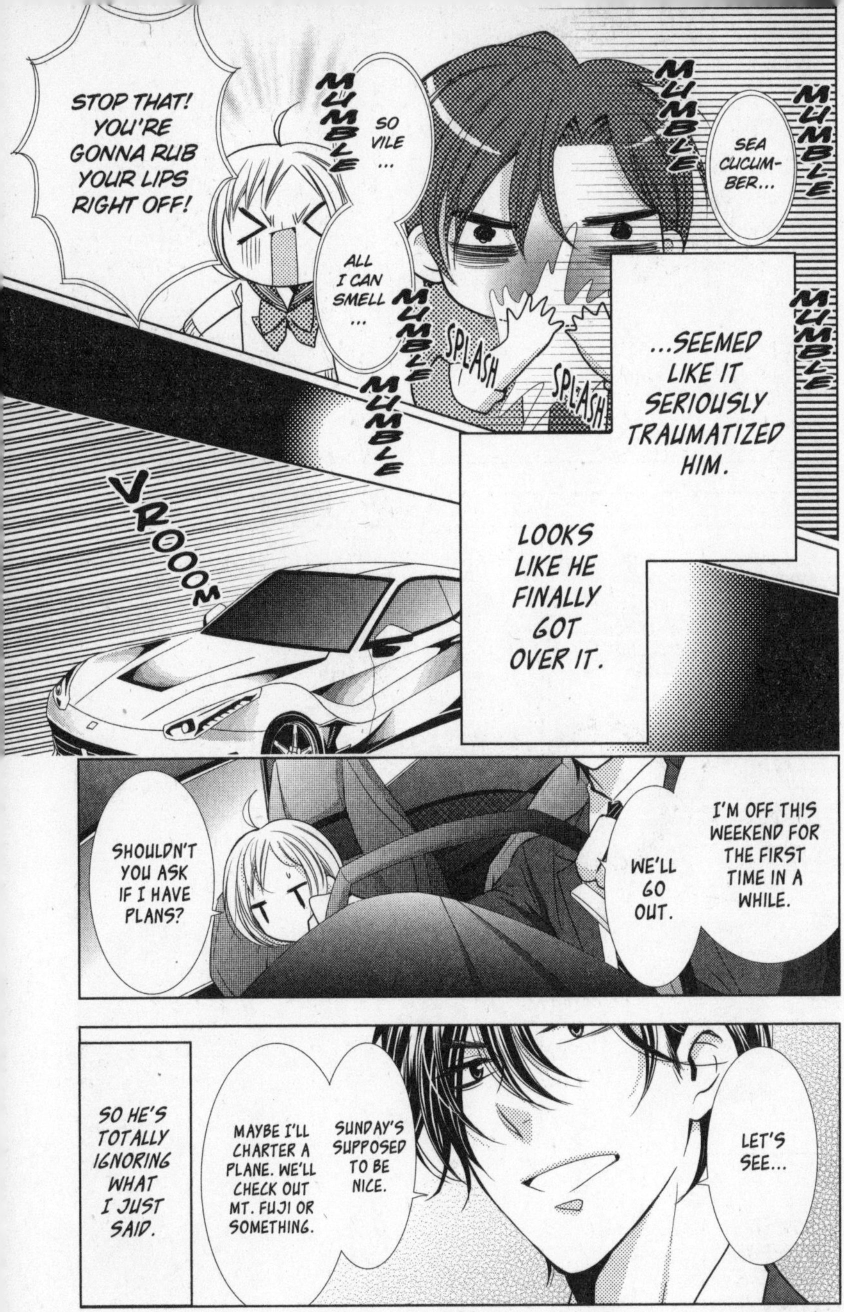
MUMBLE MUMBLE
SEA CUCUMBER...
MUMBLE
SO VILE ...
ALL I CAN SMELL ...
MUMBLE MUMBLE
SPLASH
SPLASH
STOP THAT! YOU'RE GONNA RUB YOUR LIPS RIGHT OFF!
...SEEMED LIKE IT SERIOUSLY TRAUMATIZED HIM.
MUMBLE
LOOKS LIKE HE FINALLY GOT OVER IT.
VROOOOM
I'M OFF THIS WEEKEND FOR THE FIRST TIME IN A WHILE.
WE'LL GO OUT.
SHOULDN'T YOU ASK IF I HAVE PLANS?
LET'S SEE...
SUNDAY'S SUPPOSED TO BE NICE.
MAYBE I'LL CHARTER A PLANE. WE'LL CHECK OUT MT. FUJI OR SOMETHING.
SO HE'S TOTALLY IGNORING WHAT I JUST SAID.

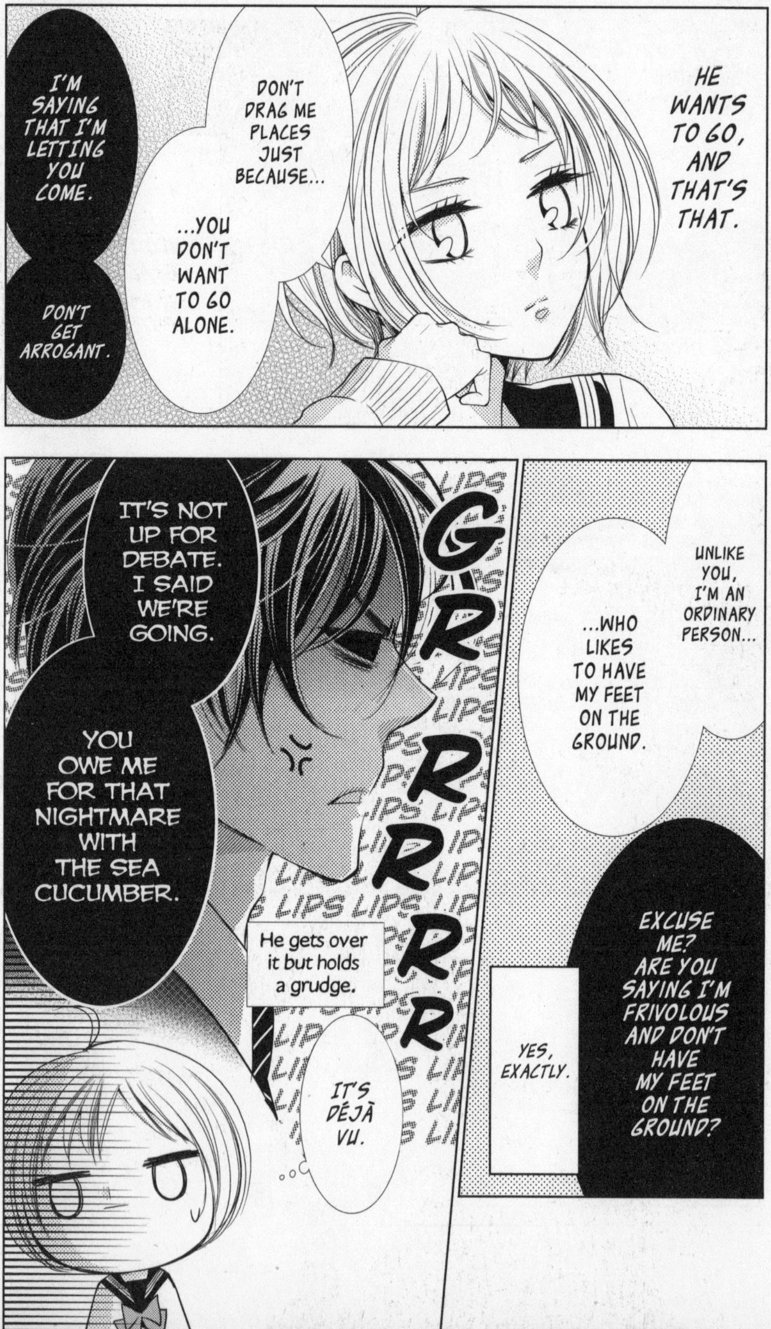
HE WANTS TO GO, AND THAT'S THAT.
DON'T DRAG ME PLACES JUST BECAUSE...
...YOU DON'T WANT TO GO ALONE.
I'M SAYING THAT I'M LETTING YOU COME.
DON'T GET ARROGANT.
UNLIKE YOU, I'M AN ORDINARY PERSON...
...WHO LIKES TO HAVE MY FEET ON THE GROUND.
EXCUSE ME? ARE YOU SAYING I'M FRIVOLOUS AND DON'T HAVE MY FEET ON THE GROUND?
YES, EXACTLY.
GRRRRR
IT'S NOT UP FOR DEBATE. I SAID WE'RE GOING.
YOU OWE ME FOR THAT NIGHTMARE WITH THE SEA CUCUMBER.
He gets over it but holds a grudge.
IT'S DÉJÀ VU.

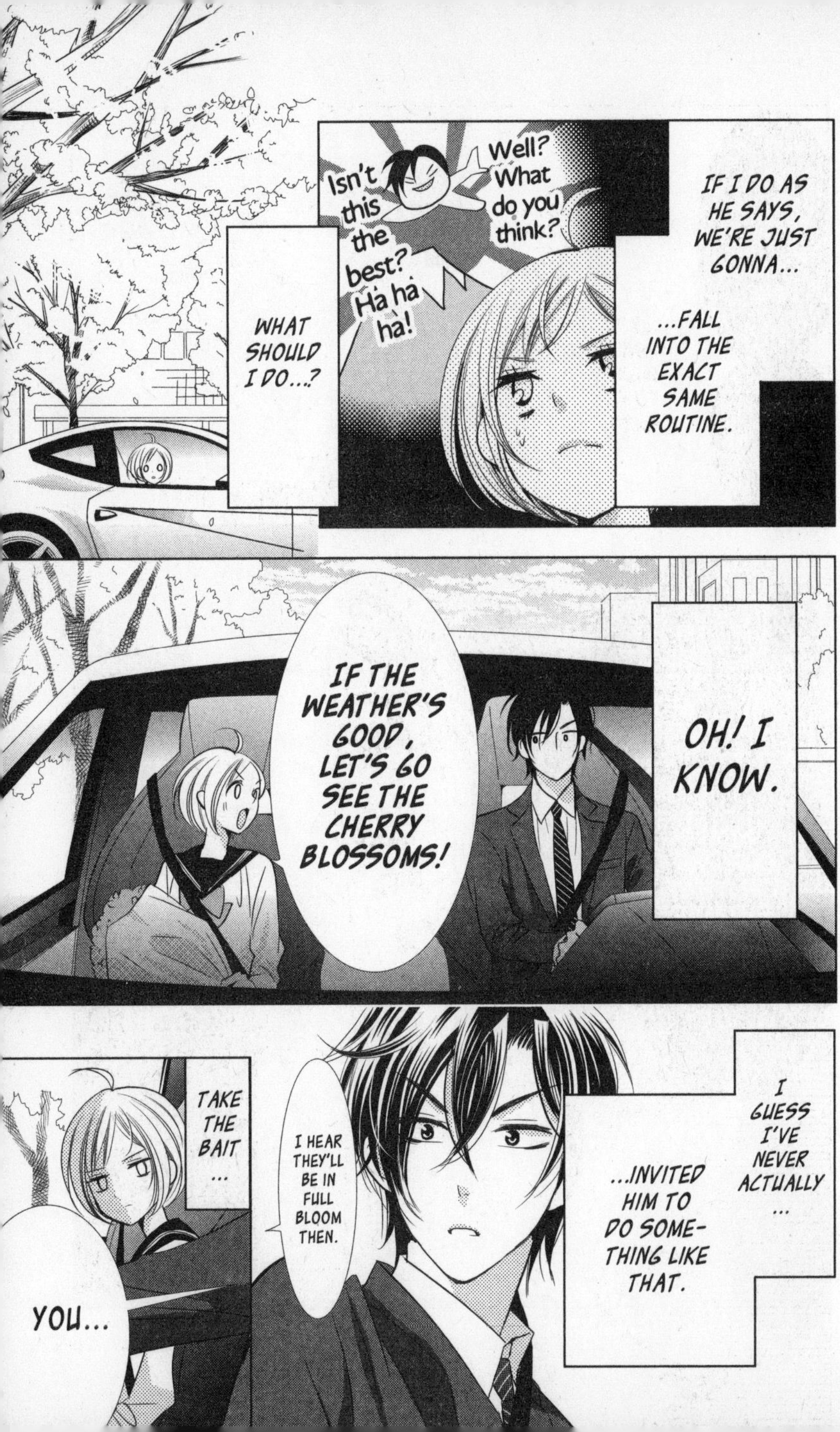
IF I DO AS HE SAYS, WE'RE JUST GONNA...
...FALL INTO THE EXACT SAME ROUTINE.
Well? What do you think?
Isn't this the best? Ha ha ha!
WHAT SHOULD I DO...?
OH! I KNOW.
IF THE WEATHER'S GOOD, LET'S GO SEE THE CHERRY BLOSSOMS!
I GUESS I'VE NEVER ACTUALLY...
...INVITED HIM TO DO SOMETHING LIKE THAT.
I HEAR THEY'LL BE IN FULL BLOOM THEN.
TAKE THE BAIT...
YOU...

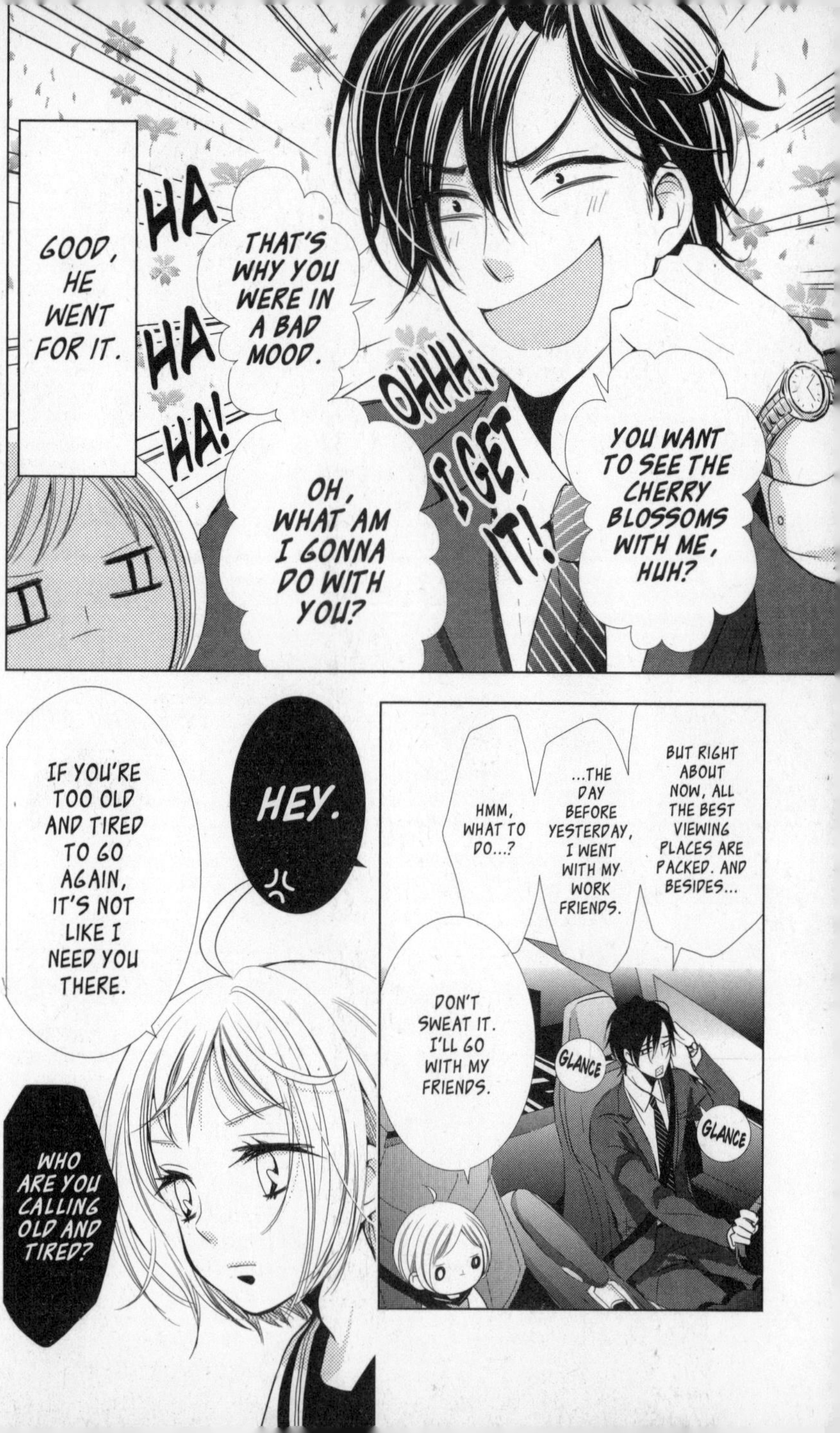
OHHH, I GET IT!
THAT'S WHY YOU WERE IN A BAD MOOD.
YOU WANT TO SEE THE CHERRY BLOSSOMS WITH ME, HUH?
OH, WHAT AM I GONNA DO WITH YOU?
HA HA HA!
GOOD, HE WENT FOR IT.
HMM, WHAT TO DO...?
...THE DAY BEFORE YESTERDAY, I WENT WITH MY WORK FRIENDS.
BUT RIGHT ABOUT NOW, ALL THE BEST VIEWING PLACES ARE PACKED. AND BESIDES...
DON'T SWEAT IT. I'LL GO WITH MY FRIENDS.
GLANCE
GLANCE
HEY.
IF YOU'RE TOO OLD AND TIRED TO GO AGAIN, IT'S NOT LIKE I NEED YOU THERE.
WHO ARE YOU CALLING OLD AND TIRED?

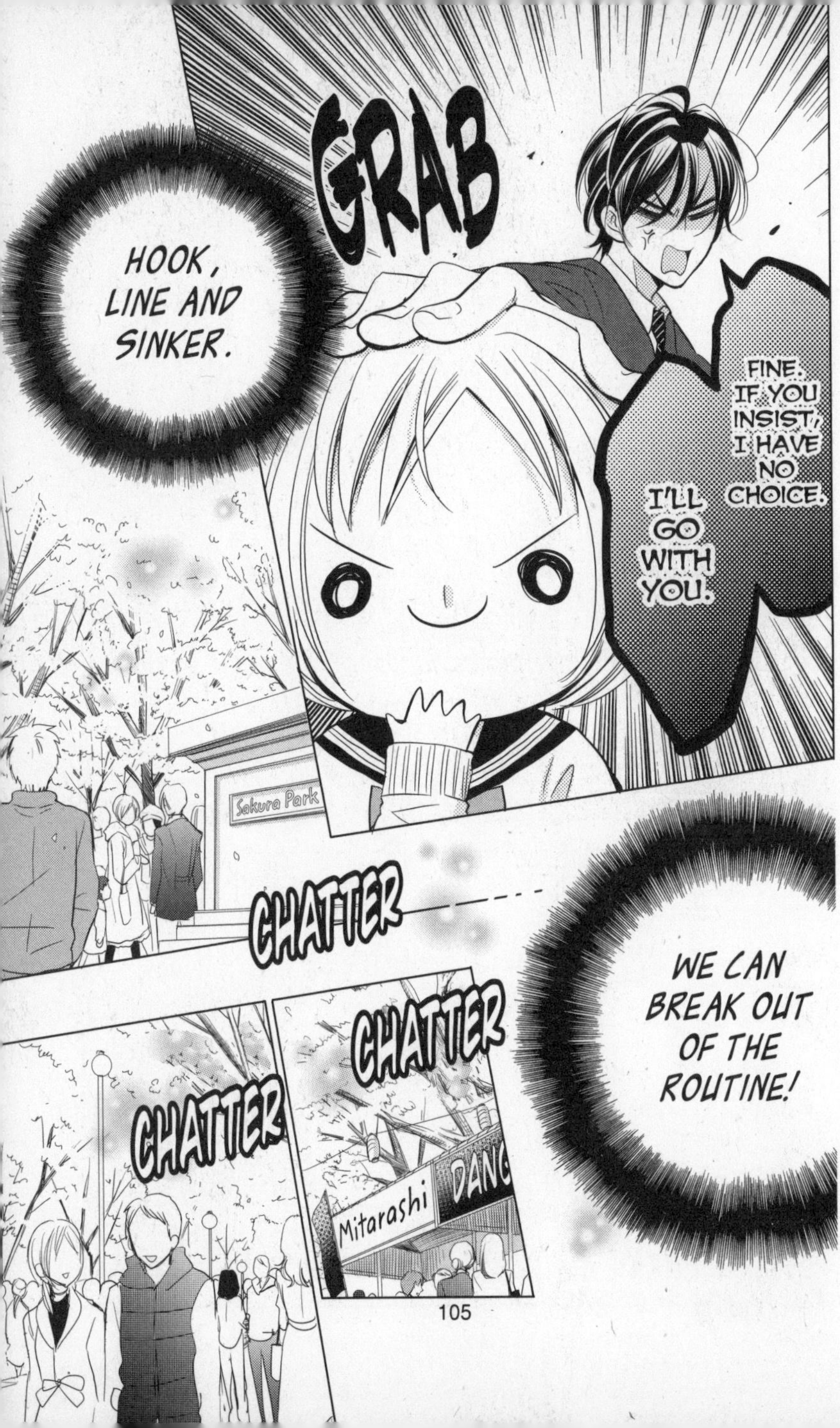
FINE. IF YOU INSIST, I HAVE NO CHOICE.
I'LL GO WITH YOU.
GRAB
HOOK, LINE AND SINKER.
WE CAN BREAK OUT OF THE ROUTINE!
Sakura Park
CHATTER
CHATTER
Mitarashi
DANG
CHATTER

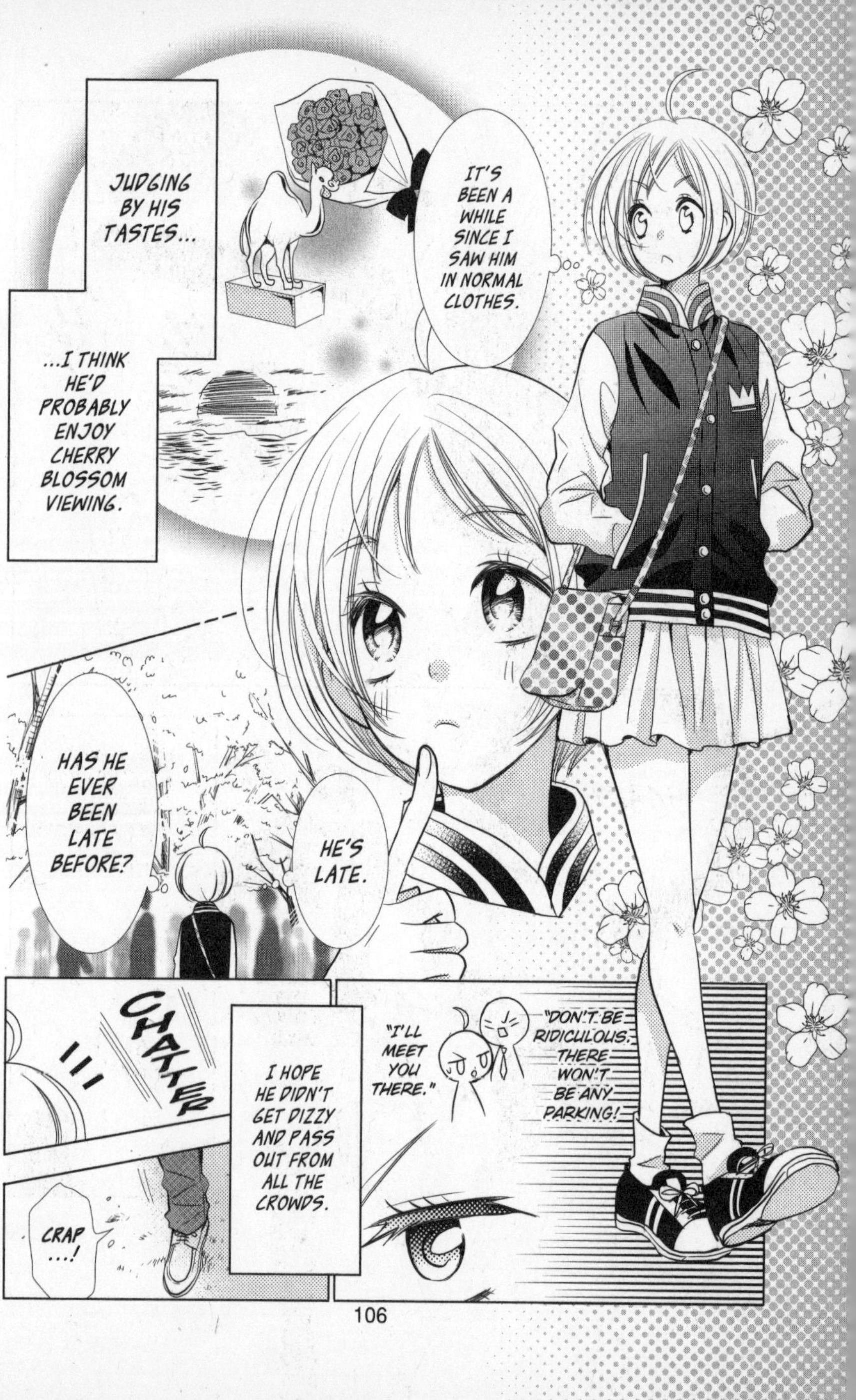
IT'S BEEN A WHILE SINCE I SAW HIM IN NORMAL CLOTHES.
JUDGING BY HIS TASTES...
...I THINK HE'D PROBABLY ENJOY CHERRY BLOSSOM VIEWING.
HE'S LATE.
HAS HE EVER BEEN LATE BEFORE?
"DON'T BE RIDICULOUS. THERE WON'T BE ANY PARKING!
"I'LL MEET YOU THERE."
I HOPE HE DIDN'T GET DIZZY AND PASS OUT FROM ALL THE CROWDS.
CHATTER
CRAP ...!

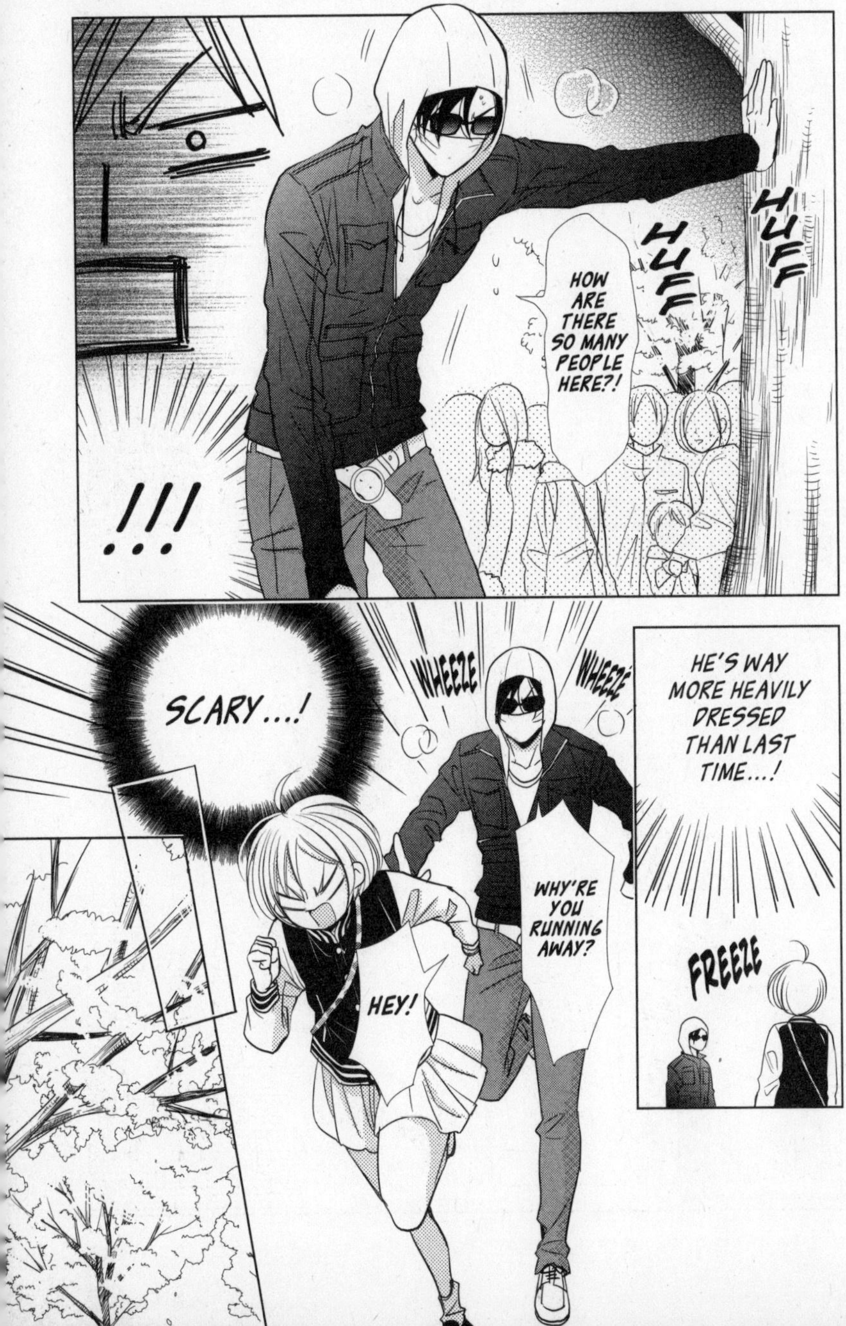
HUFF HUFF
HOW ARE THERE SO MANY PEOPLE HERE?!
!!!
HE'S WAY MORE HEAVILY DRESSED THAN LAST TIME...!
FREEZE
WHEEZE WHEEZE
SCARY...!
WHY'RE YOU RUNNING AWAY?
HEY!

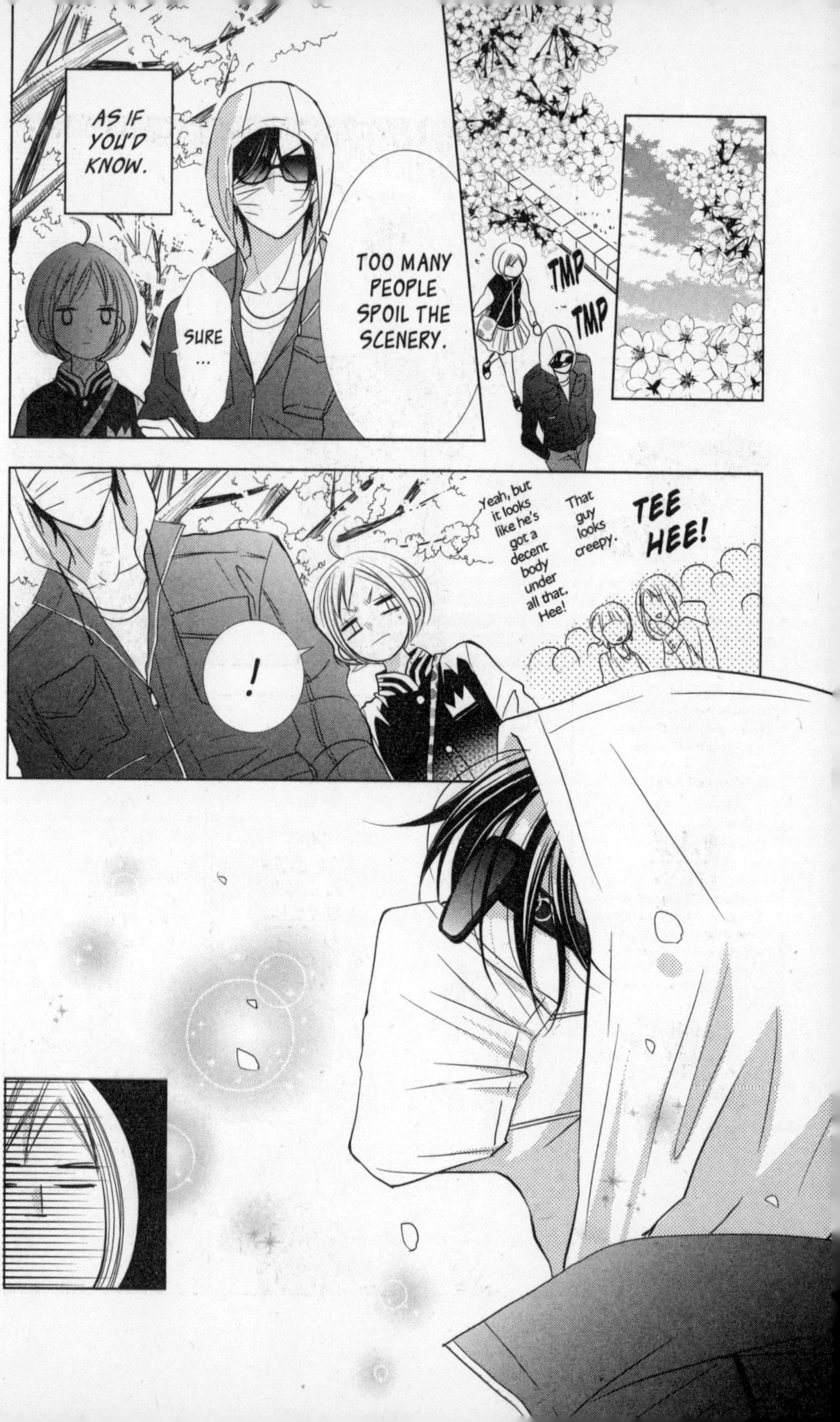
TMP
TMP
TOO MANY PEOPLE SPOIL THE SCENERY.
AS IF YOU'D KNOW.
SURE ...
TEE HEE!
That guy looks creepy.
Yeah, but it looks like he's got a decent body under all that. Hee!
!

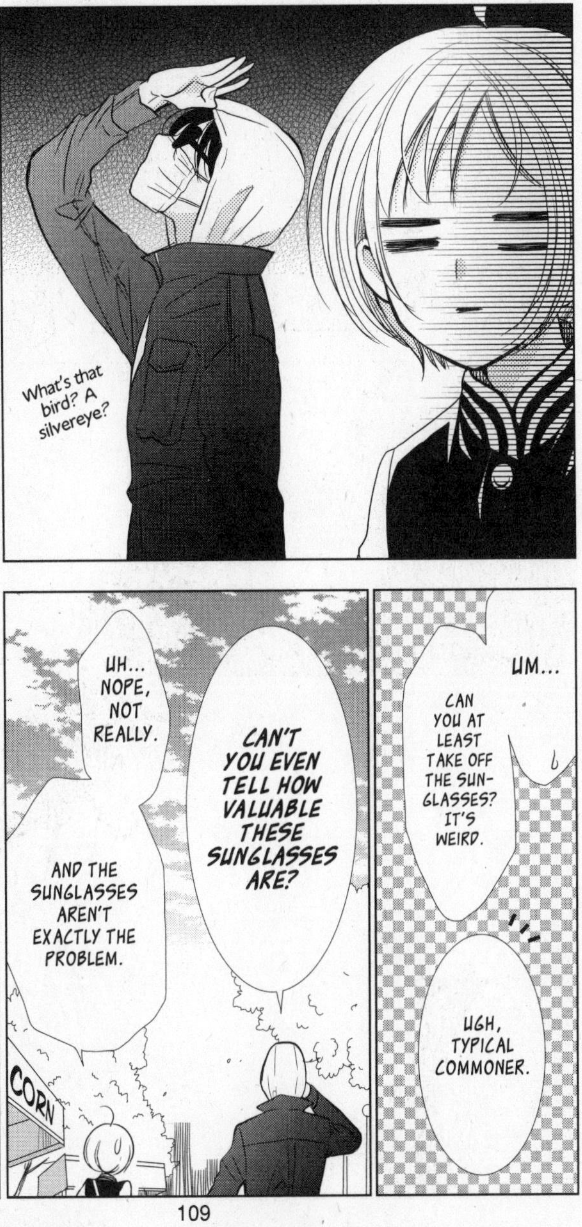
What's that bird? A silvereye?
UM...
CAN YOU AT LEAST TAKE OFF THE SUNGLASSES? IT'S WEIRD.
UGH, TYPICAL COMMONER.
CAN'T YOU EVEN TELL HOW VALUABLE THESE SUNGLASSES ARE?
UH... NOPE, NOT REALLY.
AND THE SUNGLASSES AREN'T EXACTLY THE PROBLEM.
CORN

● Hana's Regular Clothes ●

She doesn't have a specific style, but she likes clothes that are practical and boyish.

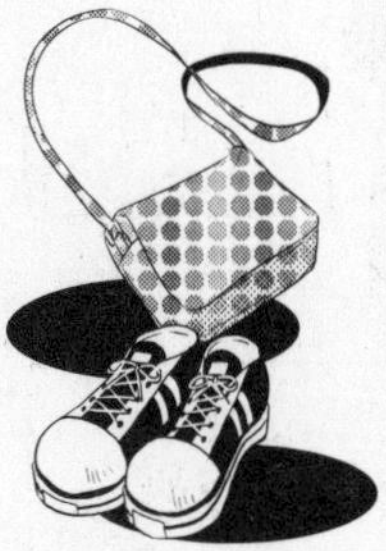

She always carries the same bags. She switches between a backpack she takes to school and this polka-dot shoulder bag.

Yukari's hand-me-downs probably aren't her style. The red sneakers she wears to school are her go-to shoes. In the summer, she also wears sandals.

LIGER

This isn't an important detail, but for this story I made this up as a popular sports brand with high school students. If you keep an eye out, you may notice other characters wearing it too.

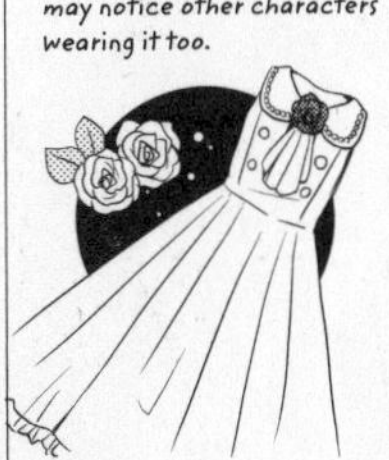

Only for appropriate occasions will she borrow the dress she's "keeping" for Takane.

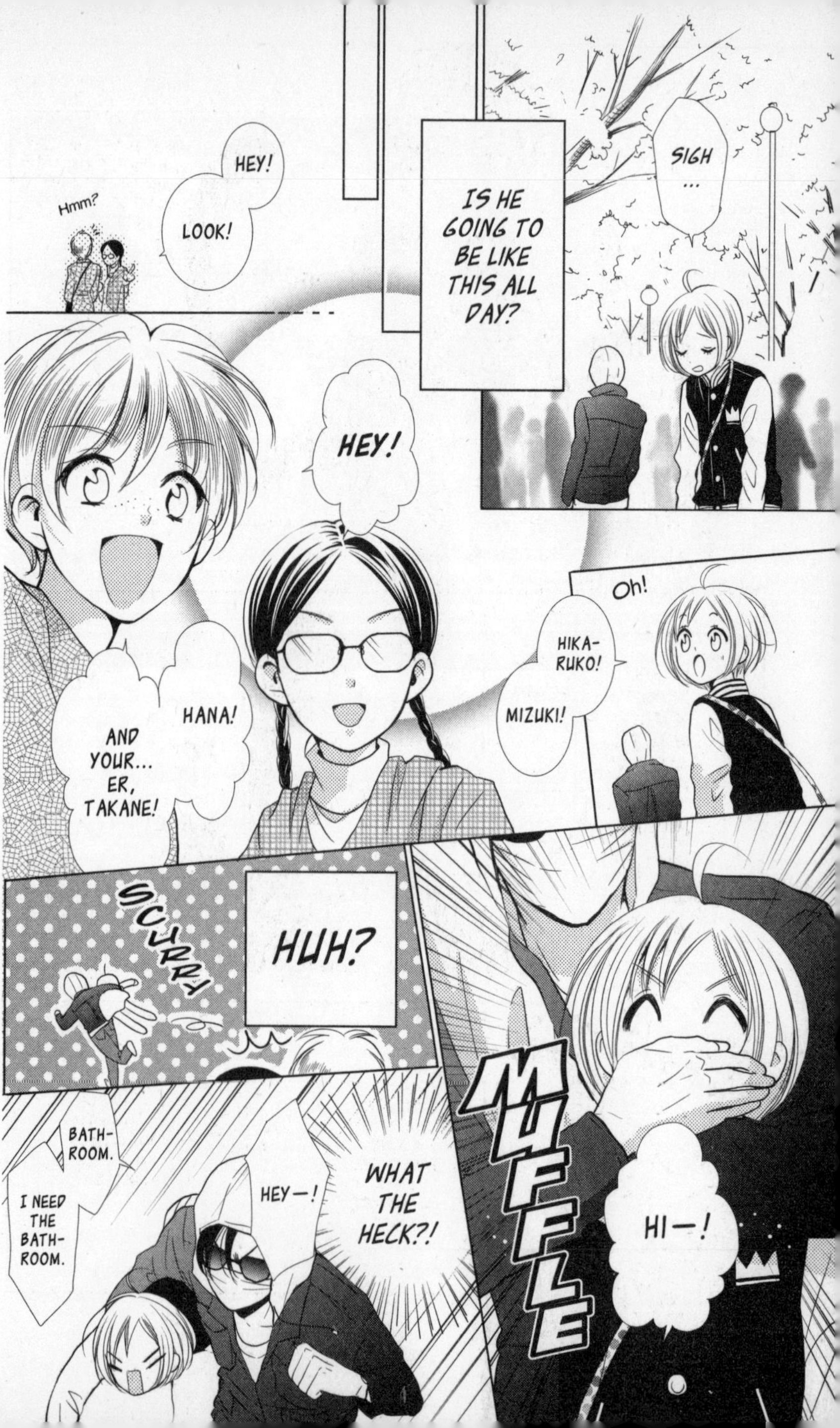
SIGH ...
IS HE GOING TO BE LIKE THIS ALL DAY?
Hmm?
HEY!
LOOK!
HEY!
Oh!
HIKA-RUKO!
MIZUKI!
HANA!
AND YOUR... ER, TAKANE!
HI—!
MUFFLE
HUH?
SCURRY
WHAT THE HECK?!
HEY—!
BATH-ROOM.
I NEED THE BATH-ROOM.

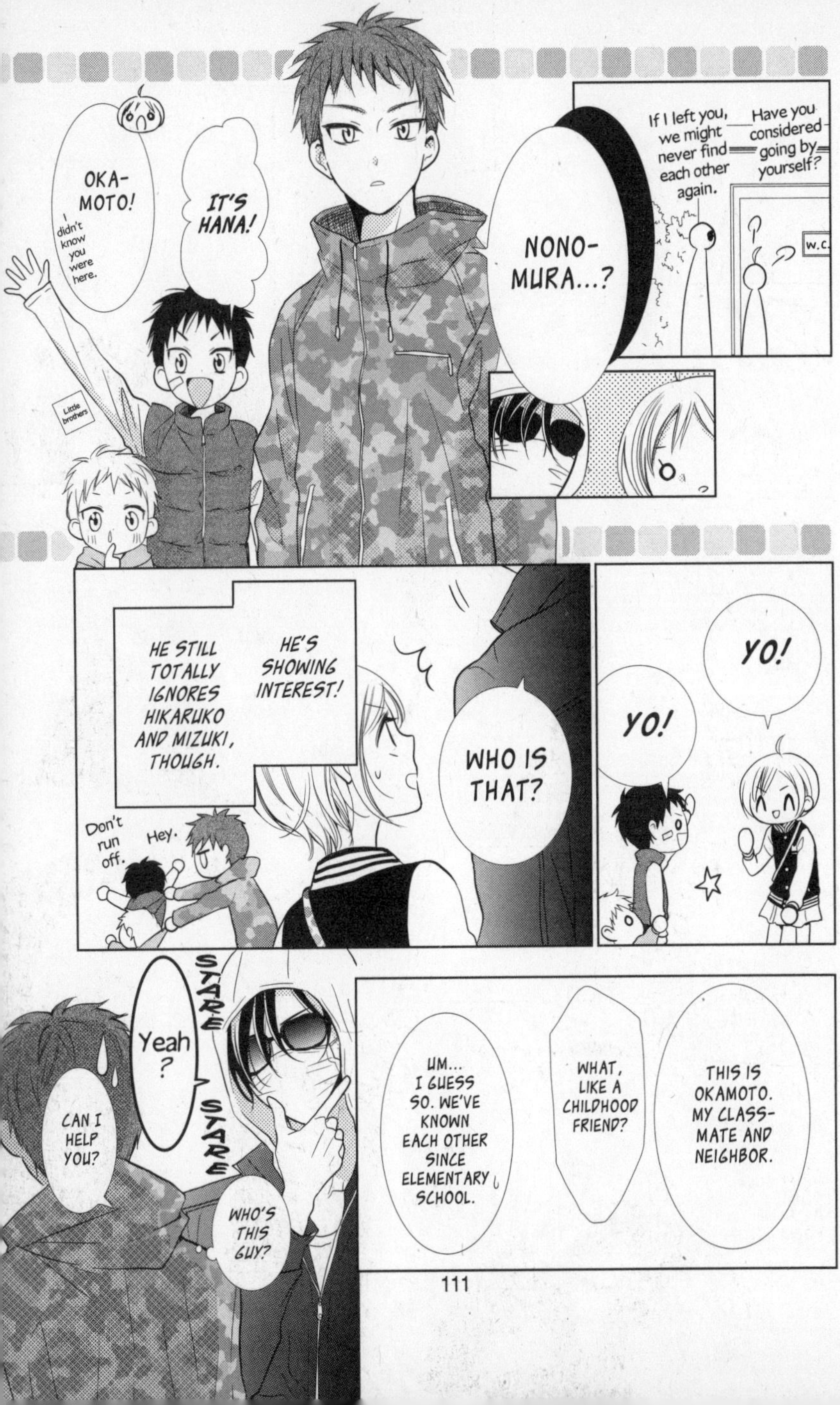
Have you considered going by yourself?
If I left you, we might never find each other again.
W.C.
NONO-MURA...?
IT'S HANA!
OKA-MOTO!
I didn't know you were here.
Little brothers
YO!
YO!
WHO IS THAT?
HE'S SHOWING INTEREST!
HE STILL TOTALLY IGNORES HIKARUKO AND MIZUKI, THOUGH.
Hey.
Don't run off.
THIS IS OKAMOTO. MY CLASS-MATE AND NEIGHBOR.
WHAT, LIKE A CHILDHOOD FRIEND?
UM... I GUESS SO. WE'VE KNOWN EACH OTHER SINCE ELEMENTARY SCHOOL.
STARE
Yeah?
STARE
CAN I HELP YOU?
WHO'S THIS GUY?

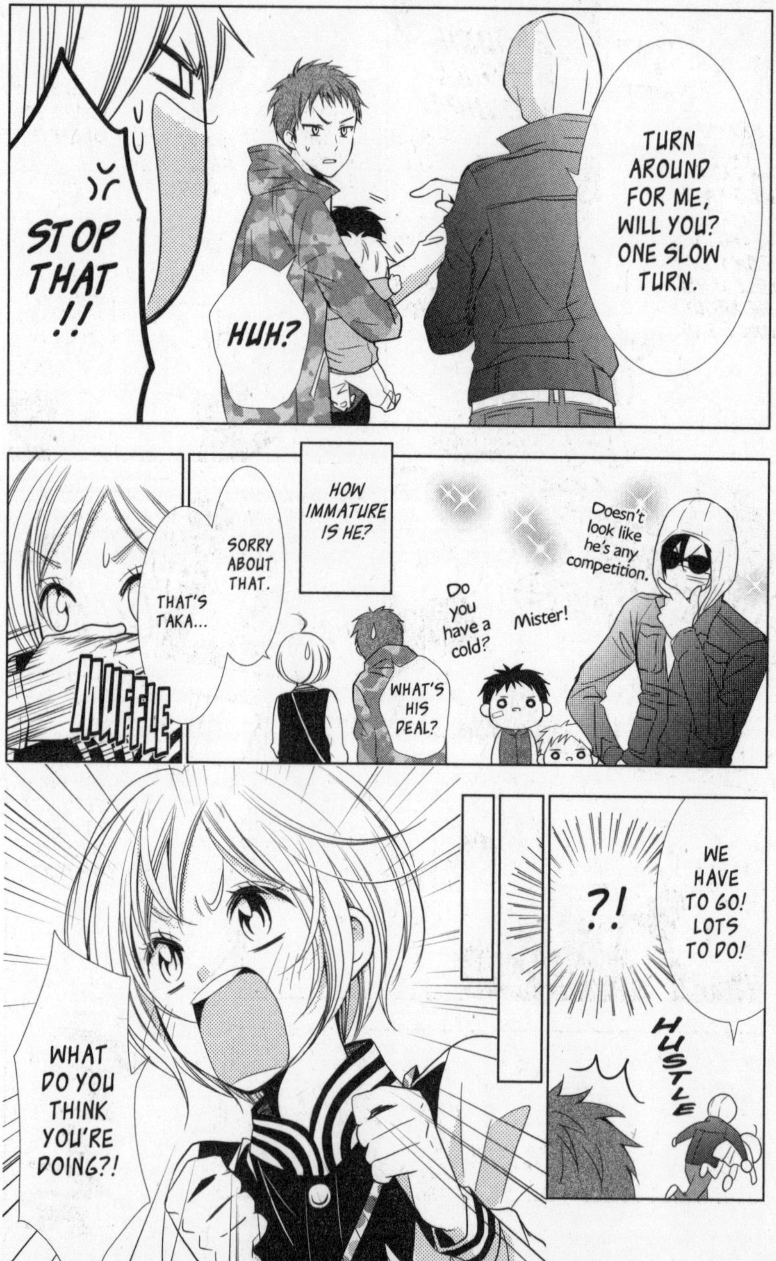
TURN AROUND FOR ME, WILL YOU? ONE SLOW TURN.
HUH?
STOP THAT!!
Doesn't look like he's any competition.
Mister!
Do you have a cold?
WHAT'S HIS DEAL?
HOW IMMATURE IS HE?
SORRY ABOUT THAT.
THAT'S TAKA...
MUFFLE
WE HAVE TO GO! LOTS TO DO!
?!
HUSTLE
WHAT DO YOU THINK YOU'RE DOING?!

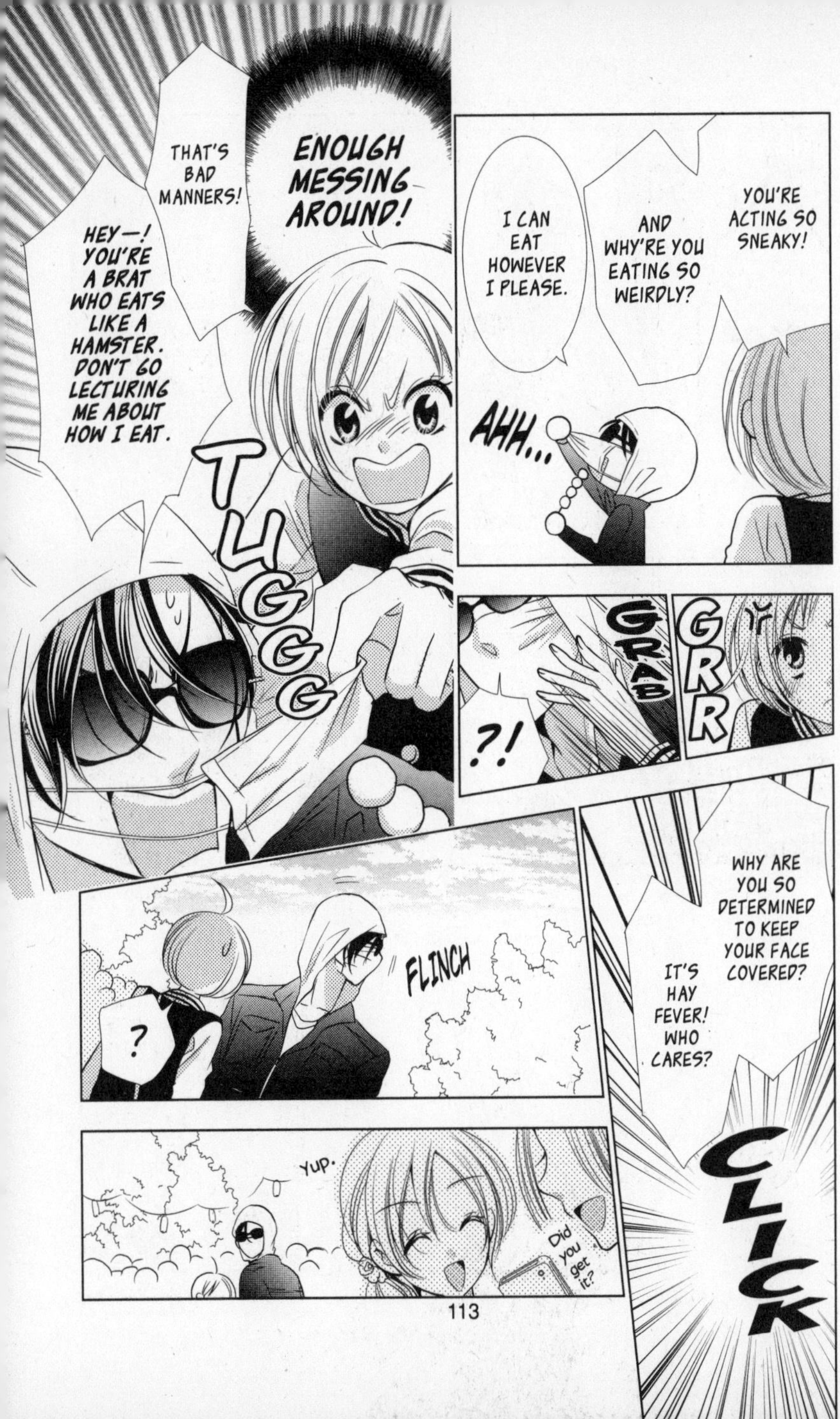
YOU'RE ACTING SO SNEAKY!
AND WHY'RE YOU EATING SO WEIRDLY?
I CAN EAT HOWEVER I PLEASE.
AHH...
GRR
GRAB
?!
ENOUGH MESSING AROUND!
THAT'S BAD MANNERS!
HEY—! YOU'RE A BRAT WHO EATS LIKE A HAMSTER. DON'T GO LECTURING ME ABOUT HOW I EAT.
TUGGG
WHY ARE YOU SO DETERMINED TO KEEP YOUR FACE COVERED?
IT'S HAY FEVER! WHO CARES?
CLICK
FLINCH
?
Did you get it?
Yup.

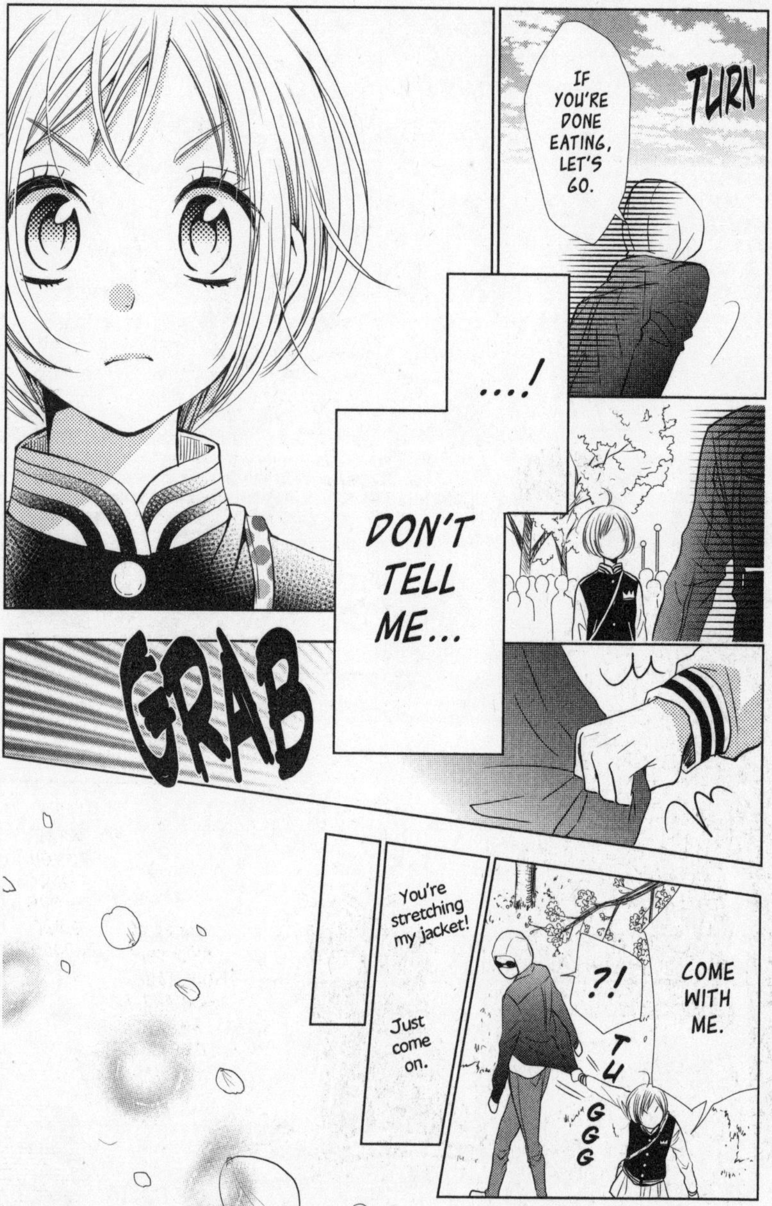

IF YOU'RE DONE EATING, LET'S GO.
TURN
...!
DON'T TELL ME...
GRAB
COME WITH ME.
?!
TUGGG
You're stretching my jacket!
Just come on.

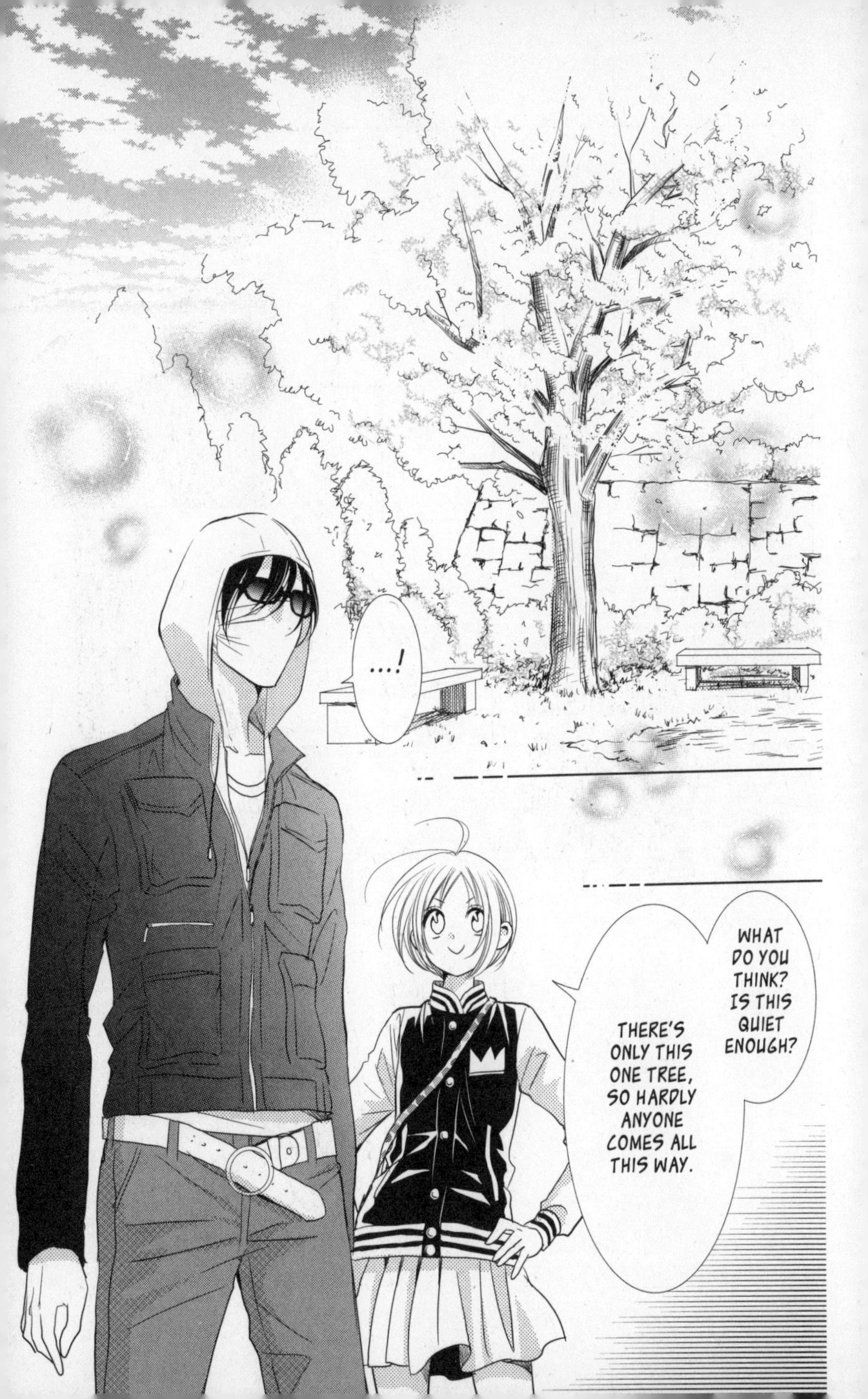
...!
WHAT DO YOU THINK? IS THIS QUIET ENOUGH?
THERE'S ONLY THIS ONE TREE, SO HARDLY ANYONE COMES ALL THIS WAY.

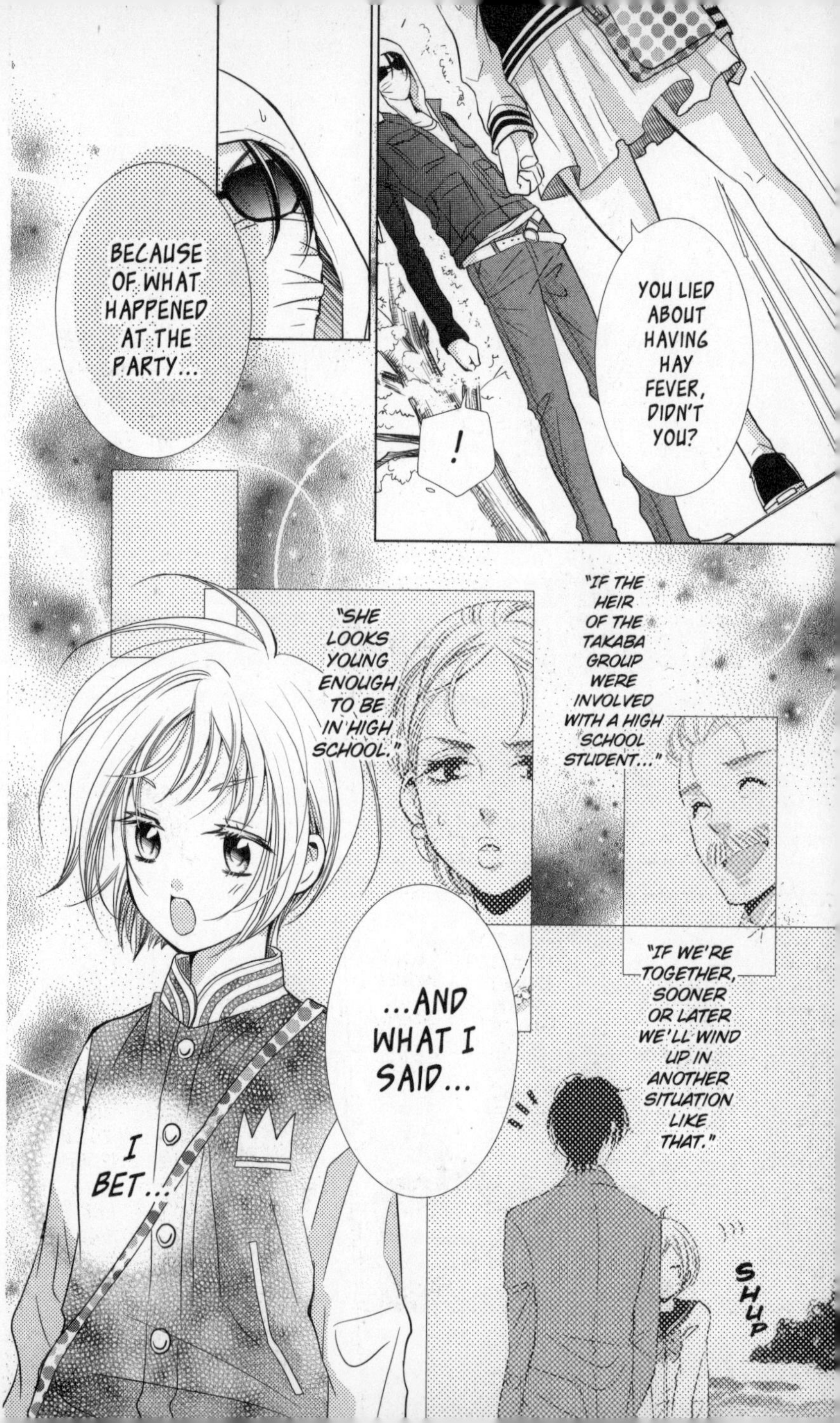
YOU LIED ABOUT HAVING HAY FEVER, DIDN'T YOU?
!
BECAUSE OF WHAT HAPPENED AT THE PARTY...
"IF THE HEIR OF THE TAKABA GROUP WERE INVOLVED WITH A HIGH SCHOOL STUDENT..."
"SHE LOOKS YOUNG ENOUGH TO BE IN HIGH SCHOOL."
"IF WE'RE TOGETHER, SOONER OR LATER WE'LL WIND UP IN ANOTHER SITUATION LIKE THAT."
...AND WHAT I SAID...
I BET...
SHUP

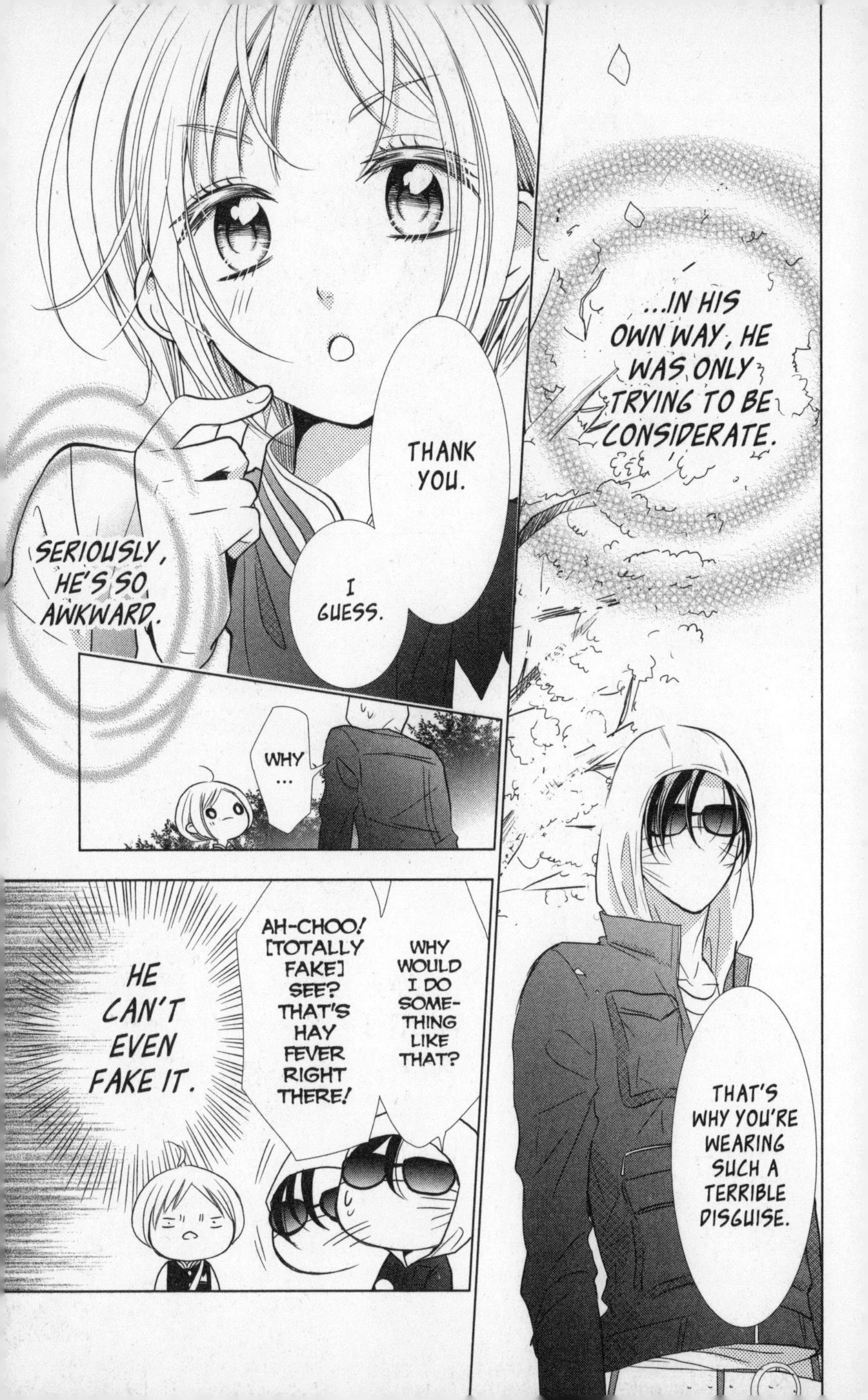
...IN HIS OWN WAY, HE WAS ONLY TRYING TO BE CONSIDERATE.
THAT'S WHY YOU'RE WEARING SUCH A TERRIBLE DISGUISE.
THANK YOU.
I GUESS.
SERIOUSLY, HE'S SO AWKWARD.
WHY...
WHY WOULD I DO SOME-THING LIKE THAT?
AH-CHOO! [TOTALLY FAKE] SEE? THAT'S HAY FEVER RIGHT THERE!
HE CAN'T EVEN FAKE IT.

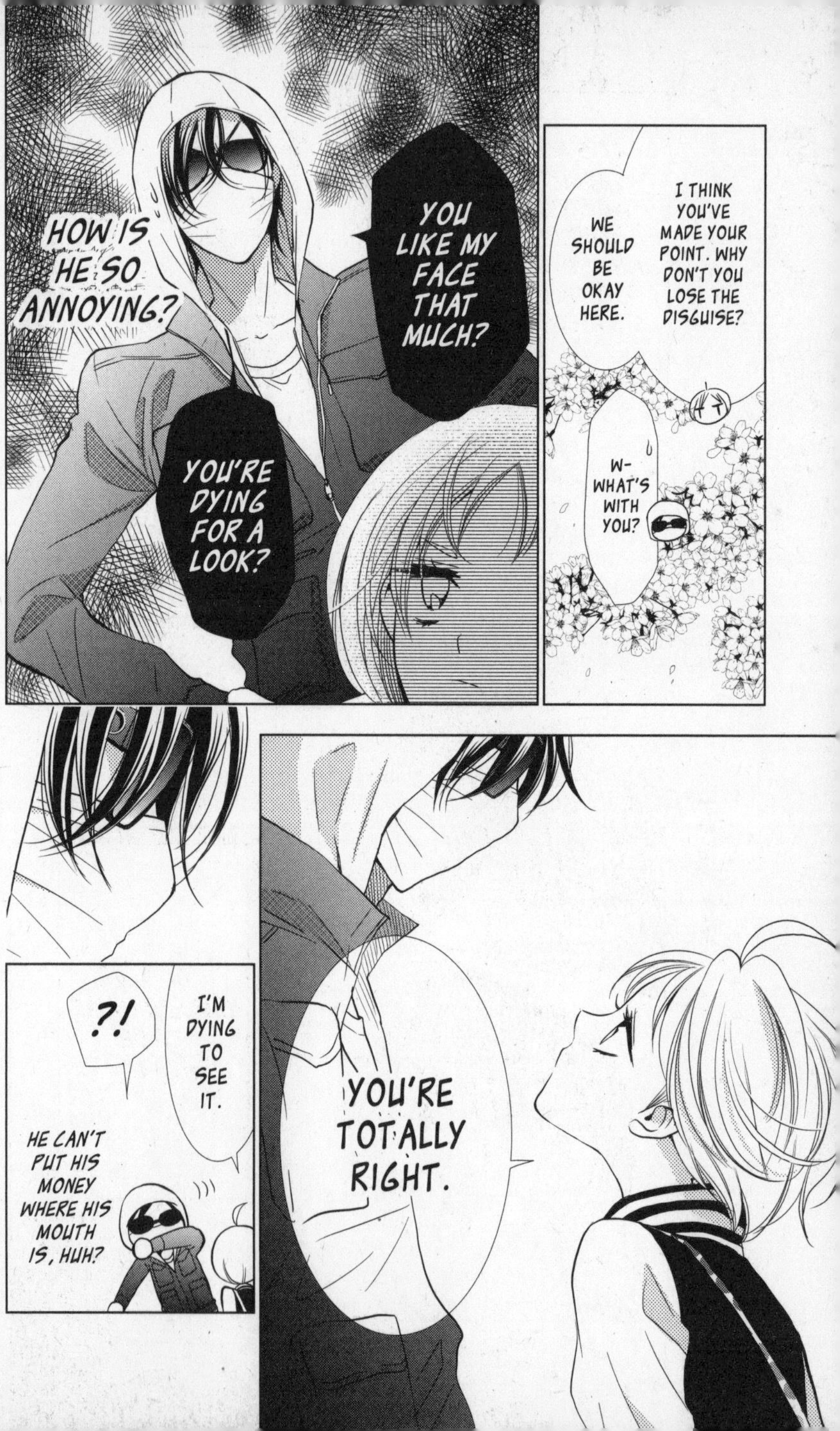
I THINK YOU'VE MADE YOUR POINT. WHY DON'T YOU LOSE THE DISGUISE?
WE SHOULD BE OKAY HERE.
W-WHAT'S WITH YOU?
YOU LIKE MY FACE THAT MUCH?
HOW IS HE SO ANNOYING?
YOU'RE DYING FOR A LOOK?
YOU'RE TOTALLY RIGHT.
I'M DYING TO SEE IT.
?!
HE CAN'T PUT HIS MONEY WHERE HIS MOUTH IS, HUH?

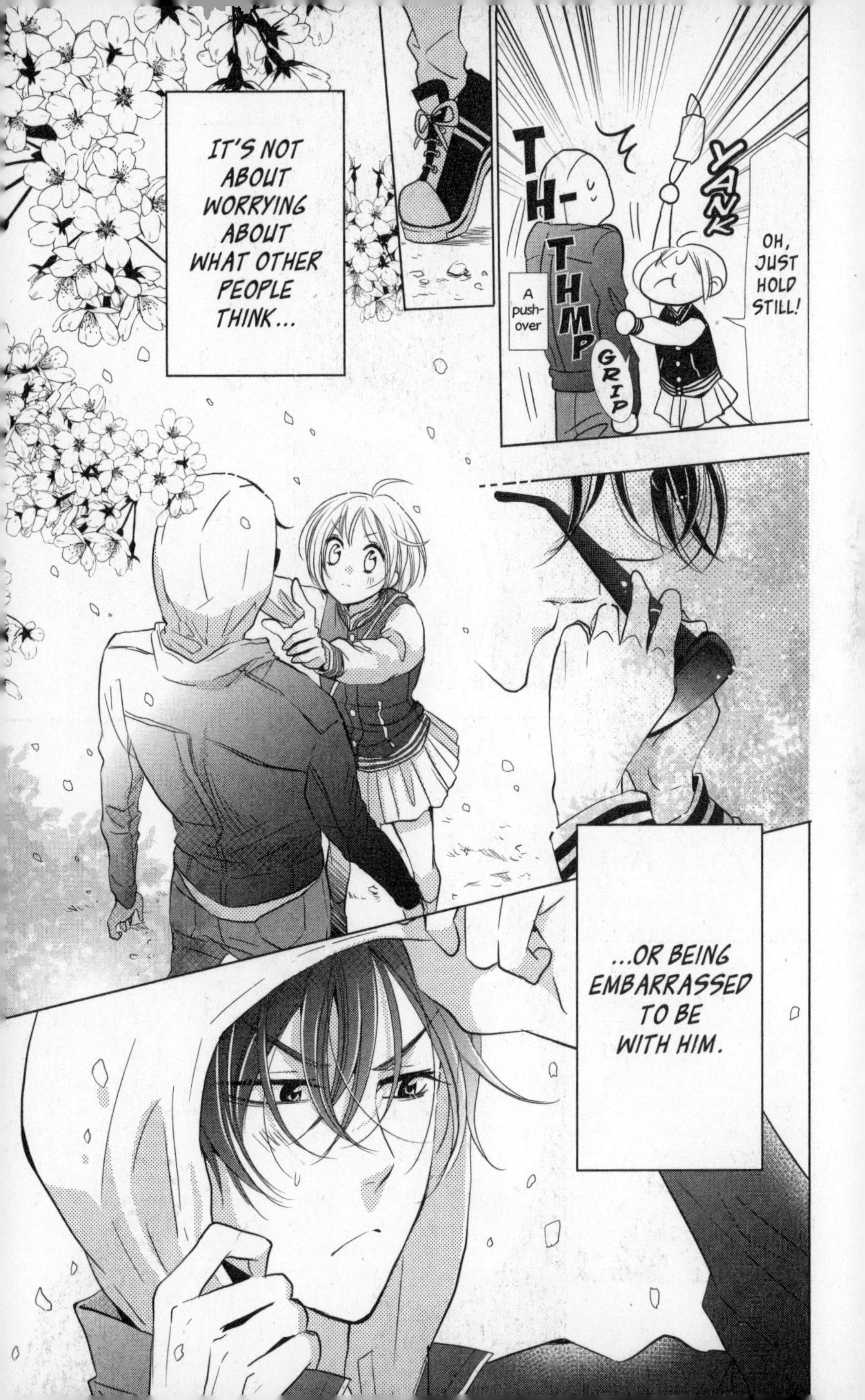
YANK
OH, JUST HOLD STILL!
TH- THMP
A push-over
GRIP
IT'S NOT ABOUT WORRYING ABOUT WHAT OTHER PEOPLE THINK...
...OR BEING EMBARRASSED TO BE WITH HIM.

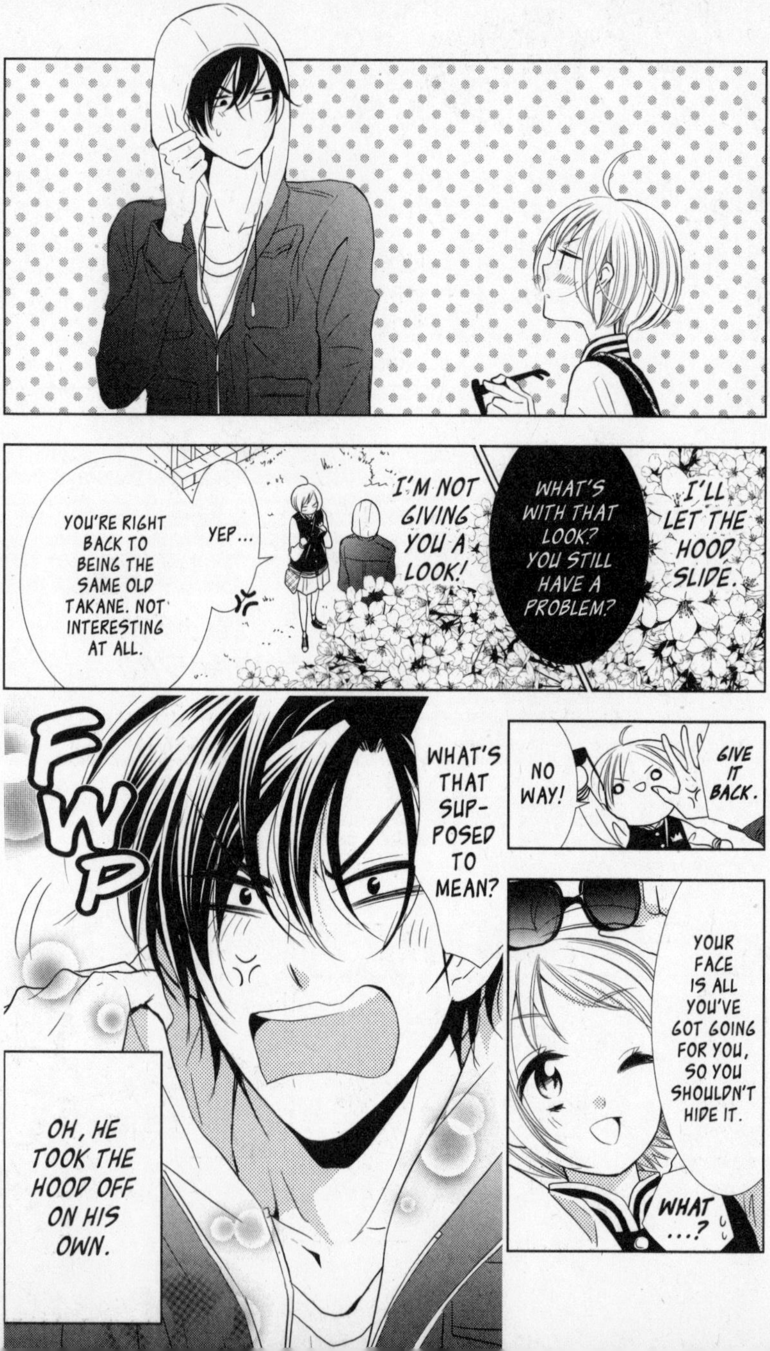
I'LL LET THE HOOD SLIDE.
WHAT'S WITH THAT LOOK? YOU STILL HAVE A PROBLEM?
I'M NOT GIVING YOU A LOOK!
YEP...
YOU'RE RIGHT BACK TO BEING THE SAME OLD TAKANE. NOT INTERESTING AT ALL.
GIVE IT BACK.
NO WAY!
YOUR FACE IS ALL YOU'VE GOT GOING FOR YOU, SO YOU SHOULDN'T HIDE IT.
WHAT...?
WHAT'S THAT SUP-POSED TO MEAN?
FWP
OH, HE TOOK THE HOOD OFF ON HIS OWN.

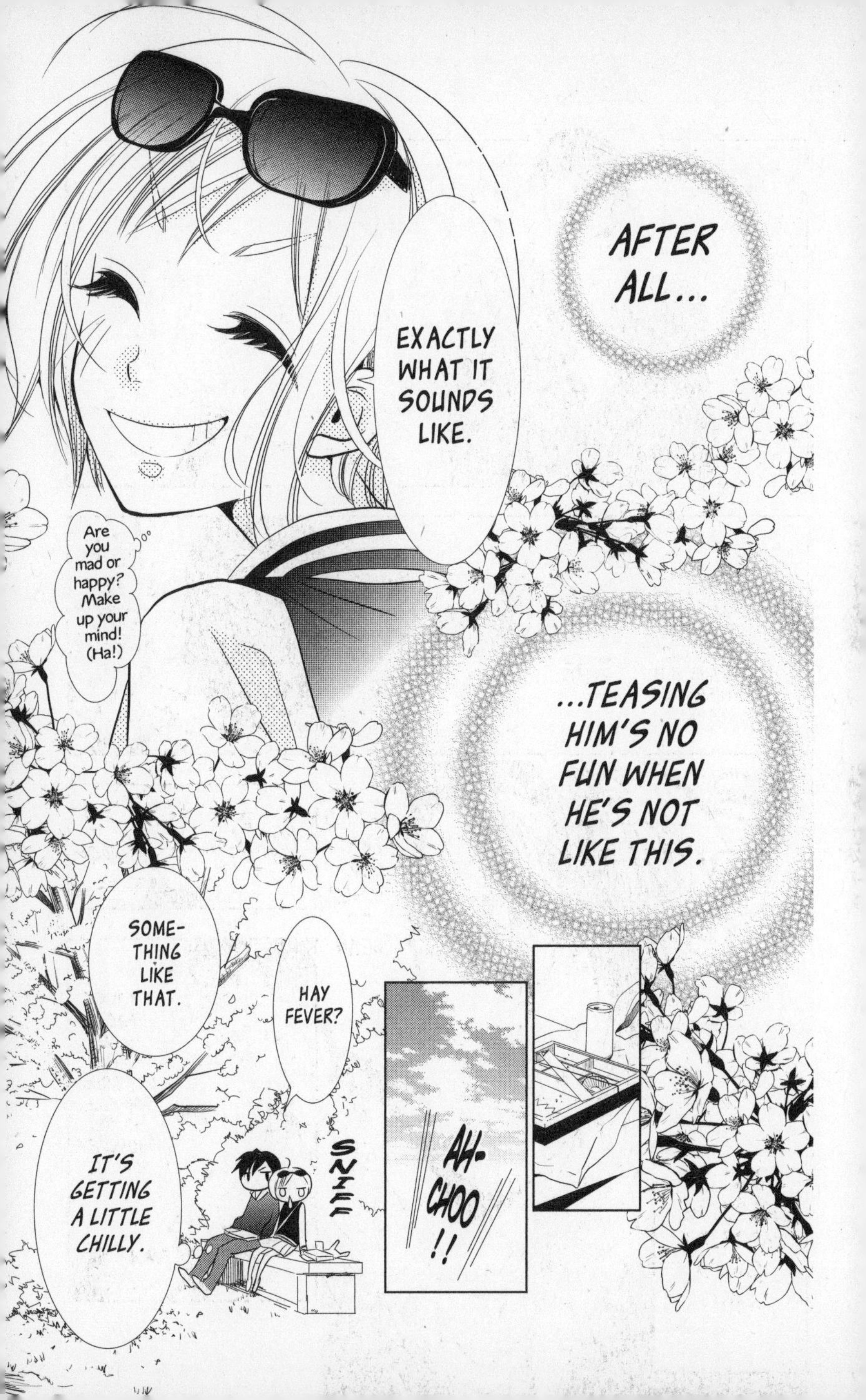
AFTER ALL...
EXACTLY WHAT IT SOUNDS LIKE.
Are you mad or happy? Make up your mind! (Ha!)
...TEASING HIM'S NO FUN WHEN HE'S NOT LIKE THIS.
AH-CHOO!!
HAY FEVER?
SOME-THING LIKE THAT.
SNIFF
IT'S GETTING A LITTLE CHILLY.

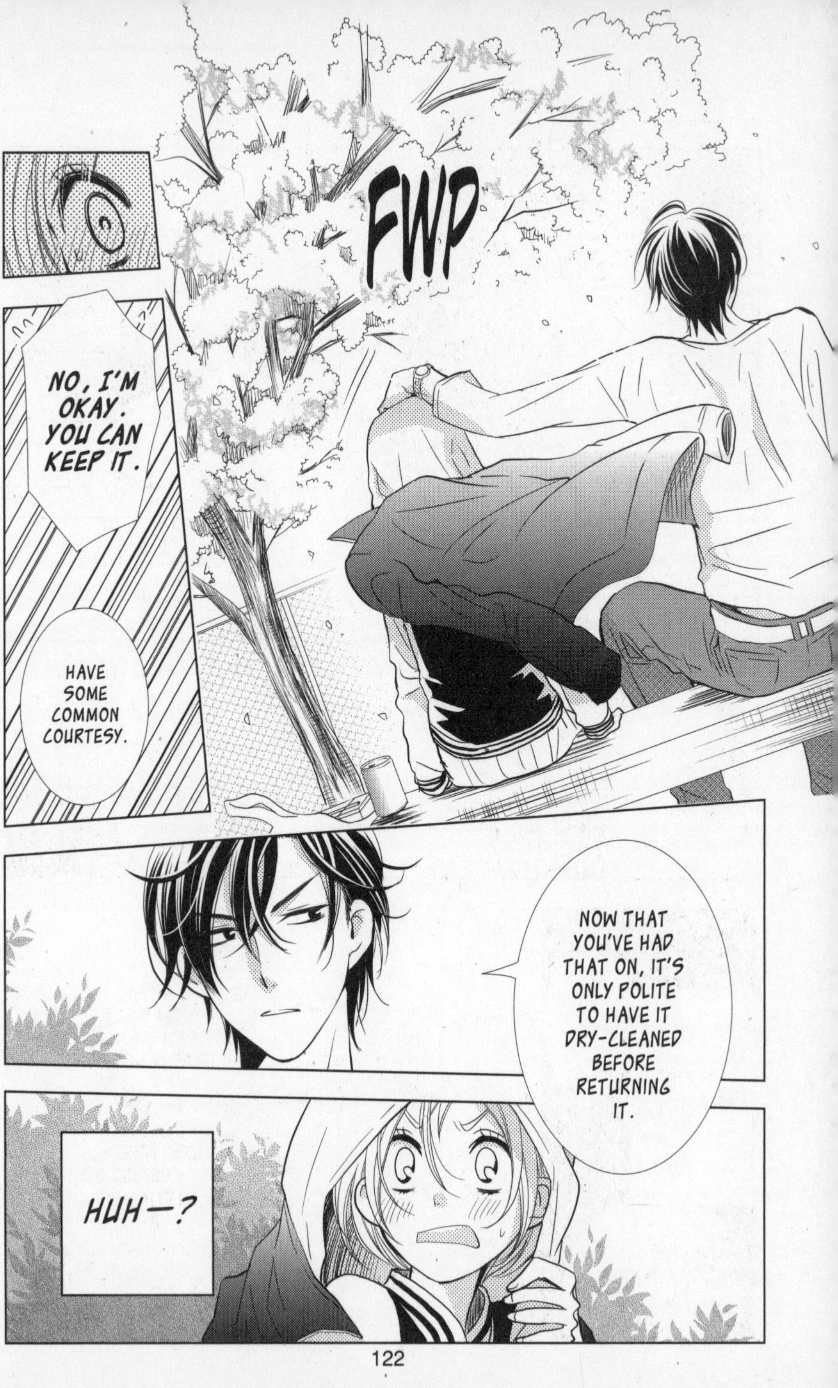
FWP
NO, I'M OKAY. YOU CAN KEEP IT.
HAVE SOME COMMON COURTESY.
NOW THAT YOU'VE HAD THAT ON, IT'S ONLY POLITE TO HAVE IT DRY-CLEANED BEFORE RETURNING IT.
HUH—?

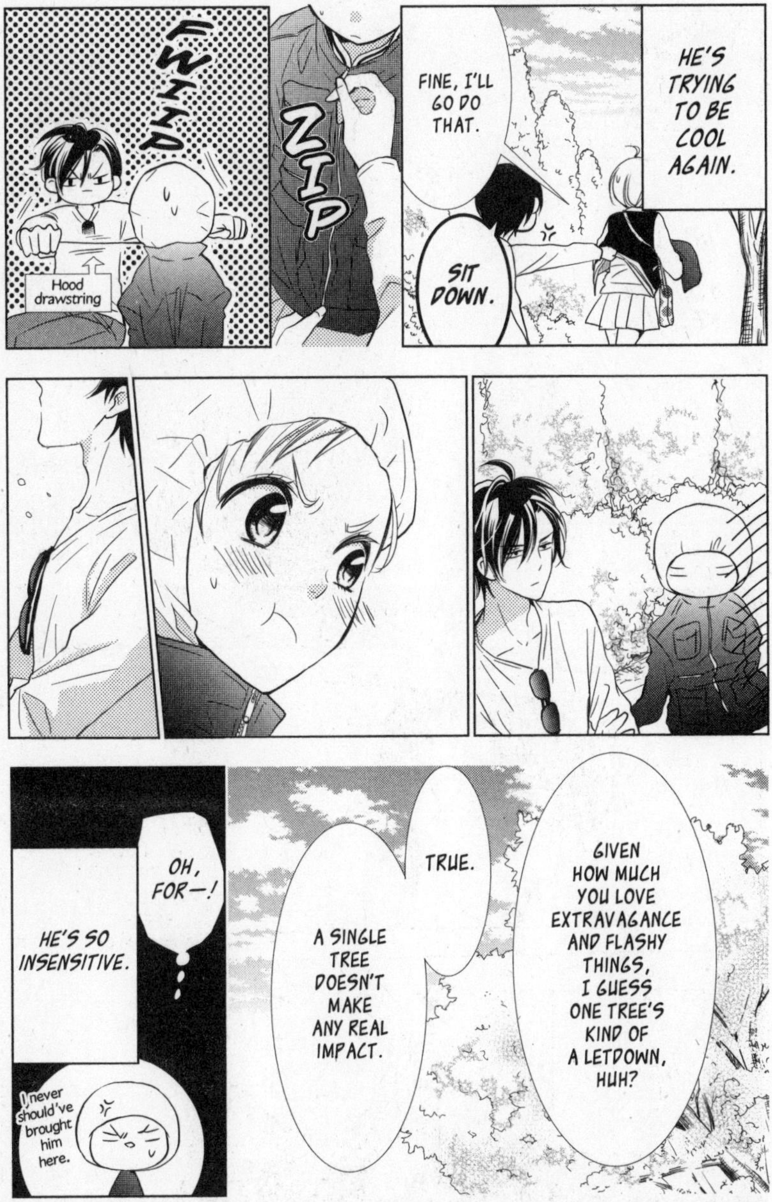
HE'S TRYING TO BE COOL AGAIN.
FINE, I'LL GO DO THAT.
SIT DOWN.
ZIP
FWIIP
Hood drawstring
GIVEN HOW MUCH YOU LOVE EXTRAVAGANCE AND FLASHY THINGS, I GUESS ONE TREE'S KIND OF A LETDOWN, HUH?
TRUE.
A SINGLE TREE DOESN'T MAKE ANY REAL IMPACT.
OH, FOR—!
HE'S SO INSENSITIVE.
I never should've brought him here.

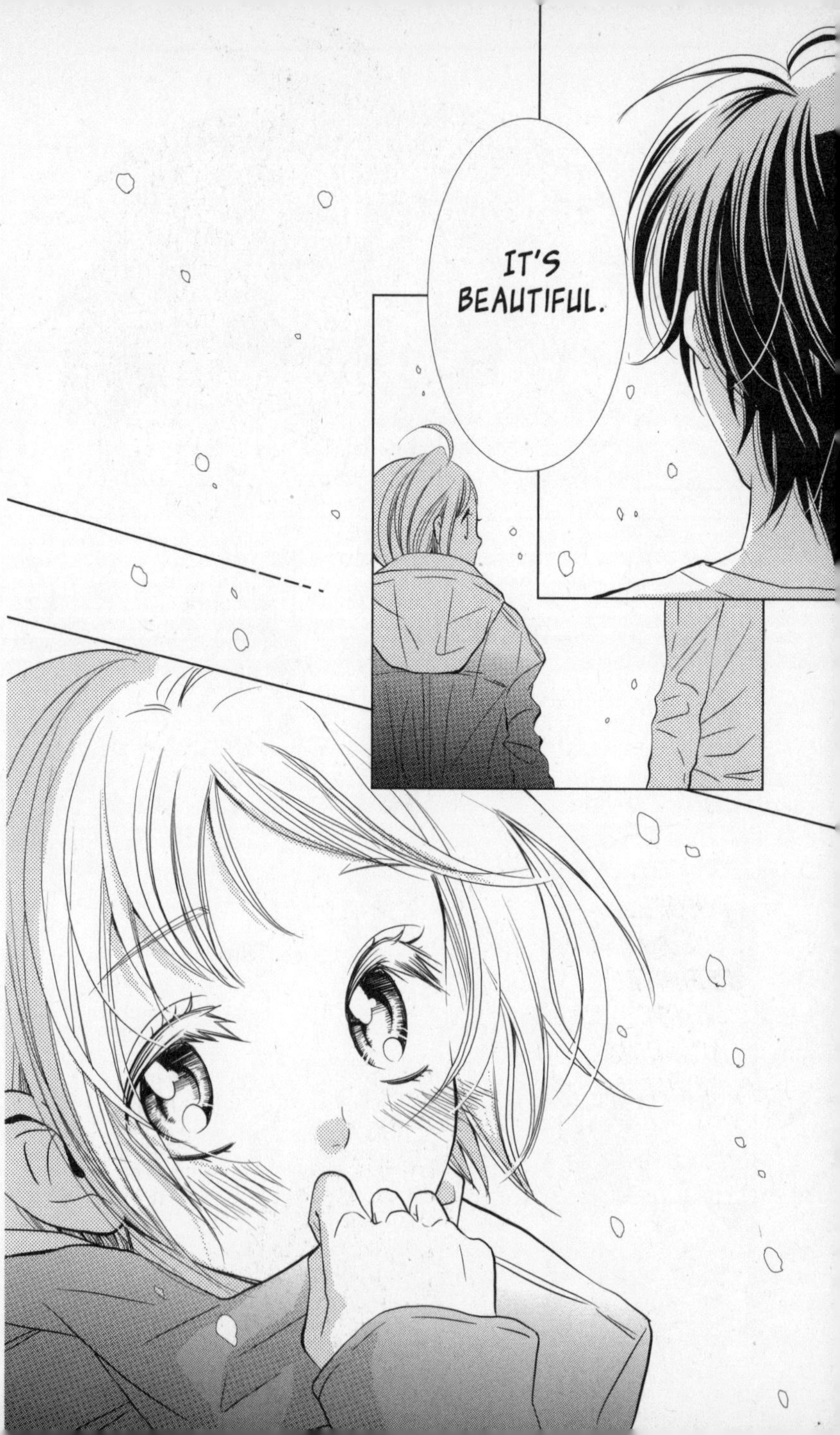
IT'S BEAUTIFUL.

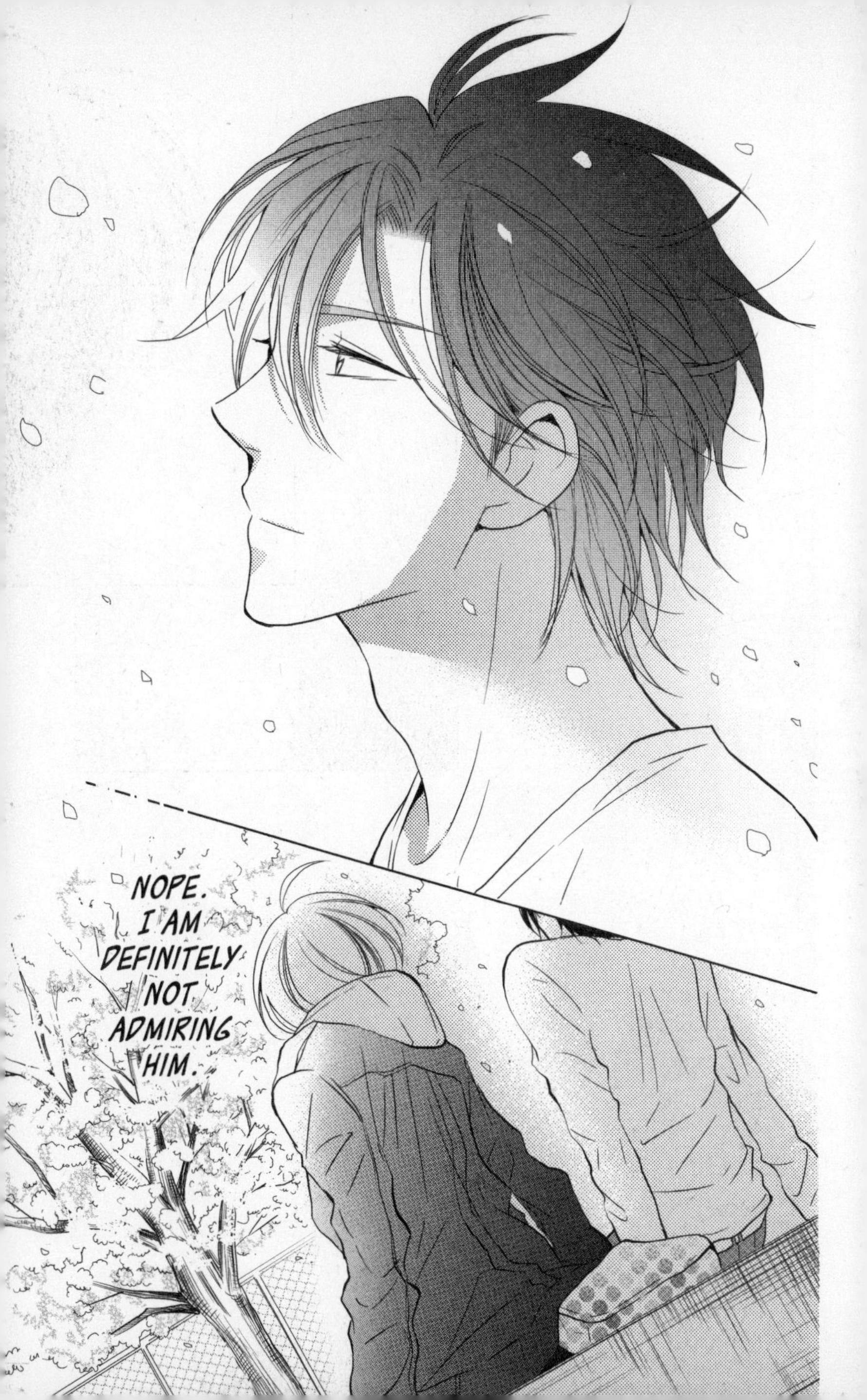
NOPE. I AM DEFINITELY NOT ADMIRING HIM.

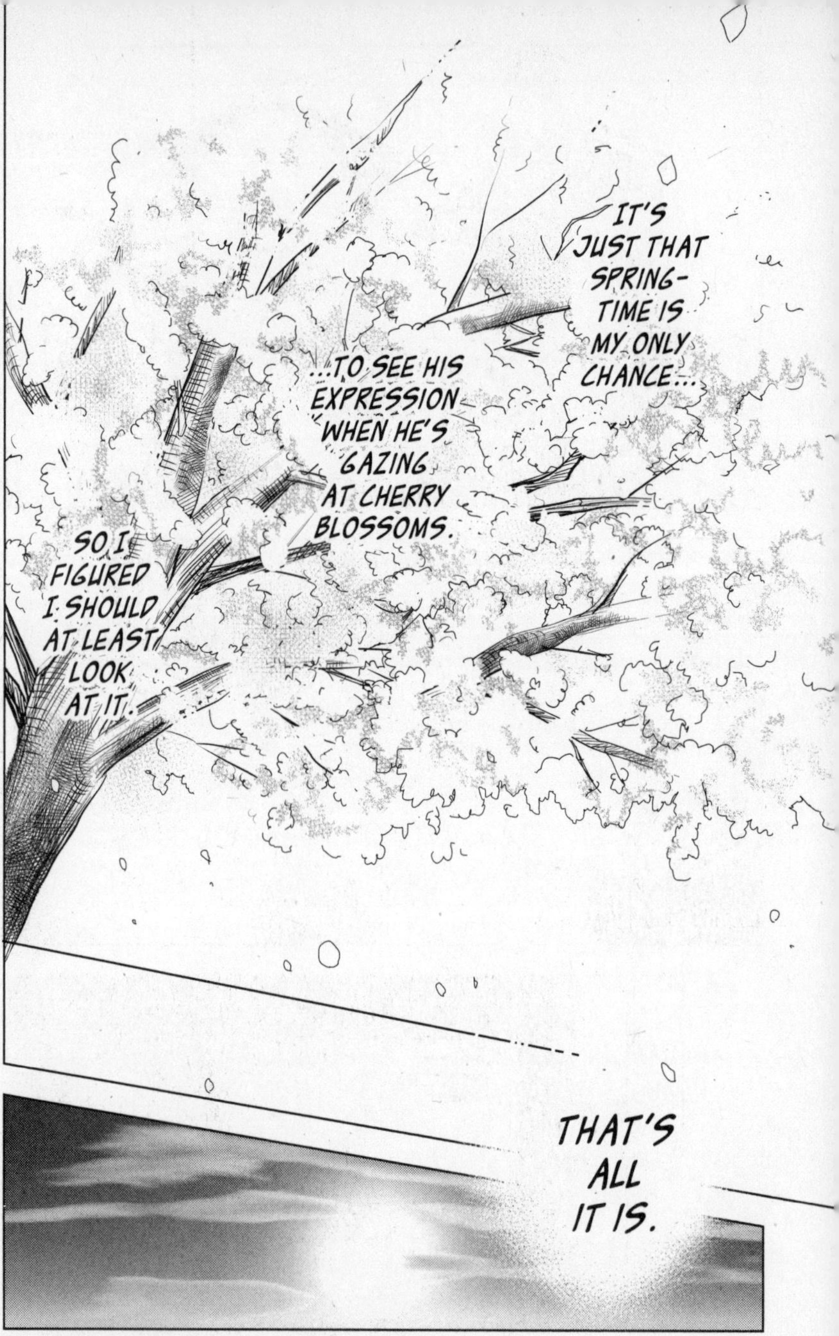
IT'S JUST THAT SPRING-TIME IS MY ONLY CHANCE...
...TO SEE HIS EXPRESSION WHEN HE'S GAZING AT CHERRY BLOSSOMS.
SO I FIGURED I SHOULD AT LEAST LOOK AT IT.
THAT'S ALL IT IS.

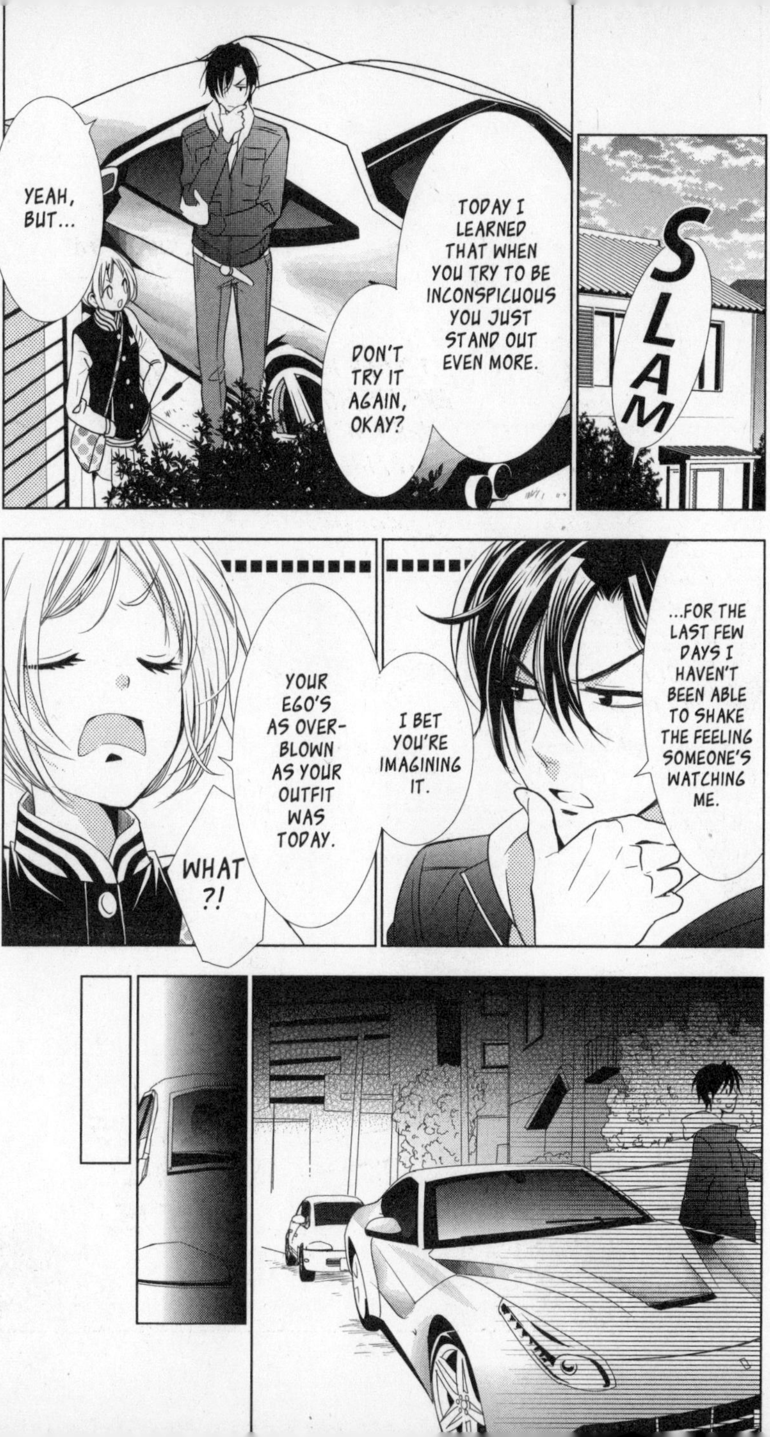
SLAM
TODAY I LEARNED THAT WHEN YOU TRY TO BE INCONSPICUOUS YOU JUST STAND OUT EVEN MORE.
DON'T TRY IT AGAIN, OKAY?
YEAH, BUT...
...FOR THE LAST FEW DAYS I HAVEN'T BEEN ABLE TO SHAKE THE FEELING SOMEONE'S WATCHING ME.
I BET YOU'RE IMAGINING IT.
YOUR EGO'S AS OVER-BLOWN AS YOUR OUTFIT WAS TODAY.
WHAT?!

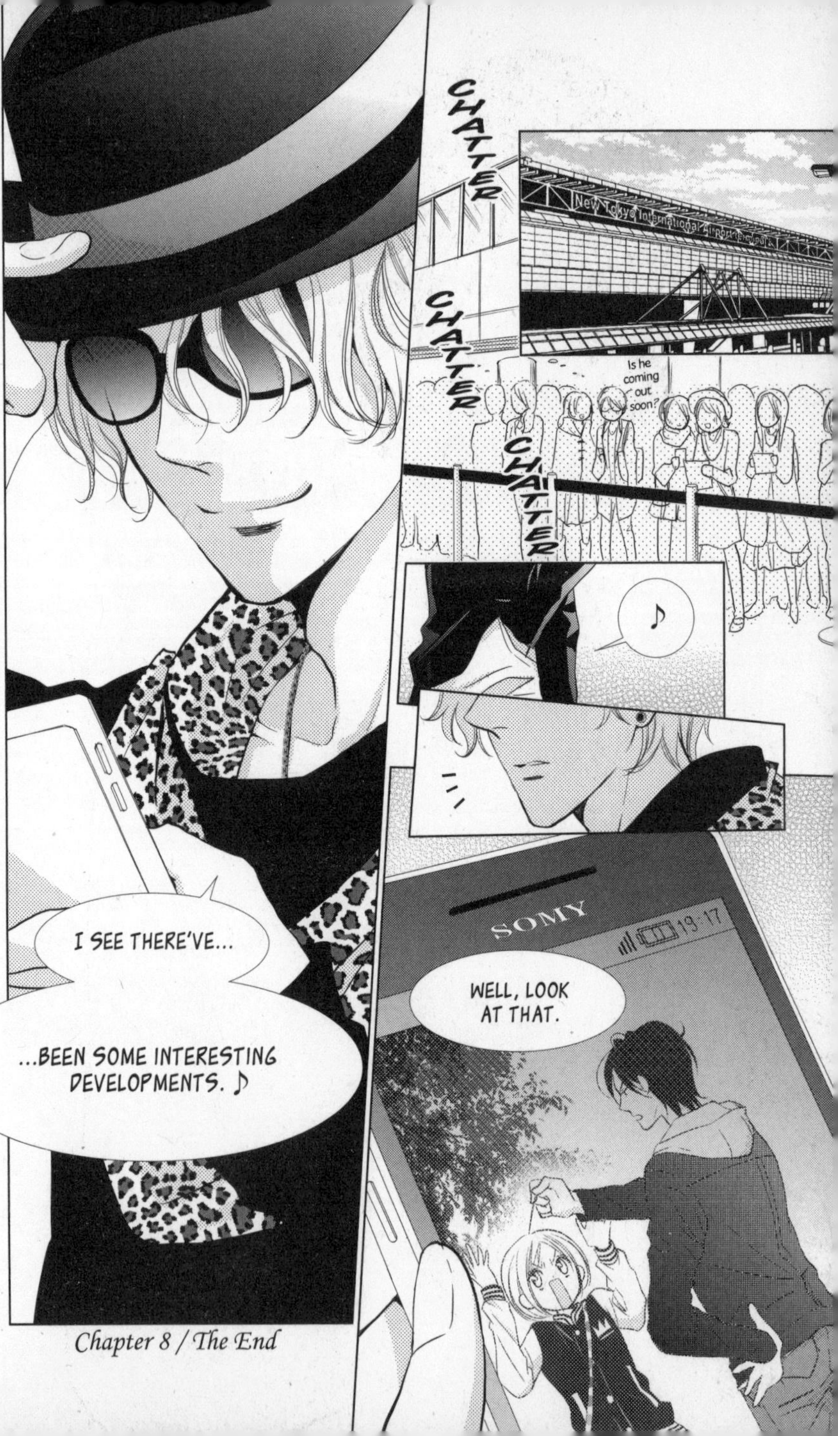
CHATTER
New Tokyo International
CHATTER
CHATTER
Is he coming out soon?
♪
SOMY
19:17
WELL, LOOK AT THAT.
I SEE THERE'VE...
...BEEN SOME INTERESTING DEVELOPMENTS. ♪

Chapter 8 / The End

Chapter 9

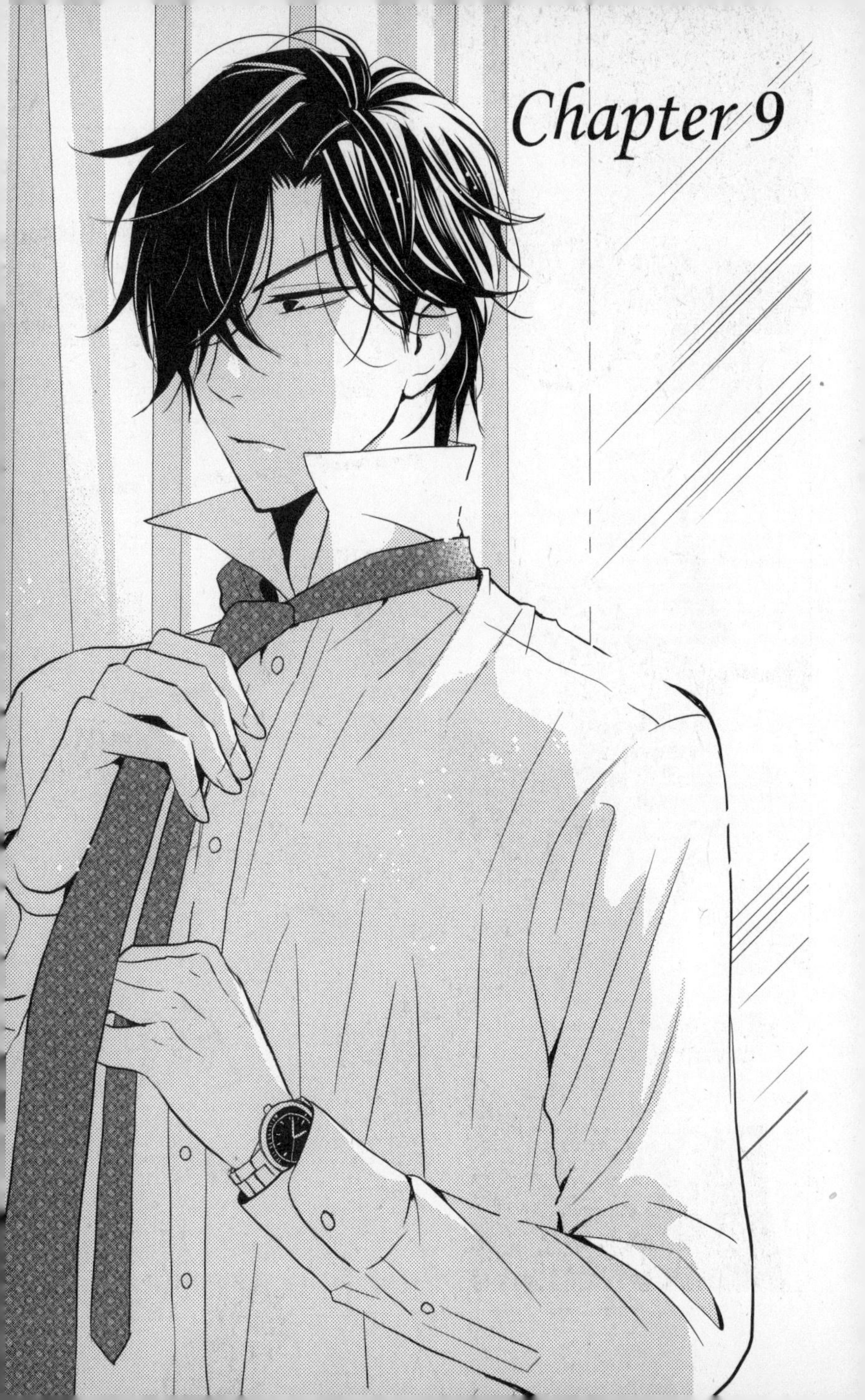

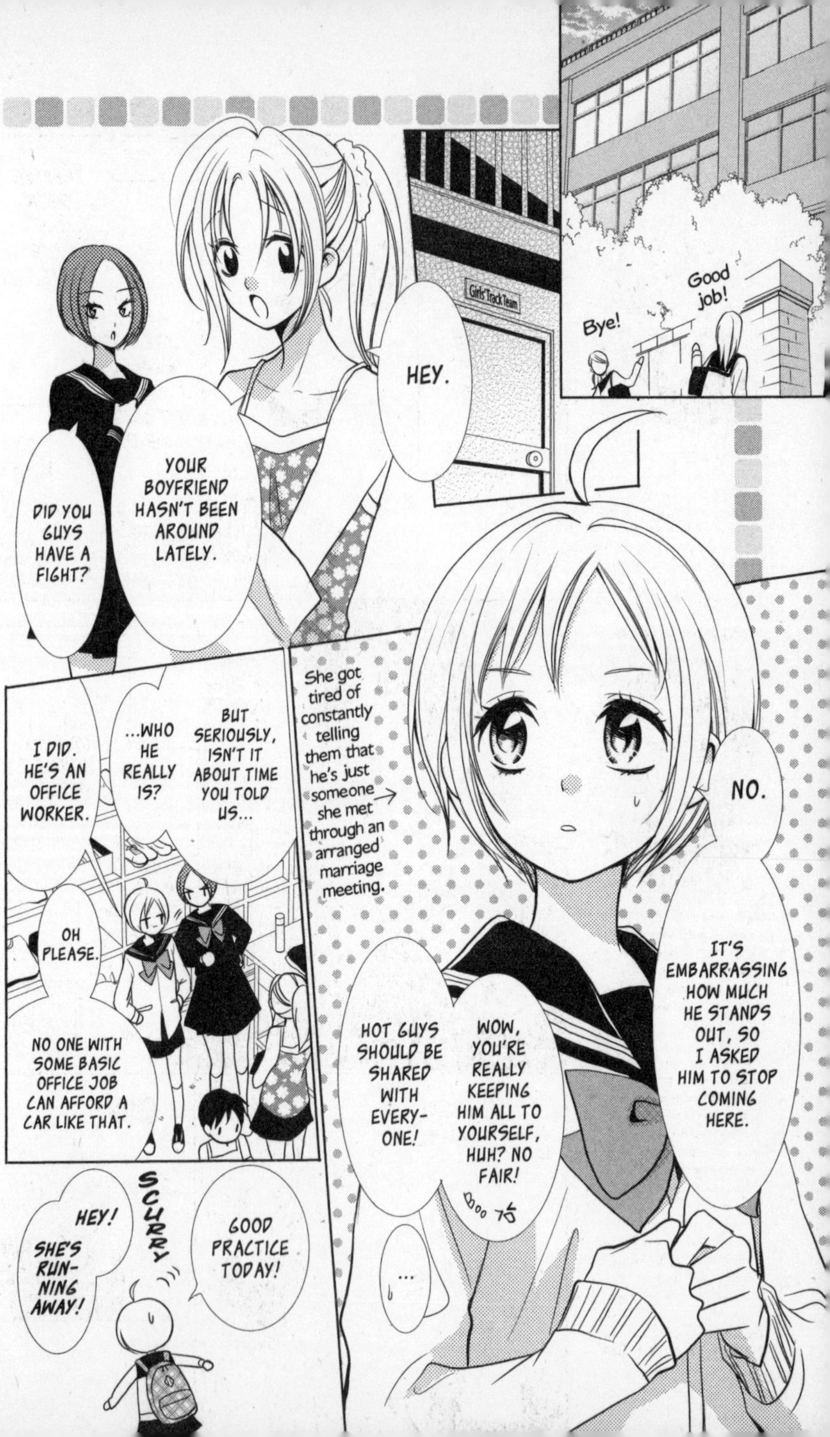
Good job!
Bye!
HEY.
YOUR BOYFRIEND HASN'T BEEN AROUND LATELY.
DID YOU GUYS HAVE A FIGHT?
NO.
IT'S EMBARRASSING HOW MUCH HE STANDS OUT, SO I ASKED HIM TO STOP COMING HERE.
WOW, YOU'RE REALLY KEEPING HIM ALL TO YOURSELF, HUH? NO FAIR!
HOT GUYS SHOULD BE SHARED WITH EVERY-ONE!
...
She got tired of constantly telling them that he's just someone she met through an arranged marriage meeting.
BUT SERIOUSLY, ISN'T IT ABOUT TIME YOU TOLD US...
...WHO HE REALLY IS?
I DID. HE'S AN OFFICE WORKER.
OH PLEASE.
NO ONE WITH SOME BASIC OFFICE JOB CAN AFFORD A CAR LIKE THAT.
GOOD PRACTICE TODAY!
SCURRY
HEY! SHE'S RUN-NING AWAY!

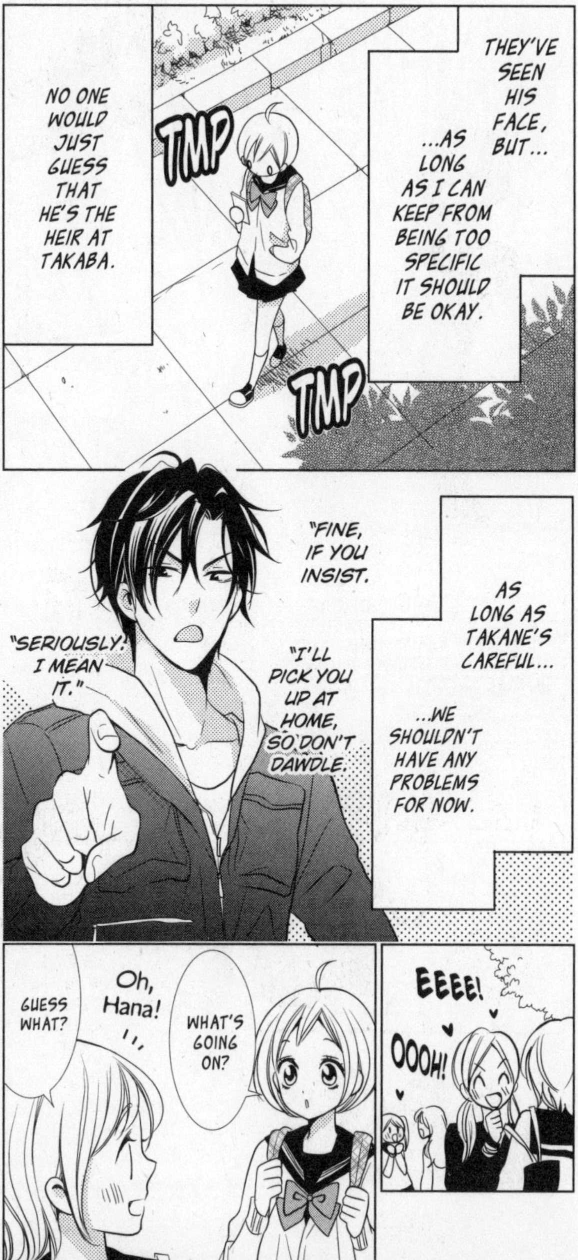
THEY'VE SEEN HIS FACE, BUT...
...AS LONG AS I CAN KEEP FROM BEING TOO SPECIFIC IT SHOULD BE OKAY.
TMP
TMP
NO ONE WOULD JUST GUESS THAT HE'S THE HEIR AT TAKABA.
AS LONG AS TAKANE'S CAREFUL...
...WE SHOULDN'T HAVE ANY PROBLEMS FOR NOW.
"FINE, IF YOU INSIST.
"I'LL PICK YOU UP AT HOME, SO DON'T DAWDLE.
"SERIOUSLY! I MEAN IT."
EEEE!
OOOH!
WHAT'S GOING ON?
Oh, Hana!
GUESS WHAT?

●Mizuki●

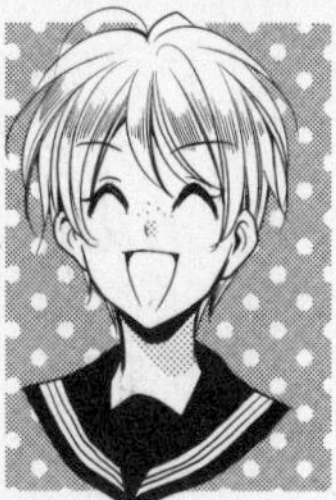

Hana, Mizu and Hikari are a trio of friends.*

Mizuki is cheerful and enjoys following trends. She's up for anything! I often forget to draw her freckles. She has a boyish look. Uses "uchi" to refer to herself [what some girls do in the Kansai region].

●Hikaruko●

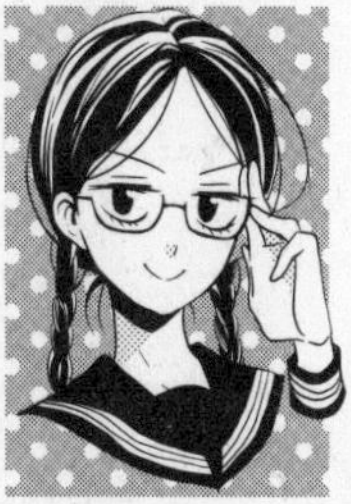

She's calm no matter what's going on and is well-informed. I didn't have enough space in volume 1 to mention that she's quite pretty when she takes off her glasses.

I don't know exactly what the future holds, but I'm hoping Hana's friends play an active part as the story goes forward. I didn't put much thought into them before introducing them as Hana's friends, but I like how they turned out.

Because she has her friends, Hana's more likely to do things that she might be hesitant to do on her own.

**Hana* means "flower," *mizu* means "water" and *hikari* means "light."

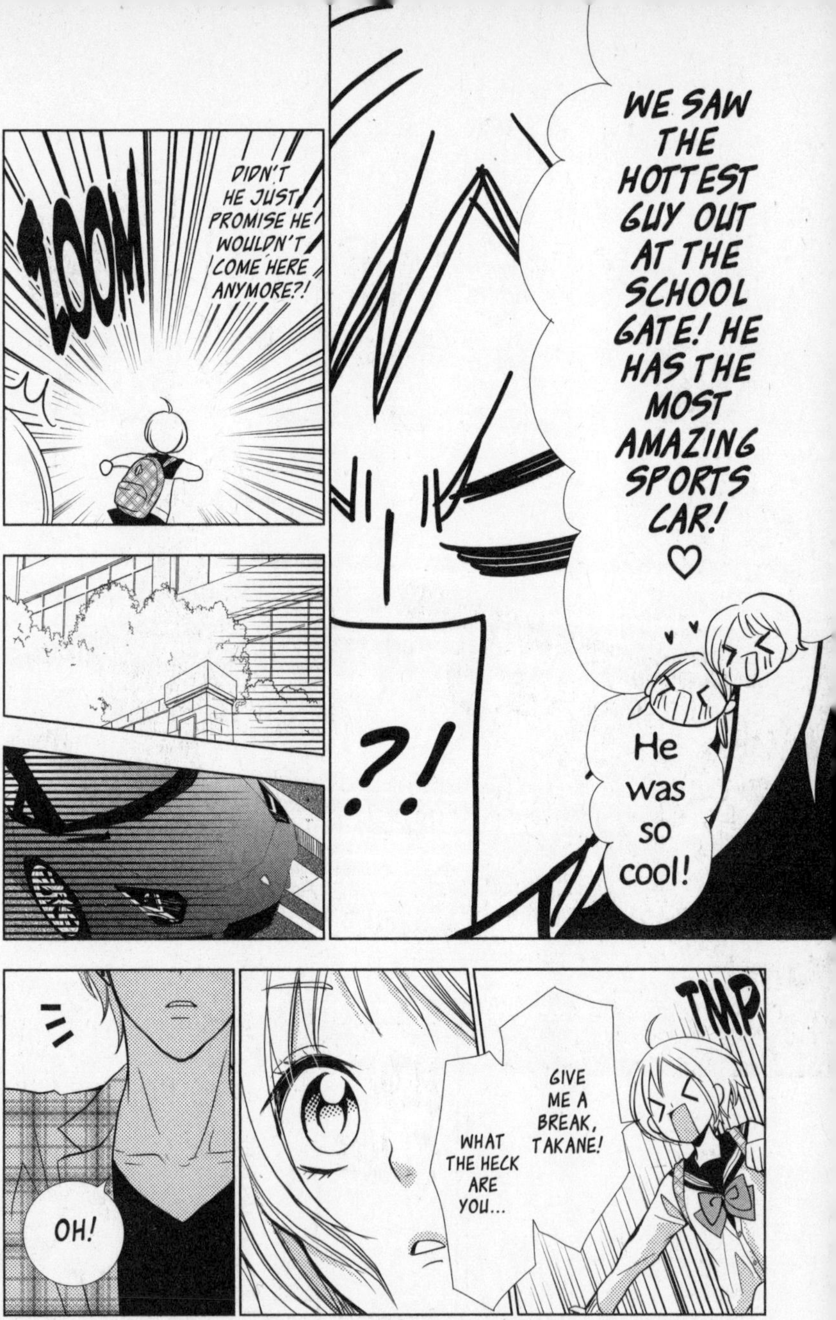
WE SAW THE HOTTEST GUY OUT AT THE SCHOOL GATE! HE HAS THE MOST AMAZING SPORTS CAR! ♡
He was so cool!
?!
DIDN'T HE JUST PROMISE HE WOULDN'T COME HERE ANYMORE?!
ZOOM
TMP
GIVE ME A BREAK, TAKANE!
WHAT THE HECK ARE YOU...
OH!

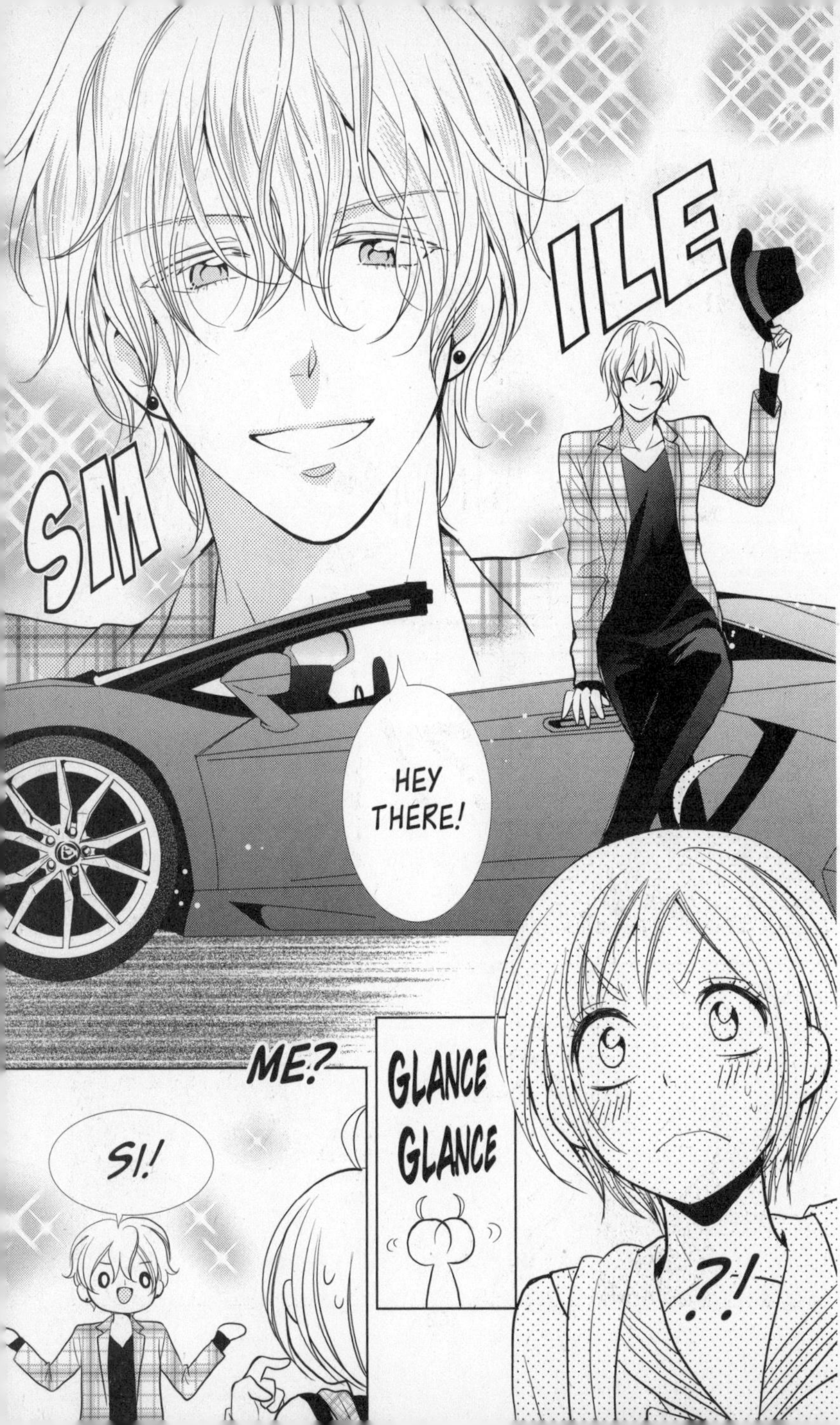
SM
ILE
HEY THERE!
?!
ME?
GLANCE
GLANCE
SI!

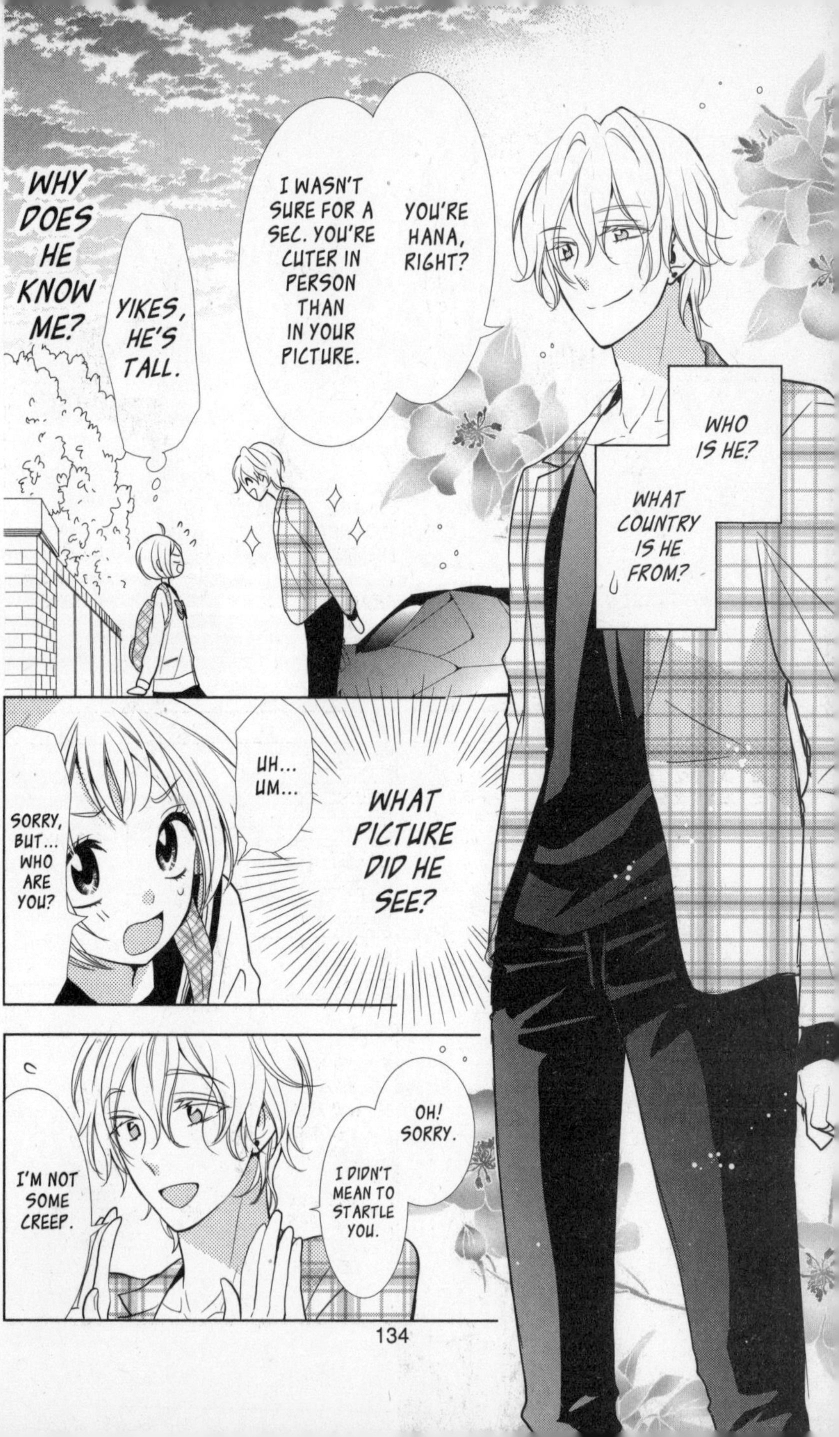
YOU'RE HANA, RIGHT?
I WASN'T SURE FOR A SEC. YOU'RE CUTER IN PERSON THAN IN YOUR PICTURE.
YIKES, HE'S TALL.
WHY DOES HE KNOW ME?
WHO IS HE?
WHAT COUNTRY IS HE FROM?
UH... UM...
WHAT PICTURE DID HE SEE?
SORRY, BUT... WHO ARE YOU?
OH! SORRY.
I DIDN'T MEAN TO STARTLE YOU.
I'M NOT SOME CREEP.

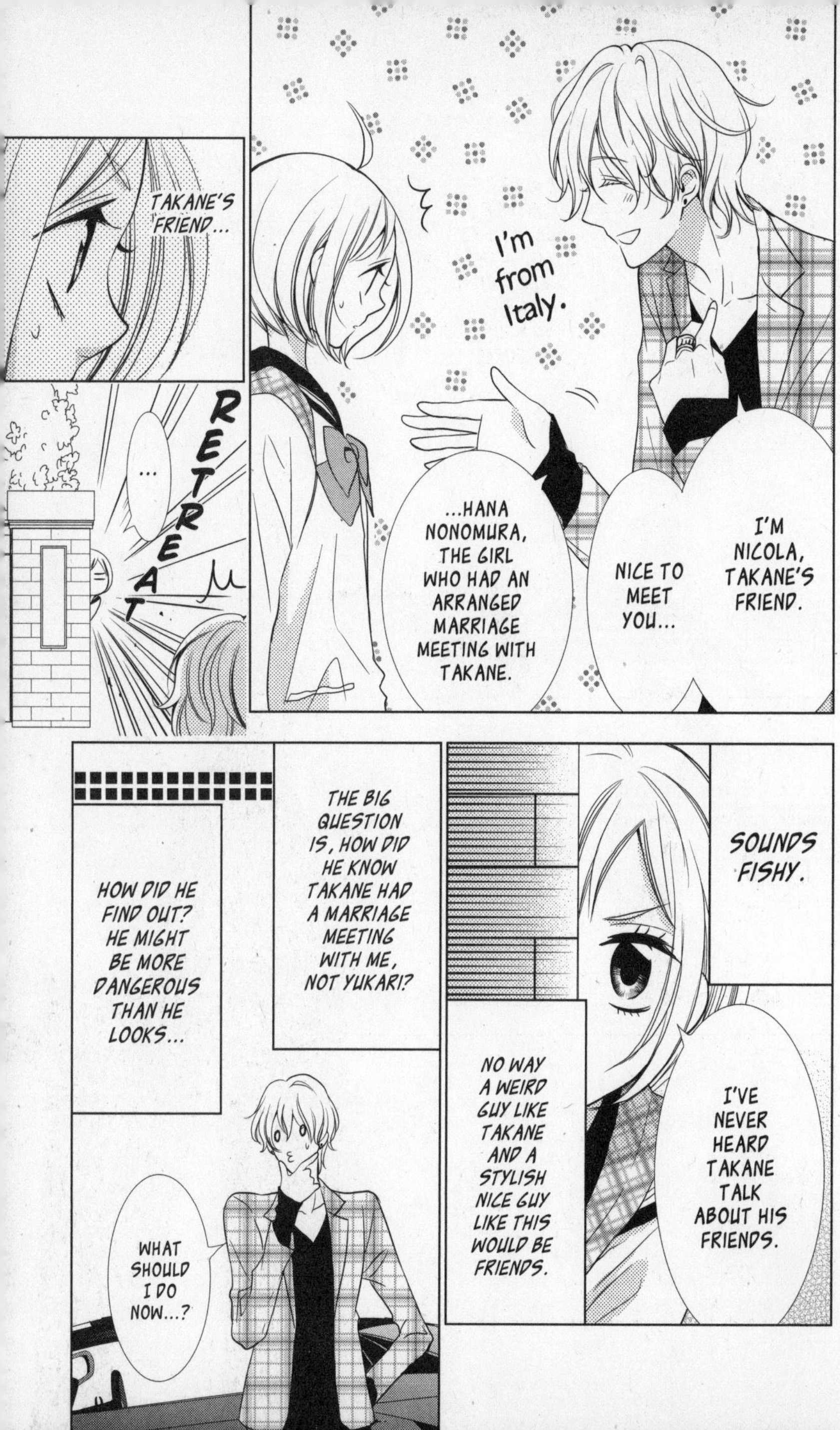
I'M NICOLA, TAKANE'S FRIEND.
NICE TO MEET YOU...
I'm from Italy.
...HANA NONOMURA, THE GIRL WHO HAD AN ARRANGED MARRIAGE MEETING WITH TAKANE.
TAKANE'S FRIEND...
...
RETREAT
SOUNDS FISHY.
I'VE NEVER HEARD TAKANE TALK ABOUT HIS FRIENDS.
NO WAY A WEIRD GUY LIKE TAKANE AND A STYLISH NICE GUY LIKE THIS WOULD BE FRIENDS.
THE BIG QUESTION IS, HOW DID HE KNOW TAKANE HAD A MARRIAGE MEETING WITH ME, NOT YUKARI?
HOW DID HE FIND OUT? HE MIGHT BE MORE DANGEROUS THAN HE LOOKS...
WHAT SHOULD I DO NOW...?

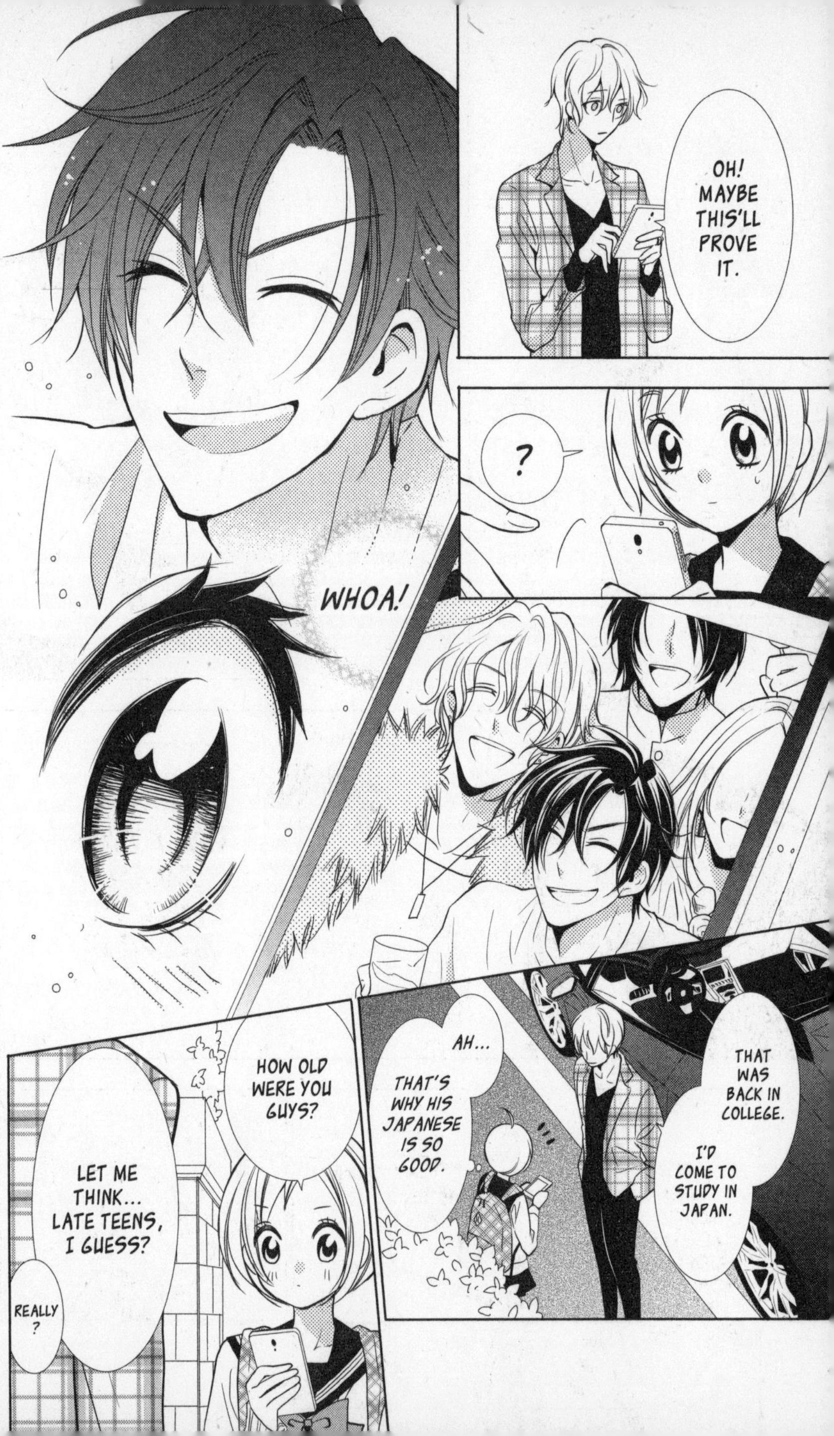
OH! MAYBE THIS'LL PROVE IT.
?
WHOA!
THAT WAS BACK IN COLLEGE.
I'D COME TO STUDY IN JAPAN.
AH...
THAT'S WHY HIS JAPANESE IS SO GOOD.
HOW OLD WERE YOU GUYS?
LET ME THINK... LATE TEENS, I GUESS?
REALLY?

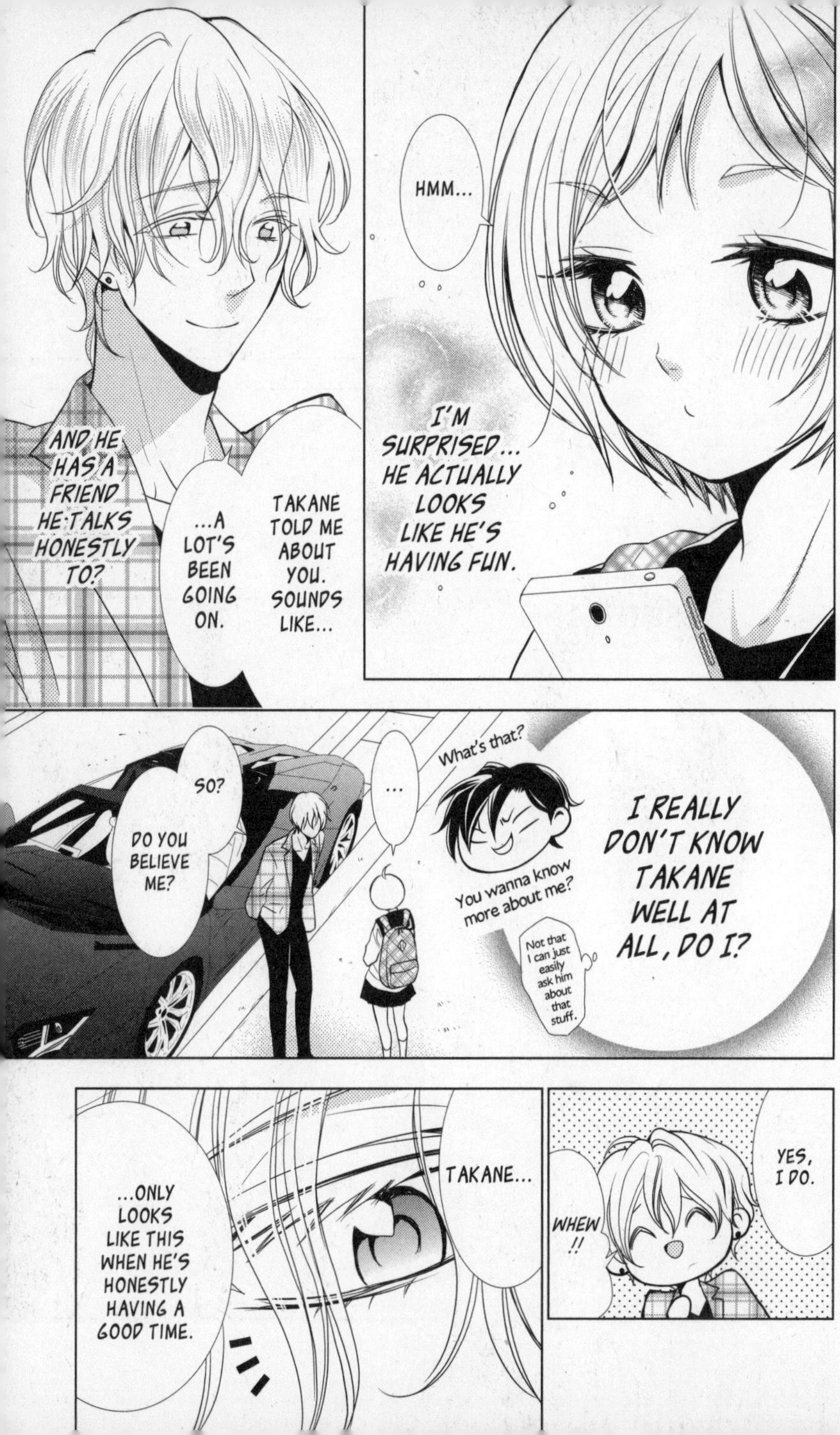
HMM...
I'M SURPRISED... HE ACTUALLY LOOKS LIKE HE'S HAVING FUN.
TAKANE TOLD ME ABOUT YOU. SOUNDS LIKE...
...A LOT'S BEEN GOING ON.
AND HE HAS A FRIEND HE TALKS HONESTLY TO?
I REALLY DON'T KNOW TAKANE WELL AT ALL, DO I?
What's that?
You wanna know more about me?
Not that I can just easily ask him about that stuff.
...
SO?
DO YOU BELIEVE ME?
YES, I DO.
WHEW!!
TAKANE...
...ONLY LOOKS LIKE THIS WHEN HE'S HONESTLY HAVING A GOOD TIME.

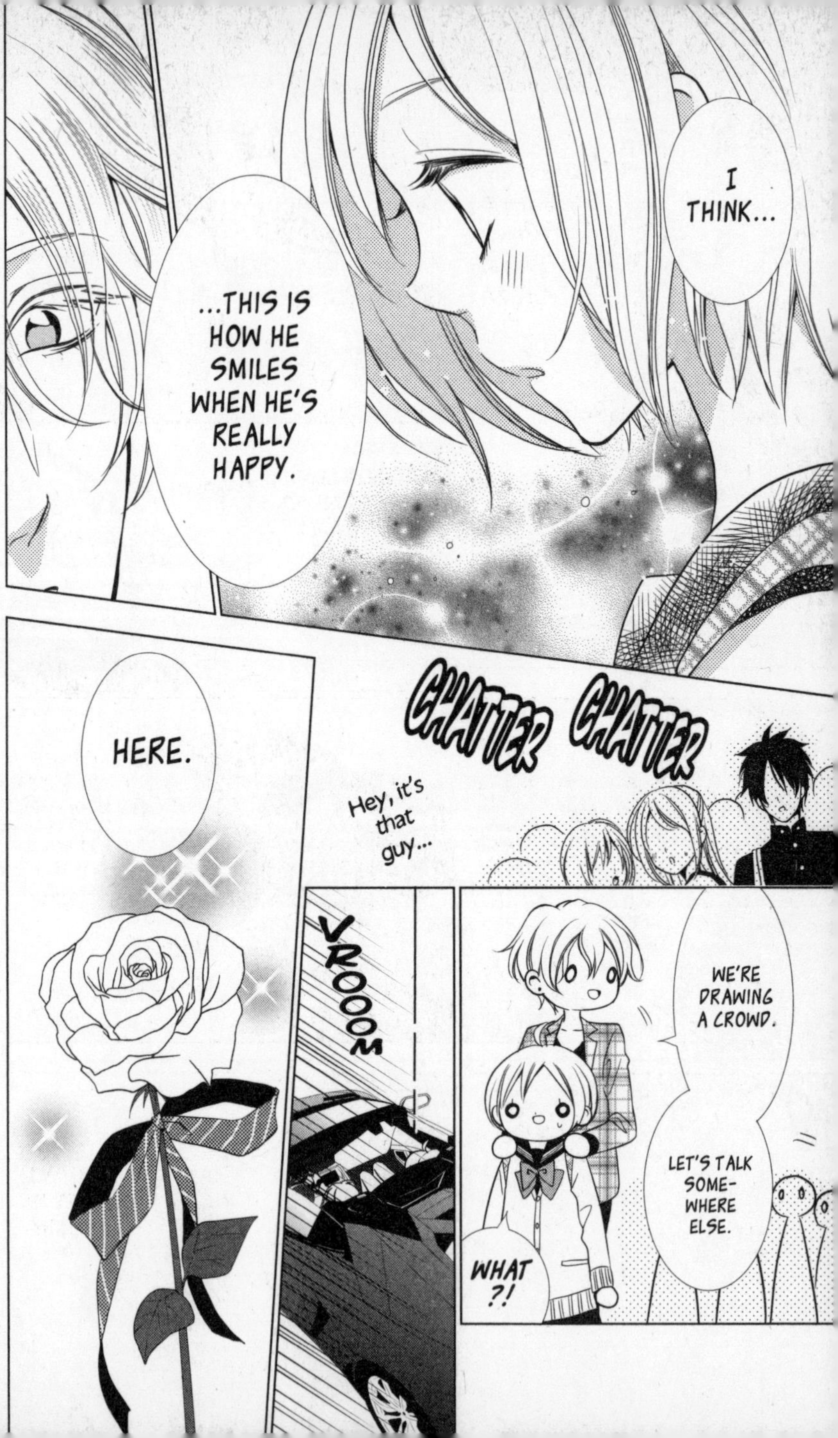
I THINK...
...THIS IS HOW HE SMILES WHEN HE'S REALLY HAPPY.
CHATTER CHATTER
Hey, it's that guy...
WE'RE DRAWING A CROWD.
LET'S TALK SOME-WHERE ELSE.
WHAT?!
VROOOM
HERE.

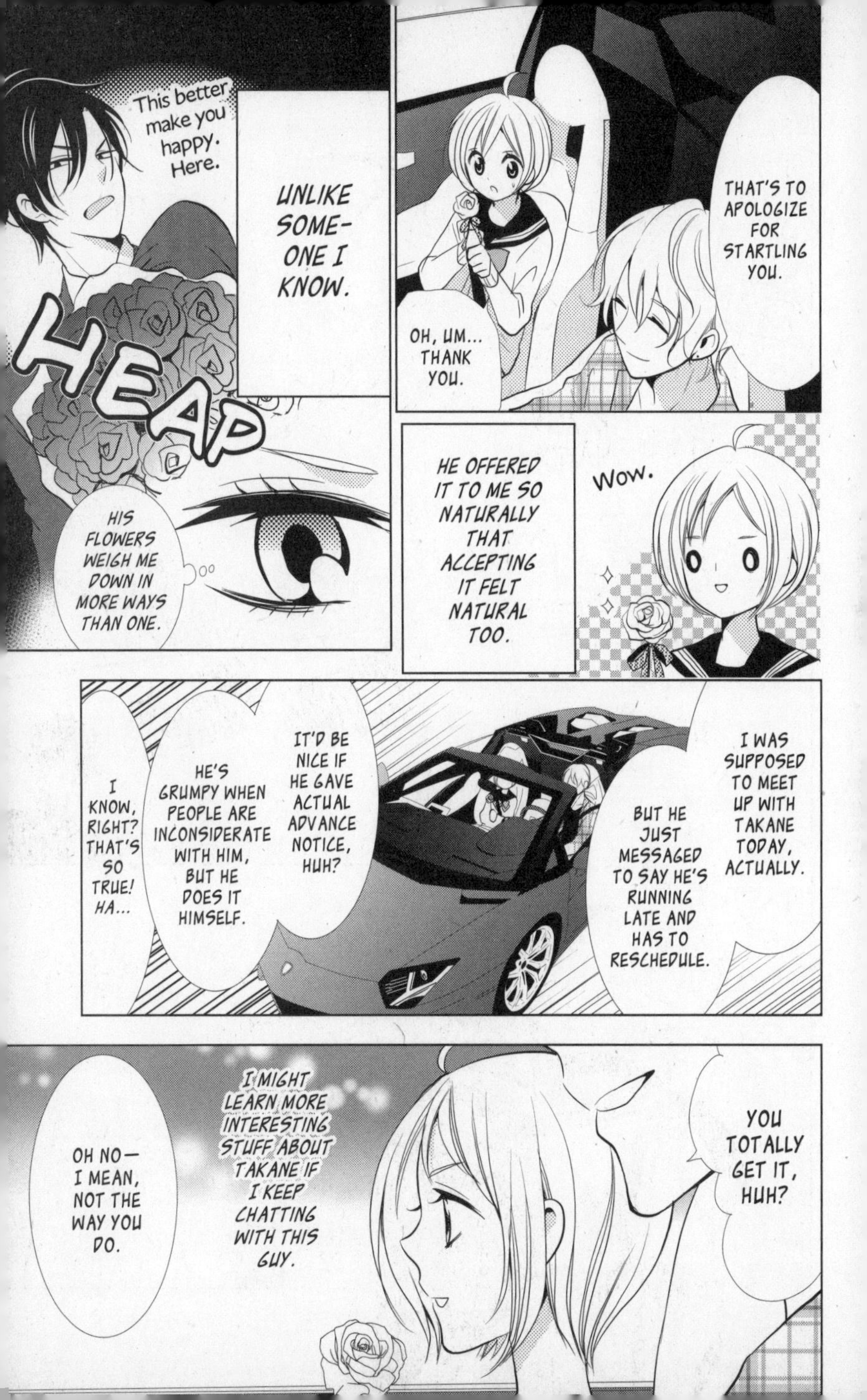
THAT'S TO APOLOGIZE FOR STARTLING YOU.
OH, UM... THANK YOU.
HE OFFERED IT TO ME SO NATURALLY THAT ACCEPTING IT FELT NATURAL TOO.
Wow.
UNLIKE SOME-ONE I KNOW.
This better make you happy. Here.
HEAP
HIS FLOWERS WEIGH ME DOWN IN MORE WAYS THAN ONE.
I WAS SUPPOSED TO MEET UP WITH TAKANE TODAY, ACTUALLY.
BUT HE JUST MESSAGED TO SAY HE'S RUNNING LATE AND HAS TO RESCHEDULE.
IT'D BE NICE IF HE GAVE ACTUAL ADVANCE NOTICE, HUH?
HE'S GRUMPY WHEN PEOPLE ARE INCONSIDERATE WITH HIM, BUT HE DOES IT HIMSELF.
I KNOW, RIGHT? THAT'S SO TRUE! HA...
YOU TOTALLY GET IT, HUH?
I MIGHT LEARN MORE INTERESTING STUFF ABOUT TAKANE IF I KEEP CHATTING WITH THIS GUY.
OH NO— I MEAN, NOT THE WAY YOU DO.

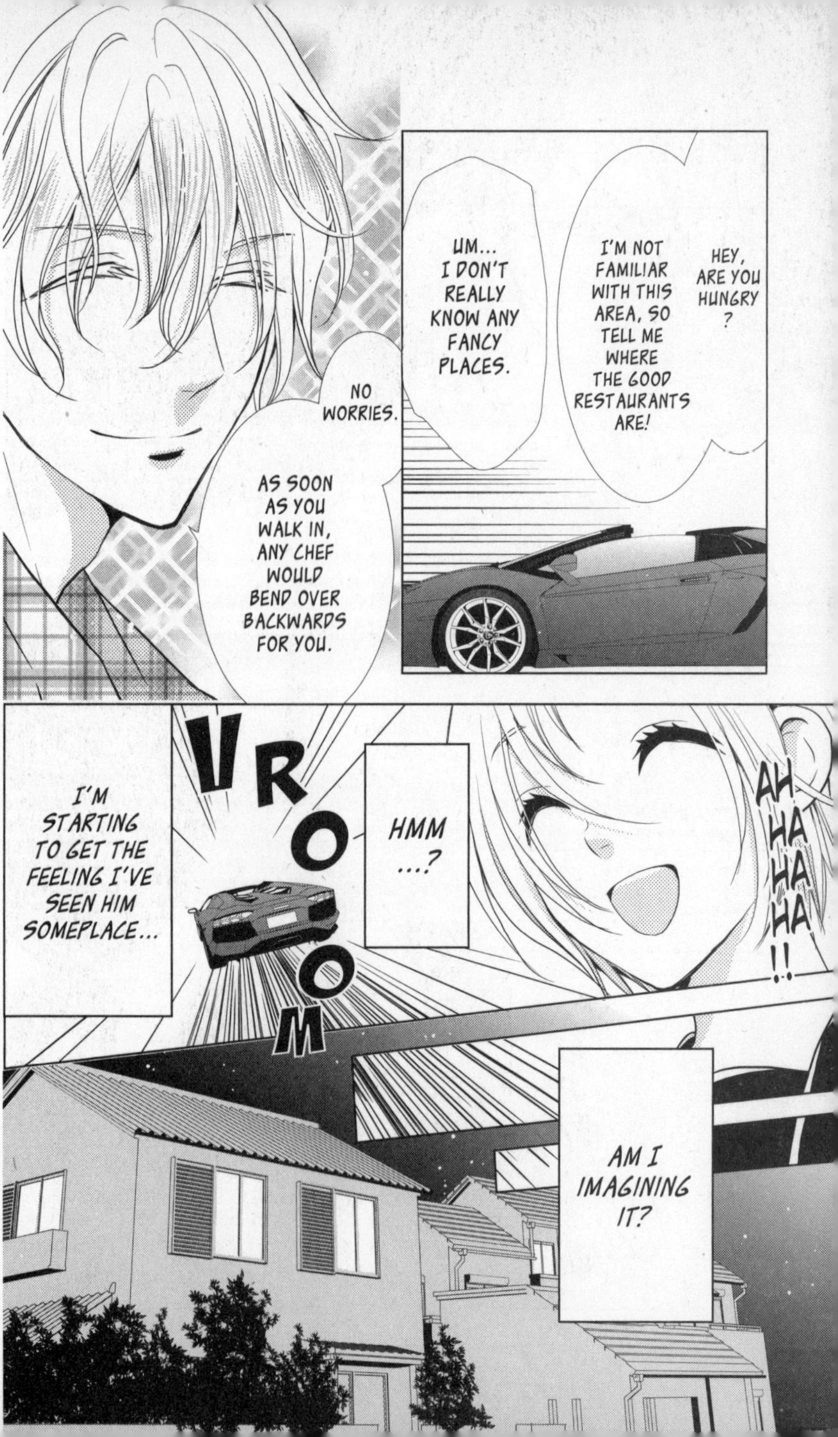
HEY, ARE YOU HUNGRY?
I'M NOT FAMILIAR WITH THIS AREA, SO TELL ME WHERE THE GOOD RESTAURANTS ARE!
UM... I DON'T REALLY KNOW ANY FANCY PLACES.
NO WORRIES.
AS SOON AS YOU WALK IN, ANY CHEF WOULD BEND OVER BACKWARDS FOR YOU.
AH HA HA HA!!
HMM ...?
VROOOM
I'M STARTING TO GET THE FEELING I'VE SEEN HIM SOMEPLACE...
AM I IMAGINING IT?

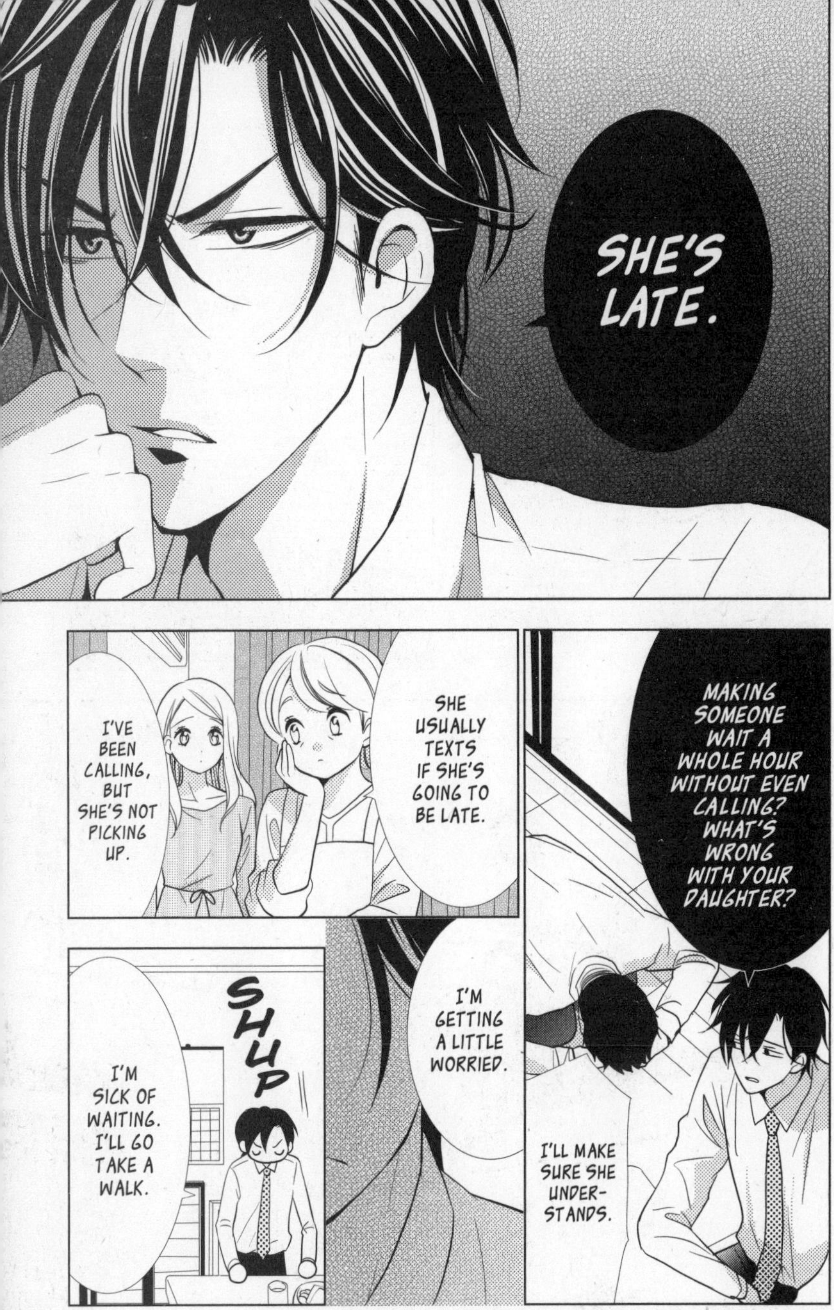
SHE'S LATE.
MAKING SOMEONE WAIT A WHOLE HOUR WITHOUT EVEN CALLING? WHAT'S WRONG WITH YOUR DAUGHTER?
I'LL MAKE SURE SHE UNDER-STANDS.
SHE USUALLY TEXTS IF SHE'S GOING TO BE LATE.
I'VE BEEN CALLING, BUT SHE'S NOT PICKING UP.
I'M GETTING A LITTLE WORRIED.
SHUP
I'M SICK OF WAITING. I'LL GO TAKE A WALK.

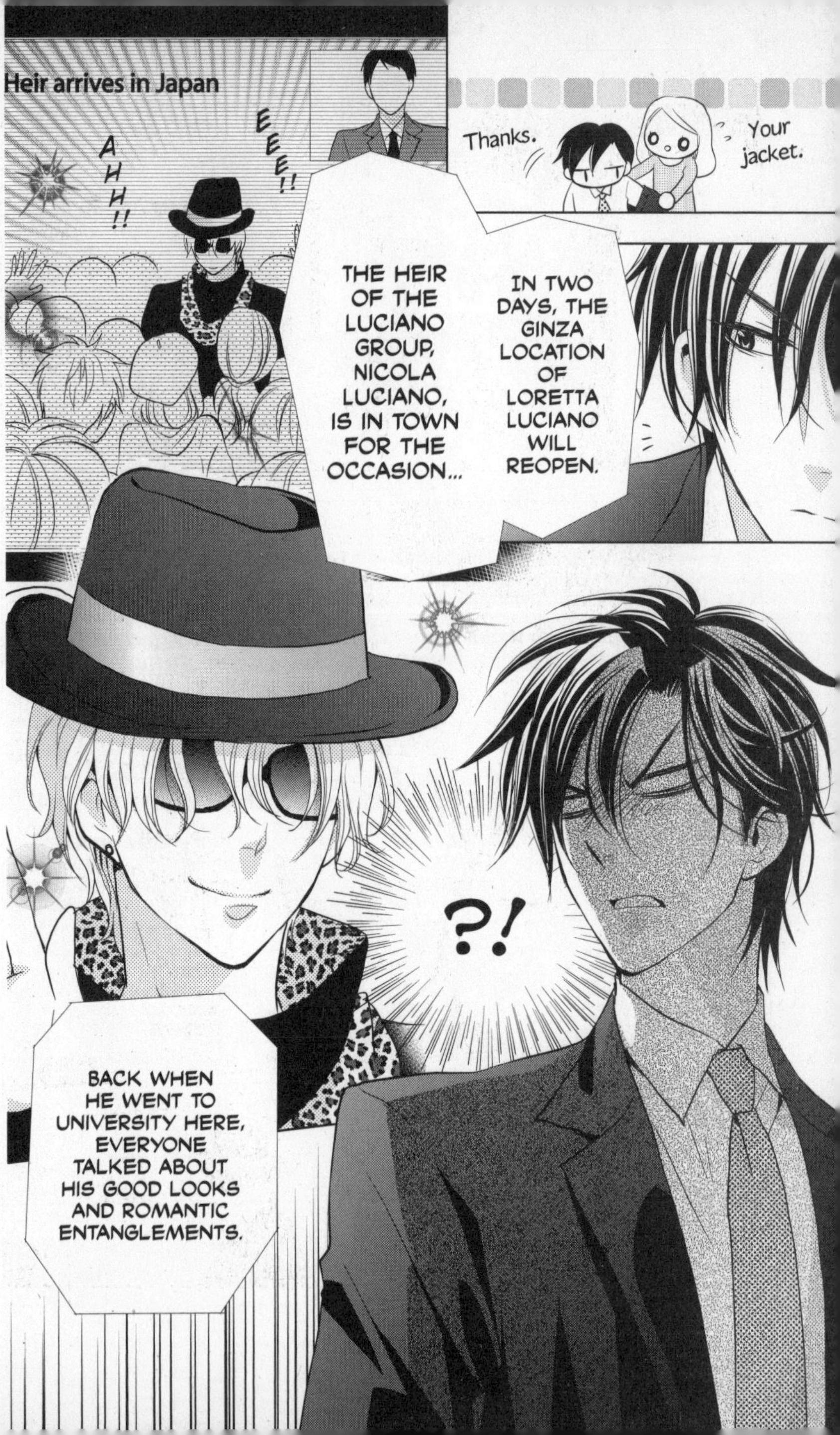
Your jacket.
Thanks.
IN TWO DAYS, THE GINZA LOCATION OF LORETTA LUCIANO WILL REOPEN.
THE HEIR OF THE LUCIANO GROUP, NICOLA LUCIANO, IS IN TOWN FOR THE OCCASION...
Heir arrives in Japan
EEE!!
AHH!!
?!
BACK WHEN HE WENT TO UNIVERSITY HERE, EVERYONE TALKED ABOUT HIS GOOD LOOKS AND ROMANTIC ENTANGLEMENTS.

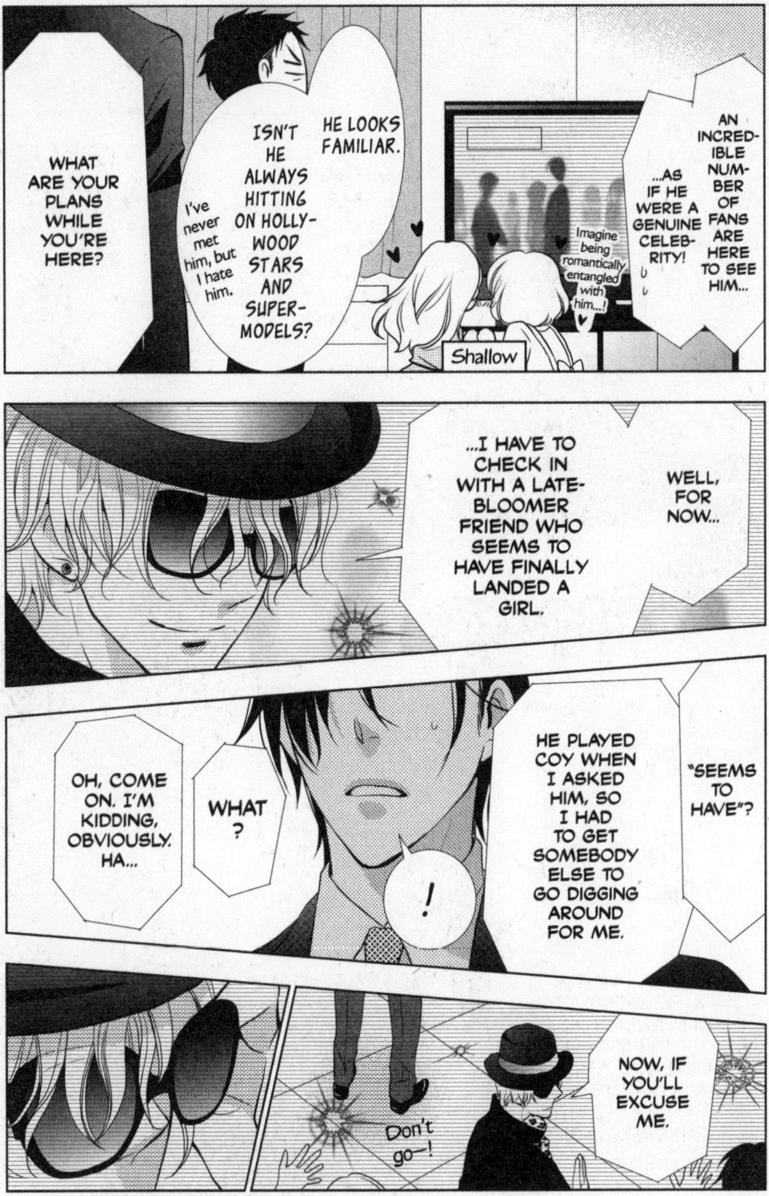
AN INCREDIBLE NUMBER OF FANS ARE HERE TO SEE HIM...
...AS IF HE WERE A GENUINE CELEBRITY!
Imagine being romantically entangled with him...!
Shallow
HE LOOKS FAMILIAR.
ISN'T HE ALWAYS HITTING ON HOLLYWOOD STARS AND SUPERMODELS?
I've never met him, but I hate him.
WHAT ARE YOUR PLANS WHILE YOU'RE HERE?
WELL, FOR NOW...
...I HAVE TO CHECK IN WITH A LATE-BLOOMER FRIEND WHO SEEMS TO HAVE FINALLY LANDED A GIRL.
"SEEMS TO HAVE"?
HE PLAYED COY WHEN I ASKED HIM, SO I HAD TO GET SOMEBODY ELSE TO GO DIGGING AROUND FOR ME.
!
WHAT?
OH, COME ON. I'M KIDDING, OBVIOUSLY. HA...
NOW, IF YOU'LL EXCUSE ME.
Don't go—!

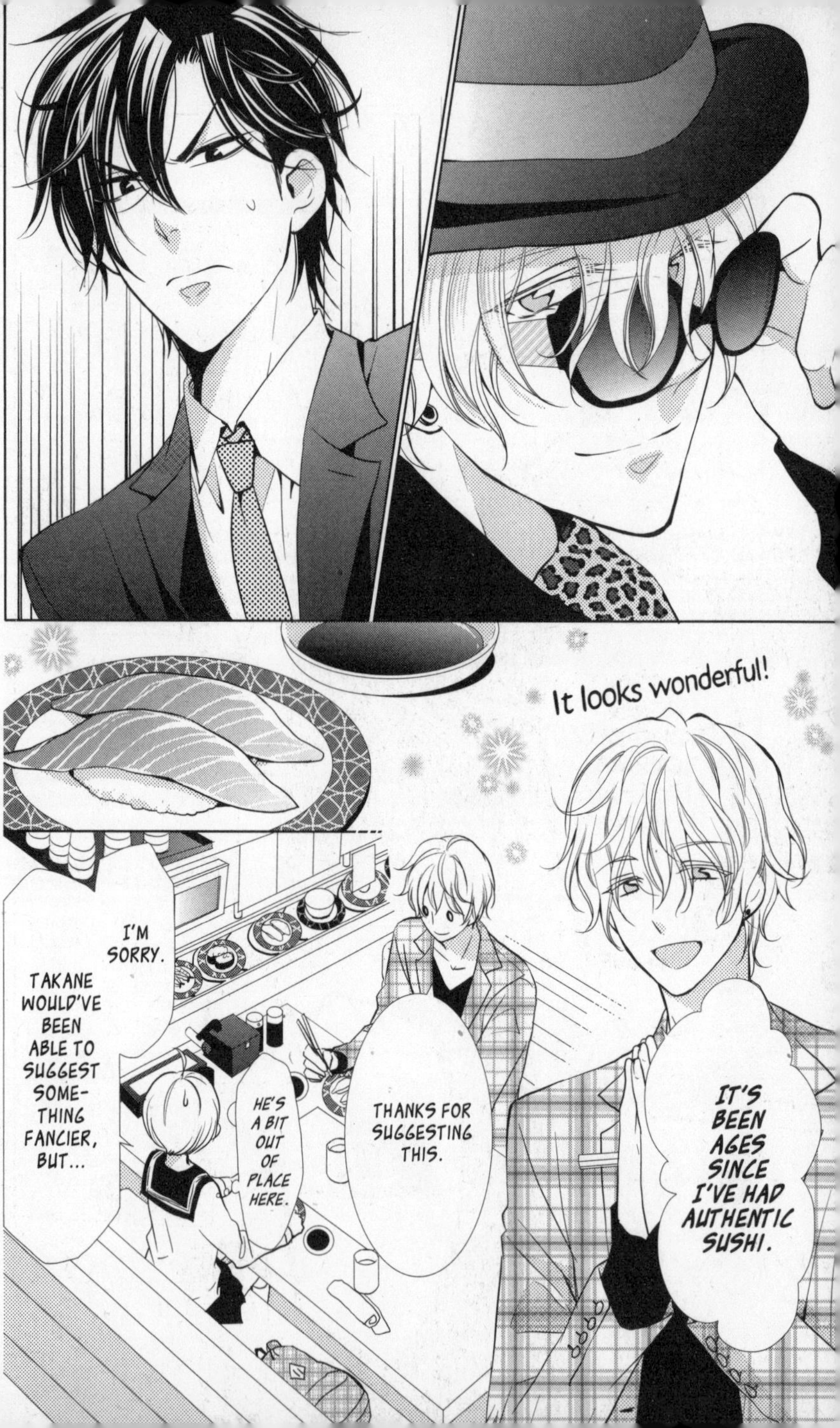
It looks wonderful!
IT'S BEEN AGES SINCE I'VE HAD AUTHENTIC SUSHI.
THANKS FOR SUGGESTING THIS.
HE'S A BIT OUT OF PLACE HERE.
I'M SORRY.
TAKANE WOULD'VE BEEN ABLE TO SUGGEST SOME-THING FANCIER, BUT...

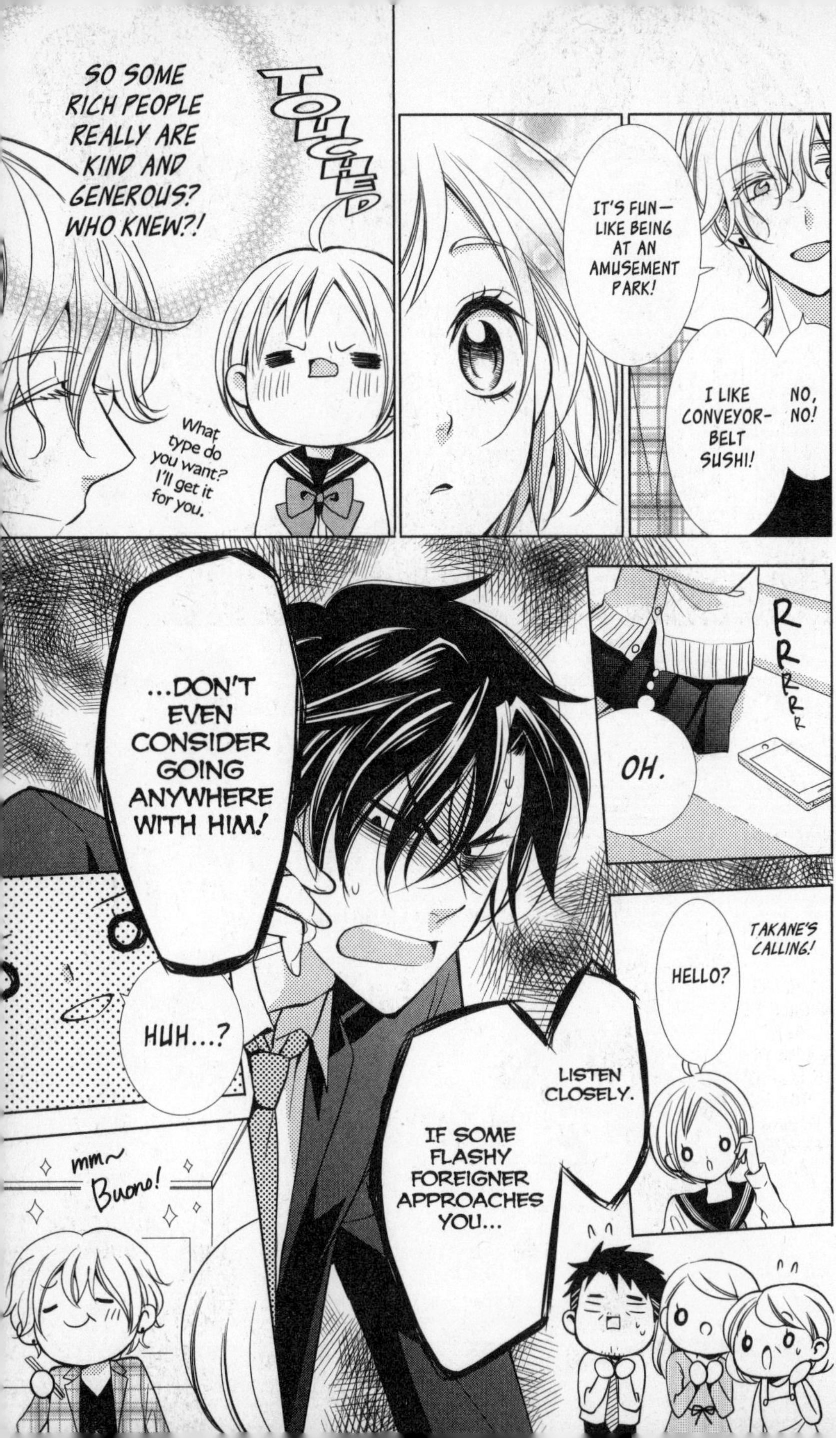

IT'S FUN—LIKE BEING AT AN AMUSEMENT PARK!
NO, NO!
I LIKE CONVEYOR-BELT SUSHI!
TOUCHED
SO SOME RICH PEOPLE REALLY ARE KIND AND GENEROUS? WHO KNEW?!
What type do you want? I'll get it for you.
RRRRR
OH.
TAKANE'S CALLING!
HELLO?
LISTEN CLOSELY.
IF SOME FLASHY FOREIGNER APPROACHES YOU...
...DON'T EVEN CONSIDER GOING ANYWHERE WITH HIM!
HUH...?
mm~ Buono!

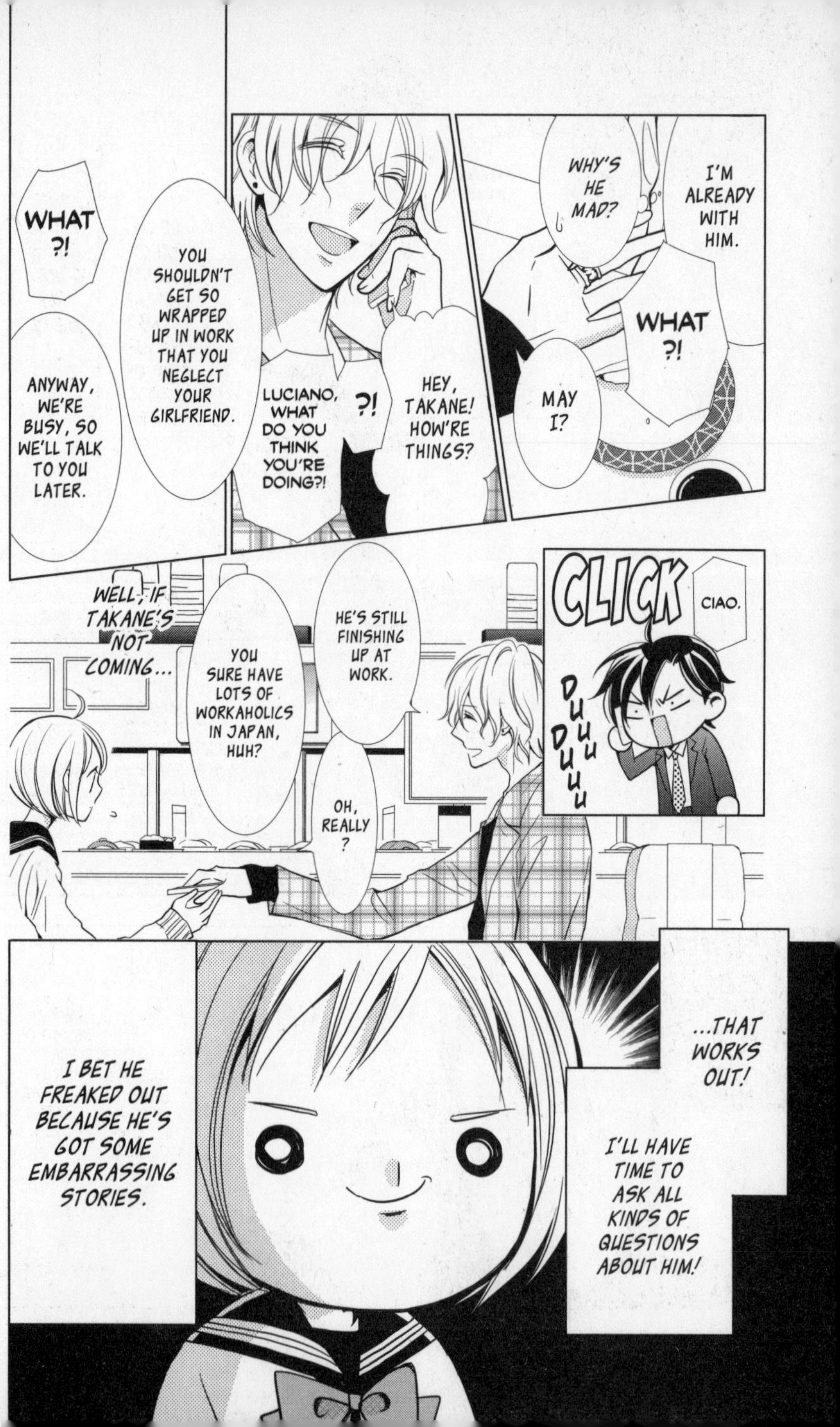
I'M ALREADY WITH HIM.
WHY'S HE MAD?
WHAT ?!
MAY I?
HEY, TAKANE! HOW'RE THINGS?
?!
LUCIANO, WHAT DO YOU THINK YOU'RE DOING?!
YOU SHOULDN'T GET SO WRAPPED UP IN WORK THAT YOU NEGLECT YOUR GIRLFRIEND.
WHAT ?!
ANYWAY, WE'RE BUSY, SO WE'LL TALK TO YOU LATER.
CLICK
CIAO.
DUUU DUUU
HE'S STILL FINISHING UP AT WORK.
OH, REALLY ?
YOU SURE HAVE LOTS OF WORKAHOLICS IN JAPAN, HUH?
WELL, IF TAKANE'S NOT COMING...
...THAT WORKS OUT!
I'LL HAVE TIME TO ASK ALL KINDS OF QUESTIONS ABOUT HIM!
I BET HE FREAKED OUT BECAUSE HE'S GOT SOME EMBARRASSING STORIES.

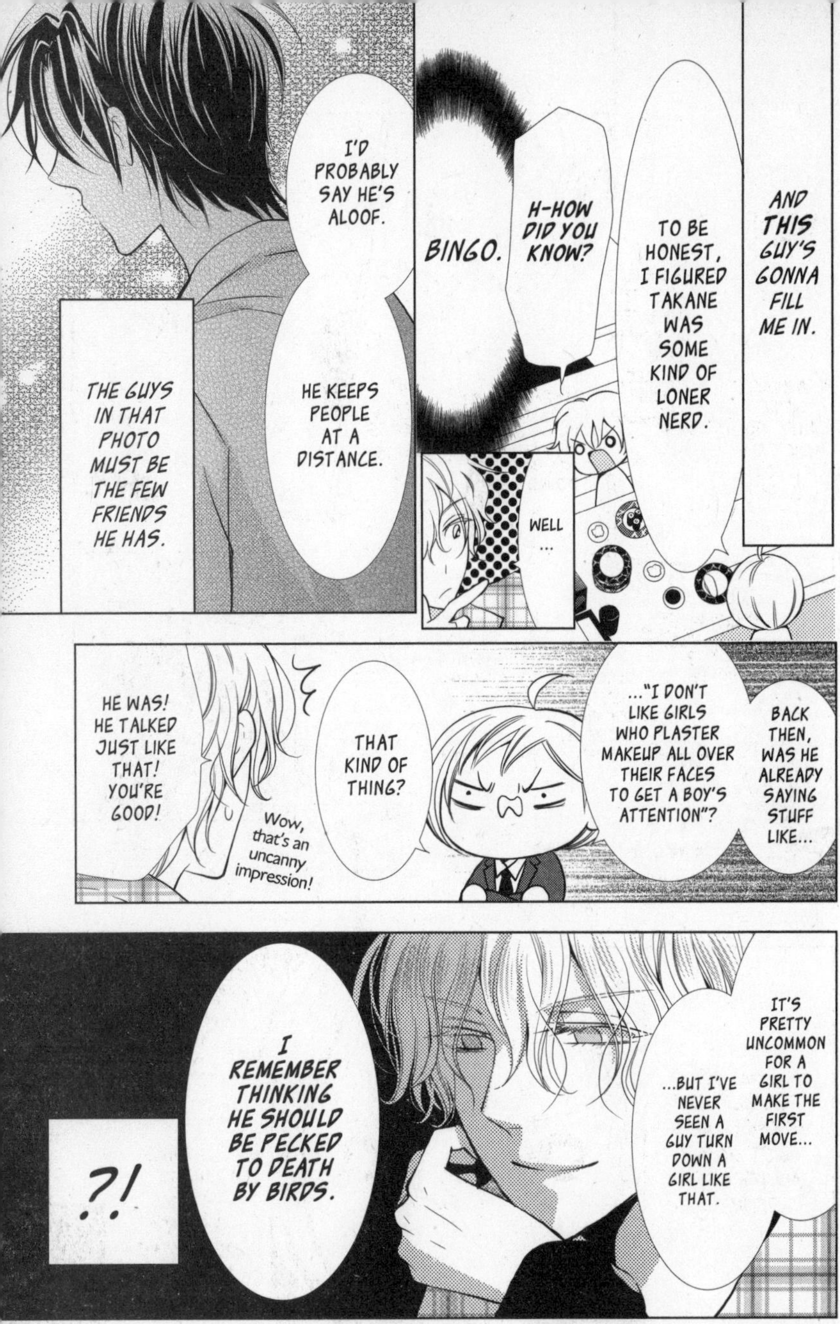
AND THIS GUY'S GONNA FILL ME IN.
TO BE HONEST, I FIGURED TAKANE WAS SOME KIND OF LONER NERD.
H-HOW DID YOU KNOW?
BINGO.
WELL...
I'D PROBABLY SAY HE'S ALOOF.
HE KEEPS PEOPLE AT A DISTANCE.
THE GUYS IN THAT PHOTO MUST BE THE FEW FRIENDS HE HAS.
BACK THEN, WAS HE ALREADY SAYING STUFF LIKE...
..."I DON'T LIKE GIRLS WHO PLASTER MAKEUP ALL OVER THEIR FACES TO GET A BOY'S ATTENTION"?
THAT KIND OF THING?
Wow, that's an uncanny impression!
HE WAS! HE TALKED JUST LIKE THAT! YOU'RE GOOD!
IT'S PRETTY UNCOMMON FOR A GIRL TO MAKE THE FIRST MOVE...
...BUT I'VE NEVER SEEN A GUY TURN DOWN A GIRL LIKE THAT.
I REMEMBER THINKING HE SHOULD BE PECKED TO DEATH BY BIRDS.
?!

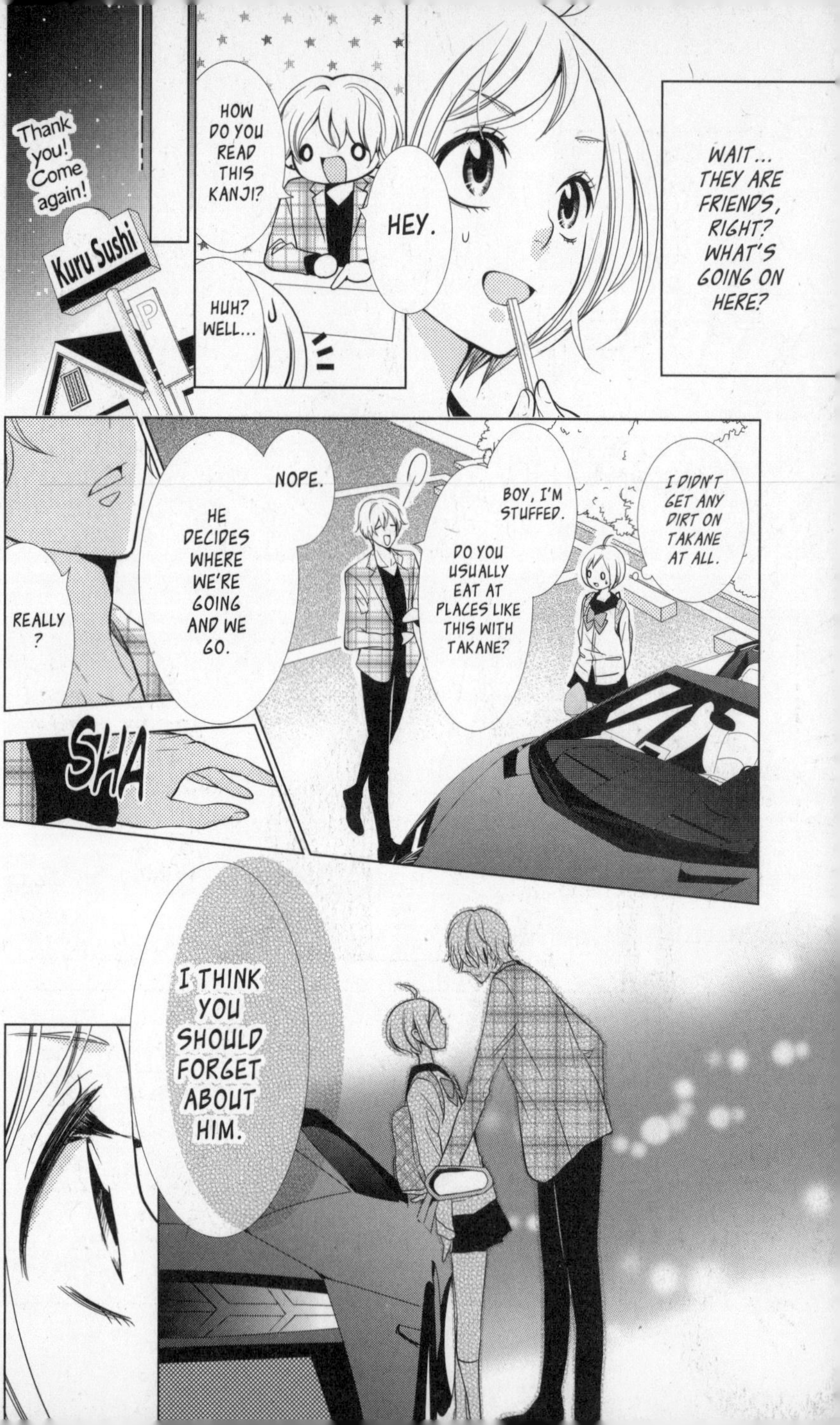
WAIT... THEY ARE FRIENDS, RIGHT? WHAT'S GOING ON HERE?
HEY.
HOW DO YOU READ THIS KANJI?
HUH? WELL...
Kuru Sushi
Thank you! Come again!
I DIDN'T GET ANY DIRT ON TAKANE AT ALL.
BOY, I'M STUFFED.
DO YOU USUALLY EAT AT PLACES LIKE THIS WITH TAKANE?
NOPE.
HE DECIDES WHERE WE'RE GOING AND WE GO.
REALLY?
SHA
I THINK YOU SHOULD FORGET ABOUT HIM.

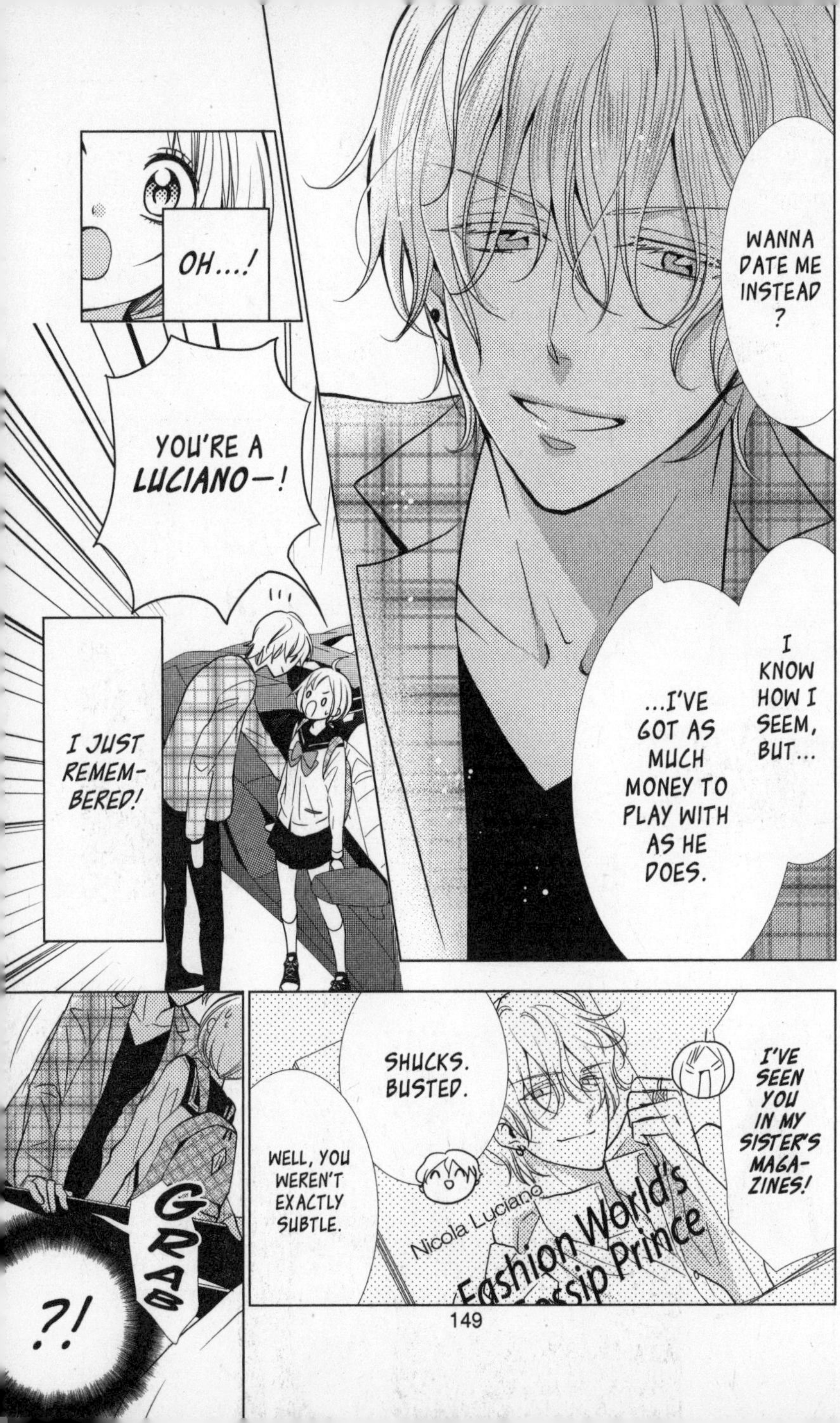
WANNA DATE ME INSTEAD ?
I KNOW HOW I SEEM, BUT...
...I'VE GOT AS MUCH MONEY TO PLAY WITH AS HE DOES.
OH...!
YOU'RE A LUCIANO—!
I JUST REMEMBERED!
I'VE SEEN YOU IN MY SISTER'S MAGAZINES!
SHUCKS. BUSTED.
WELL, YOU WEREN'T EXACTLY SUBTLE.
Nicola Luciano
Fashion World's Gossip Prince
GRAB
?!

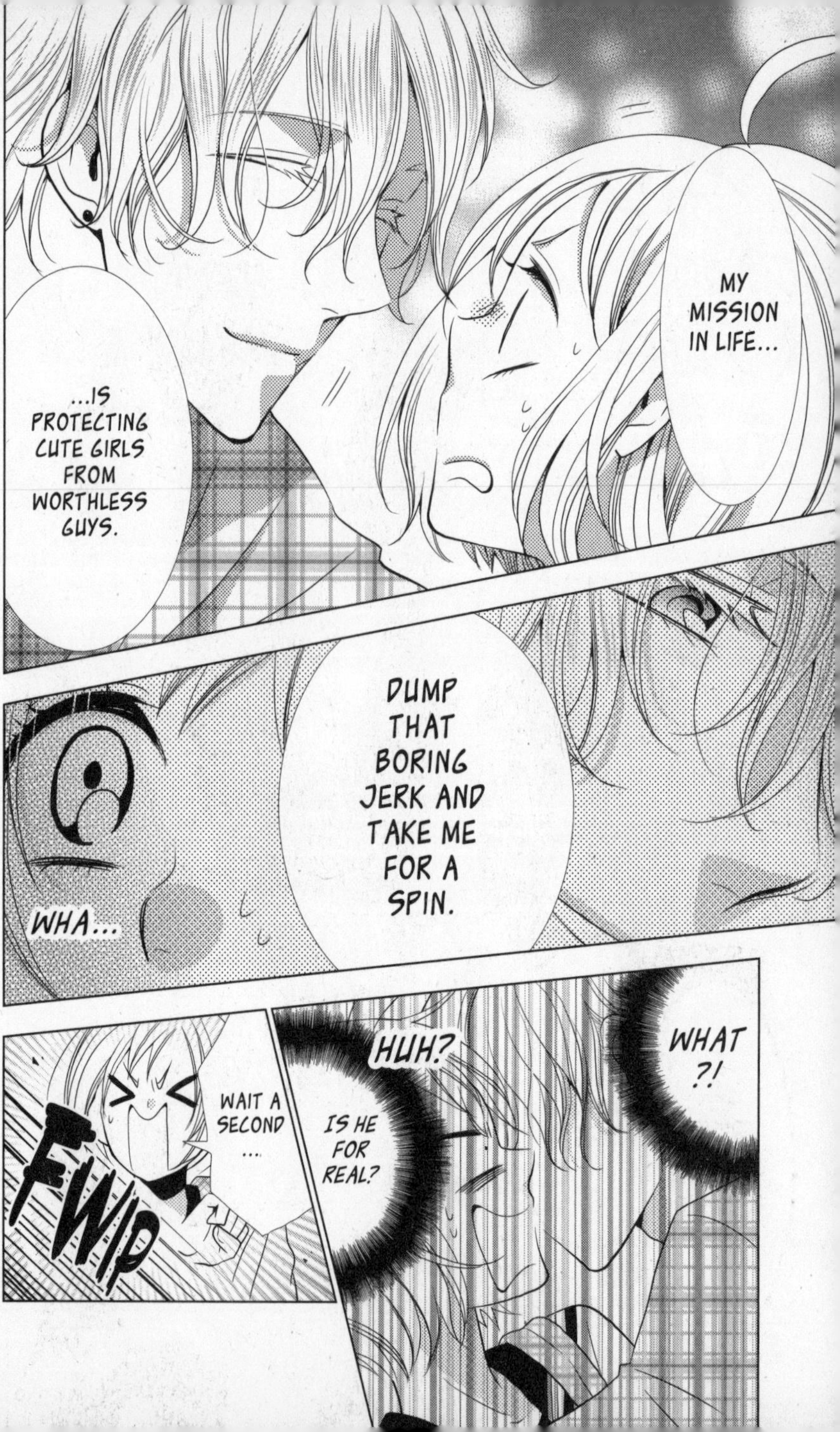
MY MISSION IN LIFE...
...IS PROTECTING CUTE GIRLS FROM WORTHLESS GUYS.
DUMP THAT BORING JERK AND TAKE ME FOR A SPIN.
WHA...
WHAT ?!
HUH?
IS HE FOR REAL?
WAIT A SECOND ....
FWIP

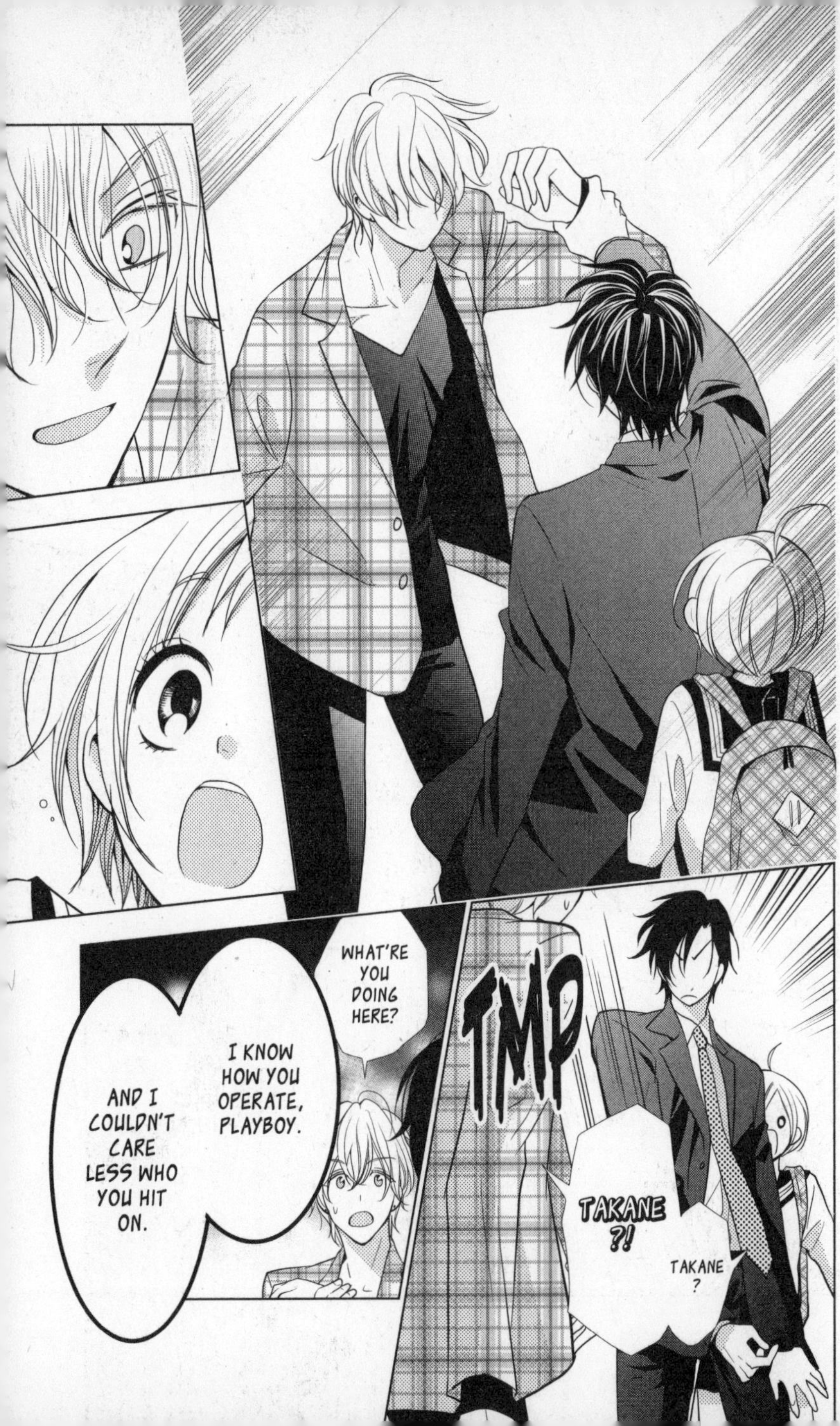
TMP
TAKANE ?!
TAKANE ?
WHAT'RE YOU DOING HERE?
I KNOW HOW YOU OPERATE, PLAYBOY.
AND I COULDN'T CARE LESS WHO YOU HIT ON.

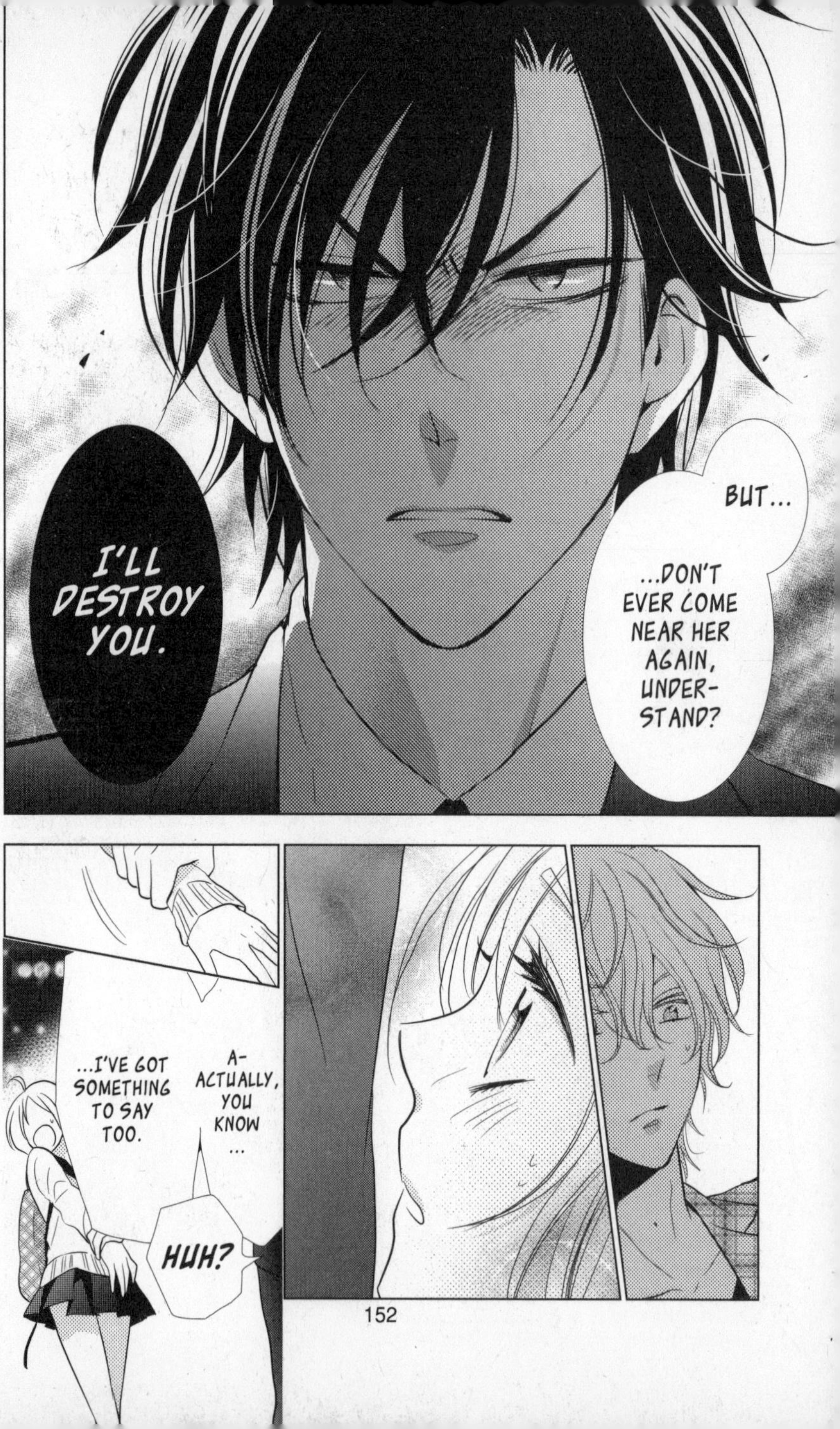
BUT...
...DON'T EVER COME NEAR HER AGAIN, UNDER-STAND?
I'LL DESTROY YOU.
A-ACTUALLY, YOU KNOW ...
...I'VE GOT SOMETHING TO SAY TOO.
HUH?

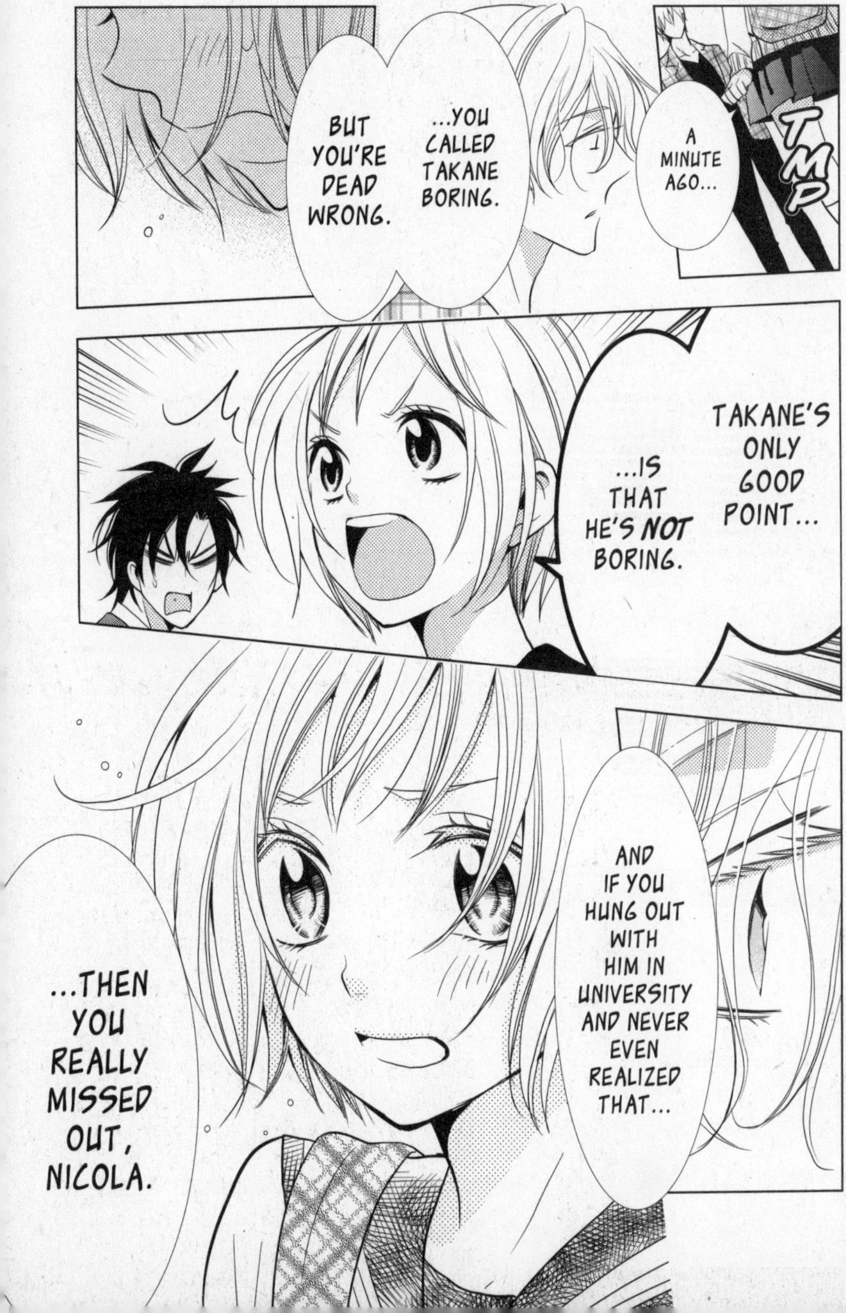
A MINUTE AGO...
TMP
...YOU CALLED TAKANE BORING.
BUT YOU'RE DEAD WRONG.
TAKANE'S ONLY GOOD POINT...
...IS THAT HE'S **NOT** BORING.
AND IF YOU HUNG OUT WITH HIM IN UNIVERSITY AND NEVER EVEN REALIZED THAT...
...THEN YOU REALLY MISSED OUT, NICOLA.

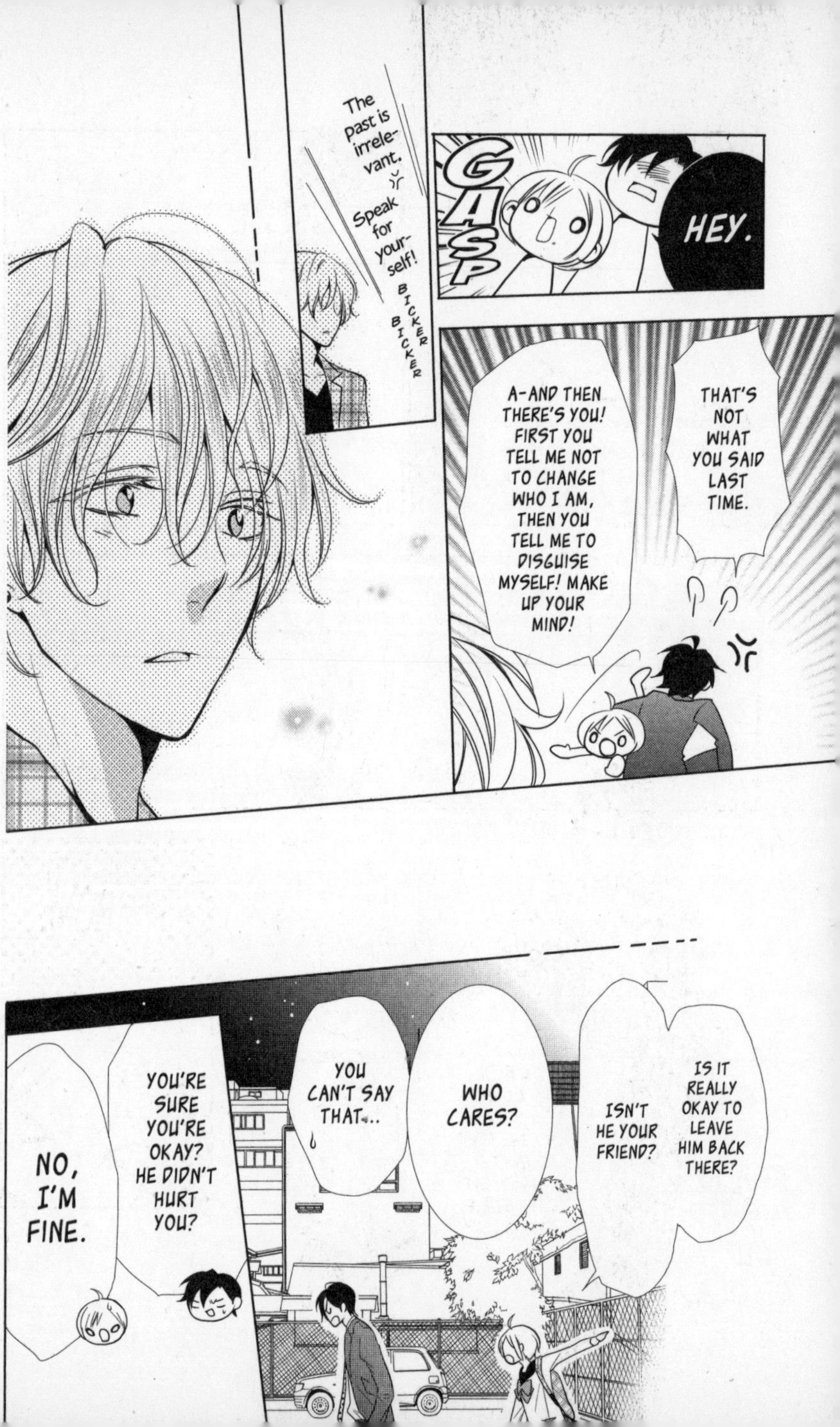
HEY.
GASP
THAT'S NOT WHAT YOU SAID LAST TIME.
A-AND THEN THERE'S YOU! FIRST YOU TELL ME NOT TO CHANGE WHO I AM, THEN YOU TELL ME TO DISGUISE MYSELF! MAKE UP YOUR MIND!
The past is irrele-vant.
Speak for your-self!
BICKER BICKER
IS IT REALLY OKAY TO LEAVE HIM BACK THERE?
ISN'T HE YOUR FRIEND?
WHO CARES?
YOU CAN'T SAY THAT...
YOU'RE SURE YOU'RE OKAY? HE DIDN'T HURT YOU?
NO, I'M FINE.

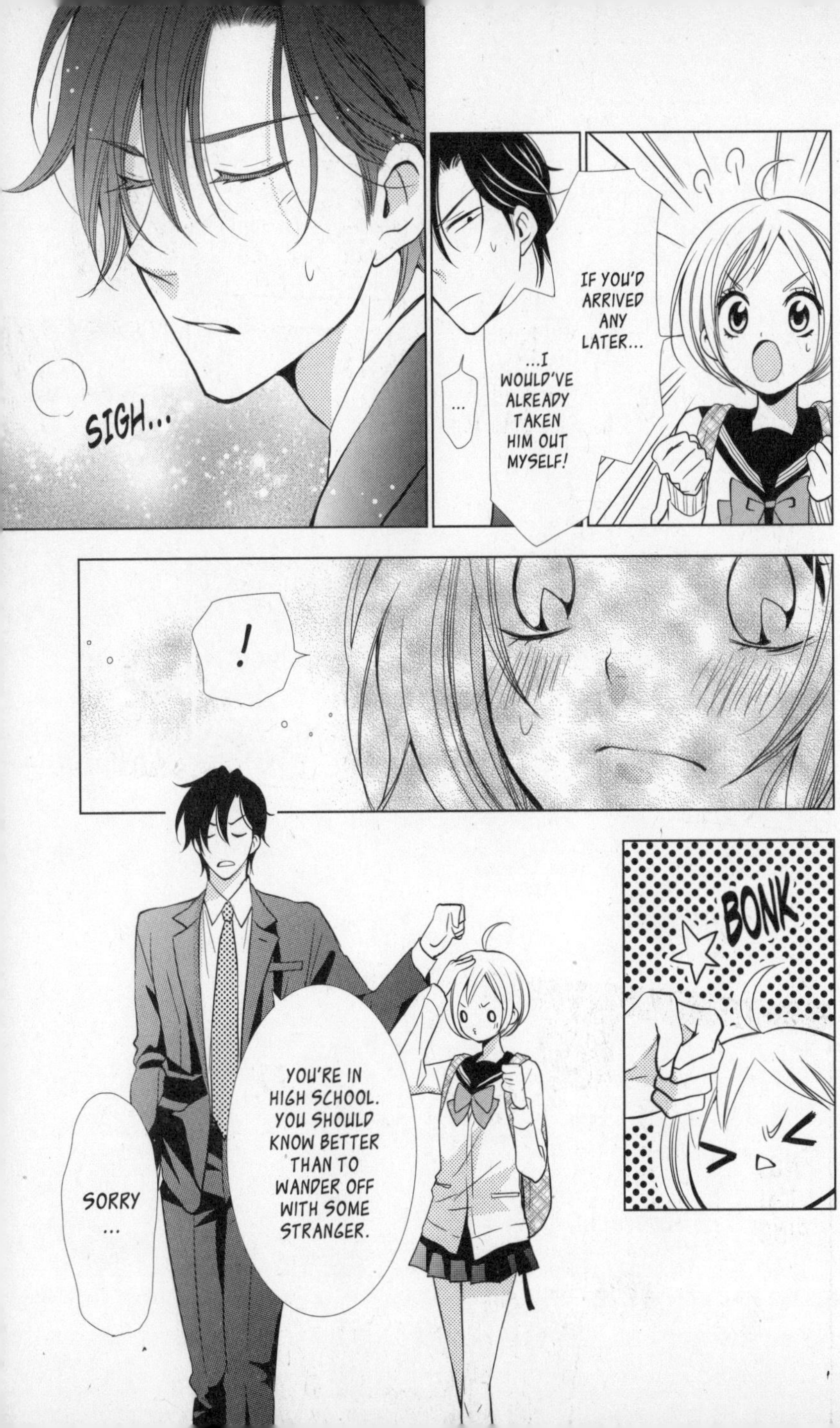
IF YOU'D ARRIVED ANY LATER...
...I WOULD'VE ALREADY TAKEN HIM OUT MYSELF!
...
SIGH...
!
BONK
YOU'RE IN HIGH SCHOOL. YOU SHOULD KNOW BETTER THAN TO WANDER OFF WITH SOME STRANGER.
SORRY...

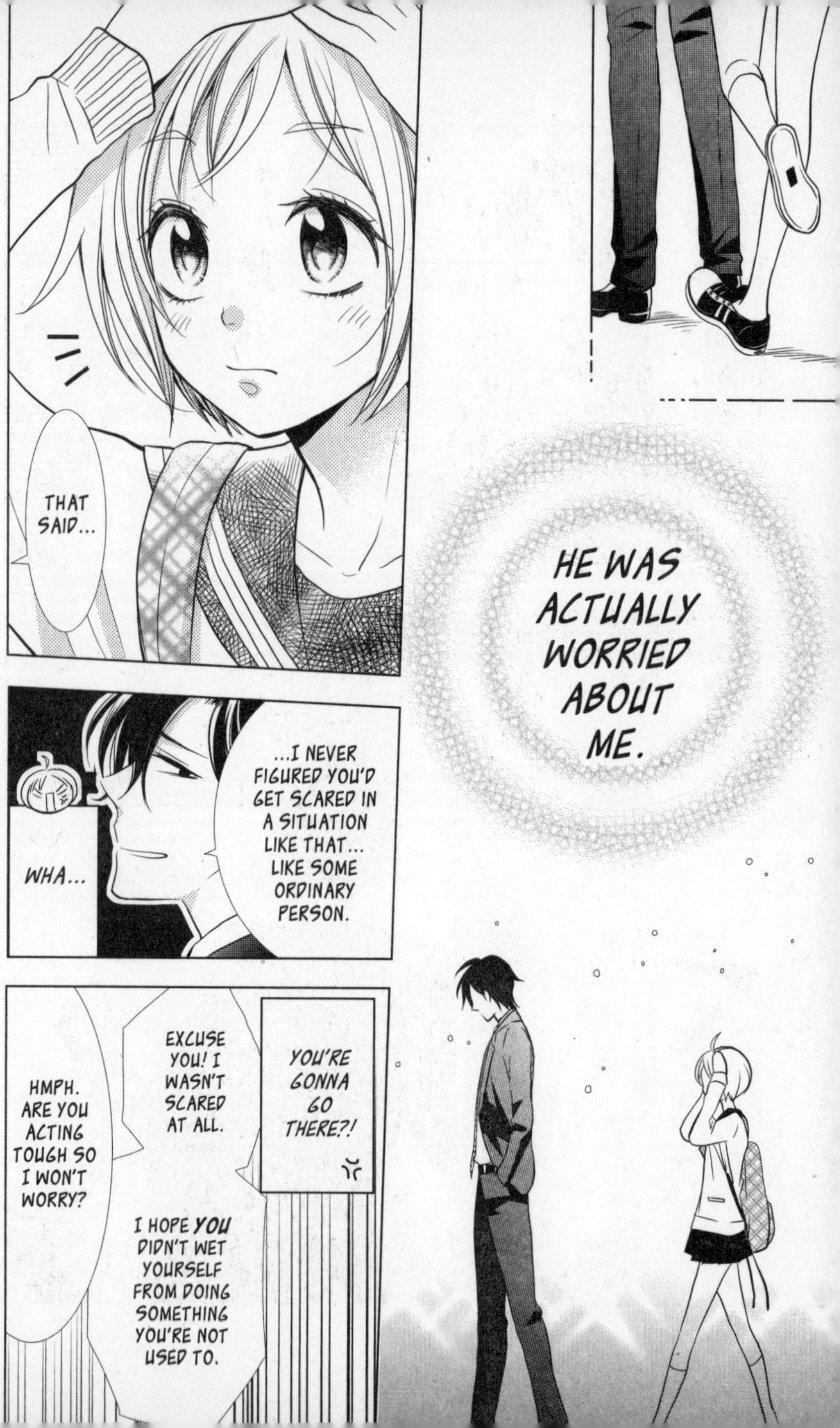

THAT SAID...
...I NEVER FIGURED YOU'D GET SCARED IN A SITUATION LIKE THAT... LIKE SOME ORDINARY PERSON.
WHA...
EXCUSE YOU! I WASN'T SCARED AT ALL.
HMPH. ARE YOU ACTING TOUGH SO I WON'T WORRY?
YOU'RE GONNA GO THERE?!
I HOPE YOU DIDN'T WET YOURSELF FROM DOING SOMETHING YOU'RE NOT USED TO.
HE WAS ACTUALLY WORRIED ABOUT ME.

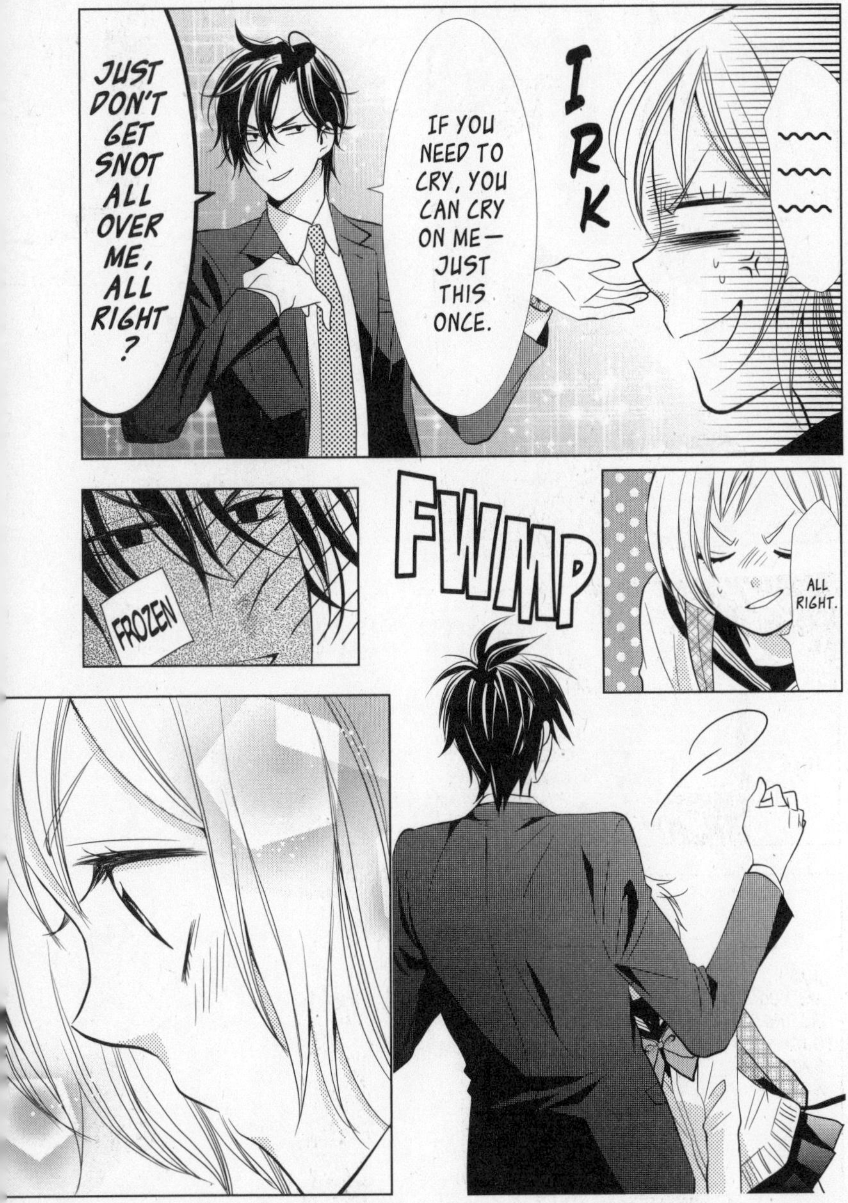
IRK
IF YOU NEED TO CRY, YOU CAN CRY ON ME—JUST THIS ONCE.
JUST DON'T GET SNOT ALL OVER ME, ALL RIGHT?
ALL RIGHT.
FWMP
FROZEN

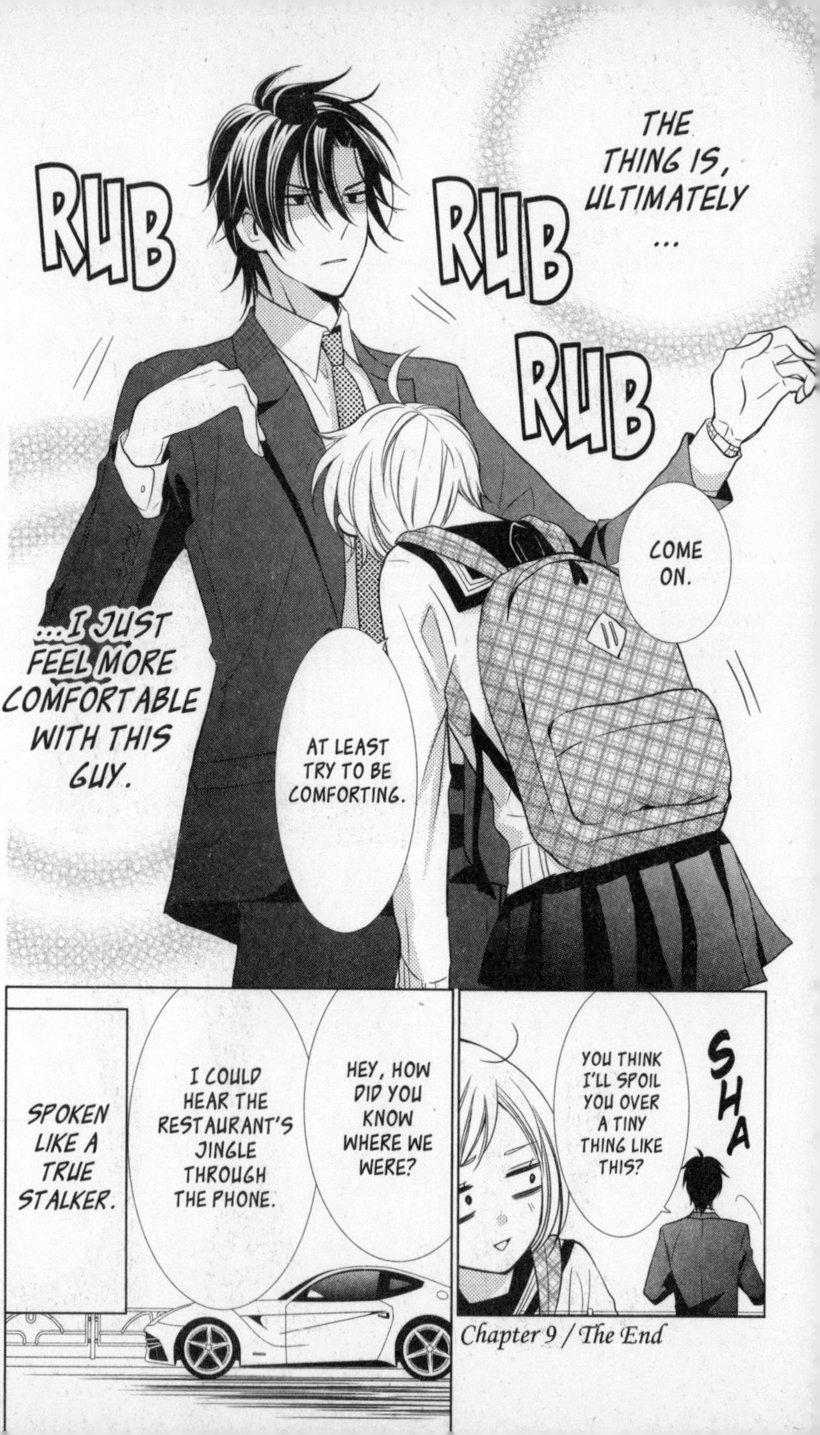
THE THING IS, ULTIMATELY ...
RUB
RUB
RUB
COME ON.
AT LEAST TRY TO BE COMFORTING.
...I JUST FEEL MORE COMFORTABLE WITH THIS GUY.
SHA
YOU THINK I'LL SPOIL YOU OVER A TINY THING LIKE THIS?
HEY, HOW DID YOU KNOW WHERE WE WERE?
I COULD HEAR THE RESTAURANT'S JINGLE THROUGH THE PHONE.
SPOKEN LIKE A TRUE STALKER.

Chapter 9 / The End

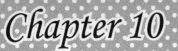

Chapter 10

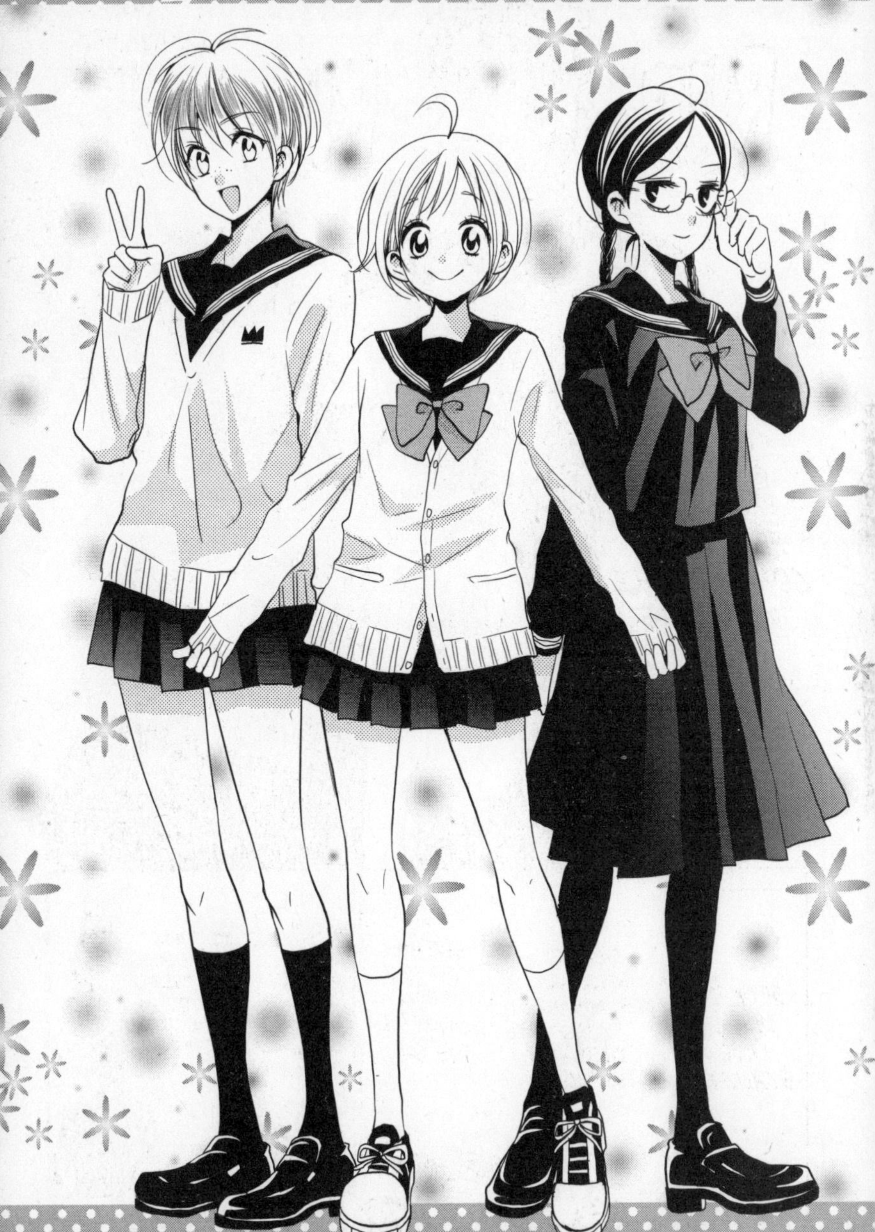

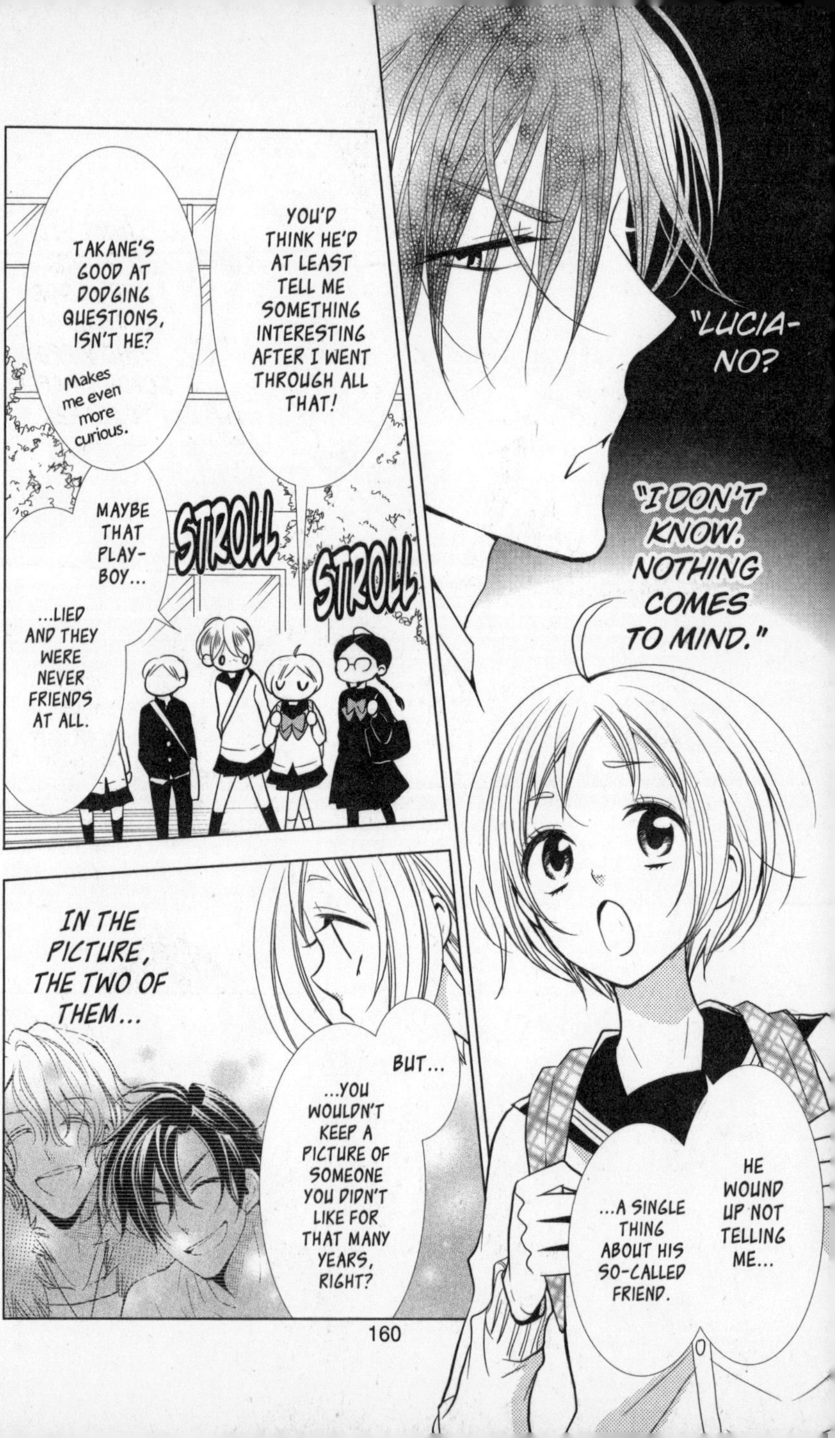
"LUCIA-NO?
"I DON'T KNOW. NOTHING COMES TO MIND."
HE WOUND UP NOT TELLING ME...
...A SINGLE THING ABOUT HIS SO-CALLED FRIEND.
YOU'D THINK HE'D AT LEAST TELL ME SOMETHING INTERESTING AFTER I WENT THROUGH ALL THAT!
TAKANE'S GOOD AT DODGING QUESTIONS, ISN'T HE?
Makes me even more curious.
STROLL
STROLL
MAYBE THAT PLAY-BOY...
...LIED AND THEY WERE NEVER FRIENDS AT ALL.
BUT...
...YOU WOULDN'T KEEP A PICTURE OF SOMEONE YOU DIDN'T LIKE FOR THAT MANY YEARS, RIGHT?
IN THE PICTURE, THE TWO OF THEM...

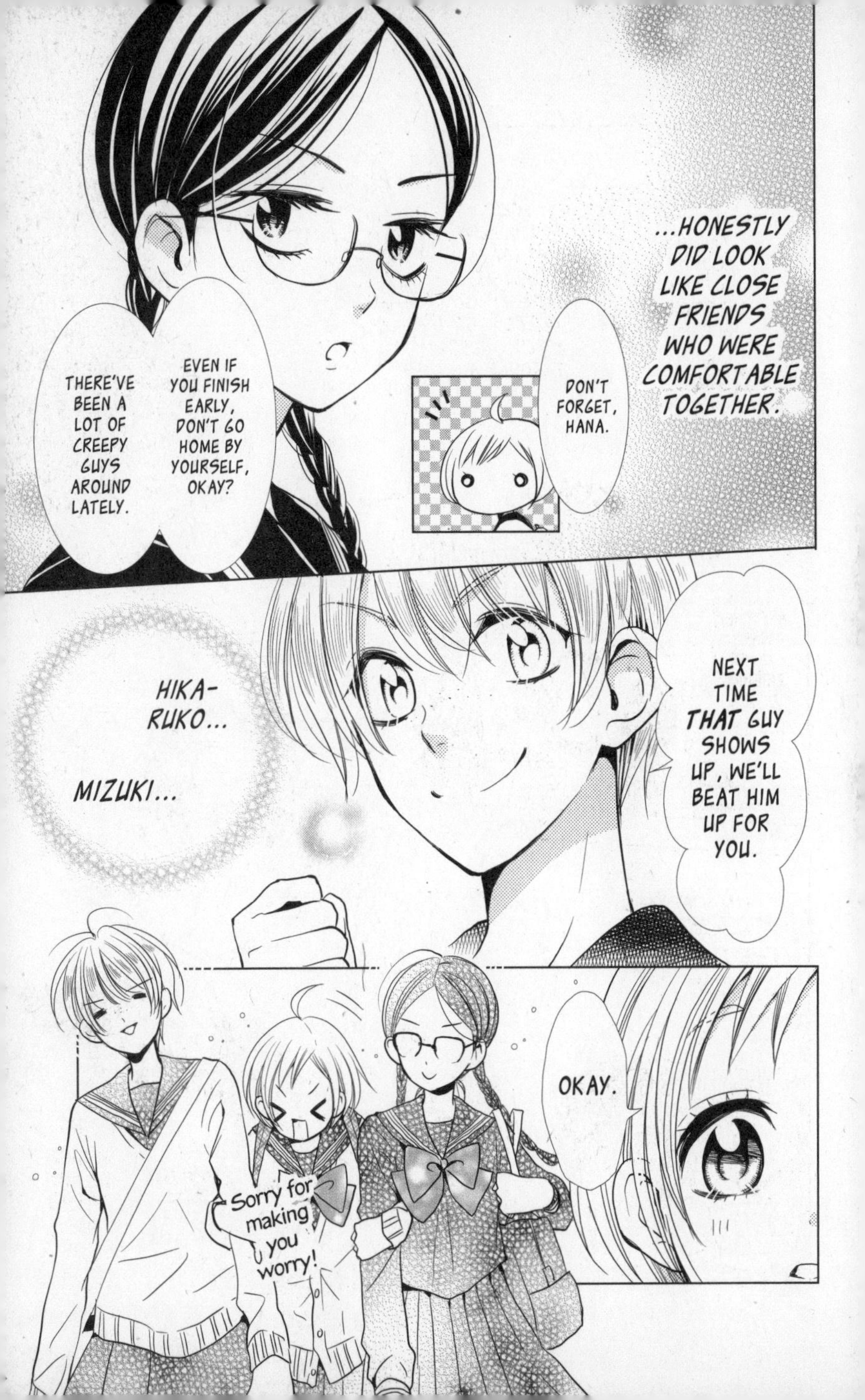
...HONESTLY DID LOOK LIKE CLOSE FRIENDS WHO WERE COMFORTABLE TOGETHER.
DON'T FORGET, HANA.
EVEN IF YOU FINISH EARLY, DON'T GO HOME BY YOURSELF, OKAY?
THERE'VE BEEN A LOT OF CREEPY GUYS AROUND LATELY.
NEXT TIME *THAT* GUY SHOWS UP, WE'LL BEAT HIM UP FOR YOU.
HIKA-RUKO...
MIZUKI...
OKAY.
Sorry for making you worry!

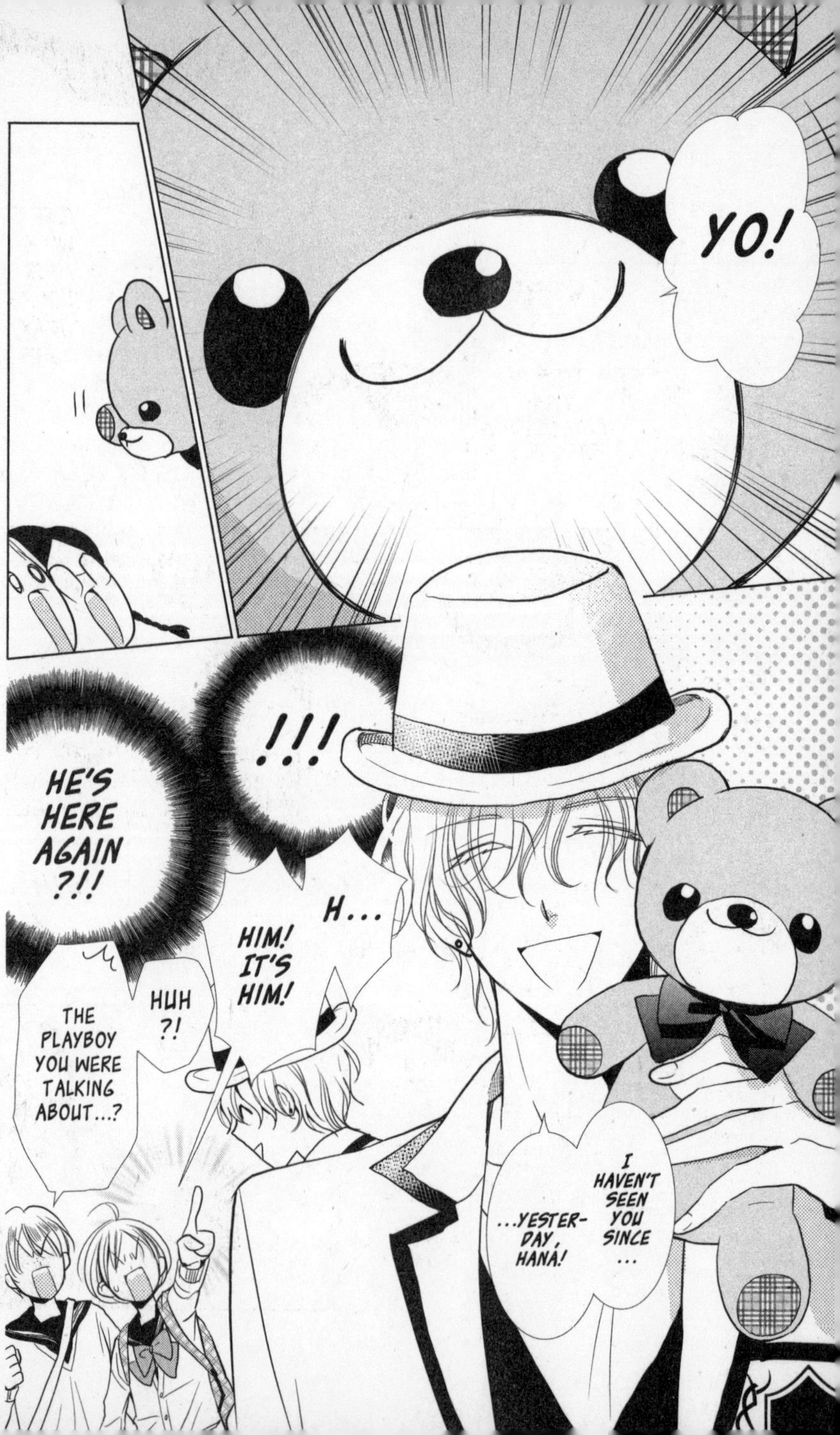
YO!
!!!
HE'S HERE AGAIN?!!
H...
HIM! IT'S HIM!
HUH?!
THE PLAYBOY YOU WERE TALKING ABOUT...?
I HAVEN'T SEEN YOU SINCE...
...YESTERDAY, HANA!

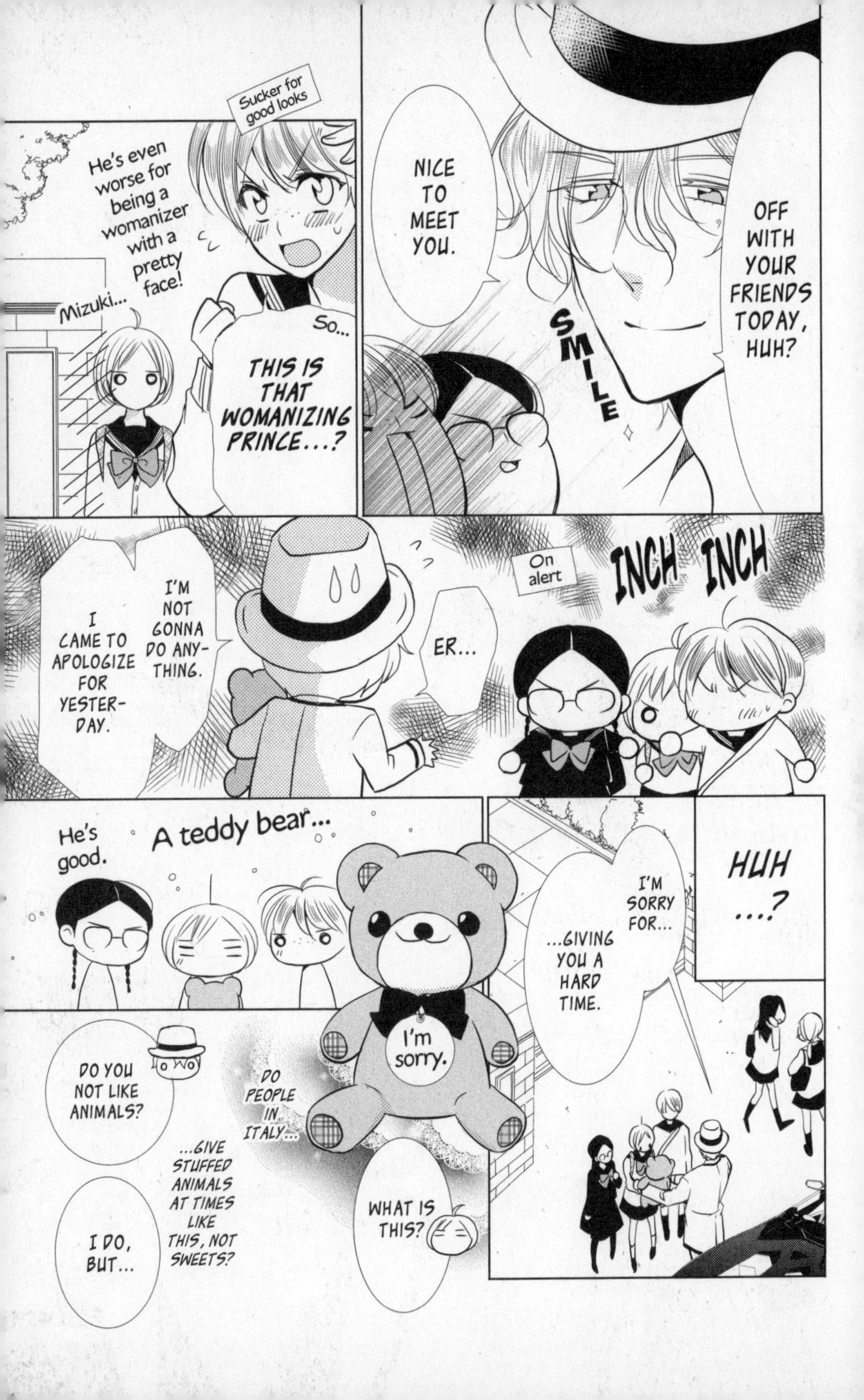
OFF WITH YOUR FRIENDS TODAY, HUH?
SMILE
NICE TO MEET YOU.
So...
THIS IS THAT WOMANIZING PRINCE...?
He's even worse for being a womanizer with a pretty face!
Sucker for good looks
Mizuki...
INCH INCH
On alert
ER...
I'M NOT GONNA DO ANYTHING.
I CAME TO APOLOGIZE FOR YESTERDAY.
HUH ...?
I'M SORRY FOR...
...GIVING YOU A HARD TIME.
A teddy bear...
He's good.
I'm sorry.
WHAT IS THIS?
DO PEOPLE IN ITALY...
...GIVE STUFFED ANIMALS AT TIMES LIKE THIS, NOT SWEETS?
DO YOU NOT LIKE ANIMALS?
I DO, BUT...

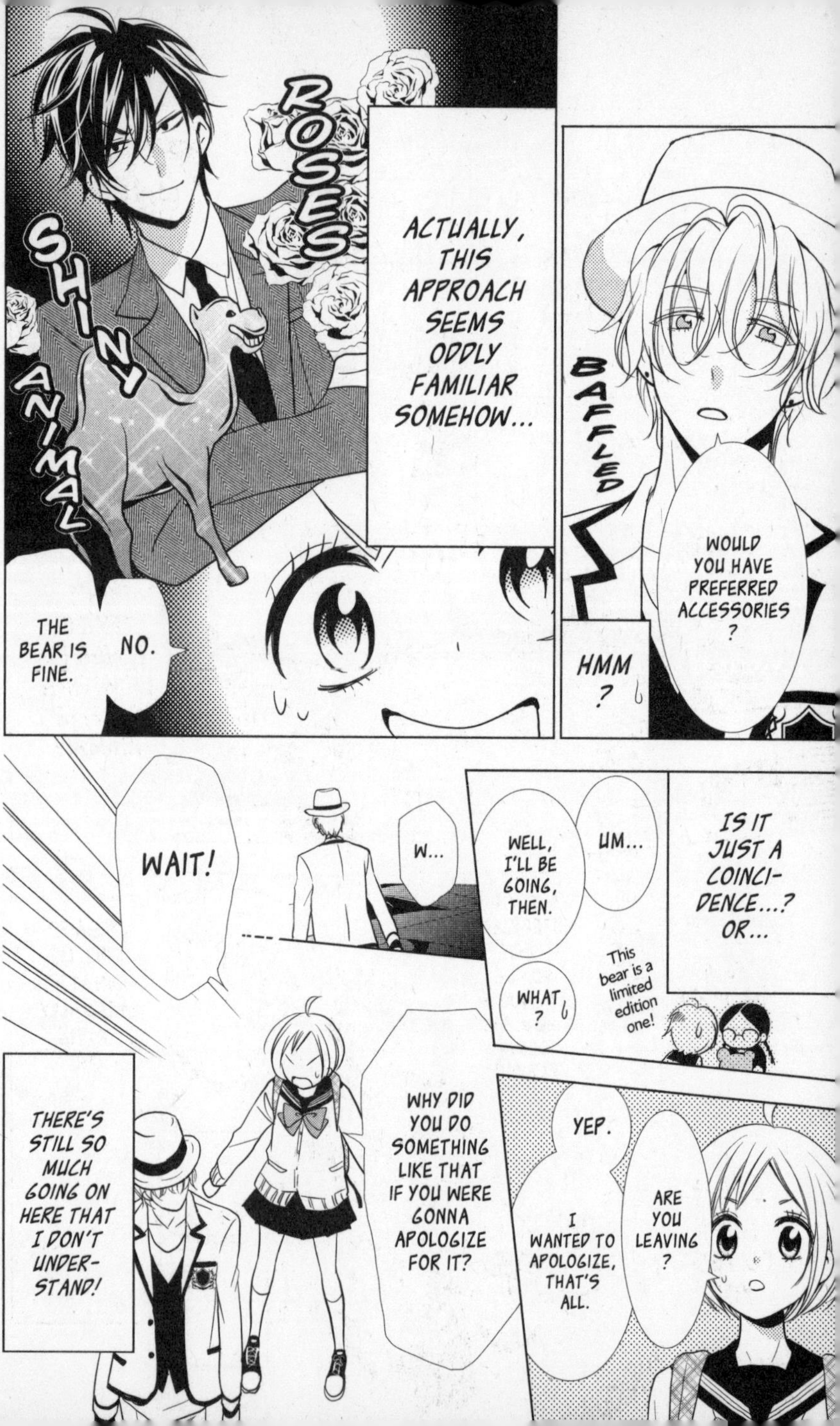
BAFFLED
WOULD YOU HAVE PREFERRED ACCESSORIES?
HMM?
ROSES
ACTUALLY, THIS APPROACH SEEMS ODDLY FAMILIAR SOMEHOW...
SHINY ANIMAL
NO.
THE BEAR IS FINE.
IS IT JUST A COINCIDENCE...? OR...
This bear is a limited edition one!
UM...
WELL, I'LL BE GOING, THEN.
WHAT?
W...
WAIT!
ARE YOU LEAVING?
YEP.
I WANTED TO APOLOGIZE, THAT'S ALL.
WHY DID YOU DO SOMETHING LIKE THAT IF YOU WERE GONNA APOLOGIZE FOR IT?
THERE'S STILL SO MUCH GOING ON HERE THAT I DON'T UNDERSTAND!

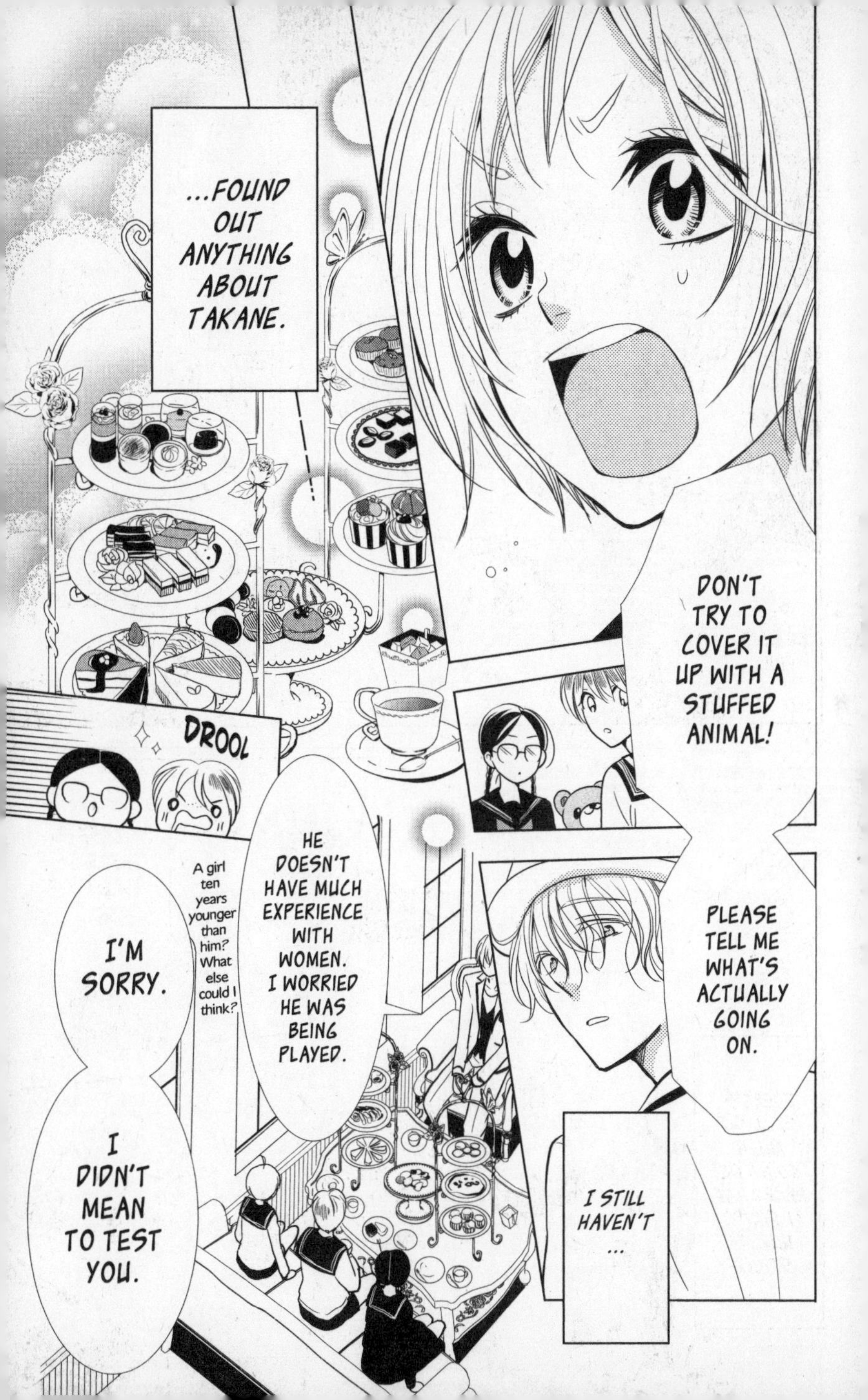
DON'T TRY TO COVER IT UP WITH A STUFFED ANIMAL!
PLEASE TELL ME WHAT'S ACTUALLY GOING ON.
I STILL HAVEN'T ...
...FOUND OUT ANYTHING ABOUT TAKANE.
DROOL
HE DOESN'T HAVE MUCH EXPERIENCE WITH WOMEN. I WORRIED HE WAS BEING PLAYED.
A girl ten years younger than him? What else could I think?
I'M SORRY.
I DIDN'T MEAN TO TEST YOU.

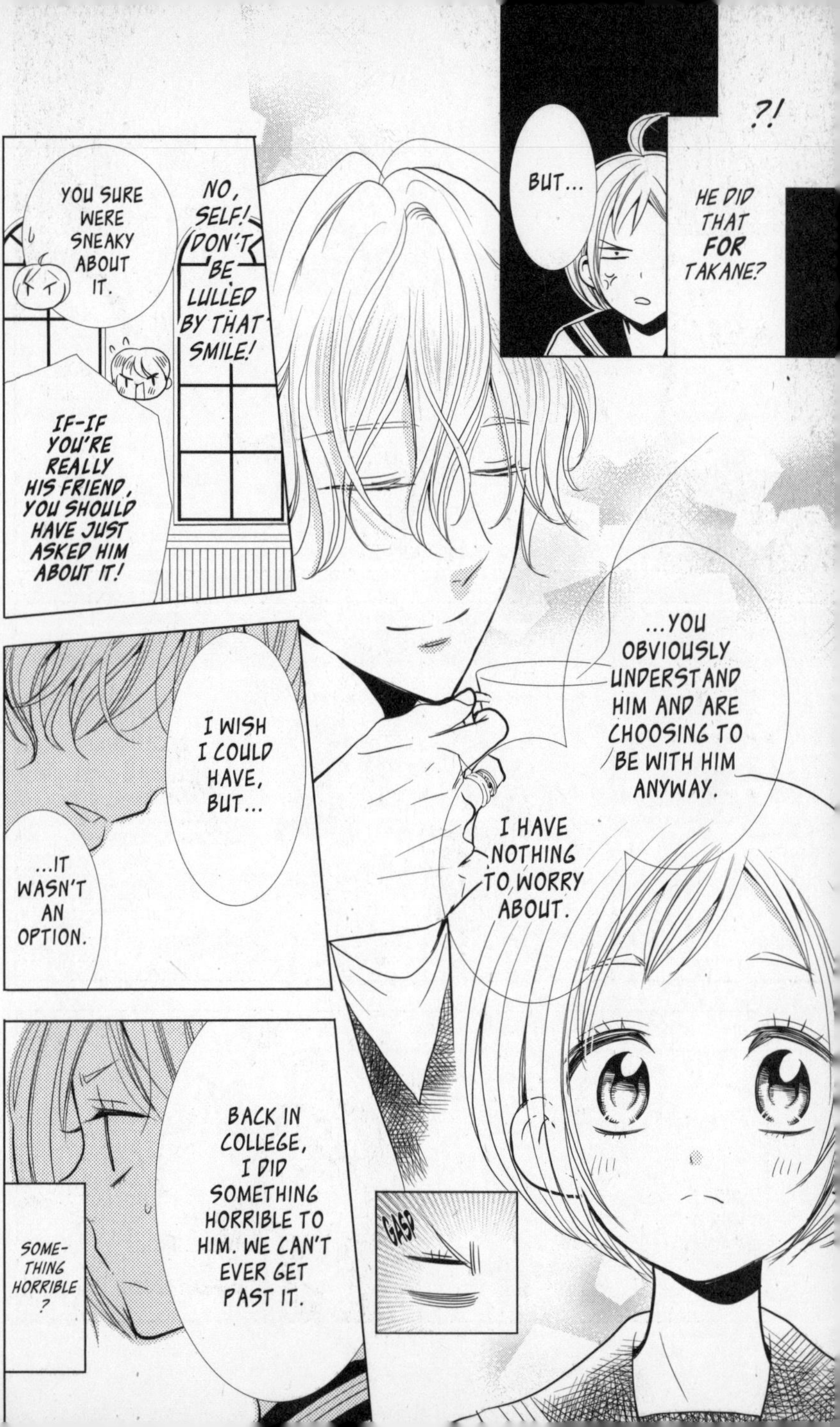
?!
HE DID THAT FOR TAKANE?
BUT...
...YOU OBVIOUSLY UNDERSTAND HIM AND ARE CHOOSING TO BE WITH HIM ANYWAY.
I HAVE NOTHING TO WORRY ABOUT.
NO, SELF! DON'T BE LULLED BY THAT SMILE!
YOU SURE WERE SNEAKY ABOUT IT.
IF-IF YOU'RE REALLY HIS FRIEND, YOU SHOULD HAVE JUST ASKED HIM ABOUT IT!
I WISH I COULD HAVE, BUT...
...IT WASN'T AN OPTION.
GASP
BACK IN COLLEGE, I DID SOMETHING HORRIBLE TO HIM. WE CAN'T EVER GET PAST IT.
SOME-THING HORRIBLE?

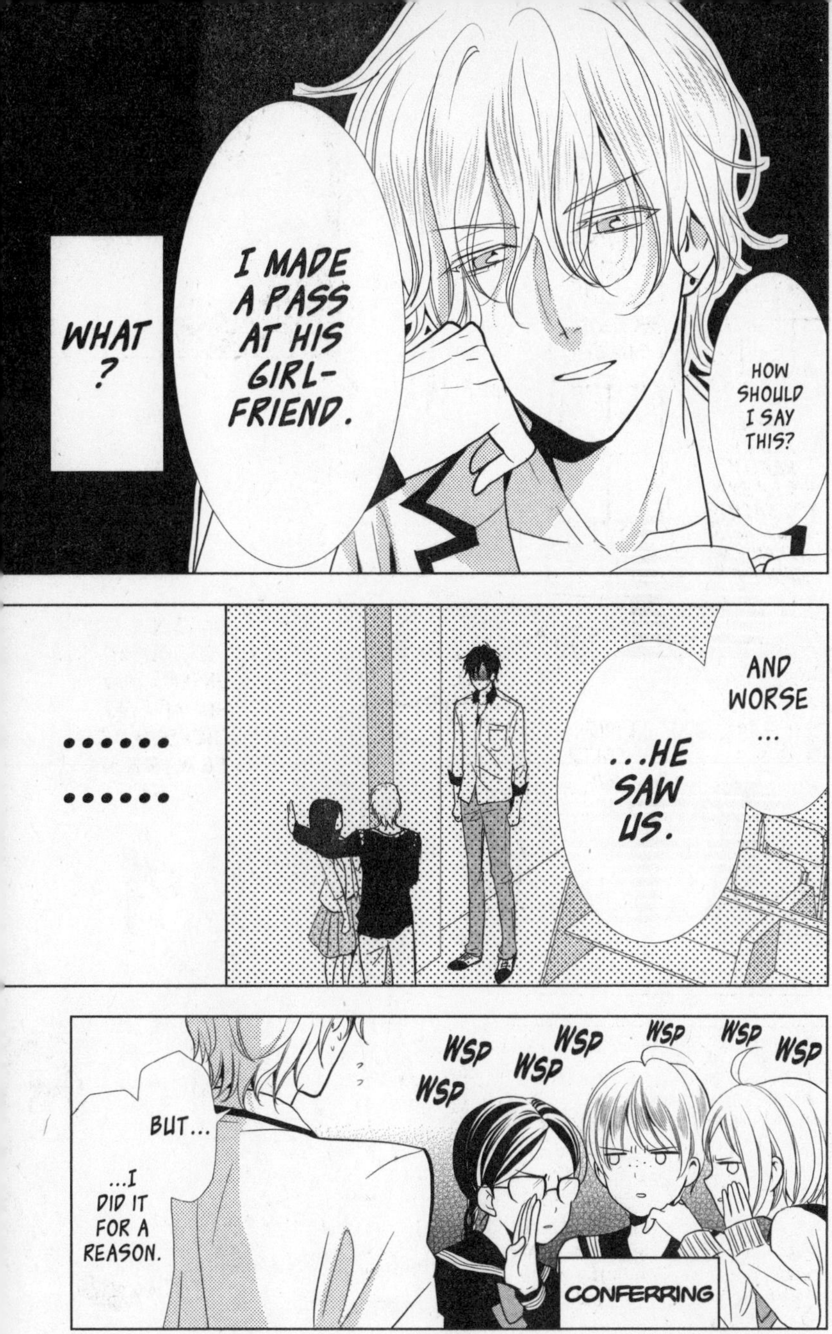
HOW SHOULD I SAY THIS?
I MADE A PASS AT HIS GIRL-FRIEND.
WHAT?
AND WORSE...
...HE SAW US.
....
WSP WSP WSP WSP WSP WSP WSP
BUT...
...I DID IT FOR A REASON.
CONFERRING

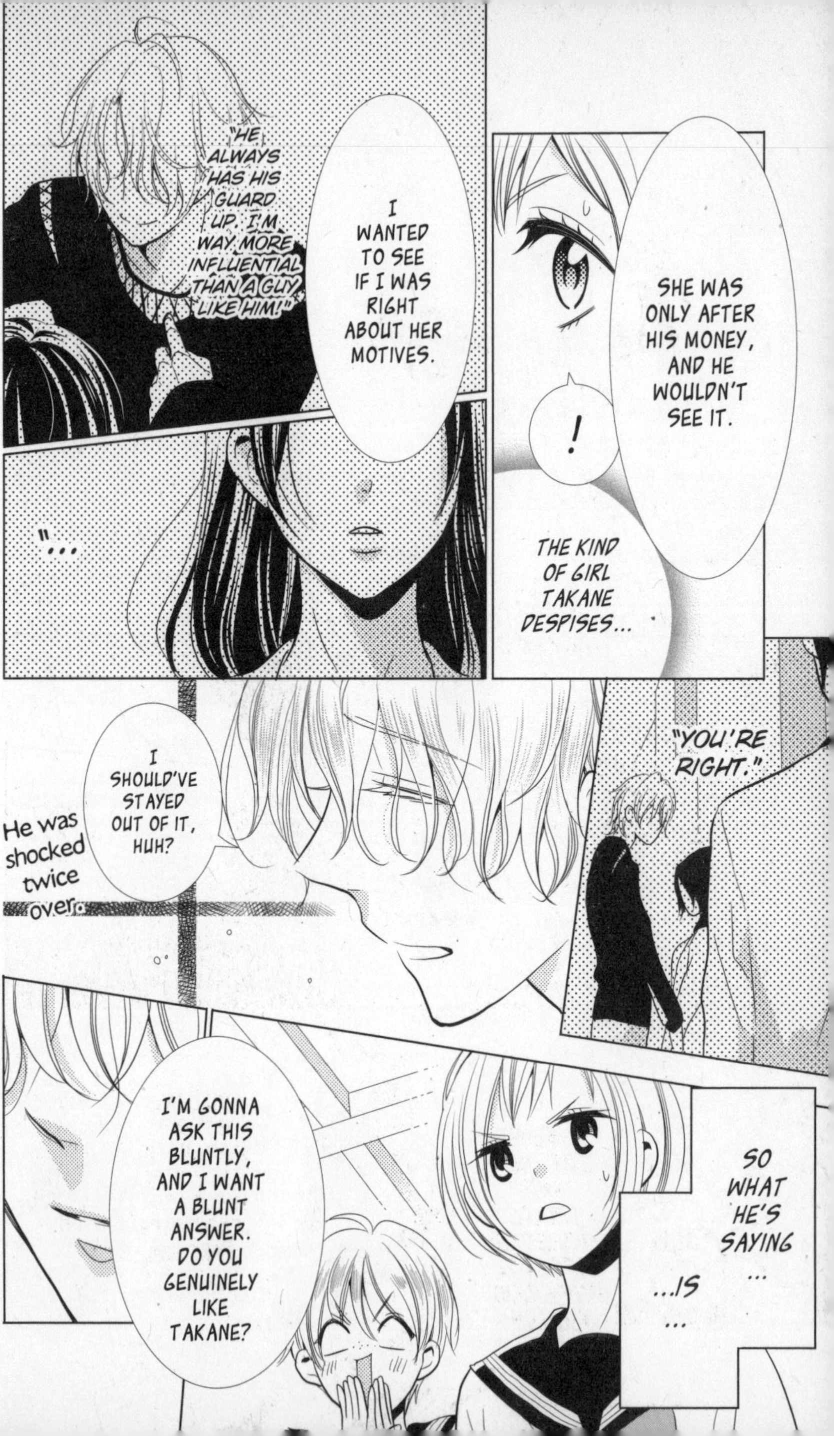
SHE WAS ONLY AFTER HIS MONEY, AND HE WOULDN'T SEE IT.
!
THE KIND OF GIRL TAKANE DESPISES...
I WANTED TO SEE IF I WAS RIGHT ABOUT HER MOTIVES.
"HE ALWAYS HAS HIS GUARD UP. I'M WAY MORE INFLUENTIAL THAN A GUY LIKE HIM!"
"...
"YOU'RE RIGHT."
I SHOULD'VE STAYED OUT OF IT, HUH?
He was shocked twice over.
SO WHAT HE'S SAYING ...
...IS ...
I'M GONNA ASK THIS BLUNTLY, AND I WANT A BLUNT ANSWER. DO YOU GENUINELY LIKE TAKANE?

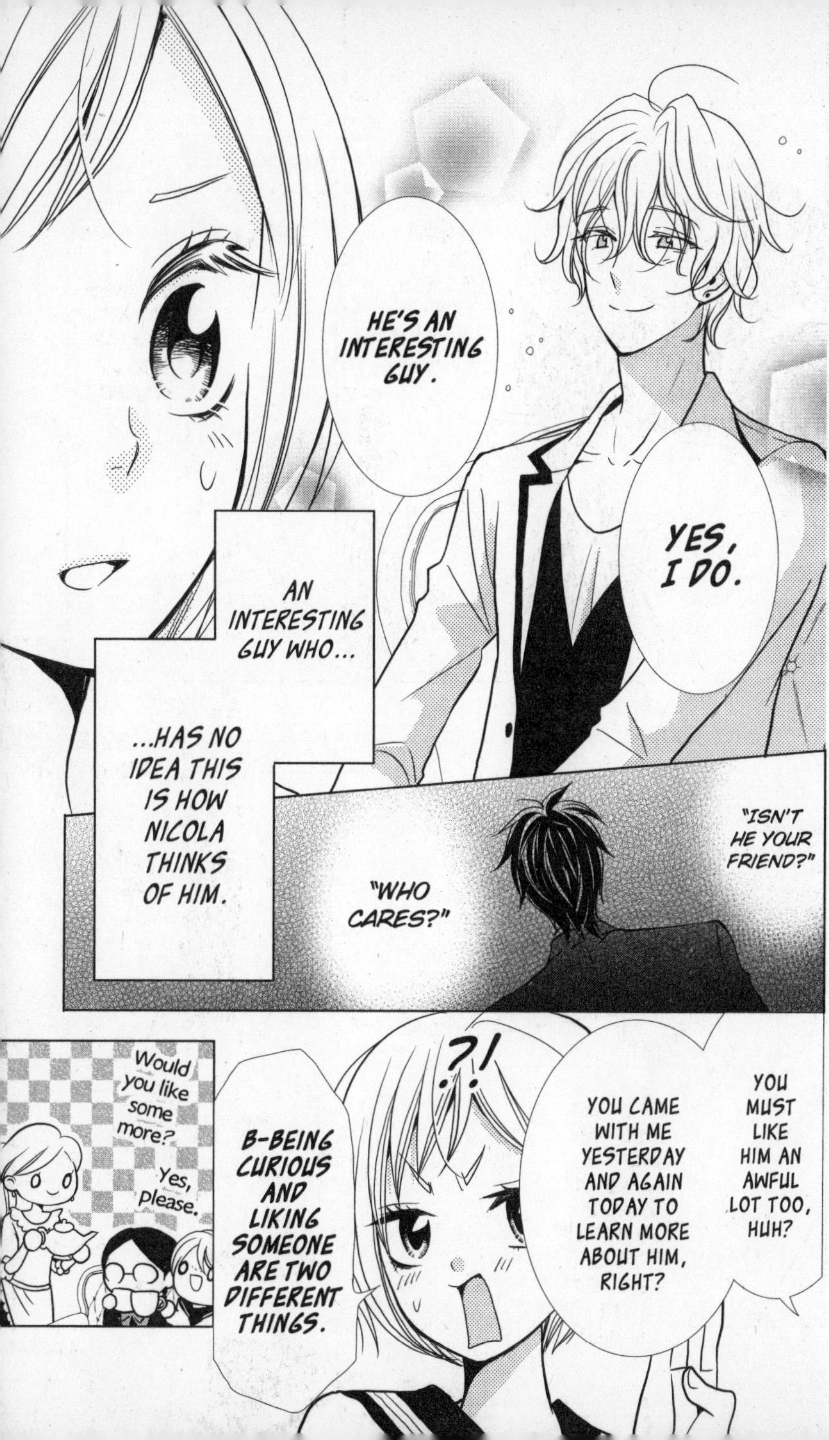
YES, I DO.
HE'S AN INTERESTING GUY.
AN INTERESTING GUY WHO...
...HAS NO IDEA THIS IS HOW NICOLA THINKS OF HIM.
"ISN'T HE YOUR FRIEND?"
"WHO CARES?"
YOU MUST LIKE HIM AN AWFUL LOT TOO, HUH?
YOU CAME WITH ME YESTERDAY AND AGAIN TODAY TO LEARN MORE ABOUT HIM, RIGHT?
?!
B-BEING CURIOUS AND LIKING SOMEONE ARE TWO DIFFERENT THINGS.
Would you like some more?
Yes, please.

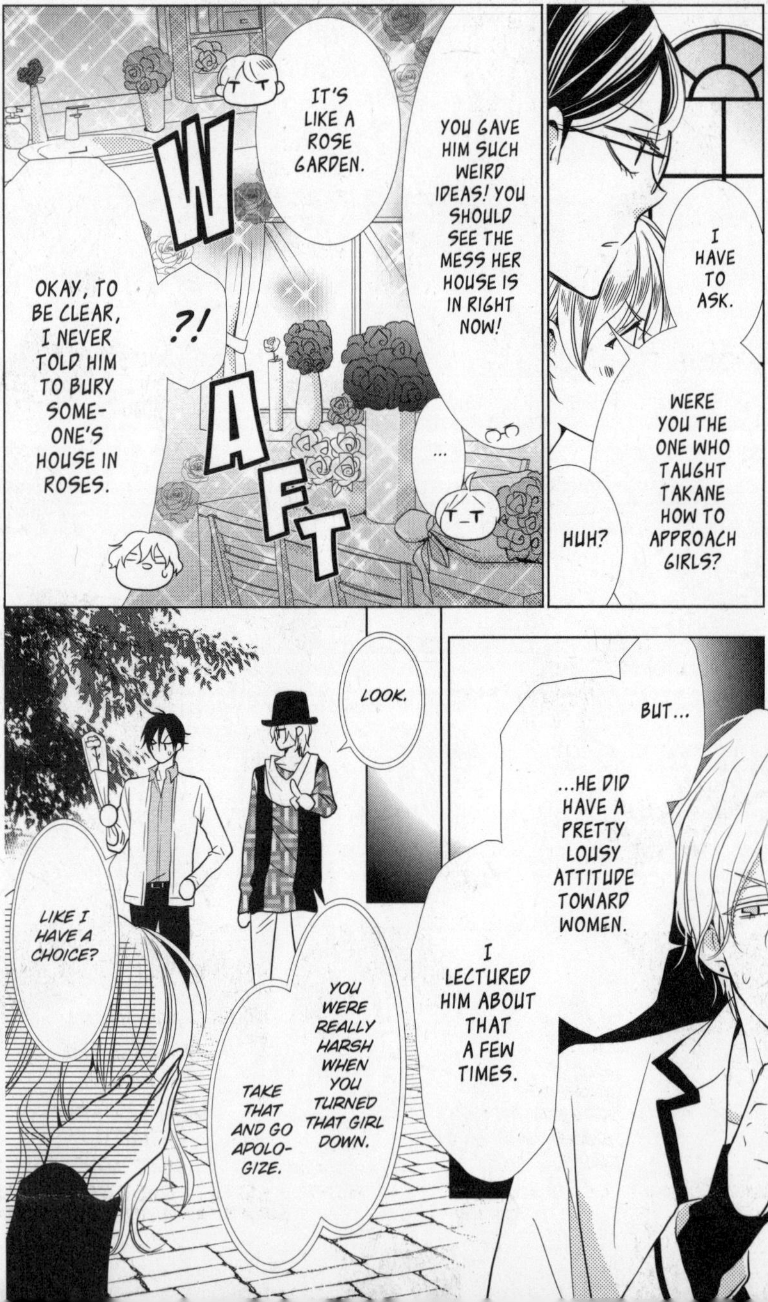
I HAVE TO ASK.
WERE YOU THE ONE WHO TAUGHT TAKANE HOW TO APPROACH GIRLS?
HUH?
YOU GAVE HIM SUCH WEIRD IDEAS! YOU SHOULD SEE THE MESS HER HOUSE IS IN RIGHT NOW!
IT'S LIKE A ROSE GARDEN.
...
WAFT
?!
OKAY, TO BE CLEAR, I NEVER TOLD HIM TO BURY SOME-ONE'S HOUSE IN ROSES.
BUT...
...HE DID HAVE A PRETTY LOUSY ATTITUDE TOWARD WOMEN.
I LECTURED HIM ABOUT THAT A FEW TIMES.
LOOK.
YOU WERE REALLY HARSH WHEN YOU TURNED THAT GIRL DOWN.
TAKE THAT AND GO APOLO-GIZE.
LIKE I HAVE A CHOICE?

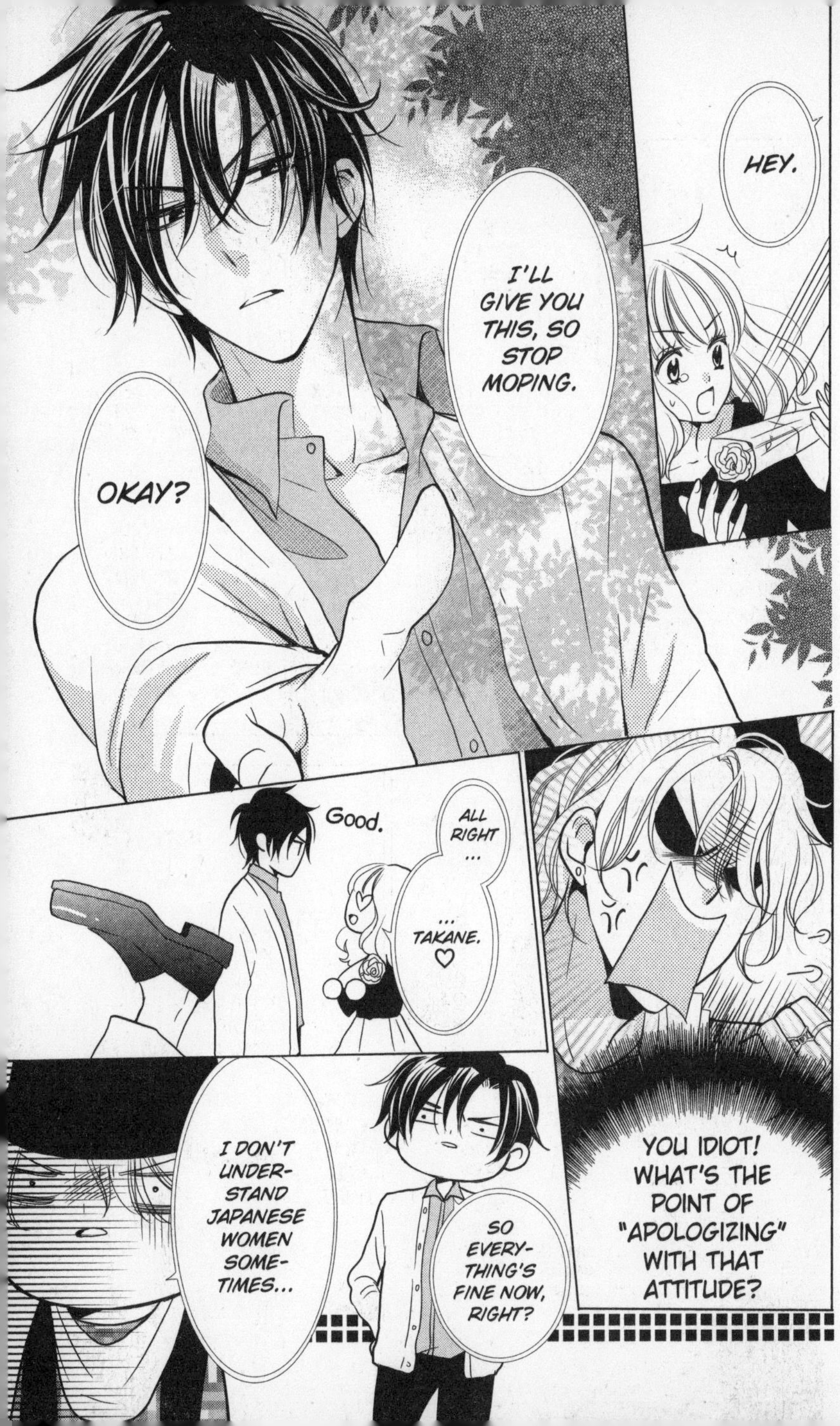
HEY.
I'LL GIVE YOU THIS, SO STOP MOPING.
OKAY?
ALL RIGHT... ...TAKANE. ♥
Good.
YOU IDIOT! WHAT'S THE POINT OF "APOLOGIZING" WITH THAT ATTITUDE?
SO EVERYTHING'S FINE NOW, RIGHT?
I DON'T UNDERSTAND JAPANESE WOMEN SOMETIMES...

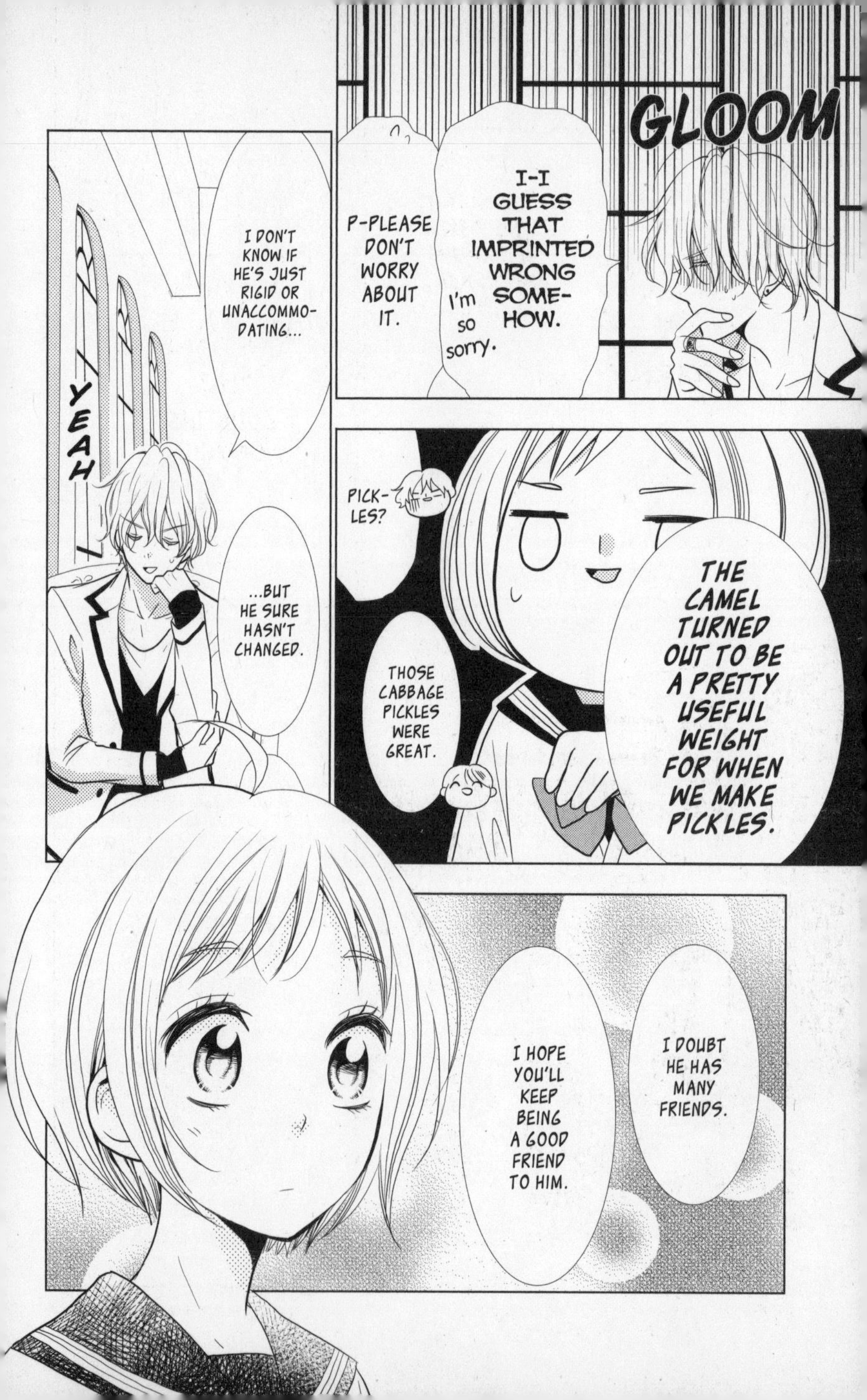
GLOOM
I-I GUESS THAT IMPRINTED WRONG SOME-HOW.
I'm so sorry.
P-PLEASE DON'T WORRY ABOUT IT.
THE CAMEL TURNED OUT TO BE A PRETTY USEFUL WEIGHT FOR WHEN WE MAKE PICKLES.
PICK-LES?
THOSE CABBAGE PICKLES WERE GREAT.
I DON'T KNOW IF HE'S JUST RIGID OR UNACCOMMO-DATING...
YEAH
...BUT HE SURE HASN'T CHANGED.
I DOUBT HE HAS MANY FRIENDS.
I HOPE YOU'LL KEEP BEING A GOOD FRIEND TO HIM.

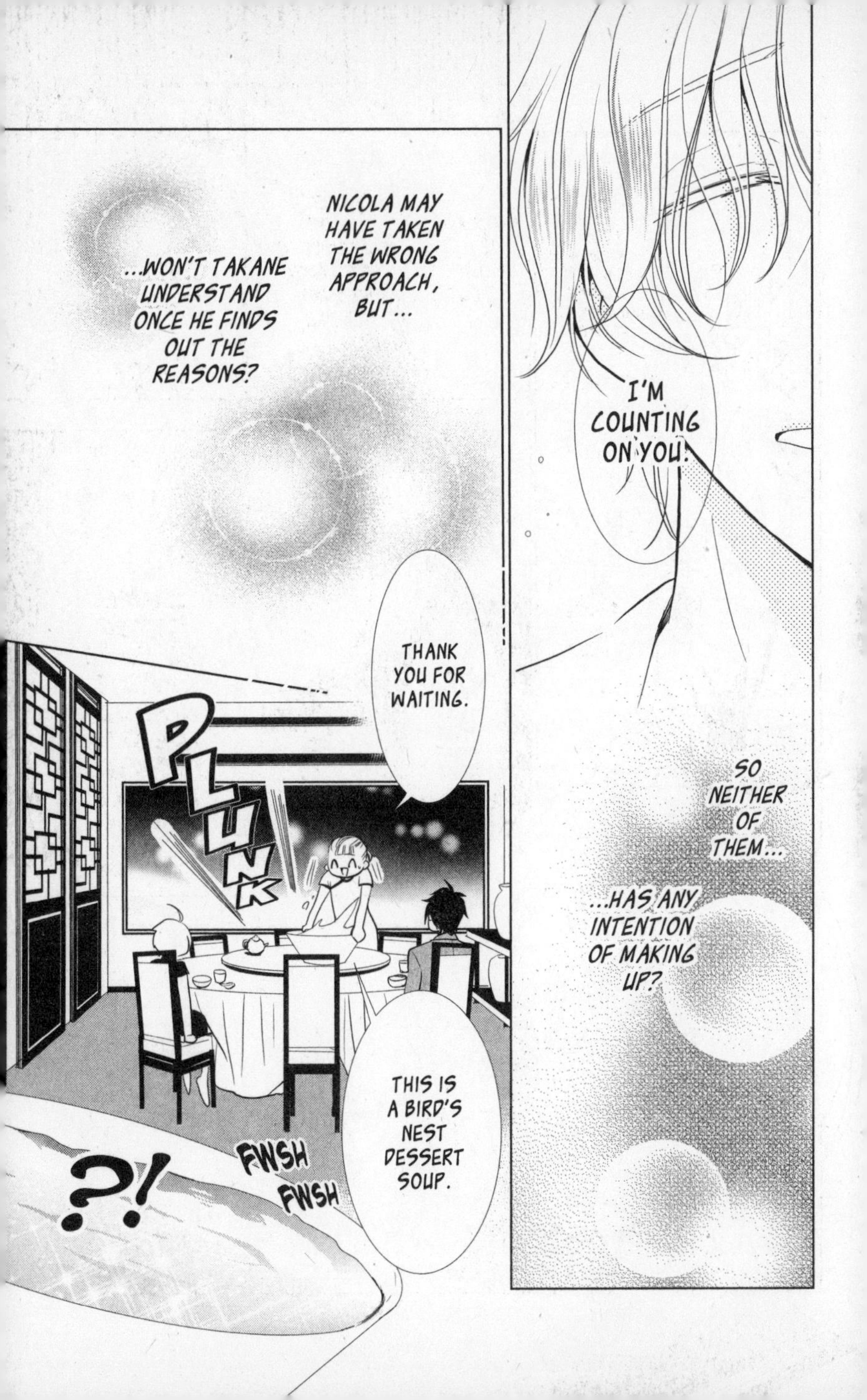
I'M COUNTING ON YOU!
SO NEITHER OF THEM...
...HAS ANY INTENTION OF MAKING UP?
NICOLA MAY HAVE TAKEN THE WRONG APPROACH, BUT...
...WON'T TAKANE UNDERSTAND ONCE HE FINDS OUT THE REASONS?
THANK YOU FOR WAITING.
PLUNK
THIS IS A BIRD'S NEST DESSERT SOUP.
FWSH FWSH
?!

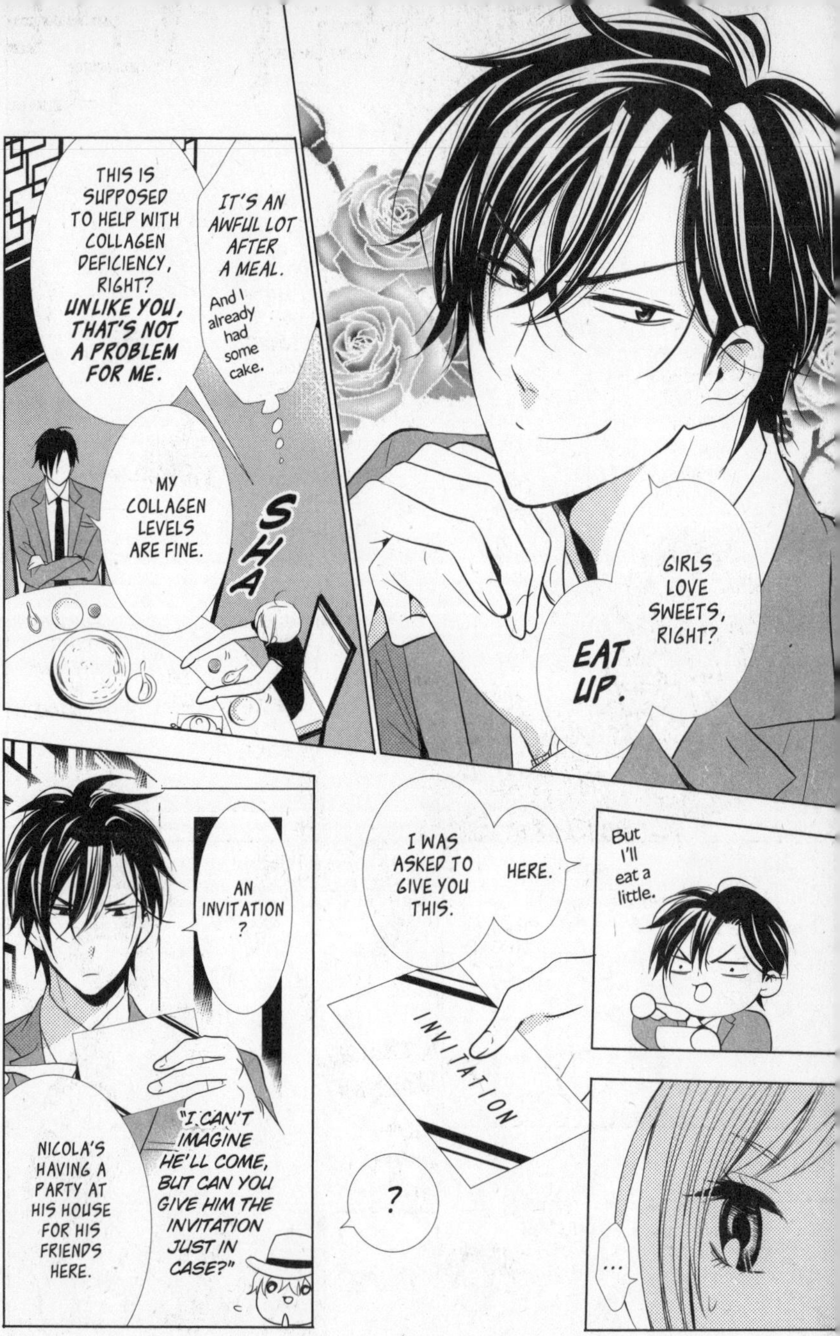
GIRLS LOVE SWEETS, RIGHT?
EAT UP.
IT'S AN AWFUL LOT AFTER A MEAL.
And I already had some cake.
THIS IS SUPPOSED TO HELP WITH COLLAGEN DEFICIENCY, RIGHT? UNLIKE YOU, THAT'S NOT A PROBLEM FOR ME.
MY COLLAGEN LEVELS ARE FINE.
SHA
But I'll eat a little.
...
HERE.
I WAS ASKED TO GIVE YOU THIS.
INVITATION
?
AN INVITATION?
"I CAN'T IMAGINE HE'LL COME, BUT CAN YOU GIVE HIM THE INVITATION JUST IN CASE?"
NICOLA'S HAVING A PARTY AT HIS HOUSE FOR HIS FRIENDS HERE.

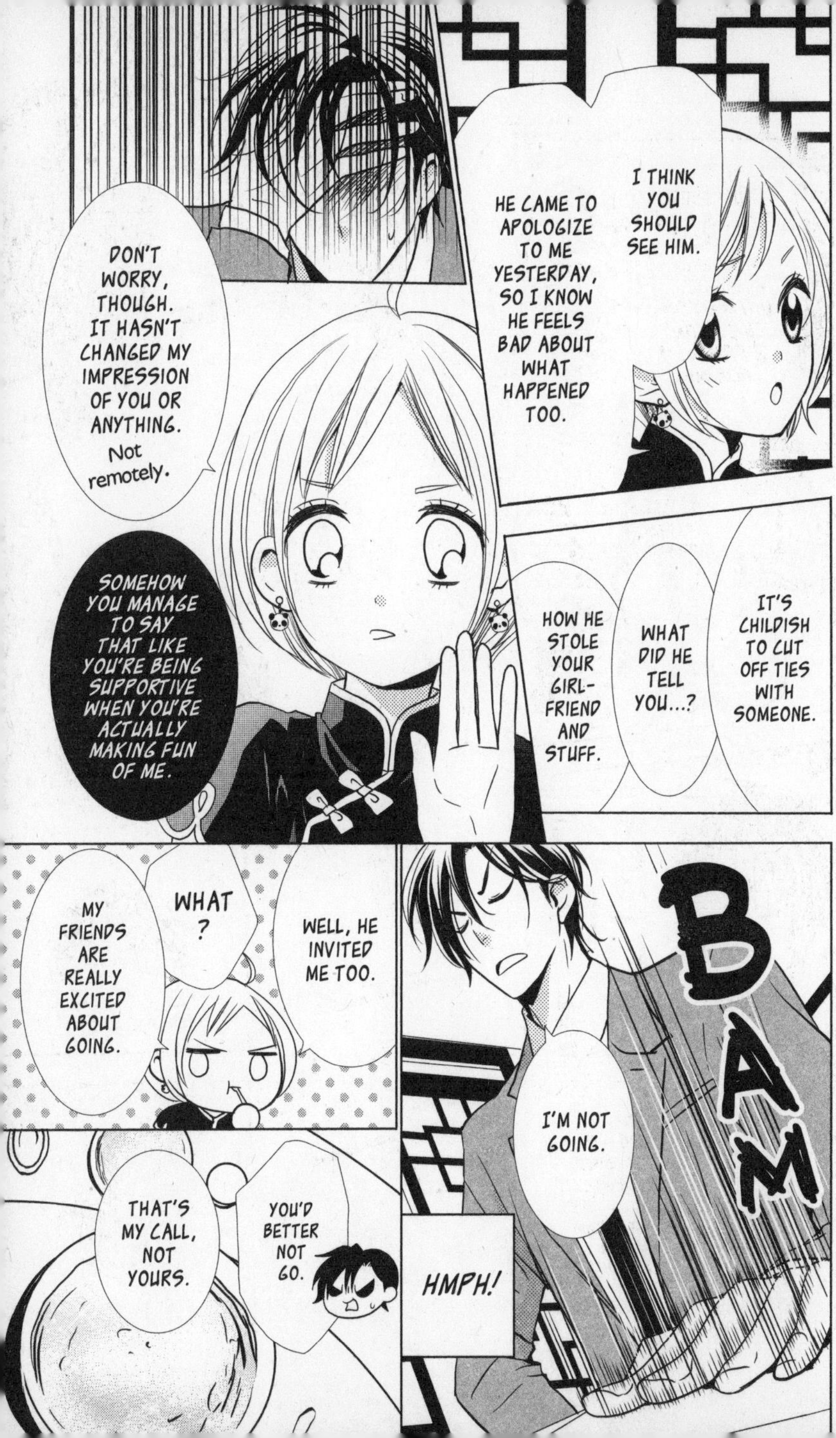
I THINK YOU SHOULD SEE HIM.
HE CAME TO APOLOGIZE TO ME YESTERDAY, SO I KNOW HE FEELS BAD ABOUT WHAT HAPPENED TOO.
IT'S CHILDISH TO CUT OFF TIES WITH SOMEONE.
WHAT DID HE TELL YOU...?
HOW HE STOLE YOUR GIRL-FRIEND AND STUFF.
DON'T WORRY, THOUGH. IT HASN'T CHANGED MY IMPRESSION OF YOU OR ANYTHING.
Not remotely.
SOMEHOW YOU MANAGE TO SAY THAT LIKE YOU'RE BEING SUPPORTIVE WHEN YOU'RE ACTUALLY MAKING FUN OF ME.
I'M NOT GOING.
BAM
WELL, HE INVITED ME TOO.
WHAT?
MY FRIENDS ARE REALLY EXCITED ABOUT GOING.
HMPH!
YOU'D BETTER NOT GO.
THAT'S MY CALL, NOT YOURS.

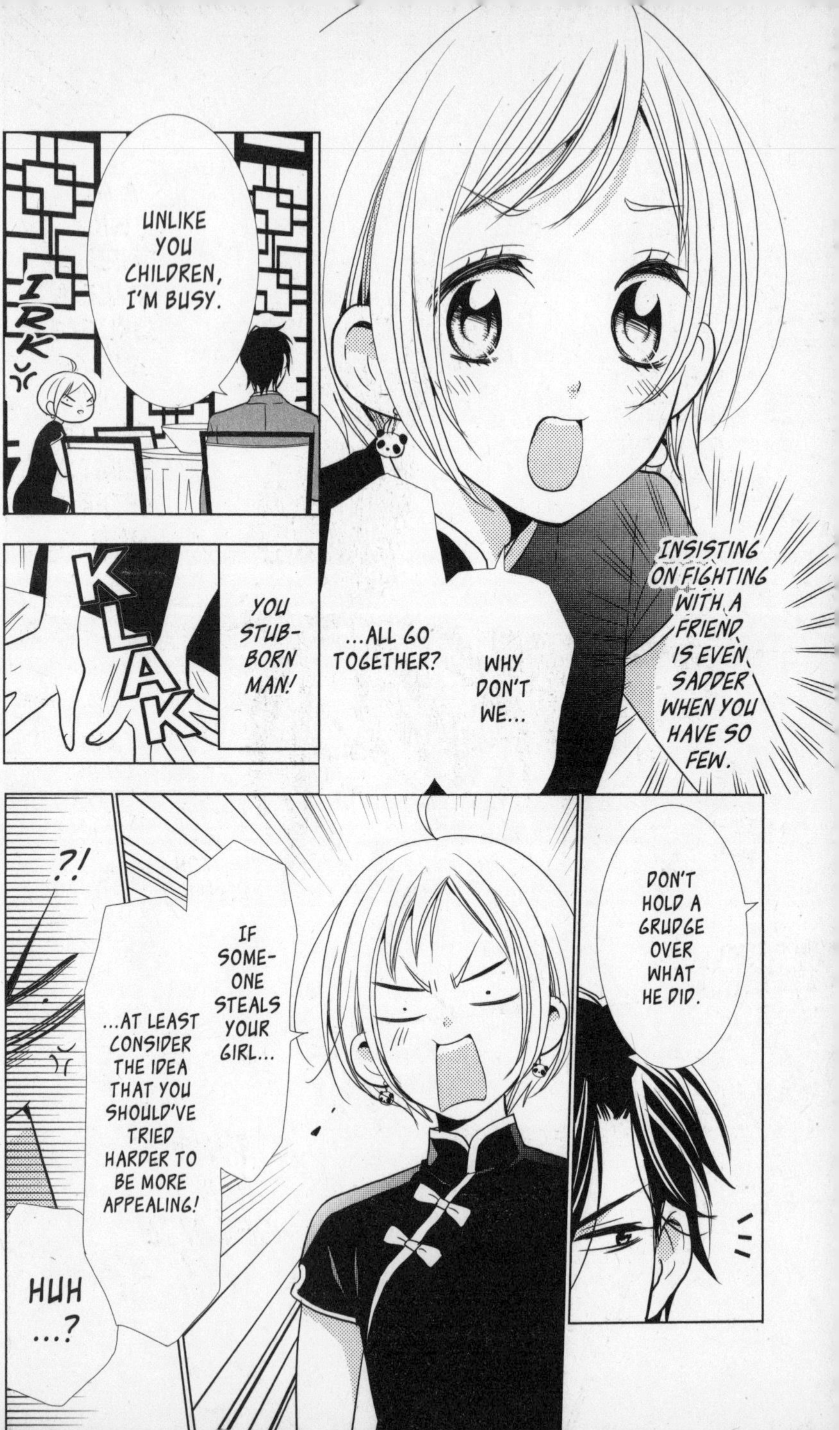
INSISTING ON FIGHTING WITH A FRIEND IS EVEN SADDER WHEN YOU HAVE SO FEW.
WHY DON'T WE...
...ALL GO TOGETHER?
UNLIKE YOU CHILDREN, I'M BUSY.
IRK
YOU STUB-BORN MAN!
KLAK
DON'T HOLD A GRUDGE OVER WHAT HE DID.
IF SOME-ONE STEALS YOUR GIRL...
...AT LEAST CONSIDER THE IDEA THAT YOU SHOULD'VE TRIED HARDER TO BE MORE APPEALING!
?!
HUH ...?

A GUY WHO TRIES TO MAKE A GIRL EAT A HUGE BOWL FULL OF GELATIN AFTER A MEAL...
...IS NEVER GONNA BEAT A GUY WHO TAKES HER TO A FANCY SWEETS SHOP!
I'M GOING TO THE PARTY!
DO WHAT YOU WANT!
WAIT!
ARE YOU KIDDING ME?!
THIS ISN'T GELATIN!!!
LET HIM EAT COLLAGEN UNTIL THAT HARD SKULL OF HIS SOFTENS!

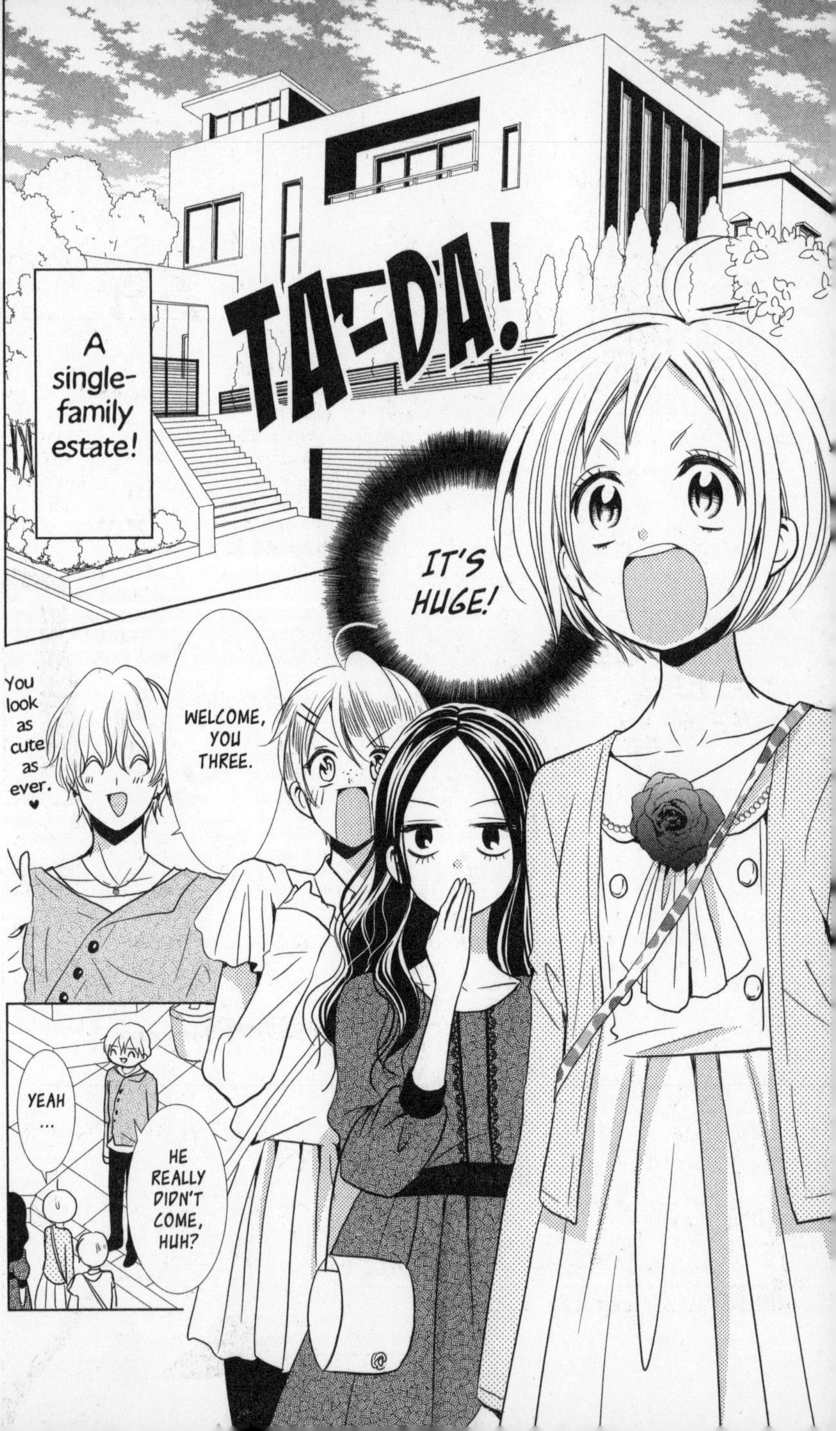
TA-DA!
A single-family estate!
IT'S HUGE!
WELCOME, YOU THREE.
You look as cute as ever. ♥
HE REALLY DIDN'T COME, HUH?
YEAH ...

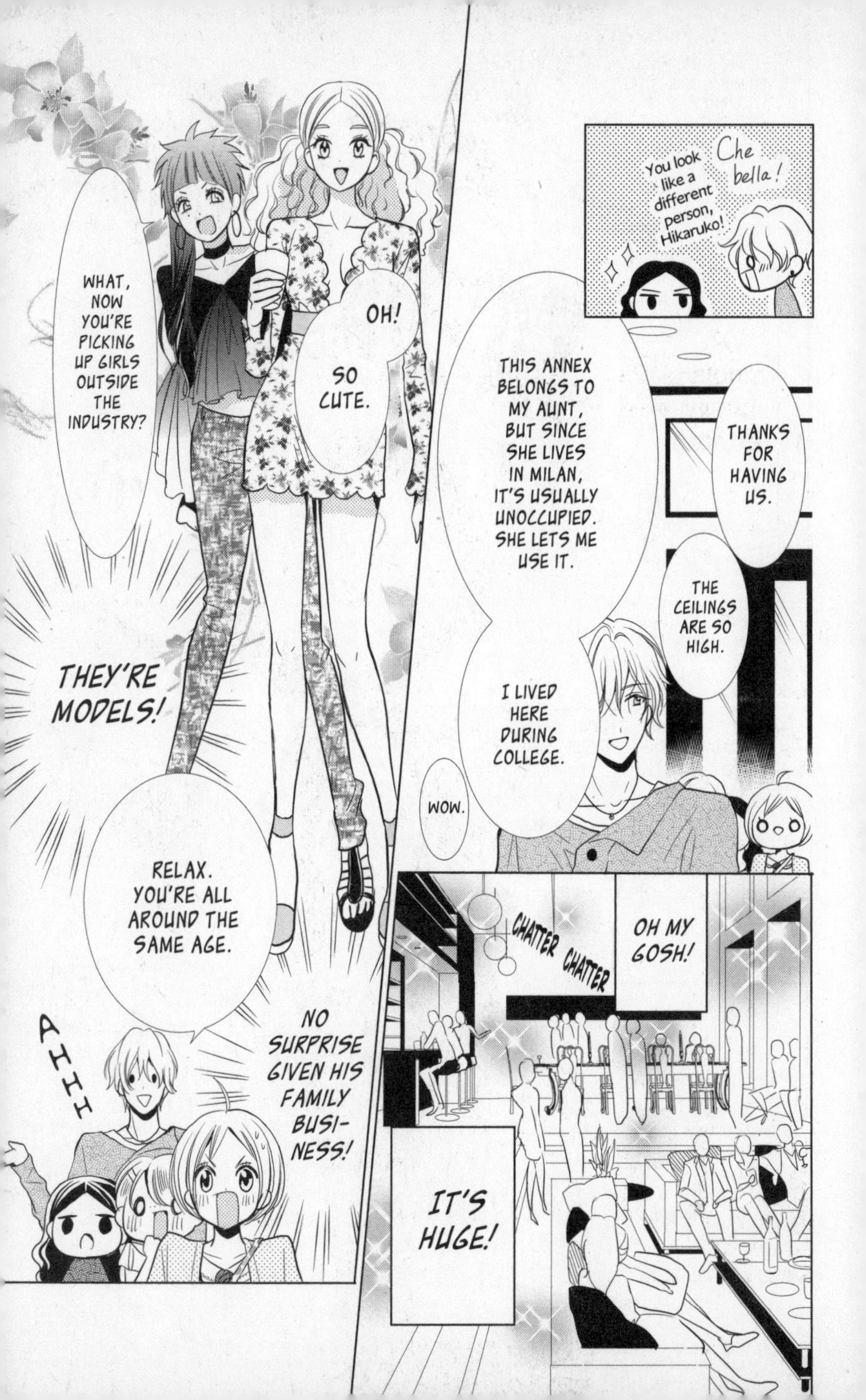
Che bella!
You look like a different person, Hikaruko!
Thanks for having us.
This annex belongs to my aunt, but since she lives in Milan, it's usually unoccupied. She lets me use it.
The ceilings are so high.
I lived here during college.
Wow.
Oh my gosh!
Chatter chatter
It's huge!
Oh!
So cute.
What, now you're picking up girls outside the industry?
They're models!
Relax. You're all around the same age.
No surprise given his family busi-ness!
AHHH

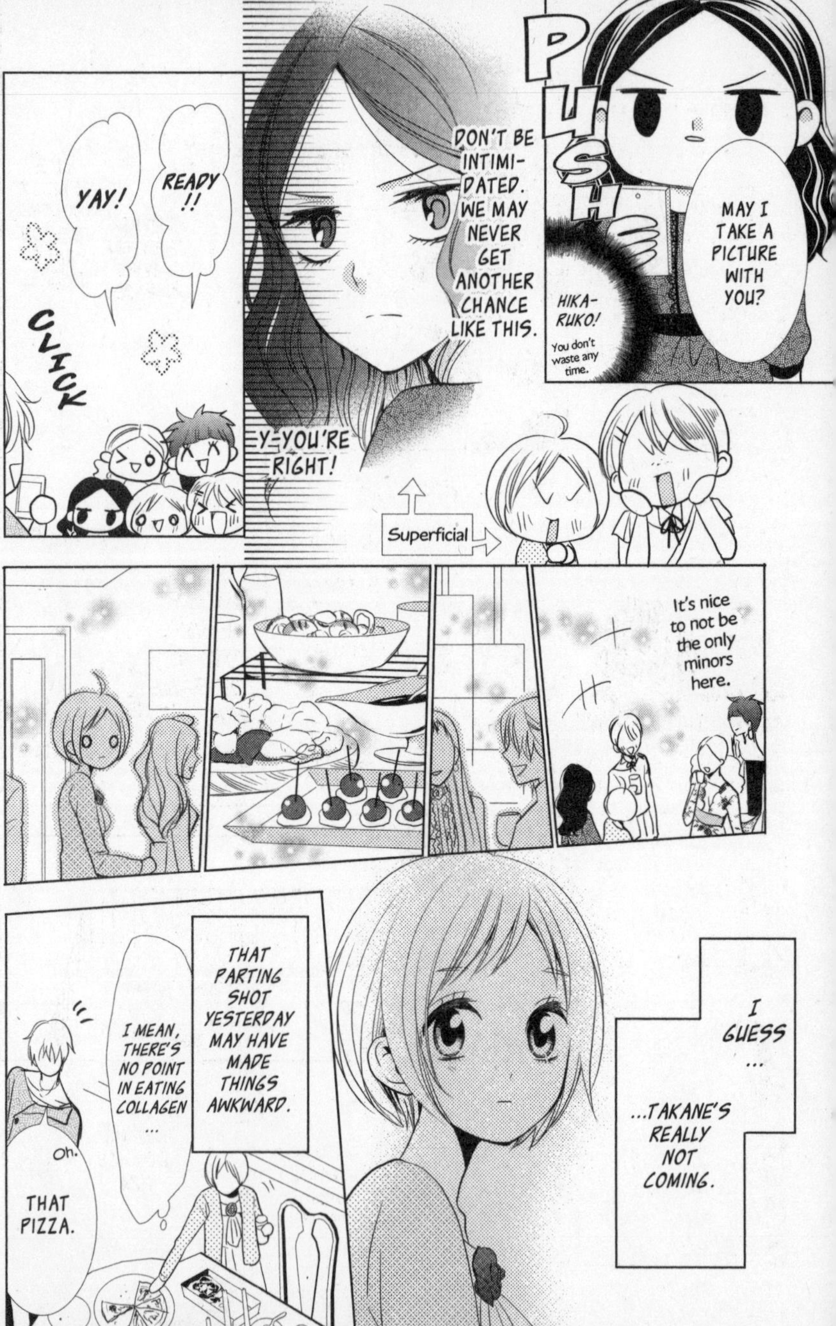

PUSH
MAY I TAKE A PICTURE WITH YOU?
HIKARUKO!
You don't waste any time.
DON'T BE INTIMIDATED. WE MAY NEVER GET ANOTHER CHANCE LIKE THIS.
Y-YOU'RE RIGHT!
Superficial
READY!!
YAY!
CLICK
It's nice to not be the only minors here.
I GUESS...
...TAKANE'S REALLY NOT COMING.
THAT PARTING SHOT YESTERDAY MAY HAVE MADE THINGS AWKWARD.
I MEAN, THERE'S NO POINT IN EATING COLLAGEN...
Oh.
THAT PIZZA.

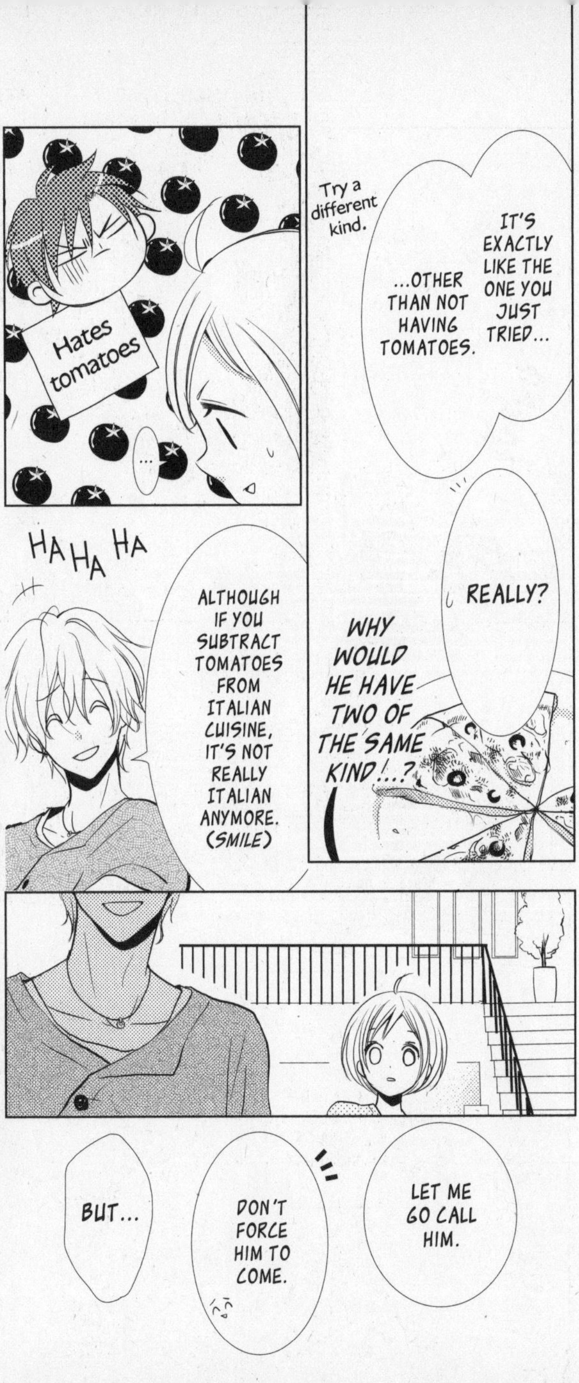
IT'S EXACTLY LIKE THE ONE YOU JUST TRIED...
...OTHER THAN NOT HAVING TOMATOES.
Try a different kind.
REALLY?
WHY WOULD HE HAVE TWO OF THE SAME KIND...?
Hates tomatoes
...
ALTHOUGH IF YOU SUBTRACT TOMATOES FROM ITALIAN CUISINE, IT'S NOT REALLY ITALIAN ANYMORE. (SMILE)
HA HA HA HA
LET ME GO CALL HIM.
DON'T FORCE HIM TO COME.
BUT...

● Special Thanks ●

- My audience, my family and my relatives
- "S," who's in charge of everything and is full of great ideas
- Everyone who handles sales and marketing
- The person in charge of the cover design

Thank you very much!

● Please Send Me Your Thoughts and Impressions! ●

Yuki Shiwasu
c/o Takane & Hana Editor
VIZ Media
P.O. Box 77010
San Francisco, CA 94107

I'll be so happy to hear from you!

While I'm at it, here's Takane in Chinese attire.

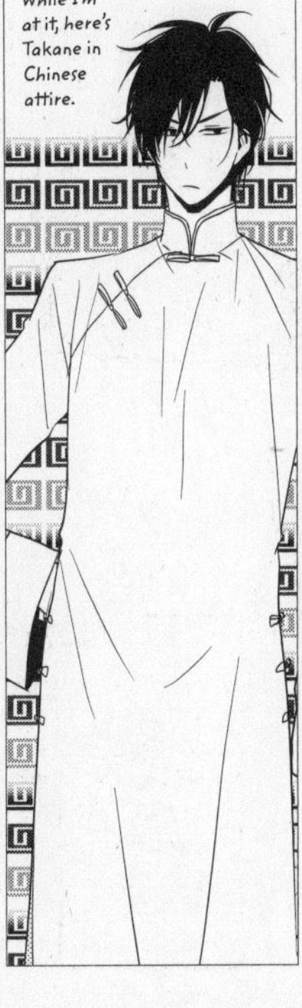

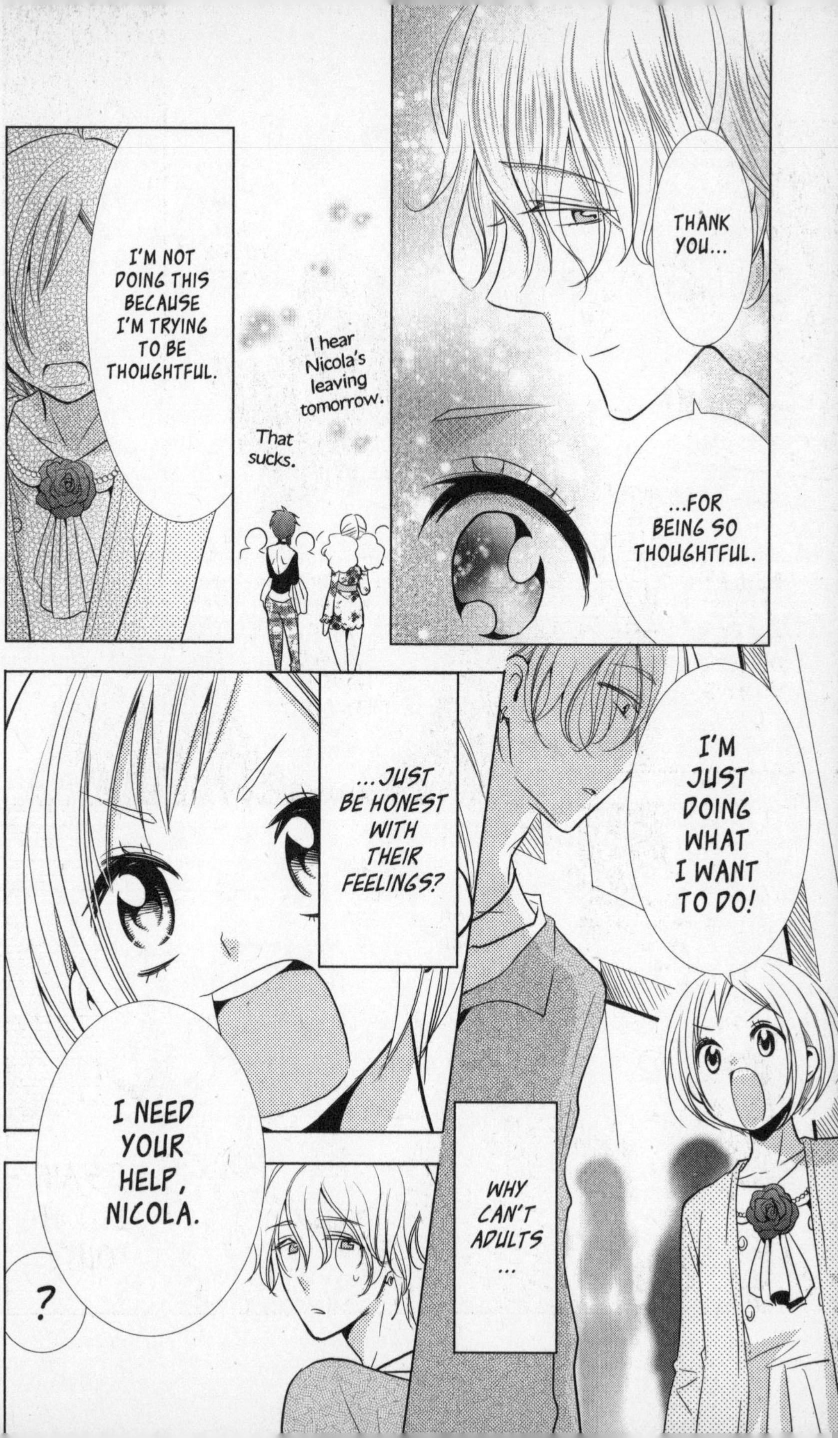
THANK YOU...
...FOR BEING SO THOUGHTFUL.
I hear Nicola's leaving tomorrow.
That sucks.
I'M NOT DOING THIS BECAUSE I'M TRYING TO BE THOUGHTFUL.
I'M JUST DOING WHAT I WANT TO DO!
WHY CAN'T ADULTS ...
...JUST BE HONEST WITH THEIR FEELINGS?
I NEED YOUR HELP, NICOLA.
?

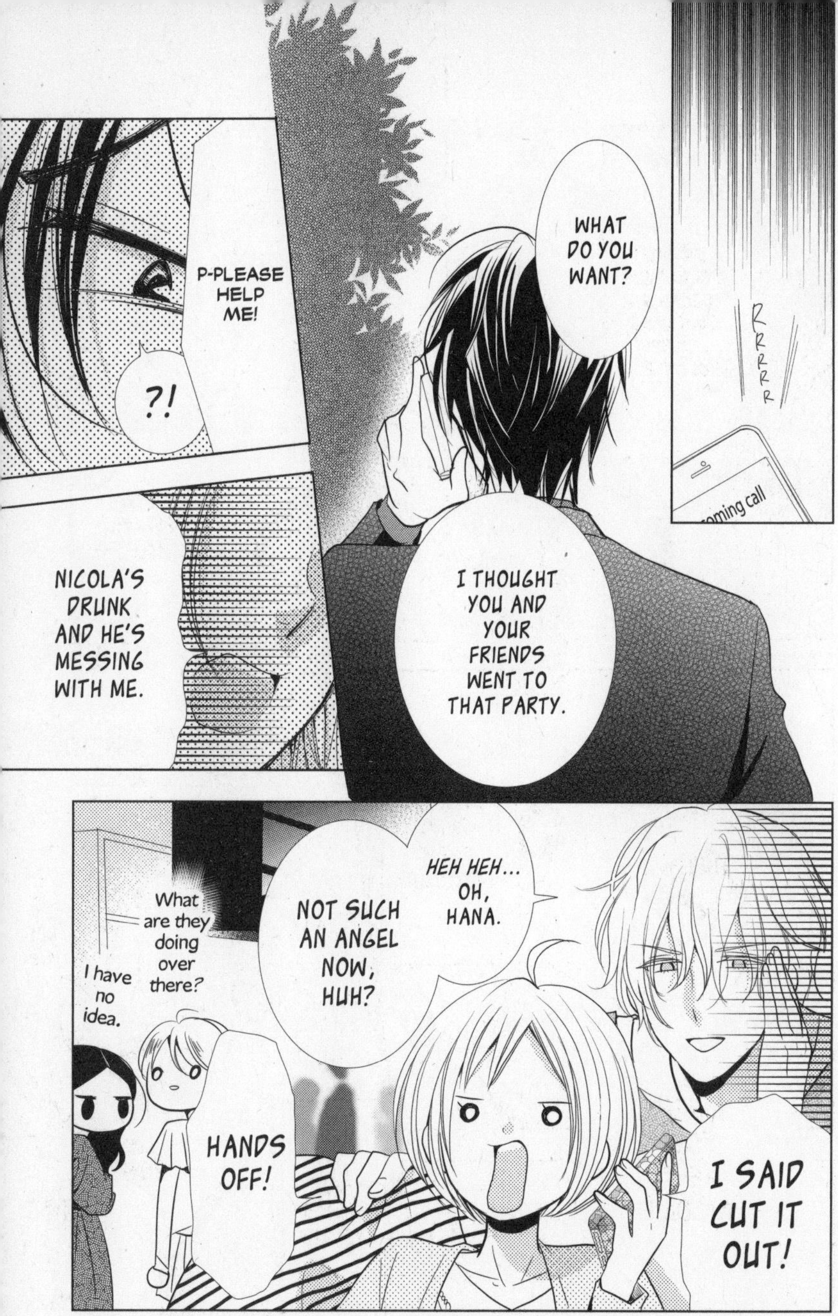
RRRRR
WHAT DO YOU WANT?
I THOUGHT YOU AND YOUR FRIENDS WENT TO THAT PARTY.
P-PLEASE HELP ME!
?!
NICOLA'S DRUNK AND HE'S MESSING WITH ME.
I SAID CUT IT OUT!
HEH HEH... OH, HANA.
NOT SUCH AN ANGEL NOW, HUH?
HANDS OFF!
What are they doing over there?
I have no idea.

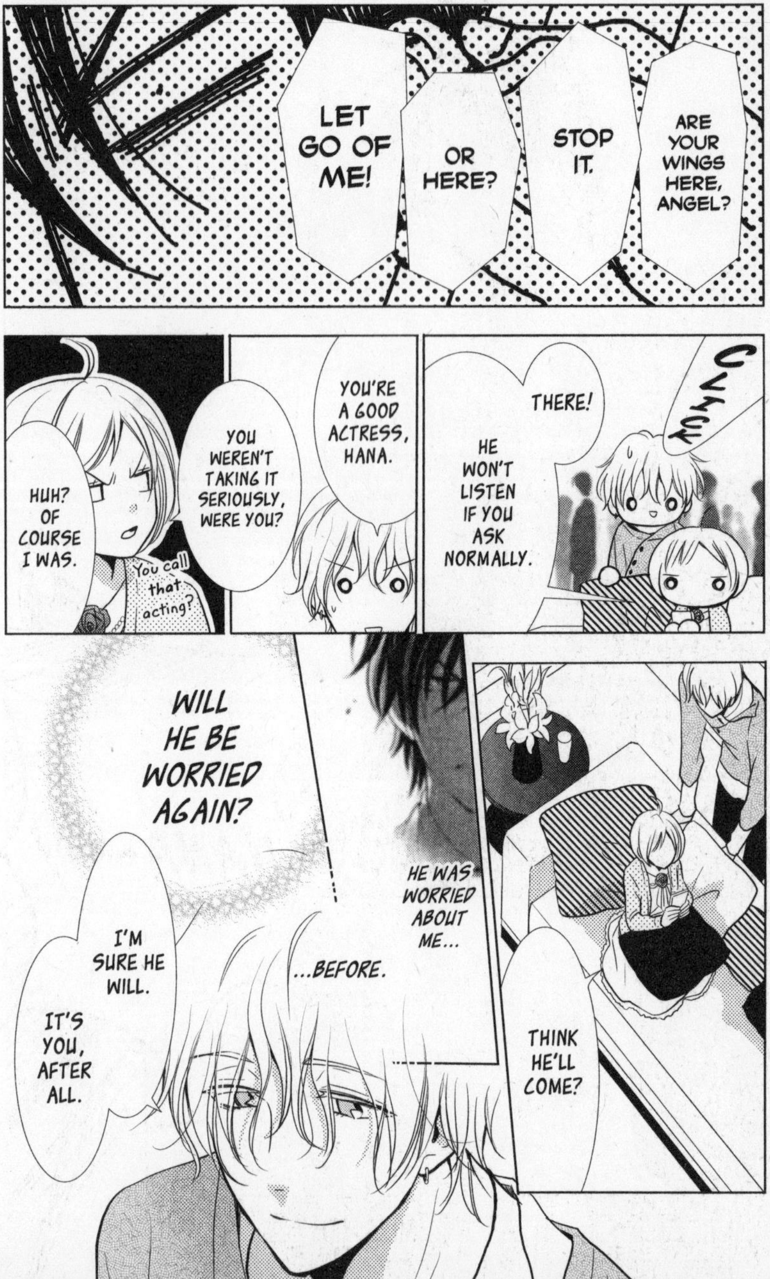
ARE YOUR WINGS HERE, ANGEL?
STOP IT.
OR HERE?
LET GO OF ME!
CLICK
THERE!
HE WON'T LISTEN IF YOU ASK NORMALLY.
YOU'RE A GOOD ACTRESS, HANA.
YOU WEREN'T TAKING IT SERIOUSLY, WERE YOU?
HUH? OF COURSE I WAS.
You call that acting?
THINK HE'LL COME?
HE WAS WORRIED ABOUT ME...
...BEFORE.
WILL HE BE WORRIED AGAIN?
I'M SURE HE WILL.
IT'S YOU, AFTER ALL.

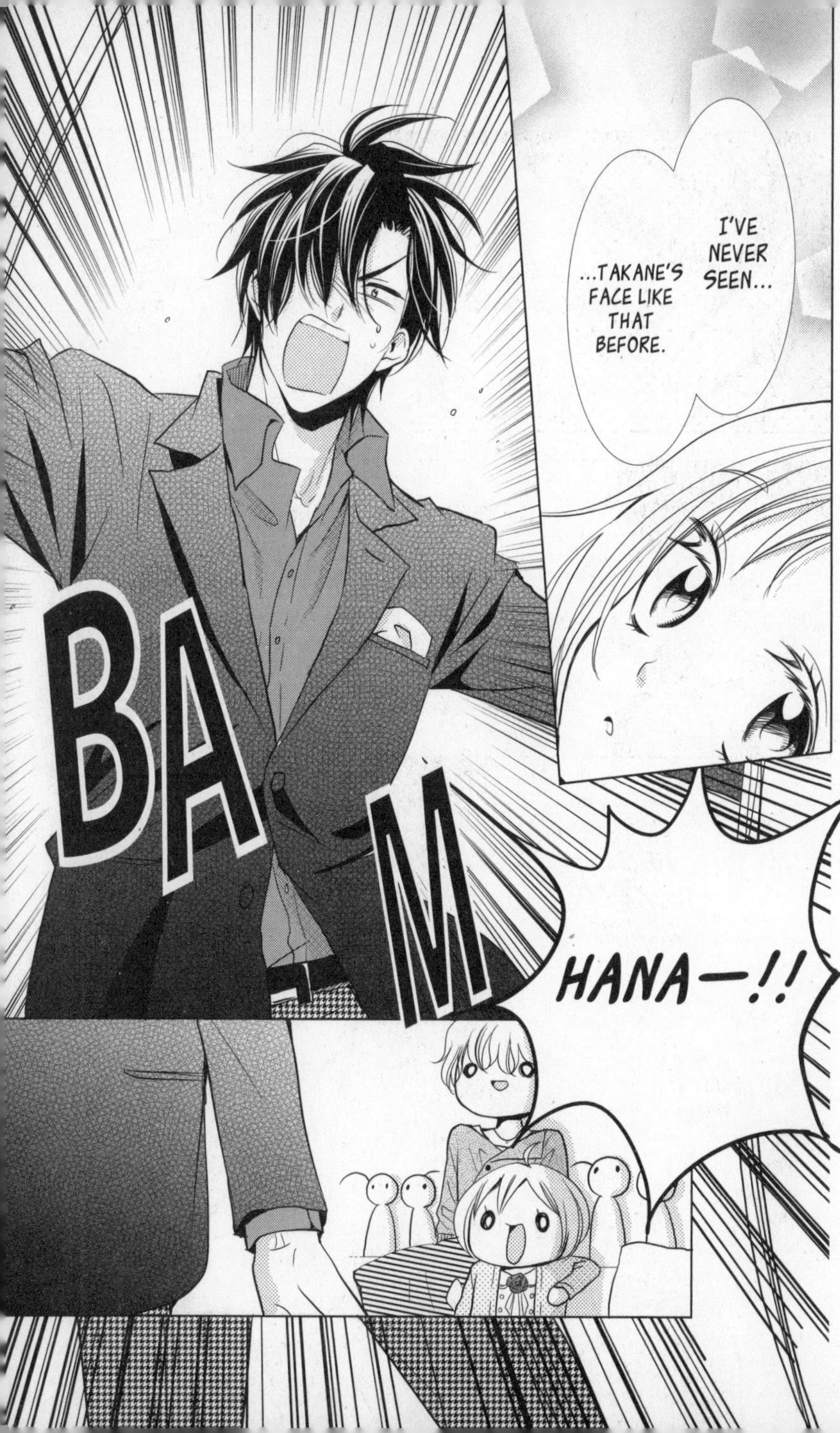
I'VE NEVER SEEN...
...TAKANE'S FACE LIKE THAT BEFORE.
HANA—!!
BAM

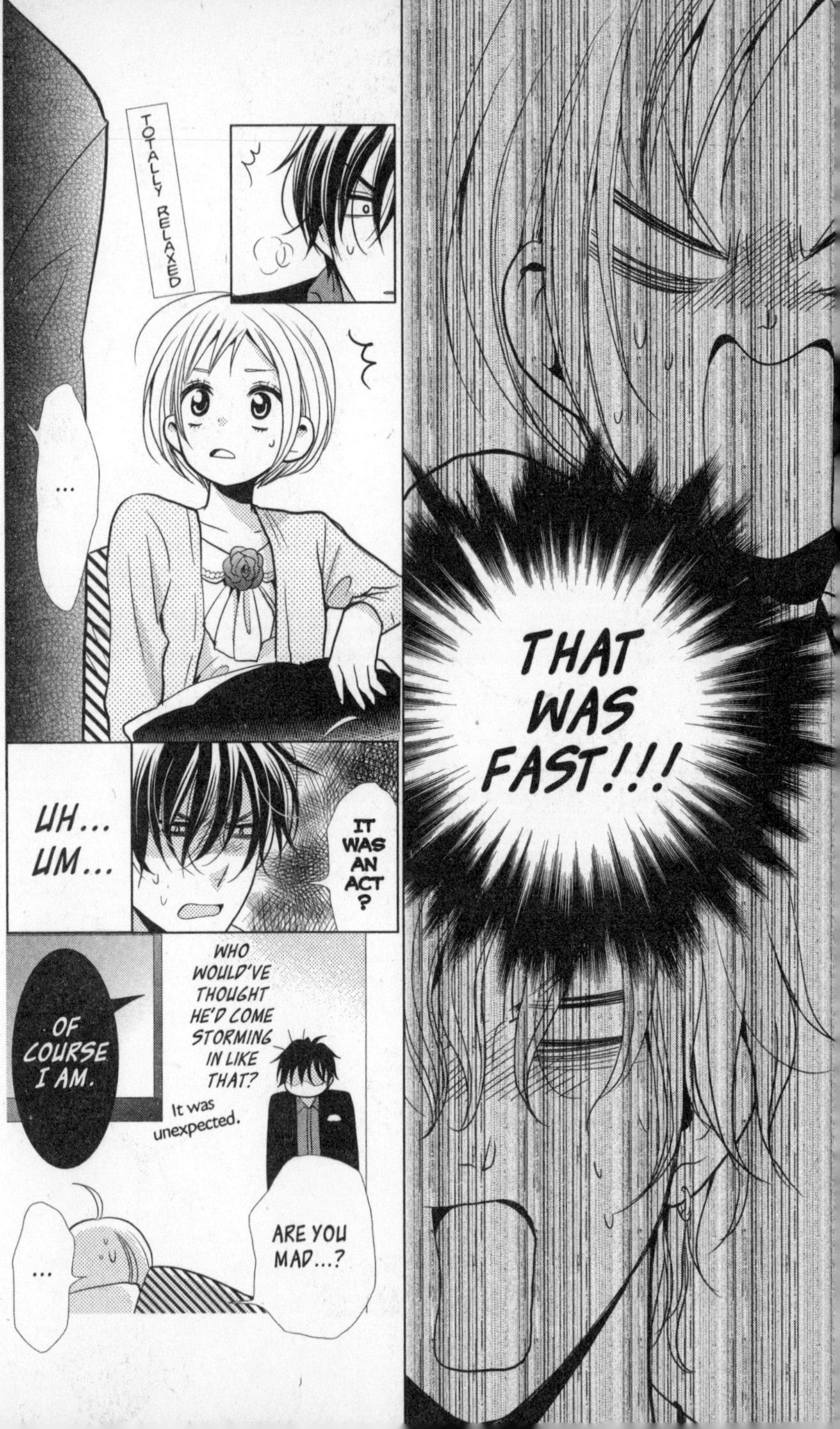
THAT WAS FAST!!!
TOTALLY RELAXED
...
IT WAS AN ACT?
UH... UM...
WHO WOULD'VE THOUGHT HE'D COME STORMING IN LIKE THAT?
It was unexpected.
OF COURSE I AM.
ARE YOU MAD...?
...

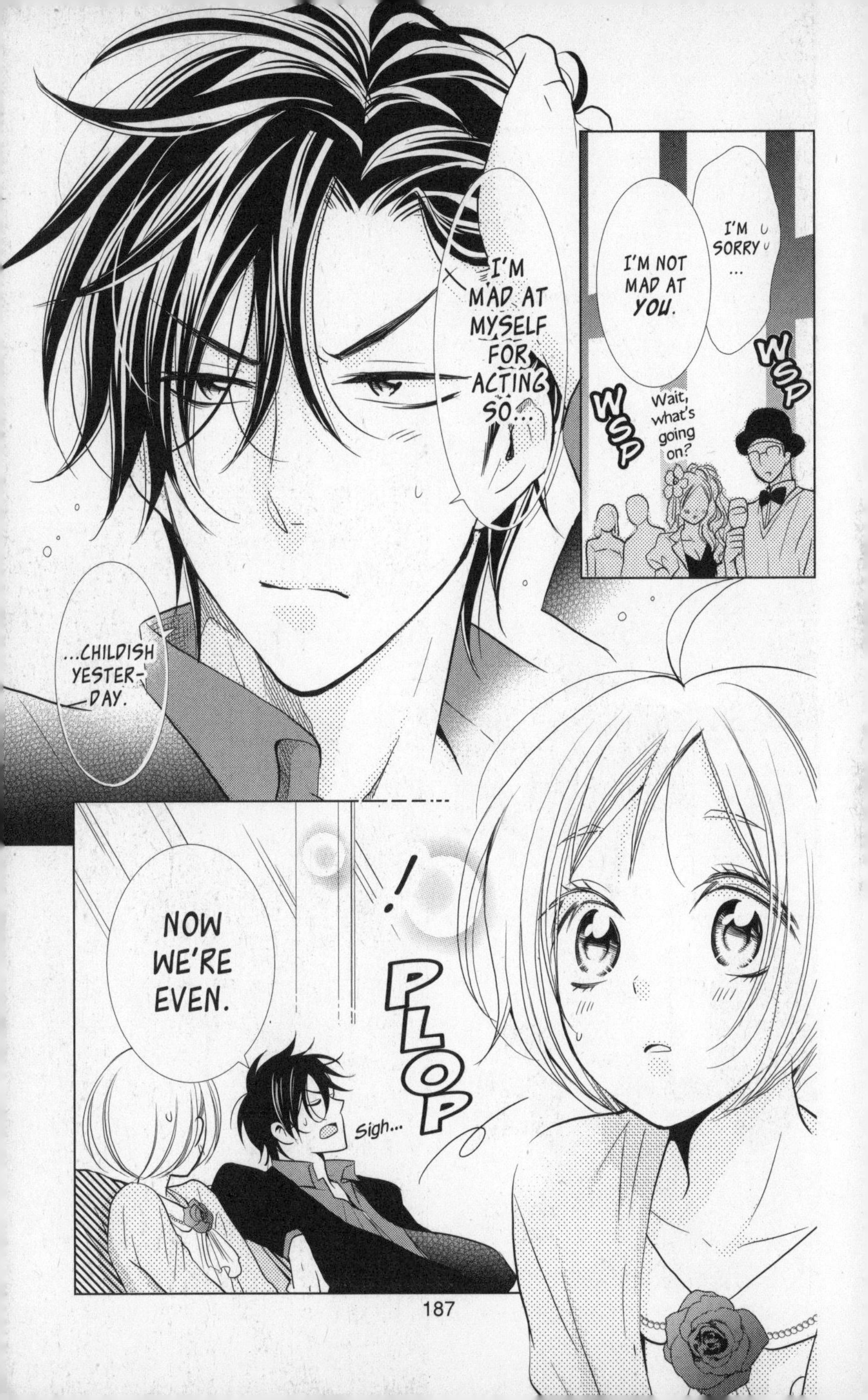
I'M SORRY...
I'M NOT MAD AT YOU.
WSP
WSP
Wait, what's going on?
I'M MAD AT MYSELF FOR ACTING SO...
...CHILDISH YESTER-DAY.
!
NOW WE'RE EVEN.
PLOP
Sigh...

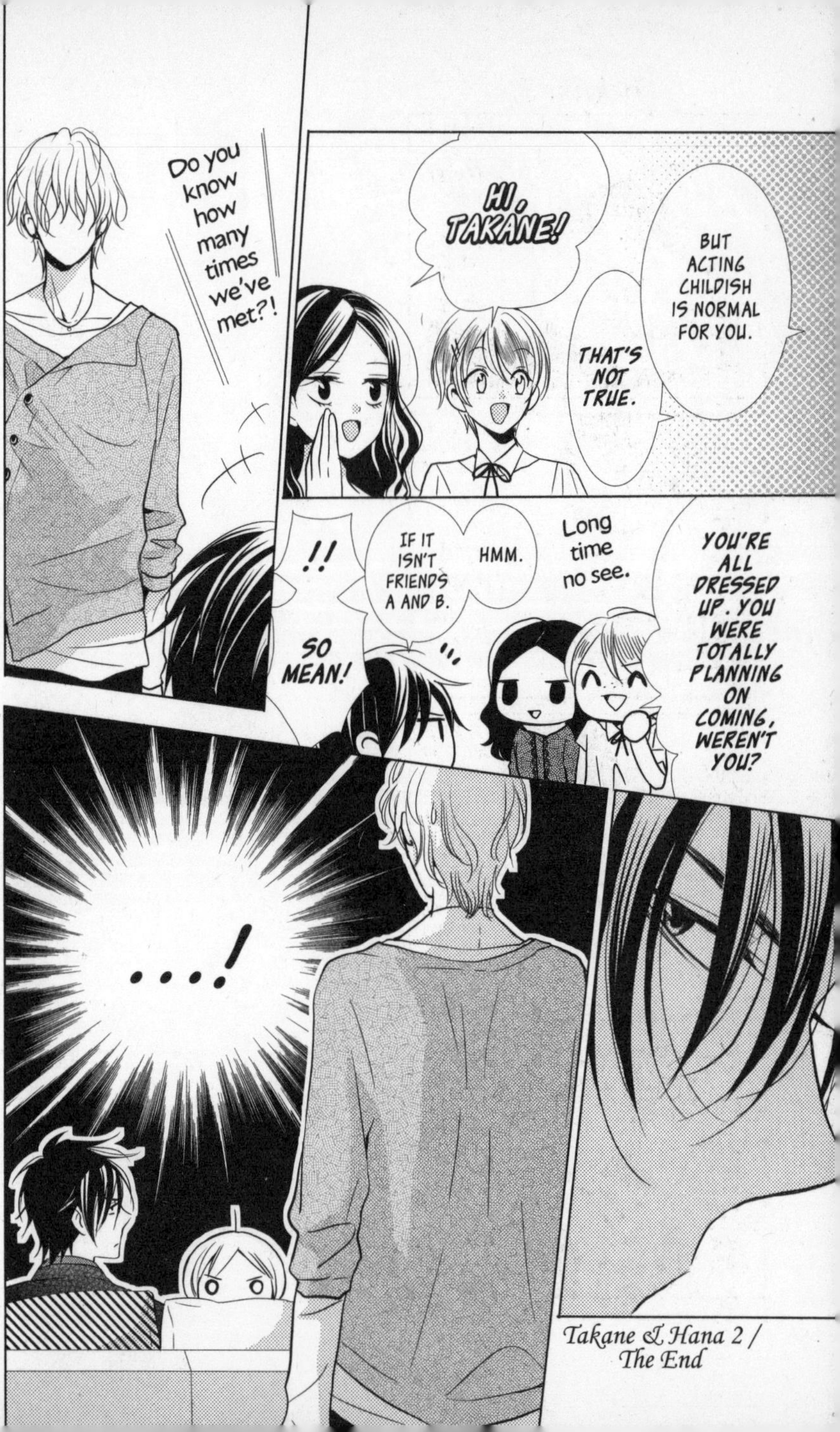
HI, TAKANE!
BUT ACTING CHILDISH IS NORMAL FOR YOU.
THAT'S NOT TRUE.
YOU'RE ALL DRESSED UP. YOU WERE TOTALLY PLANNING ON COMING, WEREN'T YOU?
Long time no see.
HMM.
IF IT ISN'T FRIENDS A AND B.
!!
SO MEAN!
Do you know how many times we've met?!
...!

Takane & Hana 2 / The End

Hikune 3

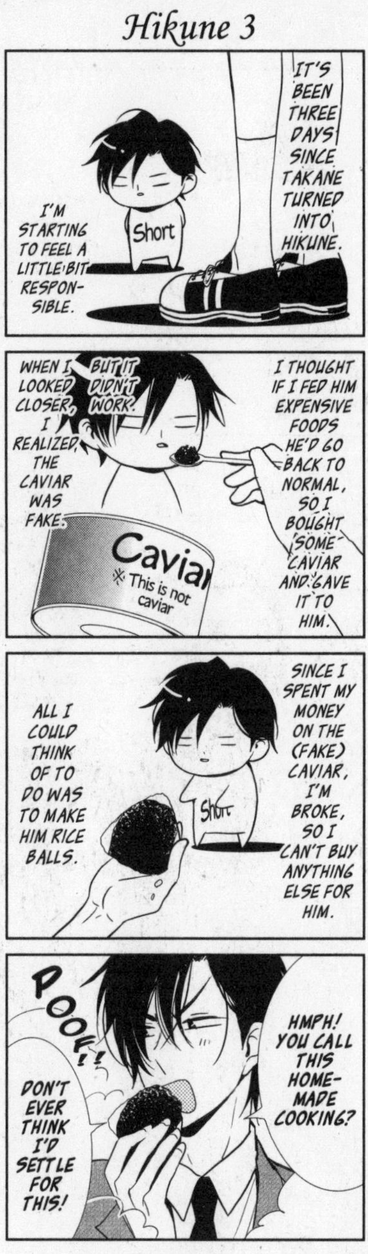
IT'S BEEN THREE DAYS SINCE TAKANE TURNED INTO HIKUNE.
I'M STARTING TO FEEL A LITTLE BIT RESPONSIBLE.
Short
I THOUGHT IF I FED HIM EXPENSIVE FOODS HE'D GO BACK TO NORMAL, SO I BOUGHT SOME CAVIAR AND GAVE IT TO HIM.
BUT IT DIDN'T WORK.
WHEN I LOOKED CLOSER, I REALIZED, THE CAVIAR WAS FAKE.
Caviar
※ This is not caviar
SINCE I SPENT MY MONEY ON THE (FAKE) CAVIAR, I'M BROKE, SO I CAN'T BUY ANYTHING ELSE FOR HIM.
Short
ALL I COULD THINK OF TO DO WAS TO MAKE HIM RICE BALLS.
HMPH! YOU CALL THIS HOME-MADE COOKING?
POOF!!
DON'T EVER THINK I'D SETTLE FOR THIS!

Bonus Story:

The Second-Best Theater in the World

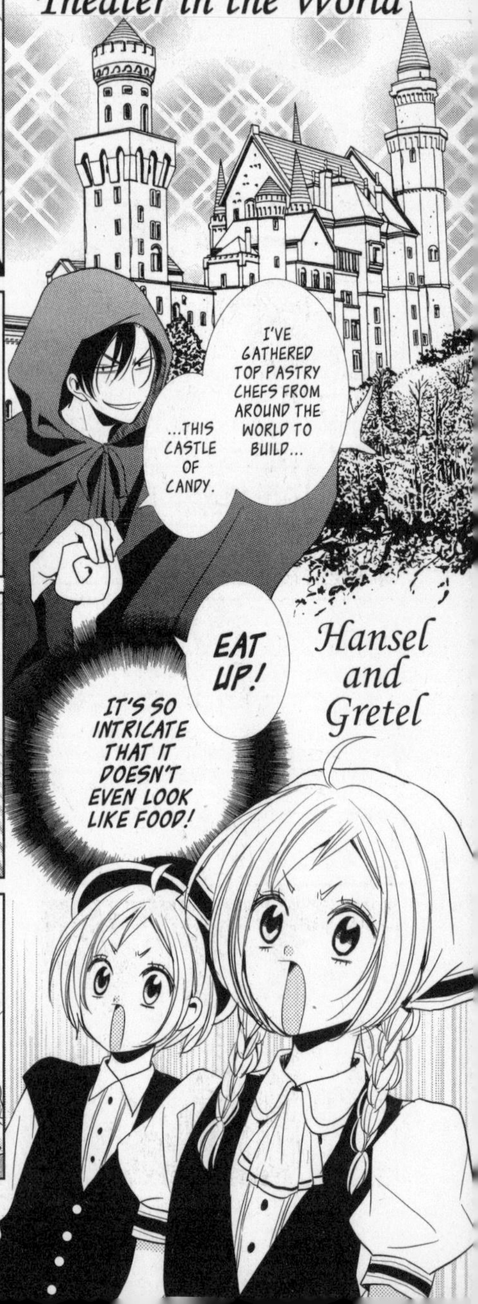
I'VE GATHERED TOP PASTRY CHEFS FROM AROUND THE WORLD TO BUILD...
...THIS CASTLE OF CANDY.
Hansel and Gretel
EAT UP!
IT'S SO INTRICATE THAT IT DOESN'T EVEN LOOK LIKE FOOD!

Cinderella

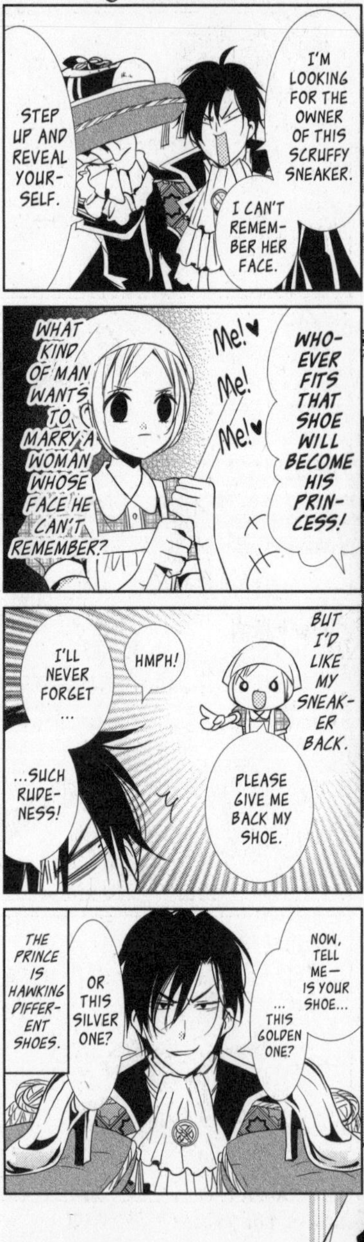
I'M LOOKING FOR THE OWNER OF THIS SCRUFFY SNEAKER.
I CAN'T REMEMBER HER FACE.
STEP UP AND REVEAL YOURSELF.
WHOEVER FITS THAT SHOE WILL BECOME HIS PRINCESS!
Me!♥
Me!
Me!♥
WHAT KIND OF MAN WANTS TO MARRY A WOMAN WHOSE FACE HE CAN'T REMEMBER?
BUT I'D LIKE MY SNEAKER BACK.
PLEASE GIVE ME BACK MY SHOE.
HMPH!
I'LL NEVER FORGET ...
...SUCH RUDENESS!
NOW, TELL ME—IS YOUR SHOE...
...THIS GOLDEN ONE?
OR THIS SILVER ONE?
THE PRINCE IS HAWKING DIFFERENT SHOES.

Peach Boy (Momotaro)

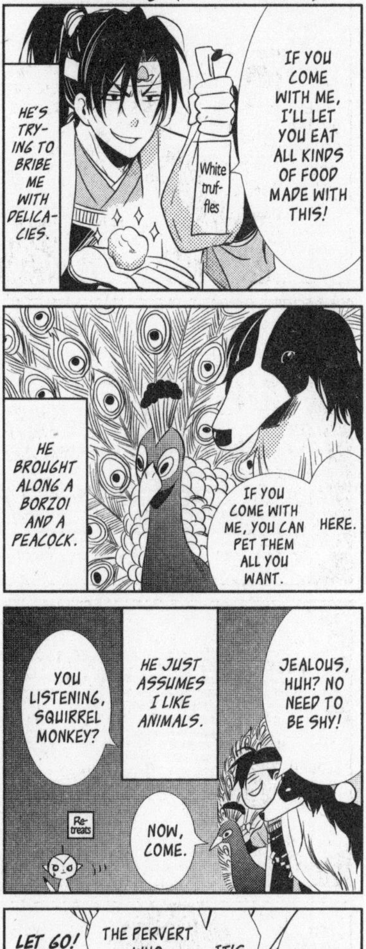
IF YOU COME WITH ME, I'LL LET YOU EAT ALL KINDS OF FOOD MADE WITH THIS!
White truffles
HE'S TRYING TO BRIBE ME WITH DELICACIES.
HERE.
IF YOU COME WITH ME, YOU CAN PET THEM ALL YOU WANT.
HE BROUGHT ALONG A BORZOI AND A PEACOCK.
JEALOUS, HUH? NO NEED TO BE SHY!
HE JUST ASSUMES I LIKE ANIMALS.
YOU LISTENING, SQUIRREL MONKEY?
NOW, COME.
Retreats
THAT'S HIM, OFFICER!
IT'S YOU!
THE PERVERT WHO SEDUCES INNOCENT ANIMALS!
LET GO! WHO DO YOU THINK I AM?!
We've got him!
He's defeated.

Aladdin and the Magic Lamp

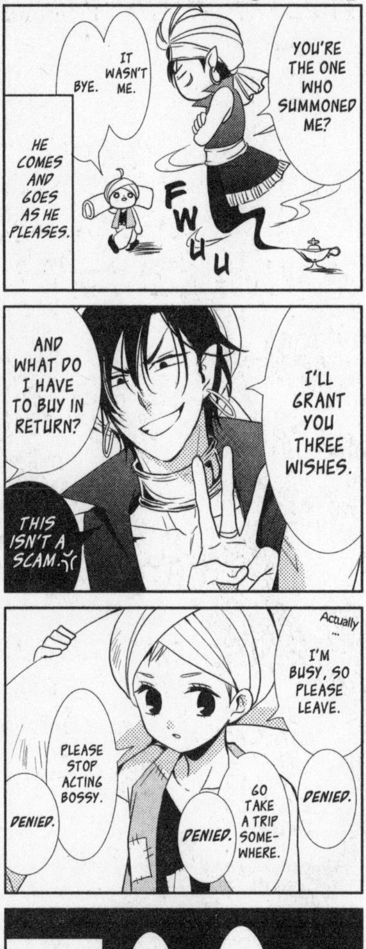
YOU'RE THE ONE WHO SUMMONED ME?
IT WASN'T ME.
BYE.
HE COMES AND GOES AS HE PLEASES.
FWUU
I'LL GRANT YOU THREE WISHES.
AND WHAT DO I HAVE TO BUY IN RETURN?
THIS ISN'T A SCAM.
Actually...
I'M BUSY, SO PLEASE LEAVE.
DENIED.
GO TAKE A TRIP SOMEWHERE.
DENIED.
PLEASE STOP ACTING BOSSY.
DENIED.
PLEASE LOOK AWAY.
DENIED.
TURN INTO A GORILLA.
DENIED.
DON'T DENY—
DENIED.
WE'RE GETTING NOWHERE.

Bonus Story: The Second-Best Theater in the World / The End

Drawing funny expressions has become
my default, so I get excessively nervous
when I have to draw more serious expressions.

—YUKI SHIWASU

Born on March 7 in Fukuoka Prefecture, Japan,
Yuki Shiwasu began her career as a manga artist
after winning the top prize in the Hakusensha Athena
Newcomers' Awards from *Hana to Yume* magazine. She
is also the author of *Furou Kyoudai* (Immortal Siblings),
which was published by Hakusensha in Japan.

Takane &Hana

VOLUME 2
SHOJO BEAT EDITION

STORY & ART BY **YUKI SHIWASU**

ENGLISH ADAPTATION **Ysabet Reinhardt MacFarlane**
TRANSLATION **JN Productions**
TOUCH-UP ART & LETTERING **Freeman Wong**
DESIGN **Shawn Carrico**
EDITOR **Amy Yu**

Takane to Hana by Yuki Shiwasu
© Yuki Shiwasu 2015
All rights reserved.
First published in Japan in 2015 by HAKUSENSHA, Inc., Tokyo.
English language translation rights arranged with HAKUSENSHA, Inc., Tokyo.

The stories, characters and incidents mentioned
in this publication are entirely fictional.

Printed in Canada

Published by VIZ Media, LLC
P.O. Box 77010
San Francisco, CA 94107

10 9 8 7 6 5 4 3 2 1
First printing, April 2018

PARENTAL ADVISORY
TAKANE & HANA is rated T for Teen and
is recommended for ages 13 and up. This
volume contains suggestive themes.

 MEDIA
viz.com

shojobeat.com

Now available in a 2-in-1 edition!

Maid-sama!

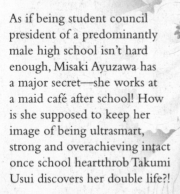

As if being student council president of a predominantly male high school isn't hard enough, Misaki Ayuzawa has a major secret—she works at a maid café after school! How is she supposed to keep her image of being ultrasmart, strong and overachieving intact once school heartthrob Takumi Usui discovers her double life?!

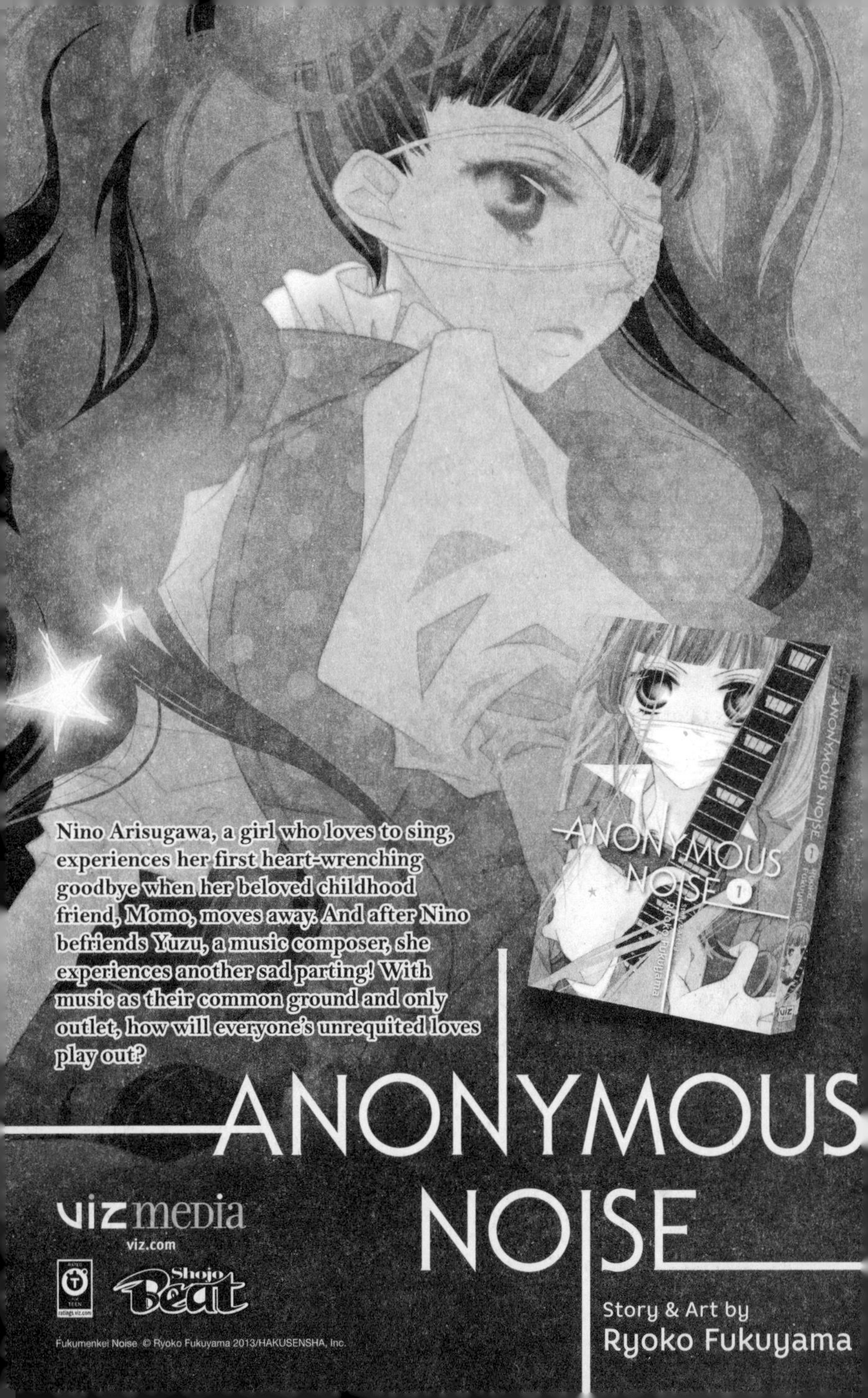
Nino Arisugawa, a girl who loves to sing, experiences her first heart-wrenching goodbye when her beloved childhood friend, Momo, moves away. And after Nino befriends Yuzu, a music composer, she experiences another sad parting! With music as their common ground and only outlet, how will everyone's unrequited loves play out?
ANONYMOUS NOISE
ANONYMOUS NOISE 1
Ryoko Fukuyama
viz media
viz.com
Shojo Beat
Story & Art by
Ryoko Fukuyama
Fukumenkei Noise © Ryoko Fukuyama 2013/HAKUSENSHA, Inc.

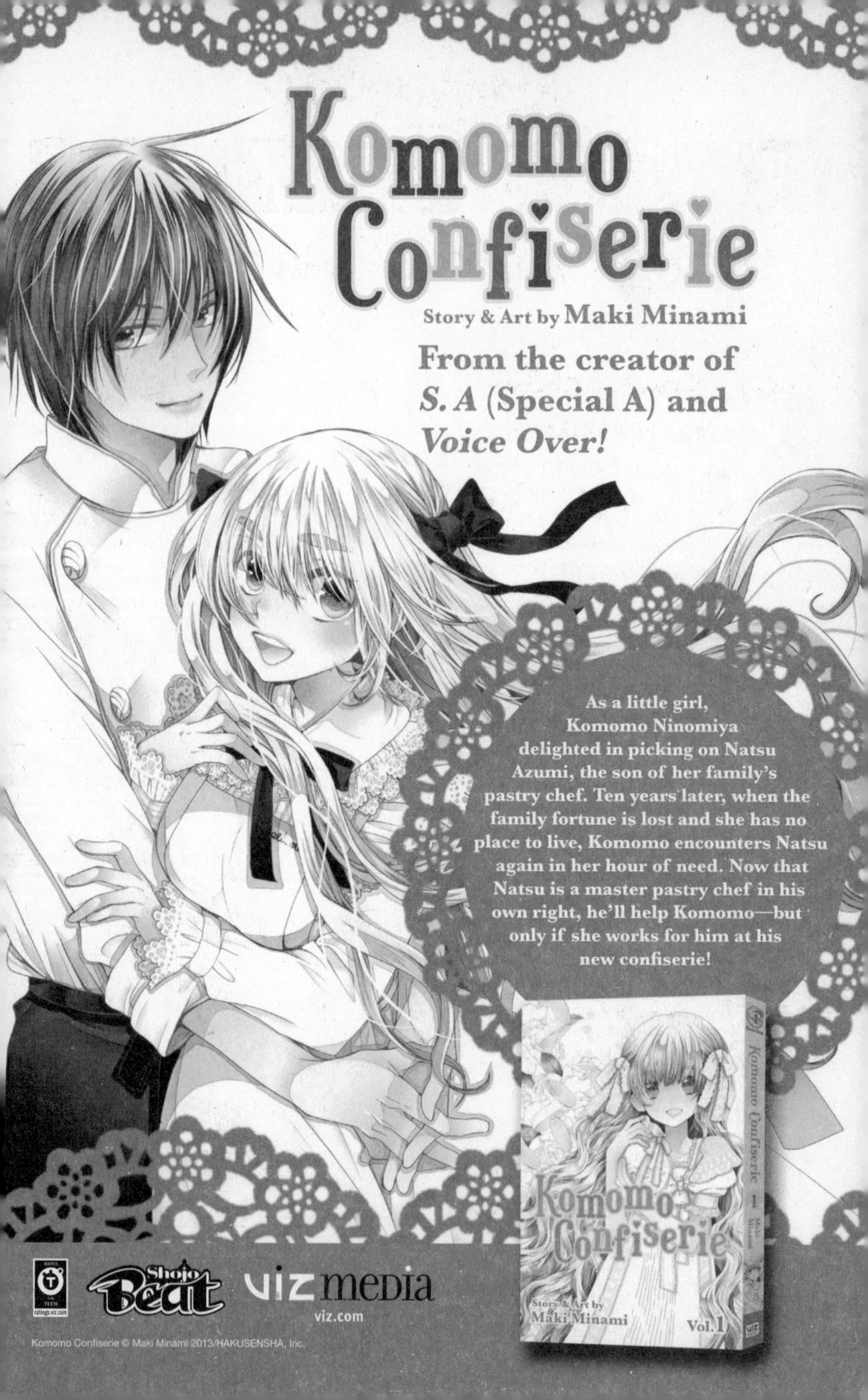
Komomo Confiserie
Story & Art by Maki Minami
From the creator of *S. A* (Special A) and *Voice Over!*
As a little girl, Komomo Ninomiya delighted in picking on Natsu Azumi, the son of her family's pastry chef. Ten years later, when the family fortune is lost and she has no place to live, Komomo encounters Natsu again in her hour of need. Now that Natsu is a master pastry chef in his own right, he'll help Komomo—but only if she works for him at his new confiserie!
Komomo Confiserie
Story & Art by Maki Minami
Vol. 1
Shojo Beat
VIZ MEDIA
viz.com
Komomo Confiserie © Maki Minami 2013/HAKUSENSHA, Inc.

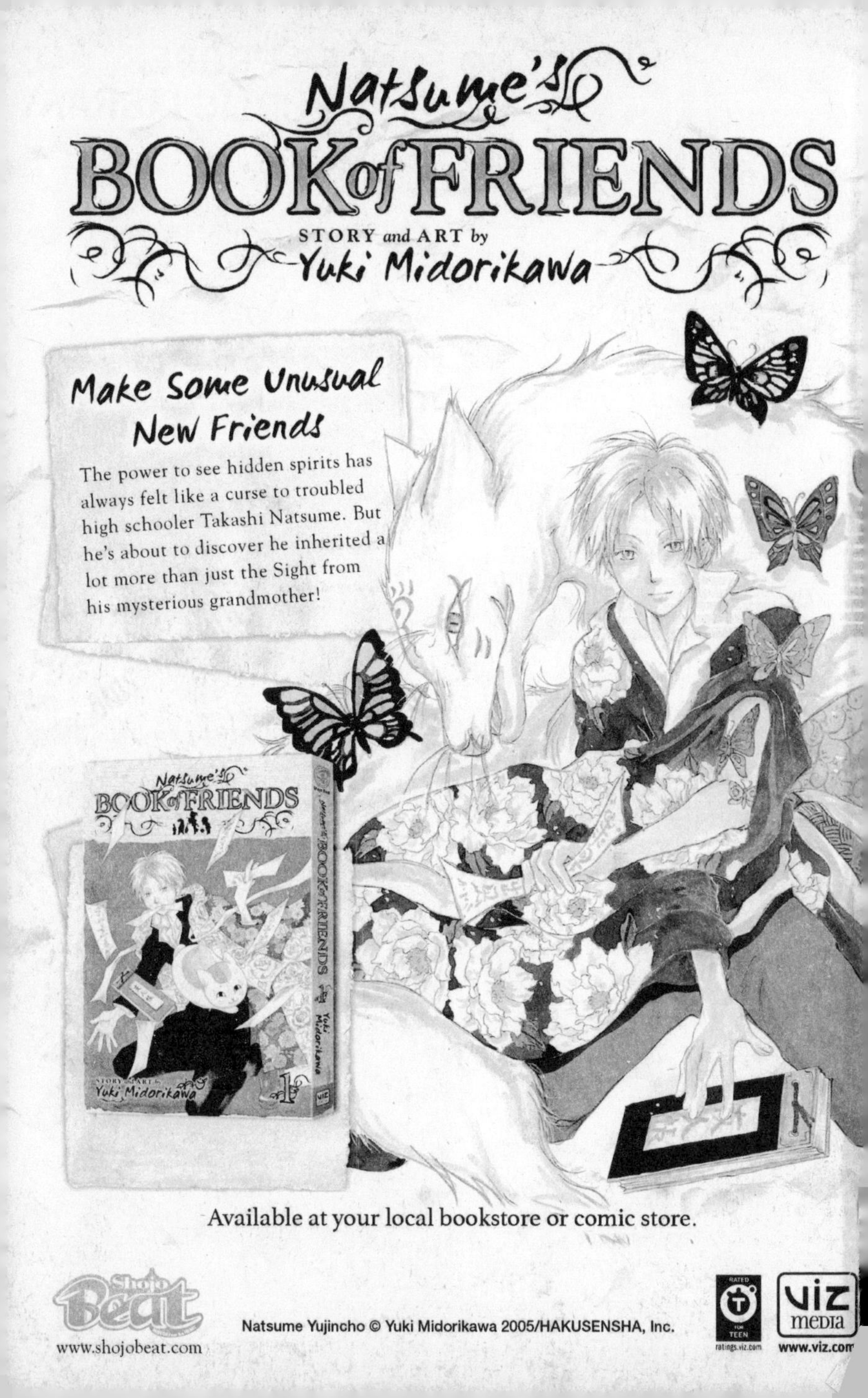
Natsume's
BOOK of FRIENDS
STORY and ART by
Yuki Midorikawa
Make Some Unusual New Friends
The power to see hidden spirits has always felt like a curse to troubled high schooler Takashi Natsume. But he's about to discover he inherited a lot more than just the Sight from his mysterious grandmother!
Natsume's BOOK of FRIENDS
STORY and ART by Yuki Midorikawa
Available at your local bookstore or comic store.
Shojo Beat
www.shojobeat.com
Natsume Yujincho © Yuki Midorikawa 2005/HAKUSENSHA, Inc.
RATED T FOR TEEN
ratings.viz.com
VIZ media
www.viz.com

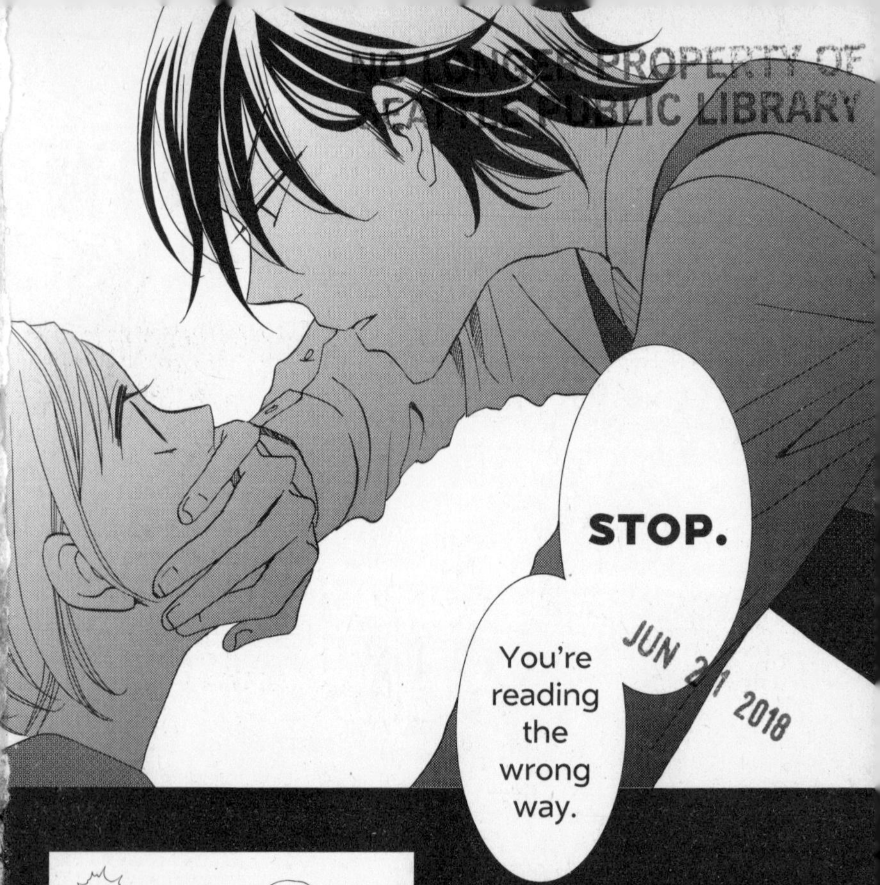
STOP.
You're reading the wrong way.

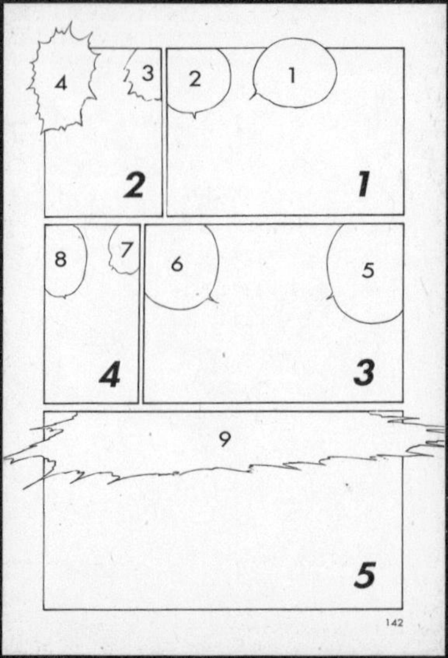
1
2
1
3
4
2
5
6
3
7
8
4
9
5
142

In keeping with the original Japanese comic format, this book reads from right to left—so action, sound effects and word balloons are completely reversed to preserve the orientation of the original artwork.

Check out the diagram shown here to get the hang of things, and then turn to the other side of the book to get started!